AF722828

Oracle8™ DBA: Database Administration The Cram Sheet

This Cram Sheet contains the distilled, key facts about Oracle8 database administration, which is the topic of the OCP-DBA Test 2 (Exam 1Z0-013). Review this information last thing before you enter the test room, paying special attention to those areas where you feel you need the most review. You can transfer any of these facts from your head onto a blank sheet of paper before beginning the exam.

ORACLE ARCHITECTURE

1. Know these Oracle8 structures:
   - **Alert log** Contains informational and error messages concerning the Oracle system and processes. It should be checked frequently, at least daily.
   - **Control files** Track database structures and ensure synchronicity of all database files via the system change number (SCN).
   - **Database datafiles** Make up the physical side of tablespaces. There are one or more datafiles per tablespace.
   - **Parameter file** Contains the initialization parameters that tell the Oracle server how to configure memory and internal resources as well as external file locations and process configurations.
   - **Redo log files** Contain the transaction journals; they are critical for database recovery. Redo log files are copied to the archive logs if archive logging is enabled.
   - **Trace files** Generated by all background processes and, if tracing is enabled, by each session. Trace files contain statistics for the process and log process messages and errors.

ADMINISTRATION TOOLS

2. Server Manager is used to perform database administration tasks. Database startup, shutdown, and recovery are Server Manager's major functions.
3. Oracle Enterprise Manager (OEM) is Oracle's new management tool. It uses a graphical user interface (GUI) to simplify database management by eliminating the need to memorize all the syntax for DBA tasks. OEM can be used to manage all the Oracle databases within an enterprise globally from a single computer.
4. OEM provides the following set of GUI tools to aid in administration:
   - **Backup Manager** Used to administer backup and recovery.
   - **Data Manager** Used to export, import, and load data.
   - **Instance Manager** Used to start up, shut down, change archive mode, change and manage initialization parameters, and get user session information.
   - **Schema Manager** Used to create, edit, and display schema objects.
   - **Security Manager** Used to create, alter, and drop users, roles, and profiles.
   - **Storage Manager** Used to create or alter tablespaces, rollback segments, and datafiles.

42. Rollback segments should have enough extents to allow each expected concurrent data manipulation language (**DML**) transaction to have its own extent.

43. Determine if you have the proper size of rollback segment extents by monitoring the **V$ROLLSTAT** view for shrinks and wraps.

44. Monitor the **V$ROLLSTAT** and **V$WAITSTAT** views for rollback (listed as **UNDO**) statistics.

45. If **V$ROLLSTAT** shows **WAITS**, you need more rollback extents allocated.

LOADING DATA

46. The Oracle SQL*Loader utility is used to load data from external files into an Oracle database. Data can be loaded via a conventional or direct path load:
    - A conventional path load uses the SQL engine to load data. This is the slower method due to the use of SQL and space management overhead as rows are inserted.
    - A direct path load writes directly to the database files above the high watermark (HWM) and is very fast because there is no database overhead.

47. SQL*Loader has five file types associated with it:
    - **Control file** Contains control information on how to load the data.
    - **Log file** Contains detailed information about the load.
    - **Bad file** Contains records that are rejected by SQL*Loader.
    - **Discard file** Contains records that did not match the selection criteria in the control file.
    - **Data file** Contains the data to be loaded.

EXPORT AND IMPORT

48. The Oracle export and import utilities are used to add flexibility to your backup strategy. An export is a logical backup of the objects in the database. The export and import utilities back up and restore database objects selectively. The export and import utilities are used also to reorganize data or move database objects from one schema to another. Objects can be exported or imported in table mode, user mode, or full database mode.

TABLES AND INDEXES

49. Tables and indexes are managed via the **CREATE**, **ALTER**, **DROP**, **TRUNCATE**, and **ANALYZE** commands. The **TRUNCATE** command removes all the rows from a table without creating any rollback information. It can be used to drop allocated storage and move the HWM or to reuse storage and keep the HWM the same. **TRUNCATE** performs much faster but cannot be rolled back. The **ANALYZE** command is used to gather statistics that can be used by the cost-based optimizer in determining the optimal execution path for SQL statements.

INTEGRITY CONSTRAINTS

50. Data integrity can be maintained through application code triggers or declared integrity constraints. The declared integrity constraints are:
    - **CHECK** Requires a specified condition to be true or unknown for every row of the table.
    - **FOREIGN KEY** Specifies the column or set of columns included in the definition of the referential integrity constraint. The foreign key column(s) can't be inserted or changed unless the primary key on the referenced table has the same key value(s).
    - **NOT NULL** Requires every row to have a value.
    - **PRIMARY KEY** Requires that no columns in the key have a null value and that the column(s) be unique in the table.
    - **UNIQUE KEY** Requires the column(s) in the key to not be duplicated in the table.

- **NORMAL** Waits for all users to exit, then shuts down.
- **IMMEDIATE** Disconnects statements that are being processed and rolls back uncommitted transactions. Sessions waiting for results are allowed to complete before being disconnected. After all users are disconnected, the database shuts down.
- **TRANSACTIONAL** Allows transactions to commit, logs out users, and then shuts down.
- **ABORT** Shuts down regardless of logins.

DATA DICTIONARY

24. The data dictionary consists at the lowest level of **X$** and **K$** C structures, not normally viewable or used by the DBA.
25. The data dictionary has **V$** virtual views, which contain variable data, such as statistics.
26. The data dictionary has dollar tables ($), which contain database metadata about tables, views, indexes, and other database structures.
27. At the uppermost layer, the data dictionary has **DBA** views about all objects, **ALL** views about all objects a user can access, and **USER** views about all objects a user owns.

USERS AND GRANTS

28. Users can be created, altered, and dropped using the **CREATE**, **ALTER**, and **DROP** commands.
29. Users are granted profiles, roles, and privileges.
30. Profiles are used to limit resource usage.
31. Roles are used to group a collection of privileges, roles, and grants that then can be granted en masse to a user or another role.
32. Grants and privileges are given at the system-, table-, or column-level.
33. The following special roles are automatically created:
    - **CONNECT** Grants the following privileges: **CREATE/ALTER SESSION**, **CREATE TABLE**, **VIEW**, **SYNONYM**, **SEQUENCE**, **CLUSTER**, and **DATABASE LINK**.
    - **DBA** Grants all system privileges with **ADMIN OPTION**.
    - **OSDBA** Grants all system privileges with **ADMIN OPTION**, **OSOPER**, and the right to create a database.
    - **OSOPER** Grants the following privileges: **STARTUP**, **SHUTDOWN**, **ALTER DATABASE OPEN/MOUNT**, **ALTER DATABASE BACKUP**, **ARCHIVE LOG**, **RECOVER DATABASE**, and **RESTRICTED SESSION**.
    - **RESOURCE** Grants the following privileges: **CREATE CLUSTER**, **PROCEDURE**, **SEQUENCE**, **TABLE**, **TRIGGER**, and **TYPE**.

DATABASE CREATION

34. File placement (control, log, archive, and datafiles) is critical to performance. Distribute I/O evenly. Use operating system tools to check for contention between Oracle and non-Oracle activities.
35. Avoid chaining—create your database with a **DB_BLOCK_SIZE** parameter that fits your largest row. The database must be re-created to change block size.
36. In addition to the **SYSTEM** tablespace, create tablespaces for temporary segments, rollback segments, data segments, and index segments.
37. Make sure the global database name is unique.

ROLLBACK SEGMENTS

38. Rollback segments store undo information. Rollback segments act as before-image journals and are critical for rollback operation, instance recovery, and read-consistency.
39. Rollback segments should be stored in their own tablespace, not with other objects.
40. Size rollback segments with **INITIAL=NEXT** and a **PCTINCREASE** of 0. The **INITIAL** size is your average transaction size. The **OPTIMAL** storage parameter is set to allow rollback segments to shrink back to an optimal size after they are caused to grow by large transactions. Set **OPTIMAL** to **MINEXTENTS*INITIAL** or to some multiple of this value.
41. For systems with large batch transactions, create an offline large rollback segment that can be put online and used when batch operations occur.

THE ORACLE INSTANCE

5. The system global area (SGA) is made up of the database buffers, shared pool, and log buffers (as well as the request and response queues in a multithreaded server [MTS] configuration).
6. The data buffer cache is where all data must pass through to get to users and back to the database. It often makes up the majority of the SGA size.
7. The shared pool stores the library cache (shared SQL area, PL/SQL procedures, and control structures), dictionary cache, and control structures.
8. The log buffers are used to store redo log entries prior to their being written to disk and usually make up the third largest section of the SGA.
9. An instance is made up of the SGA and a set of processes. The base set of processes consist of DBWn, LGWR, SMON, PMON, CKPT, ARCH, and RECO.
10. The DBWn process, known as the database writer, writes dirty (used or changed) buffers from the SGA database buffers to the disk.
11. The LGWR process, known as the log writer, writes redo log entries from the log buffers to the redo logs.
12. The SMON process, known as the system monitor, cleans up sort memory areas and recovers instances after instance failures as well as coalesces contiguous chunks of free space in datafiles.
13. The PMON process, known as the process monitor, cleans up after failed processes.
14. The CKPT process, known as the checkpoint process, signals the DBWn at checkpoints and updates all the datafiles and control files with the current checkpoint information.
15. The ARCH process, known as the archiver, copies the online redo log files to the location where archive files are written.
16. The RECO process, known as recoverer, recovers failed distributed transactions.
17. An instance can have several optional processes: Dnnn, LCKn, SNPn, and QMNn.
18. The Dnnn processes, known as the dispatcher processes, monitor connections in the MTS environment and distribute them to shared server (Snnn) processes.
19. The LCKn processes, known as the lock processes, perform inter-instance locking in an Oracle Parallel Server environment.
20. The SNPn process, known as the snapshot process, is only set up if the **JOB_QUEUE** parameter is set to a non-zero value. The SNPn processes (up to nine) wake up at specified intervals, check the job tables, and, if a job is due, run it.
21. The QMNn processes, known as the queue monitor, monitor the message queues for Oracle Advanced Queuing. You can have up to 10 QMNn processes.

ORACLE STARTUP AND SHUTDOWN

22. To start up an Oracle instance, the general procedure is:
    1. Start Server Manager (for example, on Unix: **svrmgrl**).
    2. Issue the **CONNECT INTERNAL** connec tion command.
    3. Issue the **STARTUP** command with the appropriate option:
        - **OPEN** Does a **NOMOUNT**, **MOUNT**, and **OPEN EXCLUSIVE** (default).
        - **MOUNT** Starts instance processes but doesn't open the database for use.
        - **NOMOUNT** Used only for database and control file creation.
        - **SHARED** or **PARALLEL** Used only if the database has the parallel option installed. Allows more than one instance to access the same database files.
    4. Start up proceeds from **NOMOUNT** to **MOUNT** to **OPEN** status.
23. To shut down an Oracle instance, the usual procedure is:
    1. Start Server Manager.
    2. Issue the **CONNECT INTERNAL** connection command.
    3. Issue the **SHUTDOWN** command with the appropriate option:

EXAM CRAM™

Oracle8™ DBA: Database Administration

Paul Collins

CORIOLIS™

Oracle8™ DBA: Database Administration Exam Cram

The Coriolis Group, LLC
14455 N. Hayden Road
Suite 220
Scottsdale, Arizona 85260

480/483-0192
FAX 480/483-0193
http://www.coriolis.com

Library of Congress Cataloging-in-Publication Data
Collins, Paul, 1959-
Oracle8 DBA: database administration exam cram / by Paul Collins.
p. cm.
Includes index.
ISBN 1-57610-603-9
1. Electronic data processing personnel--Certification. 2. Database management--Examinations--Study guides. 3. Oracle (Computer file) I. Title.
QA76.3.C655 2000
005.75'85--dc21 00-022938
CIP

President, CEO
Keith Weiskamp

Publisher
Steve Sayre

Acquisitions Editor
Jeff Kellum

Marketing Specialist
Cynthia Caldwell

Project Editor
Pat DuMoulin

Technical Reviewer
Pete Sharman

Production Coordinator
Laura Wellander

Cover Designer
Jesse Dunn

Layout Designer
April Nielsen

Printed in the United States of America
10 9 8 7 6 5 4 3 2 1

CORIOLIS

14455 North Hayden Road • Suite 220 • Scottsdale, Arizona 85260

Coriolis: The Smartest Way To Get Certified™

To help you reach your goals, we've listened to readers like you, and we've designed our entire product line around you and the way you like to study, learn, and master challenging subjects.

In addition to our highly popular *Exam Cram* and *Exam Prep* books, we offer several other products to help you pass certification exams. Our *Practice Tests* and *Flash Cards* are designed to make your studying fun and productive. Our *Audio Reviews* have received rave reviews from our customers—and they're the perfect way to make the most of your drive time!

The newest way to get certified is the *Exam Cram Personal Trainer*—a highly interactive, personalized self-study course based on the best-selling *Exam Cram* series. It's the first certification-specific product to completely link a customizable learning tool, exclusive *Exam Cram* content, and multiple testing techniques so you can study what, how, and when you want.

Exam Cram Insider—a biweekly newsletter containing the latest in certification news, study tips, and announcements from Certification Insider Press—gives you an ongoing look at the hottest certification programs. (To subscribe, send an email to **eci@coriolis.com** and type "subscribe insider" in the body of the email.) We also sponsor the Certified Crammer Society and the Coriolis Help Center—two other resources that will help you get certified even faster!

Help us continue to provide the very best certification study materials possible. Write us or email us at **cipq@coriolis.com** and let us know how our books have helped you study. Tell us about new features that you'd like us to add. Send us a story about how we've helped you; if we use it in one of our books, we'll send you an official Coriolis shirt!

Good luck with your certification exam and your career. Thank you for allowing us to help you achieve your goals.

Keith Weiskamp

Keith Weiskamp
President and CEO

Look For These Other Books From The Coriolis Group:

I would like to dedicate this book to my children Justin and Jordan. I know doing this book was hardest on them because they did not get to see Daddy as much as they are used to. So I want to give both of you special thanks for understanding.

❧

About The Author

Paul Collins specializes in Oracle database design and administration for Skyler-Marks Consulting. He has over 10 years of Oracle experience and has been a speaker at Oracle Open World and IOUG-Alive conferences. Paul is one of the database administrators who helped develop the first Oracle Database Administration Certification test for Oracle7. Paul is OCP certified and is coauthor of *Oracle DBA Exam Cram: Test 3 and Test 4* for Oracle7.

Acknowledgments

I would like to acknowledge the team that helped me write this book. Their expertise helped me immensely, and they improved the quality of the book significantly. So, thanks to Jeff Kellum, my acquisitions editor for his professionalism; Pat DuMoulin, my project editor who held everything together even when I was missing my deadlines; Pete Sharman, the technical reviewer who did a great job finding all my mistakes; Ellen Strader, my copyeditor; and Louise Leahy and Jill Batistick, the proofreaders who corrected everything else. And thanks to the rest of the team for their excellent work: production coordinator, Laura Wellander; marketing specialist, Cynthia Caldwell; cover designer, Jesse Dunn; and layout designer, April Nielsen.

Also, a special thanks to Penny Miles who helped me review the book.

Contents At A Glance

Table Of Contents

Introduction

Welcome to *Oracle8 DBA: Database Administration Exam Cram*! This book will help you get ready to take—and pass—the second of the five-part series of exams for Oracle Certified Professional-Oracle8 Certified Database Administrator (OCP-DBA) certification. In this Introduction, I talk about Oracle's certification programs in general and how the *Exam Cram* series can help you prepare for Oracle8's certification exams.

Exam Cram books help you understand and appreciate the subjects and materials you need to pass Oracle certification exams. The books are aimed strictly at test preparation and review. They do not teach you everything you need to know about a topic. Instead, I present and dissect the questions and problems that you're likely to encounter on a test.

Nevertheless, to completely prepare yourself for any Oracle test, I recommend that you begin by taking the Self-Assessment included in this book immediately following this Introduction. This tool will help you evaluate your knowledge base against the requirements for an OCP-DBA under both ideal and real circumstances.

Based on what you learn from that exercise, you might decide to begin your studies with some classroom training or by reading one of the many DBA guides available from Oracle and third-party vendors. I also strongly recommend that you install, configure, and fool around with the software or environment that you'll be tested on, because nothing beats hands-on experience and familiarity when it comes to understanding the questions you're likely to encounter on a certification test. Book learning is essential, but hands-on experience is the best teacher of all!

The Oracle Certified Professional (OCP) Program

The OCP program for DBA certification currently includes five separate tests. A brief description of each test follows, and Table 1 shows the required exams for the OCP-DBA certification:

Table 1 OCP-DBA Requirements*

All 5 of these tests are required		
Test 1	Exam 1Z0-001	Introduction to Oracle: SQL and PL/SQL
➤ Test 2	Exam 1Z0-013	Oracle8: Database Administration
Test 3	Exam 1Z0-015	Oracle8: Backup and Recovery
Test 4	Exam 1Z0-014	Oracle8: Performance Tuning
Test 5	Exam 1Z0-016	Oracle8: Network Administration

* If you are currently an OCP certified in Oracle7.3, you need take only the upgrade exam (Oracle8: New Features for Administrators, Exam 1Z0-010) to be certified in Oracle8.

- *Introduction to Oracle: SQL And PL/SQL (Exam 1Z0-001)*—Test 1 is the base test for the series. Knowledge tested in Test 1 will also be used in all other tests in the DBA series. Besides testing knowledge of SQL and PL/SQL language constructs, syntax, and usage, Test 1 covers Data Definition Language (DDL), Data Manipulation Language (DML), and Data Control Language (DCL). Also covered in Test 1 are basic data modeling and database design.
- *Oracle8: Database Administration (Exam 1Z0-013)*—Test 2 deals with all levels of database administration in Oracle8 (primarily version 8.0.5 and above). Topics include architecture, startup and shutdown, database creation, managing database internal and external constructs (such as redo logs, rollback segments, and tablespaces), and all other Oracle structures. Database auditing, use of National Language Support (NLS) features, and use of SQL*Loader and other utilities are also covered.
- *Oracle8: Backup And Recovery (Exam 1Z0-015)*—Test 3 covers one of the most important parts of the Oracle DBA's job: database backup and recovery operations. Test 3 tests knowledge in backup and recovery motives, architecture as it relates to backup and recovery, backup methods, failure scenarios, recovery methodologies, archive logging, supporting 24x7 shops, troubleshooting, and use of Oracle8's standby database features. The test also covers the use of the Recovery Manager (RMAN) product from Oracle, new in Oracle8.
- *Oracle8: Performance Tuning (Exam 1Z0-014)*—Test 4 covers all aspects of tuning an Oracle8 database. Topics in both application and database tuning are covered. The exam tests knowledge in diagnosis of tuning problems, database optimal configuration, shared pool tuning, buffer cache tuning, Oracle block usage, tuning rollback segments and redo mechanisms, monitoring and detecting lock contention, tuning sorts, load optimization, and tuning in OLTP, DSS, and mixed environments.

- *Oracle8: Network Administration (Exam 1Z0-016)*—Test 5 covers all parts of the Net8 product: NET8, Oracle Names Server, the listener process, lsnrctl (the listener control utility), and the NET8 configuration files sqlnet.ora, tnsnames.ora, and listener.ora.

To obtain an OCP certificate in database administration, an individual must pass all five exams. You do not have to take the tests in any particular order. However, it is usually better to take the examinations in order because the knowledge tested builds from each exam. The core exams require individuals to demonstrate competence with all phases of Oracle8 database lifetime activities. If you already have your Oracle7.3 certification, you need to take only one exam—Oracle8: New Features for Administrators (Exam 1Z0-010)—to upgrade your status.

It's not uncommon for the entire process to take a year or so, and many individuals find that they must take a test more than once to pass. The primary goal of the *Exam Cram* series is to make it possible, given proper study and preparation, to pass all of the OCP-DBA tests on the first try.

Finally, certification is an ongoing activity. Once an Oracle version becomes obsolete, OCP-DBAs (and other OCPs) typically have a six-month time frame in which they can become recertified on current product versions. (If an individual does not get recertified within the specified time period, his certification becomes invalid.) Because technology keeps changing and new products continually supplant old ones, this should come as no surprise.

The best place to keep tabs on the OCP program and its various certifications is on the Oracle Web site. The current root URL for the OCP program is at **http://education.oracle.com/certification**. Oracle's certification Web site changes frequently, so if this URL doesn't work, try using the Search tool on Oracle's site (**www.oracle.com**) with either "OCP" or the quoted phrase "Oracle Certified Professional Program" as the search string. This will help you find the latest and most accurate information about the company's certification programs.

Taking A Certification Exam

Alas, testing is not free. You'll be charged $125 for each test you take, whether you pass or fail. In the United States and Canada, tests are administered by Sylvan Prometric. Sylvan Prometric can be reached at 1-800-891-3926, any time from 7:00 A.M. to 6:00 P.M., Central Time, Monday through Friday. If you can't get through at this number, try 1-612-896-7000 or 1-612-820-5707.

To schedule an exam, call at least one day in advance. To cancel or reschedule an exam, you must call at least one day before the scheduled test time (or you may be charged the $125 fee). When calling Sylvan Prometric, please have the following information ready for the telesales staffer who handles your call:

- Your name, organization, and mailing address.
- The name of the exam you want to take.
- A method of payment. (The most convenient approach is to supply a valid credit card number with sufficient available credit. Otherwise, payments by check, money order, or purchase order must be received before a test can be scheduled. If the latter methods are required, ask your order-taker for more details.)

An appointment confirmation will be sent to you by mail if you register more than five days before an exam, or it will be sent by fax if less than five days before the exam. A Candidate Agreement letter, which you must sign to take the examination, will also be provided.

On the day of the test, try to arrive at least 15 minutes before the scheduled time slot. You must supply two forms of identification, one of which must be a photo ID.

All exams are completely closed book. In fact, you will not be permitted to take anything with you into the testing area. I suggest that you review the most critical information about the test you're taking just before the test. (*Exam Cram* books provide a brief reference—The Cram Sheet, located inside the front of this book—that lists the essential information from the book in distilled form.) You will have some time to compose yourself, to mentally review this critical information, and even to take a sample orientation exam before you begin the real thing. I suggest you take the orientation test before taking your first exam; they're all more or less identical in layout, behavior, and controls, so you probably won't need to do this more than once.

When you complete an Oracle8 certification exam, the testing software will tell you whether you've passed or failed. Results are broken into several topical areas. Whether you pass or fail, I suggest you ask for—and keep—the detailed report that the test administrator prints for you. You can use the report to help you prepare for another go-round, if necessary, and even if you pass, the report shows areas you may need to review to keep your edge. If you need to retake an exam, you'll have to call Sylvan Prometric, schedule a new test date, and pay another $125.

Tracking OCP Status

Oracle generates transcripts that indicate the exams you have passed and your corresponding test scores. After you pass the necessary set of five exams, you'll be certified as an Oracle8 DBA. Official certification normally takes anywhere from four to six weeks (generally within 30 days), so don't expect to get your credentials overnight. Once certified, you will receive a package with a Welcome Kit that contains a number of elements:

- An OCP-DBA certificate, suitable for framing.
- A license agreement to use the OCP logo. Once it is sent into Oracle and your packet of logo information is received, the license agreement allows you to use the logo for advertisements, promotions, documents, letterhead, business cards, and so on. An OCP logo sheet, which includes camera-ready artwork, comes with the license.

Many people believe that the benefits of OCP certification go well beyond the perks that Oracle provides to newly anointed members of this elite group. I am starting to see more job listings that request or require applicants to have an OCP-DBA certification, and many individuals who complete the program can qualify for increases in pay and/or responsibility. As an official recognition of hard work and broad knowledge, OCP certification is a badge of honor in many IT organizations.

How To Prepare For An Exam

At a minimum, preparing for OCP-DBA exams requires that you obtain and study the following materials:

- The Oracle8 Server version 8.0.5 Documentation Set on CD-ROM.
- The exam preparation materials, practice tests, and self-assessment exams on the Oracle certification page (**http://education.oracle.com/certification**). Find the materials, download them, and use them!
- This *Exam Cram* book. It's the first and last thing you should read before taking the exam.

In addition, you'll probably find any or all of the following materials useful in your quest for Oracle8 DBA expertise:

- *OCP resource kits*—Oracle Corporation has a CD-ROM with example questions and materials to help with the exam; generally, these are provided free by requesting them from your Oracle representative. They have also been offered free for the taking at most Oracle conventions, such as IOUGA-Alive! and Oracle Open World.

- *Classroom training*—Oracle, TUSC, LearningTree, and many others offer classroom and computer based training-type material that you will find useful to help you prepare for the exam. But a word of warning: these classes are fairly expensive (in the range of $300 per day of training). However, they do offer a condensed form of learning to help you brush up on your Oracle knowledge. The tests are closely tied to the classroom training provided by Oracle, so I would suggest taking at least the introductory classes to get the Oracle-specific (and classroom-specific) terminology under your belt.
- *Other publications*—You'll find direct references to other publications and resources in this book, and there's no shortage of materials available about Oracle8 DBA topics. To help you sift through some of the publications out there, I end each chapter with a "Need To Know More?" section that provides pointers to more complete and exhaustive resources covering the chapter's subject matter. This section tells you where to look for further details.
- *The Oracle Support CD-ROM*—Oracle provides a Support CD-ROM on a quarterly basis. This CD-ROM contains useful white papers, bug reports, technical bulletins, and information about release-specific bugs, fixes, and new features. Contact your Oracle representative for a copy.
- *The Oracle Administrator and PL/SQL Developer*—These are online references from RevealNet, Inc., an Oracle and database online reference provider. These online references provide instant lookup on thousands of database and developmental topics and are an invaluable resource for study and learning about Oracle. Demo copies can be downloaded from **www.revealnet.com**. Also available at the RevealNet Web site are the DBA and PL/SQL Pipelines, online discussion groups where you can obtain expert information from Oracle DBAs worldwide. The costs of these applications run about $400 each (current pricing is available on the Web site) and are worth every cent.

These required and recommended materials represent a nonpareil collection of sources and resources for Oracle8 DBA topics and software. In the section that follows, I explain how this book works and give you some good reasons why this book should also be on your required and recommended materials list.

About This Book

Each topical *Exam Cram* chapter follows a regular structure, along with graphical cues about especially important or useful material. Here's the structure of a typical chapter:

- *Opening hotlists*—Each chapter begins with lists of the terms, tools, and techniques that you must learn and understand before you can be fully conversant with the chapter's subject matter. I follow the hotlists with one or two introductory paragraphs to set the stage for the rest of the chapter.
- *Topical coverage*—After the opening hotlists, each chapter covers a series of topics related to the chapter's subject. Throughout this section, I highlight material most likely to appear on a test using a special Exam Alert layout, like this:

  This is what an Exam Alert looks like. Normally, an Exam Alert stresses concepts, terms, software, or activities that will most likely appear in one or more certification test questions. For that reason, any information found offset in Exam Alert format is worthy of unusual attentiveness on your part. Indeed, most of the facts appearing in The Cram Sheet appear as Exam Alerts within the text.

  Occasionally in *Exam Crams*, you'll see tables called "Vital Statistics." The contents of Vital Statistics tables are worthy of an extra once-over. These tables contain informational tidbits that might show up in a test question.

  Even if material isn't flagged as an Exam Alert or included in a Vital Statistics table, *all* the contents of this book are associated, at least tangentially, to something test-related. This book is tightly focused for quick test preparation, so you'll find that what appears in the meat of each chapter is critical knowledge.

  I have also provided tips that will help build a better foundation of data administration knowledge. Although the information may not be on the exam, it is highly relevant and will help you become a better test-taker.

  This is how tips are formatted. Keep your eyes open for these, and you'll become a test guru in no time!

- *Practice questions*—A section at the end of each chapter presents a series of mock test questions and explanations of both correct and incorrect answers. I also try to point out especially tricky questions by using a special icon, like this:

  Ordinarily, this icon flags the presence of an especially devious question, if not an outright trick question. Trick questions are calculated to "trap" you if you don't read them carefully, and more than once at that. Although they're not ubiquitous, such questions make regular appearances in the Oracle8 exams. That's why exam questions are as much about reading comprehension as they are about knowing DBA material inside out and backward.

- *Details and resources*—Every chapter ends with a section titled "Need To Know More?". This section provides direct pointers to Oracle and third-party resources that offer further details on the chapter's subject matter. In addition, this section tries to rate the quality and thoroughness of each topic's coverage. If you find a resource you like in this collection, use it, but don't feel compelled to use all these resources. On the other hand, I recommend only resources I use on a regular basis, so none of my recommendations will be a waste of your time or money.

The bulk of the book follows this chapter structure slavishly, but there are a few other elements that I would like to point out. Chapter 15 includes a sample test that provides a good review of the material presented throughout the book to ensure you're ready for the exam. Chapter 16 provides an answer key to the sample test. In addition, you'll find a handy glossary and an index.

Finally, look for The Cram Sheet, which appears inside the front of this *Exam Cram* book. It is a valuable tool that represents a condensed and compiled collection of facts, figures, and tips that I think you should memorize before taking the test. Because you can dump this information out of your head onto a piece of paper before answering any exam questions, you can master this information by brute force—you need to remember it only long enough to write it down when you walk into the test room. You might even want to look at it in the car or in the lobby of the testing center just before you walk in to take the test.

How To Use This Book

If you're prepping for a first-time test, I've structured the topics in this book to build on one another. Therefore, some topics in later chapters make more sense after you've read earlier chapters. That's why I suggest you read this book from front to back for your initial test preparation.

If you need to brush up on a topic or you have to bone up for a second try, use the index or table of contents to go straight to the topics and questions that you need to study. Beyond the tests, I think you'll find this book useful as a tightly focused reference to some of the most important aspects of topics associated with being a DBA, as implemented under Oracle8.

Given all the book's elements and its specialized focus, I've tried to create a tool that you can use to prepare for—and pass—the Oracle OCP-DBA set of examinations. Please share your feedback on the book with me, especially if you have ideas about how I can improve it for future test-takers. I'll consider everything you say carefully, and I try to respond to all suggestions. You can reach me via email at **paulcollins@compuserve.com**. Or you can send your questions or comments to **cipq@coriolis.com**. Please remember to include the title of the book in your message; otherwise, I'll be forced to guess which book of mine you're making a suggestion about. Also, be sure to check out the Web pages at **www.coriolis.com**, where you'll find information updates, commentary, and certification information.

Thanks, and enjoy the book!

Self-Assessment

I've included a Self-Assessment in this *Exam Cram* to help you evaluate your readiness to tackle Oracle Certified Professional-Oracle8 Certified Database Administrator (OCP-DBA) certification. It should also help you understand what you need to master the topic of this book—namely, Exam 1Z0-013 (Test 2), "Oracle8 DBA: Database Administration." But before you tackle this Self-Assessment, let's talk about the concerns you may face when pursuing an Oracle8 OCP-DBA certification, and what an ideal Oracle8 OCP-DBA candidate might look like.

Oracle8 OCP-DBAs In The Real World

In the next section, I describe an ideal Oracle8 OCP-DBA candidate, knowing full well that only a few actual candidates meet this ideal. In fact, my description of that ideal candidate might seem downright scary. But take heart, because, although the requirements to obtain an Oracle8 OCP-DBA may seem pretty formidable, they are by no means impossible to meet. However, you should be keenly aware that it does take time, requires some expense, and consumes a substantial effort.

You can get all the real-world motivation you need from knowing that many others have gone before you. You can follow in their footsteps. If you're willing to tackle the process seriously and do what it takes to obtain the necessary experience and knowledge, you can take—and pass—the certification tests. In fact, the *Exam Crams* and the companion *Exam Preps* are designed to make it as easy as possible for you to prepare for these exams. But prepare you must!

The same, of course, is true for other Oracle certifications, including:

- Oracle7.3 OCP-DBA, which is like the Oracle8 OCP-DBA certification but requires only four core exams.
- Application Developer, Oracle Developer Rel 1 OCP, which is aimed at software developers and requires five exams.
- Application Developer, Oracle Developer Rel 2 OCP, which is aimed at software developers and requires five exams.

- Oracle Database Operators OCP, which is aimed at database operators and requires only one exam.
- Oracle Java Technology Certification OCP, which is aimed at Java developers and requires five exams.

The Ideal Oracle8 OCP-DBA Candidate

Just to give you some idea of what an ideal Oracle8 OCP-DBA candidate is like, here are some relevant statistics about the background and experience such an individual might have. Don't worry if you don't meet these qualifications (or, indeed, if you don't even come close), because this world is far from ideal, and where you fall short is simply where you'll have more work to do. The ideal candidate will have:

- Academic or professional training in relational databases, Structured Query Language (SQL), performance tuning, backup and recovery, and Net8 administration.
- Three-plus years of professional database administration experience, including experience installing and upgrading Oracle executables, creating and tuning databases, troubleshooting connection problems, creating users, and managing backup and recovery scenarios.

I believe that well under half of all certification candidates meet these requirements. In fact, most probably meet less than half of these requirements (that is, at least when they begin the certification process). But, because all those who have their certifications already survived this ordeal, you can survive it, too—especially if you heed what this Self-Assessment can tell you about what you already know and what you need to learn.

Put Yourself To The Test

The following series of questions and observations is designed to help you figure out how much work you'll face in pursuing Oracle certification and what kinds of resources you may consult on your quest. Be absolutely honest in your answers, or you'll end up wasting money on exams you're not ready to take. There are no right or wrong answers, only steps along the path to certification. Only you can decide where you really belong in the broad spectrum of aspiring candidates.

Two things should be clear from the outset, however:

- Even a modest background in computer science will be helpful.

- Hands-on experience with Oracle products and technologies is an essential ingredient to certification success.

Educational Background

1. Have you ever taken any computer-related classes? [Yes or No]

   If yes, proceed to question 2; if no, proceed to question 4.

2. Have you taken any classes on relational databases? [Yes or No]

   If yes, you will probably be able to handle Oracle's architecture and network administration discussions. If you're rusty, brush up on the basic concepts of databases and networks. If the answer is no, consider some basic reading in this area. I strongly recommend a good Oracle database administration book such as *Oracle8 Administration and Management* by Michael Ault (Wiley, 1998). Or, if this title doesn't appeal to you, check out reviews for other, similar titles at your favorite online bookstore.

3. Have you taken any database administration classes? [Yes or No]

   If yes, you will probably be able to handle Oracle's terminology, concepts, and technologies (but brace yourself for frequent departures from normal usage). If you're rusty, brush up on basic concepts and terminology. If your answer is no, you might want to check out the Oracle technet web site (**http://technet.oracle.com**) and read some of the white papers on Oracle8. If you have access to the Oracle MetaLink website, download the Oracle8 Database Administration manual.

4. Have you done any reading on relational databases? [Yes or No]

   If yes, review the requirements from questions 2 and 3. If you meet those, move to the next section, "Hands-On Experience." If you answered no, consult the recommended reading for both topics. This kind of strong background will be of great help in preparing you for the Oracle exams.

Hands-On Experience

Another important key to success on all of the Oracle tests is hands-on experience. If I leave you with only one realization after taking this Self-Assessment, it should be that there's no substitute for time spent installing, configuring, and using the various Oracle products upon which you'll be tested repeatedly and in depth.

5. Have you installed, configured, and worked with Oracle8? [Yes or No]

If yes, make sure you understand basic concepts as covered in Exam 1Z0-013, "Oracle8: Database Administration" (Test 2) and advanced concepts as covered in Exam 1Z0-014, "Oracle8: Performance Tuning" (Test 4). You should also study for Exam 1Z0-001 (Test 1), "Introduction to Oracle: SQL and PL/SQL."

TIP: You can download the candidate certification guide, objectives, practice exams, and other information about Oracle exams from the company's Training and Certification page on the Web at **http://education.oracle.com/certification**.

If you haven't worked with Oracle, you must obtain a copy of Oracle8 or Personal Oracle8. Then, learn about Oracle databases.

TIP: For any and all of these Oracle exams, the candidate guides for the topics involved are a good study resource. You can download them free from the Oracle Web site (**education.oracle.com**). You can also download information on purchasing additional exam practice tests ($99 per exam).

If you have the funds or your employer will pay your way, consider taking a class at an Oracle training and education center.

Before you even think about taking any Oracle exam, make sure you've spent enough time with Oracle8 to understand how it may be installed and configured, how to maintain such an installation, and how to troubleshoot the software when things go wrong. This will help you in the exam—as well as in real life.

Testing Your Exam-Readiness

Whether you attend a formal class on a specific topic to get ready for an exam or use written materials to study on your own, some preparation for the Oracle certification exams is essential. At $125 a try, pass or fail, you want to do everything you can to pass on your first try. That's where studying comes in.

I have included in this book several practice exam questions for each chapter and a sample test, so if you don't score well on the chapter questions, you can study more and then tackle the sample test at the end of the book. If you don't earn a score of at least 70 percent after this test, you'll want to investigate the other practice test resources I mention in this section.

For any given subject, consider taking a class if you've tackled self-study materials, taken the test, and failed anyway. If you can afford the privilege, the opportunity to interact with an instructor and fellow students can make all the difference in the world. For information about Oracle classes, visit the Training and Certification page at **http://education.oracle.com**.

If you can't afford to take a class, visit the Training and Certification page anyway, because it also includes free practice exams that you can download. Even if you can't afford to spend much at all, you should still invest in some low-cost practice exams from commercial vendors, because they can help you assess your readiness to pass a test better than any other tool. The following company offers practice exams on its Web site for less than $100 apiece (and some for significantly less than that):

- Selftest Software at **www.selftestsoftware.com**

6. Have you taken a practice exam on your chosen test subject? [Yes or No]

   If yes—and you scored 70 percent or better—you're probably ready to tackle the real thing. If your score isn't above that crucial threshold, keep at it until you break that barrier. If you answered no, obtain all the free and low-budget practice tests you can find (or afford) and get to work. Keep at it until you can comfortably break the passing threshold.

> **TIP** There is no better way to assess your test readiness than to take a good-quality practice exam and pass with a score of 70 percent or better. When I'm preparing, I shoot for 80-plus percent, just to leave room for the "weirdness factor" that sometimes shows up on Oracle exams.

Assessing Your Readiness For Exam 1Z0-013 (Test 2)

In addition to the general exam-readiness information in the previous section, other resources are available to help you prepare for the Oracle8: Database Administration exam. For starters, visit the Revealnet pipeline (**www.revealnet.com**) or **technet.oracle.com**. These are great places to ask questions and get good answers, or simply to observe the questions that others ask (along with the answers, of course).

Oracle exam mavens also recommend checking the Oracle Knowledge Base from Revealnet. You can get information on purchasing the Revealnet software at **www.revealnet.com**.

For Introduction to Oracle: SQL and PL/SQL preparation in particular, I'd also like to recommend that you check out one or more of these books as you prepare to take the exam:

- Ault, Michael. *Oracle8 Administration and Management.* Wiley, 1998.
- Loney, Kevin. *Oracle8 DBA Handbook.* Oracle Press, 1998.
- Kreines, David C., and Laskey, Brian. *Oracle Database Administration.* O'Reilly, 1999.
- Toledo, Hugo. *Oracle Networking*. Oracle Press, 1996.

Stop by your favorite bookstore or online bookseller to check out one or more of these books. The first two are—in my opinion—the best general all-around references on Oracle8 available, and the third complements the contents of this *Exam Cram* very nicely. The fourth book provides excellent basic information on networking.

One last note: Hopefully, it makes sense to stress the importance of hands-on experience in the context of the Database Administration exam. As you review the material for that exam, you'll realize that hands-on experience with Oracle8 commands, tools, and utilities is invaluable.

Onward, Through The Fog!

Once you've assessed your readiness, undertaken the right background studies, obtained the hands-on experience that will help you understand the products and technologies at work, and reviewed the many sources of information to help you prepare for a test, you'll be ready to take a round of practice tests. When your scores come back positive enough to get you through the exam, you're ready to go after the real thing. If you follow my assessment regime, you'll not only know what you need to study, but when you're ready to make a test date at Sylvan. Good luck!

1

Oracle OCP Certification Exams

Terms you'll need to understand:

- ✓ Radio button
- ✓ Checkbox
- ✓ Exhibit
- ✓ Multiple-choice question formats
- ✓ Careful reading
- ✓ Process of elimination

Techniques you'll need to master:

- ✓ Assessing your exam-readiness
- ✓ Preparing to take a certification exam
- ✓ Practicing (to make perfect)
- ✓ Making the best use of the testing software
- ✓ Budgeting your time
- ✓ Saving the hardest questions until last
- ✓ Guessing (as a last resort)

As experiences go, test-taking is not something that most people anticipate eagerly, no matter how well they're prepared. In most cases, familiarity helps ameliorate test anxiety. In plain English, this means you probably won't be as nervous when you take your fourth or fifth Oracle certification exam as you will be when you take your first one.

But no matter whether it's your first test or your tenth, understanding the exam-taking particulars (how much time to spend on questions, the setting you'll be in, and so on) and the testing software will help you concentrate on the material rather than on the environment. Likewise, mastering a few basic test-taking skills should help you recognize—and perhaps even outfox—some of the tricks and gotchas you're bound to find in some of the Oracle test questions.

In this chapter, I'll explain the testing environment and software, as well as describe some proven test-taking strategies you should be able to use to your advantage.

Assessing Exam-Readiness

Before you take any Oracle exam, I strongly recommend that you read through and take the Self-Assessment included with this book (it appears just before this chapter, in fact). This will help you compare your knowledge base to the requirements for obtaining an OCP, and it will also help you identify parts of your background or experience that may be in need of improvement, enhancement, or further learning. If you get the right set of basics under your belt, obtaining Oracle certification will be that much easier.

Once you've gone through the Self-Assessment, you can remedy those topical areas where your background or experience may not measure up to an ideal certification candidate. But you can also tackle subject matter for individual tests at the same time, so you can continue making progress while you're catching up in some areas.

Once you've worked through an *Exam Cram*, read the supplementary materials, and taken the practice test at the end of the book, you'll have a pretty clear idea of when you should be ready to take the real exam. Although I strongly recommend that you keep practicing until your scores top the 70 percent mark, 75 percent would be a good goal to give yourself some margin for error in a real exam situation (where stress will play more of a role than when you practice). Once you hit that point, you should be ready to go. But if you get through the practice exam in this book without attaining that score, you should keep taking practice tests and studying the materials until you get there. You'll find more information about other practice test vendors in the

Self-Assessment, along with even more pointers on how to study and prepare. But now, on to the exam itself!

The Testing Situation

When you arrive at the Sylvan Prometric Testing Center where you scheduled your test, you'll need to sign in with a test coordinator. He or she will ask you to produce two forms of identification, one of which must be a photo ID. Once you've signed in and your time slot arrives, you'll be asked to leave any books, bags, or other items you brought with you, and you'll be escorted into a closed room. Typically, that room will be furnished with anywhere from one to half a dozen computers, and each workstation is separated from the others by dividers designed to keep you from seeing what's happening on someone else's computer.

You'll be furnished with a pen or pencil and a blank sheet of paper or, in some cases, an erasable plastic sheet and an erasable felt-tip pen. You're allowed to write down any information you want on this sheet, and you can write stuff on both sides of the page. I suggest that you memorize as much as possible of the material that appears on The Cram Sheet (inside the front of this book), and then write that information down on the blank sheet as soon as you sit down in front of the test machine. You can refer to the sheet any time you like during the test, but you'll have to surrender it when you leave the room.

Most test rooms feature a wall with a large window. This allows the test coordinator to monitor the room, to prevent test-takers from talking to one another, and to observe anything out of the ordinary that might go on. The test coordinator will have preloaded the Oracle certification test you've signed up for, and you'll be permitted to start as soon as you're seated in front of the machine.

All Oracle certification exams permit you to take up to a certain maximum amount of time (usually 90 minutes) to complete the test (the test itself will tell you, and it maintains an on-screen counter/clock so you can check the time remaining any time you like). Each exam consists of between 60 and 70 questions, randomly selected from a pool of questions.

> **TIP** The passing score varies per exam and the questions selected. For Exam 1Z0-013, the passing score is 68 percent.

All Oracle certification exams are computer generated and use a multiple-choice format. Although this might sound easy, the questions are constructed not just to check your mastery of basic facts and figures about Oracle8 DBA topics, but also require you to evaluate one or more sets of circumstances or requirements. Often, you'll be asked to give more than one answer to a question; likewise, you may be asked to select the best or most effective solution to a problem from a range of choices, all of which technically are correct. The tests are quite an adventure, and they involve real thinking. This book will show you what to expect and how to deal with the problems, puzzles, and predicaments you're likely to find on the tests—in particular, Exam 1Z0-013 (Test 2), "Oracle8 DBA: Database Administration."

Test Layout And Design

A typical test question is depicted in Question 1. It's a multiple-choice question that requires you to select a single correct answer. Following the question is a brief summary of each potential answer and why it was either right or wrong.

Question 1

If an instance fails, which type of segment is used to recover uncommitted transactions?

❍ a. Table

❍ b. Index

❍ c. Rollback

❍ d. Temporary

Answer c is correct. Transaction recovery occurs after an instance failure. All uncommitted transactions are rolled back using the redo log files and the before images stored in rollback segments. Table is a data segment and is not used in recovery. Index is an index segment and is not used in recovery either. Temporary segments are used for sorting, not for recovery.

This sample question corresponds closely to those you'll see on Oracle certification tests. To select the correct answer during the test, you would position the cursor over the radio button next to answer c and click the mouse to select that particular choice. The only difference between the certification test and this question is that the real questions are not immediately followed by the answers.

Next, I'll examine a question where one or more answers are possible. This type of question provides checkboxes, rather than radio buttons, for marking all appropriate selections.

Question 2

Which dynamic performance views would you join to display the current size of the R03 rollback segment? [Choose two]

- ❑ a. **V$SESSION**
- ❑ b. **V$ROLLNAME**
- ❑ c. **V$ROLLSTAT**
- ❑ d. **V$PARAMETER**
- ❑ e. **V$DATAFILE**
- ❑ f. **V$TRANSACTION**
- ❑ g. **V$DATAFILE_HEADER**

Answers b and c are correct. **V$ROLLNAME** displays the name and USN of each rollback segment. **V$ROLLSTAT** displays the USN, status, optimal size, current size, HWM, and the current and active extent of each rollback segment. Answers a, d, e, f, and g do not show any rollback size information.

For this type of question, one or more answers must be selected to answer the question correctly. For Question 2, you would have to select the checkboxes next to items b and c to obtain credit for a correct answer.

These two basic types of questions can appear in many forms. They constitute the foundation on which all the Oracle certification exam questions rest. More complex questions may include so-called "exhibits," which are usually tables or data-content layouts of one form or another. You'll be expected to use the information displayed in the exhibit to guide your answer to the question.

Other questions involving exhibits may use charts or diagrams to help document a workplace scenario that you'll be asked to troubleshoot or configure. Paying careful attention to such exhibits is the key to success—be prepared to toggle between the picture and the question as you work. Often, both are complex enough that you might not be able to remember all of either one.

Using Oracle's Test Software Effectively

A well-known test-taking principle is to read over the entire test from start to finish first, but to answer only those questions that you feel absolutely sure of on the first pass. On subsequent passes, you can dive into more complex questions, knowing how many such questions you have to deal with.

Fortunately, Oracle test software makes this approach easy to implement. At the bottom of each question, you'll find a checkbox that permits you to mark that question for a later visit. (Note that marking questions makes review easier, but you can return to any question by clicking the Forward and Back buttons repeatedly until you get to the question.) As you read each question, if you answer only those you're sure of and mark for review those that you're not, you can keep going through a decreasing list of open questions as you knock the trickier ones off.

> **TIP** There's at least one potential benefit to reading the test over completely before answering the trickier questions: Sometimes, you find information in later questions that sheds more light on earlier ones. Other times, information you read in later questions might jog your memory about Oracle8 DBA facts, figures, or behavior that also will help with earlier questions. Either way, you'll come out ahead if you defer those questions about which you're not absolutely sure of the answer(s).

Keep working on the questions until you are absolutely sure of all your answers or until you know you'll run out of time. If there are still unanswered questions, you'll want to zip through them and guess. No answer guarantees no credit for a question, and a guess has at least a chance of being correct. (Oracle scores blank answers and incorrect answers as equally wrong.)

> **TIP** At the very end of your test period, you're better off guessing than leaving questions blank or unanswered.

Taking Testing Seriously

The most important advice I can give you about taking any Oracle test is this: Read each question carefully. Some questions are deliberately ambiguous; some use double negatives; others use terminology in incredibly precise ways. I've taken numerous practice tests and real tests myself, and in nearly every test I've missed at least one question because I didn't read it closely or carefully enough.

Here are some suggestions on how to deal with the tendency to jump to an answer too quickly:

- Make sure you read every word in the question. If you find yourself jumping ahead impatiently, go back and start over.
- As you read, try to restate the question in your own terms. If you can do this, you should be able to pick the correct answer(s) much more easily.
- When returning to a question after your initial read-through, reread every word again—otherwise, the mind falls quickly into a rut. Sometimes, seeing a question afresh after turning your attention elsewhere lets you see something you missed before, but the strong tendency is to see what you've seen before. Try to avoid that tendency at all costs.
- If you return to a question more than twice, try to articulate to yourself what you don't understand about the question, why the answers don't appear to make sense, or what appears to be missing. If you chew on the subject for a while, your subconscious might provide the details that are lacking, or you may notice a "trick" that will point to the right answer.

Above all, try to deal with each question by thinking through what you know about being an Oracle8 DBA—utilities, characteristics, behaviors, facts, and figures involved. By reviewing what you know (and what you've written down on your information sheet), you'll often recall or understand things sufficiently to determine the answer to the question.

Question-Handling Strategies

Based on the tests I've taken, a couple of interesting trends in the answers have become apparent. For those questions that take only a single answer, usually two or three of the answers will be obviously incorrect, and two of the answers will be plausible. But, of course, only one can be correct. Unless the answer leaps out at you (and if it does, reread the question to look for a trick; sometimes those are the ones you're most likely to get wrong), begin the process of answering by eliminating those answers that are obviously wrong.

Things to look for in the "obviously wrong" category include spurious command choices or table or view names, nonexistent software or command options, and terminology you've never seen before. If you've done your homework for a test, no valid information should be completely new to you. In that case, unfamiliar or bizarre terminology probably indicates a totally bogus answer. As long as you're sure what's right, it's easy to eliminate what's wrong.

Numerous questions assume that the default behavior of a particular Oracle utility (such as Oracle Enterprise Manager [OEM] or SQL*Loader) is in effect. It's essential, therefore, to know and understand the default settings for

OEM, SQL*Loader, and Server Manager utilities. If you know the defaults and understand what they mean, this knowledge will help you cut through many Gordian knots.

Likewise, when dealing with questions that require multiple answers, you must know and select all the correct options to get credit. This, too, qualifies as an example of why careful reading is so important.

As you work your way through the test, another counter that Oracle thankfully provides will come in handy—the number of questions completed and questions outstanding. Budget your time by making sure that you've completed one-fourth of the questions one-quarter of the way through the test period (between 13 and 17 questions in the first 22 or 23 minutes). Check again three-quarters of the way through (between 39 and 51 questions in the first 66 to 69 minutes).

If you're not through after 85 minutes, use the last five minutes to guess your way through the remaining questions. Remember, guesses are potentially more valuable than blank answers, because blanks are always wrong, but a guess might turn out to be right. If you haven't a clue with any of the remaining questions, pick answers at random, or choose all a's, b's, and so on. The important thing is to submit a test for scoring that has an answer for every question.

Mastering The Inner Game

In the final analysis, knowledge breeds confidence, and confidence breeds success. If you study the materials in this book carefully and review the questions at the end of each chapter, you should be aware of those areas where additional studying is required.

Next, follow up by reading some or all of the materials recommended in the "Need To Know More?" section at the end of each chapter. The idea is to become familiar enough with the concepts and situations that you find in the sample questions to be able to reason your way through similar situations on a real test. If you know the material, you have every right to be confident that you can pass the test.

Once you've worked your way through the book, take the practice test in Chapter 15. The test will provide a reality check and will help you identify areas you need to study further. Make sure you follow up and review materials related to the questions you miss before scheduling a real test. Only when you've covered all the ground and feel comfortable with the whole scope of the practice test, should you take a real test.

TIP: If you take the practice test (Chapter 15) and don't score at least 75 percent correct, you'll want to practice further. At a minimum, download the practice tests and the self-assessment tests from the Oracle Education Web site's download page (its location appears in the next section). If you're more ambitious or better funded, you might want to purchase a practice test from one of the third-party vendors that offers them.

Armed with the information in this book and with the determination to augment your knowledge, you should be able to pass the certification exam. But if you don't work at it, you'll spend the test fee more than once before you finally pass. If you prepare seriously, the execution should go flawlessly. Good luck!

Additional Resources

By far, the best source of information about Oracle certification tests comes from Oracle itself. Because its products and technologies—and the tests that go with them—change frequently, the best place to go for exam-related information is online.

If you haven't already visited the Oracle certification pages, do so right now. As I'm writing this chapter, the certification home page resides at **http://education.oracle.com/certification/** (see Figure 1.1).

> *Note: It might not be there by the time you read this, or it may have been replaced by something new and different, because things change regularly on the Oracle site. Should this happen, please read the section titled "Coping With Change On The Web," later in this chapter.*

The menu options in the left column of the page point to the most important sources of information in the certification pages. Here's what to check out:

- *FAQs*—Frequently Asked Questions; yours might be answered here.
- *What's New*—Any new tests are described here.
- *Test Information*—This is a detailed section that provides many jump points to detailed test descriptions for the several OCP certifications.
- *Practice Tests*—This section is a source for practice tests.
- *Test Registration*—This section provides information for phone registration and a link to the Prometric Web page for online registration. Also, this section provides a list of testing sites outside of the U.S.

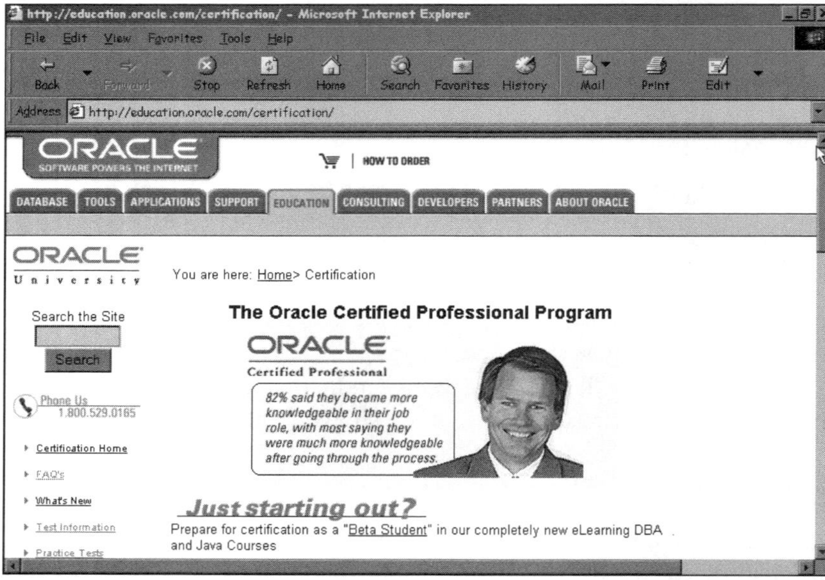

Figure 1.1 The Oracle certification page should be your starting point for further investigation of the most current exam and preparation information.

- *Candidate Agreements*—Just what are you agreeing to be by becoming Oracle certified?
- *OCP Logo*—After you receive your certification, you can go to this page to download OCP graphics.
- *Oracle Partners*—This link provides information about test discounts and other offers for Oracle Partner companies.

Of course, these are just the high points of what's available in the Oracle certification pages. As you browse through them—and I strongly recommend that you do—you'll probably find other things I didn't mention here that are every bit as interesting and compelling.

Coping With Change On The Web

Sooner or later, all the specifics I've shared with you about the Oracle certification pages, and all the other Web-based resources I mention throughout the rest of this book, will go stale or be replaced by newer information. In some cases, the URLs you find here might lead you to their replacements; in other cases, the URLs will go nowhere, leaving you with the dreaded "404 File not found" error message.

When that happens, please don't give up. There's always a way to find what you want on the Web—if you're willing to invest some time and energy. To begin with, most large or complex Web sites—and Oracle's qualifies on both counts—offer a search engine. As long as you can get to Oracle's home page (and I'm sure that it will stay at **www.oracle.com** for a long while yet), you can use this tool to help you find what you need.

The more particular or focused you can make a search request, the more likely it is that the results will include information you can use. For instance, you can search the string "training and certification" to produce a lot of data about the subject in general, but, if you're looking for the Preparation Guide for the Oracle DBA tests, you'll be more likely to get there quickly if you use a search string such as this:

```
"DBA" AND "preparation guide"
```

Likewise, if you want to find the training and certification downloads, try a search string such as this one:

```
"training and certification" AND "download page"
```

Finally, don't be afraid to use general search tools, such as **www.search.com**, **www.altavista.com**, or **www.excite.com**, to search for related information. Even though Oracle offers the best information about its certification exams online, there are plenty of third-party sources of information, training, and assistance in this area that do not have to follow a party line like Oracle does. The bottom line is this: If you can't find something where the book says it lives, start looking around. If worse comes to worse, you can always email me! I just might have a clue. My email address is **paulcollins@compuserve.com**.

2

Oracle Architectural Components

Terms you'll need to understand:

- √ Oracle instance
- √ Oracle database
- √ System global area (SGA)
- √ Shared pool
- √ Program global area (PGA)
- √ Background processes
- √ Buffer
- √ Tablespace
- √ Schema
- √ Segment
- √ Extent
- √ Data block
- √ Datafile

Techniques you'll need to master:

- √ Understanding the structures of the SGA
- √ Understanding the interrelations of Oracle processes
- √ Understanding the physical structure of an Oracle database
- √ Understanding how a commit is processed

Understanding the Oracle architecture and how it works will help you in all your future database administrator (DBA) tasks. Your abilities to troubleshoot, tune, and recover the database are especially enhanced with this knowledge. In this chapter, I'll explain the Oracle architectural components and explore the differences between an Oracle instance and an Oracle database. An intimate and complete understanding of how both the Oracle internal structures and the Oracle processes interact with each other is vital to your success as a DBA.

The Oracle Instance And The System Global Area (SGA)

All too often the concepts of an Oracle *instance* and an Oracle *database* are confused. To really understand Oracle, you must understand the internal structures that make up an Oracle instance and an Oracle database.

All running Oracle databases are associated with an Oracle instance. When a database is started, Oracle allocates a memory area called the *system global area (SGA)* and starts one or more Oracle processes. The SGA and the Oracle processes make up an Oracle instance.

Figure 2.1 shows the Oracle processes. Use this diagram of Oracle processes, files, and SGA components to help understand the interrelationships described in this chapter.

The SGA is made up of several memory components, and the largest of these is usually the database buffer cache, followed by the shared pool area and the redo log buffers. The shared pool consists of the following components:

- *The shared SQL area* (also known as the *library cache*)—Where SQL and PL/SQL statements are kept.
- *The data dictionary cache*—Where data dictionary-related entries are kept.
- *Control structures*—These structures include latches, locks, character set data, and, if multithreaded server (MTS) is being used, request and response queues.

Figure 2.1 graphically depicts these SGA components and their relationships to the Oracle datafiles. The SGA also contains the sort extent pool (SEP) in non-MTS instances; in MTS instances, the user global area (UGA) contains the SEP.

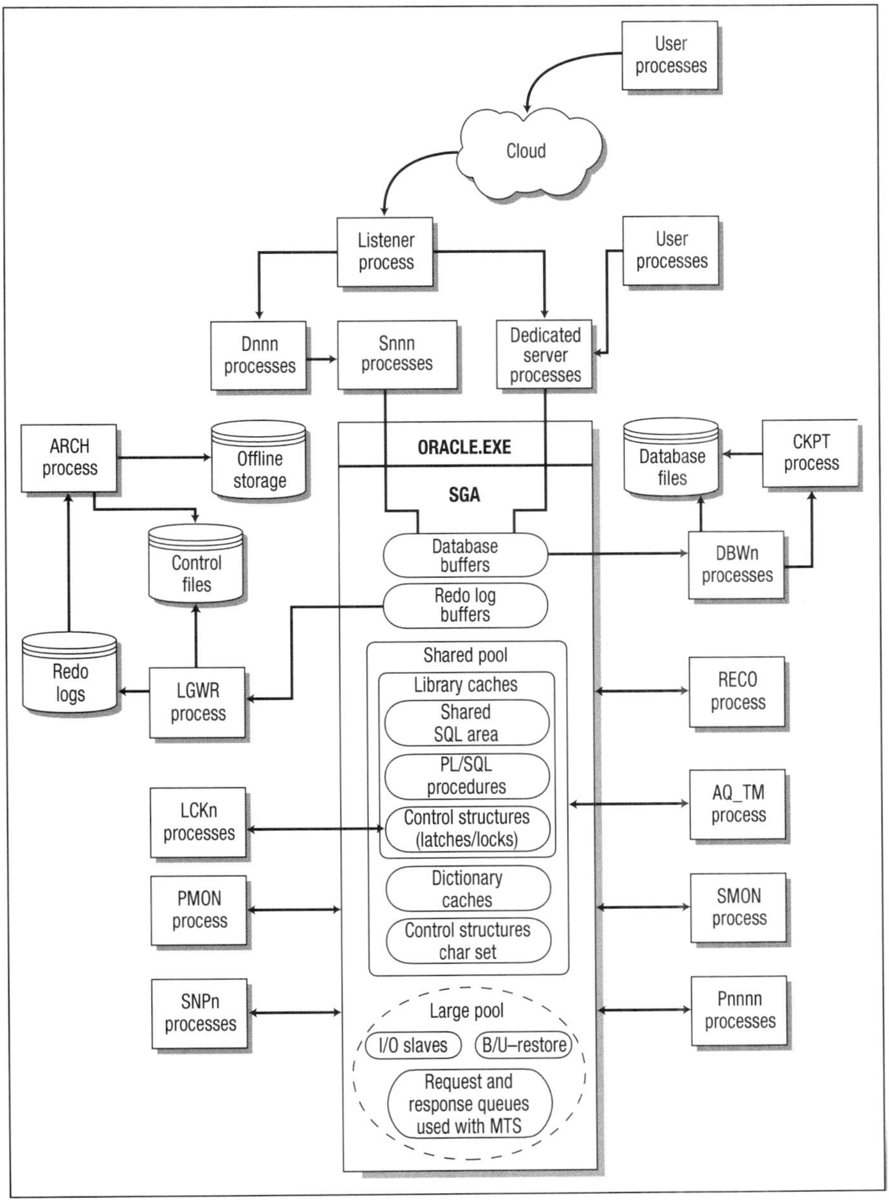

Figure 2.1 Oracle processes.

The SGA is read-write; all users connected to a multiple-user instance can read information from the instance's SGA, and multiple processes write to the SGA during execution. Figure 2.2 shows which processes read and write to the SGA.

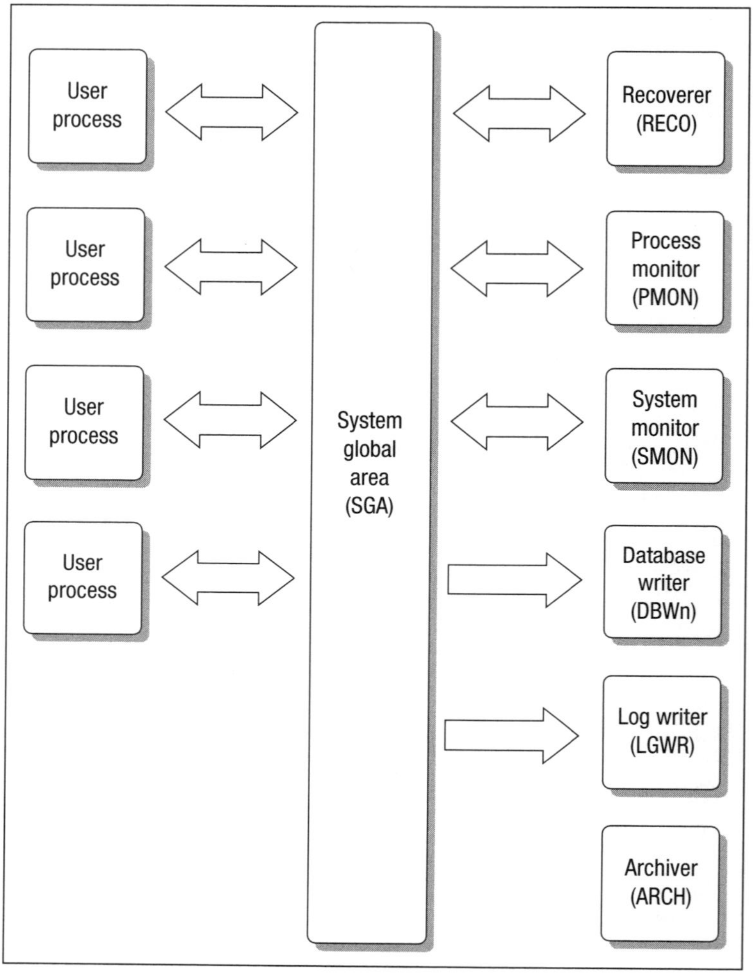

Figure 2.2 SGA and user process interaction.

The SGA also includes information communicated between processes, such as locking information. If the system uses an MTS architecture, the request and response queues as well as some user session information are kept in the SGA. (See the "Program Global Area (PGA)" section later in this chapter.)

The Database Buffer Cache

The database buffer cache is normally the largest component of the SGA, which is controlled by the initialization parameters **DB_BLOCK_SIZE** and **DB_BLOCK_BUFFERS**. The **DB_BLOCK_SIZE** sets the size of database blocks used in all other components of the SGA. The **DB_BLOCK_SIZE** is a multiple of the operating system (OS) block size, which is usually a multiple of 512 bytes. On most systems, the **DB_BLOCK_SIZE** is a minimum of 2K.

The database buffer area is divided into the *dirty list* (buffers that have been modified and are waiting to be written to disk) and the least recently used (LRU) list. Buffers that are unmodified and can be used are called *free buffers*. If an Oracle server (user) process attempts to move a buffer to the dirty list and the list is full, it signals the database writer (DBWn) process, which writes the dirty buffers back to disk, placing them on the free list. The only action that adds a data block to the database buffer cache is a read by a server process at the request of a user. The database buffer cache stores copies of data blocks and is shared by all users.

When an Oracle process accesses a buffer, the buffer is moved to the most recently used (MRU) end of the LRU list. As more buffers are moved to the MRU end of the LRU list, dirty buffers move towards the LRU end of the LRU list.

When a user process asks for a piece of data the first time, it searches for the data in the database buffer cache. If the data is found in the cache (a cache hit), it is read from cache memory, which is very fast. If the data can't be found in the cache (a cache miss), the data must be copied from a datafile on disk to the buffer cache before it can be used by the user process.

To read a data block into the buffer cache, the process must find a free buffer. The process must search the LRU list, starting at the LRU end of the list, until it finds a free buffer or until it has searched the limit of buffers. If a buffer is not dirty, it does not need to be written to disk before a new block can be read into the buffer. As the process searches the LRU, it moves dirty buffers to the dirty list. When it finds a free buffer, it reads the data block from disk into the buffer and moves the buffer to the MRU end of the LRU. If a process searches without finding a free buffer, the process signals the DBWn background process to write some of the dirty buffers to disk.

A full table scan reads the blocks of a table and puts them on the LRU end of the LRU list instead of on the MRU end. This helps performance because it is normally not desirable to keep blocks from a full table scan in the buffer cache.

To change the way Oracle treats a full table scan, use the **CACHE** clause when creating or altering a table. This will cause blocks to be put on the MRU end of the list. This might be desirable for small code tables or large static tables that have heavy input/output (I/O).

You can configure the database buffer cache with separate buffer pools. This allows different database objects (tables, clusters, indexes, and partitions) to age out of the buffer cache differently. When a database object is created, it is assigned to an appropriate buffer pool to control the way its data blocks age out of the cache. The **KEEP** buffer pool retains the schema object's data blocks in memory. The **RECYCLE** buffer pool eliminates data blocks from memory as soon as they are no longer needed. The **DEFAULT** buffer pool contains data blocks from schema objects that are not assigned to the **KEEP** or **RECYCLE** buffer pool, as well as schema objects that are explicitly assigned to the **DEFAULT** pool. The initialization parameters that configure the **KEEP** and **RECYCLE** buffer pools are **BUFFER_POOL_KEEP** and **BUFFER_POOL_RECYCLE**.

The Redo Log Buffer

The *redo log buffer* is contained within the SGA and holds information about database changes. These changes consisting of inserts, updates, deletes, creates, alters, or drops are stored in *redo entries*. Redo entries can be used for recovery when needed. The circular process of the redo log buffer is started when the background process log writer (LGWR) writes the redo log buffer to the active online redo log file on disk, allowing the server processes to write new data to the redo log buffer. The **LOG_BUFFER** initialization parameter sets the size of the redo log buffer in bytes.

The Shared Pool

The second largest component of the SGA is the *shared pool*; it is controlled in size by the initialization parameter **SHARED_POOL_SIZE**. This parameter is set in bytes and is generally set to 10 to 20 percent of available memory; however, in some heavy ad hoc environments, it can be much larger. In dedicated server environments, the shared pool can be smaller than the equivalent MTS environment. This happens because, in a dedicated server system, the sort areas used by each process are kept in the user's program global area (PGA), whereas in an MTS environment, the UGA extents used for sorting are tracked using the SEP, which is a part of the shared pool. Any time a process needs a temporary segment for sorting, it checks the SEP first before allocating a new segment.

The shared pool portion of the SGA contains three memory structures: the library cache, dictionary cache, and control structures. Figure 2.3 shows the contents of the shared pool.

Library Cache

The shared SQL areas, private SQL areas, PL/SQL procedures and packages, and control structures (i.e., locks and library cache handles) are located in the *library cache*. The size of the shared pool is used in determining the size of the

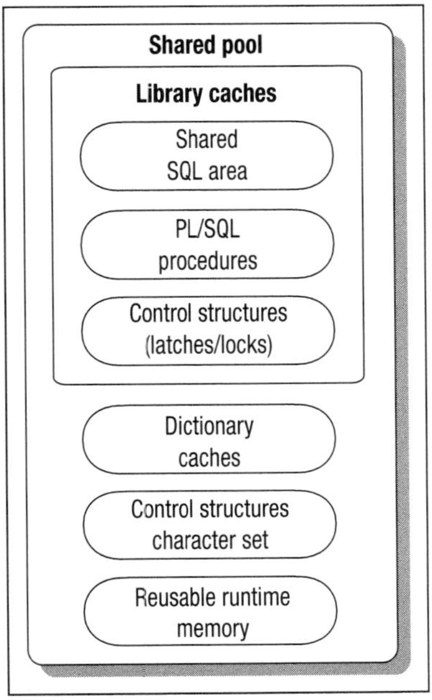

Figure 2.3 The contents and organization of the shared pool.

library cache. The parse tree and execution plan for a single SQL statement is contained in the shared SQL area. Memory is saved in Oracle by using one shared SQL area for identical data manipulation language (DML) statements. Oracle manages the shared SQL area using a modified LRU algorithm. If a SQL statement requires a new shared SQL area and the shared pool is fully allocated, items are deallocated from the pool until enough free space is available for the new statement in the shared SQL area. If Oracle deallocates a shared SQL area, the SQL statement must be reparsed and reassigned to another shared SQL area when it is re-executed.

Oracle processes PL/SQL programs, procedures, functions, packages, anonymous blocks, and database triggers the same way it processes individual SQL statements. A shared SQL area is allocated to hold the parsed compiled form of a program. If more than one user executes the same program, then a single shared area is used by all users.

The shared SQL area is managed via a modified LRU algorithm. A shared SQL area remains in the shared pool even if the original process that used it is terminated. If a SQL area is not used, it ages out of the shared pool. This reduces the overhead of processing SQL statements on a multiuser system.

Oracle flushes the shared SQL area from the shared pool in the following circumstances:

- When new statistics are generated with the **ANALYZE** command, all shared SQL areas that contain statements referencing the analyzed object are flushed from the shared pool. When statements are re-executed, they are assigned a new shared SQL area and use the new statistics.
- When an object is altered, all the shared SQL area that references the object is marked invalid and will be reparsed the next time it is executed.
- When the global database name is changed, the entire shared pool is flushed.
- When the DBA manually flushes all information in the shared pool.

Data Dictionary Cache

The *data dictionary* is a set of database tables and views containing metadata about the database. Oracle frequently accesses the data dictionary. The data dictionary cache holds data as rows instead of as buffers, which hold entire blocks of data.

Control Structures

The memory for control structures in the shared pool is set automatically by Oracle. This space is used for character set conversion, network security attributes, and other Oracle control mechanisms.

Program Global Area (PGA)

The *program global area (PGA)* contains the user's session variables, session information, and arrays. Each user is assigned a PGA and, in MTS systems, a UGA. Though not a defined part of the SGA, the user's PGA interacts intimately with the SGA. A PGA is allocated when an Oracle user connects to the database and a session is created. The PGA contains a stack space to hold variables, arrays, and other information.

In a dedicated server environment, the PGA also contains information about the user's session, such as private SQL areas. If the instance is running in MTS mode, the session information is allocated in the SGA.

Background Processes

It is very important to understand how the Oracle background processes interact with the SGA. The *background processes* are part of every Oracle instance.

There are four mandatory processes that must be present at all times for Oracle to function: DBWn, LGWR, system monitor (SMON), and process monitor (PMON). Other processes will become active depending on the options of Oracle installed or the initialization parameters used. On Unix, the Oracle background processes show up as separate processes and are easy to see. On Windows NT, which is a threaded OS, only the Oracle process is displayed on the Windows NT process monitor. The background processes are still present and are threads of the Oracle process.

> You must know how each of the Oracle mandatory background processes work and how they interact with other processes. Be sure to study the following sections carefully.

Database Writer (DBWn)

The *DBWn processes* write modified or dirty blocks from the database buffer cache to the disk files. Blocks aren't written on commit; only the rollback segment and header are affected by a commit. In general, DBWn writes only when more data needs to be read into the SGA and too few database buffers are free. The LRU data is written to the datafiles first. DBWn's entire purpose is to manage the database buffer cache so the server processes can always find free buffers.

> Remember, DBWn writes to datafiles but does not read from them.

DBWn behavior is controlled by initialization parameters. The parameter **DB_WRITER_PROCESSES** specifies the number of DBWn processes (DBW0, ..., DBW9) to use for improving write performance. The **DISK_ASYNCH_IO** parameter, or **ASYNC_WRITE** on some systems, tells DBWn to enable asynchronous writing to database files on systems that allow this to be switched. On systems in which asynchronous writes are the normal mode, **DISK_ASYNCH_IO** isn't required to be set.

By using write-ahead logging, DBWn does not need to write blocks when a transaction commits. Instead, DBWn batch writes with high efficiency. In the most cases, DBWn writes only when more data needs to be read into the SGA and not enough database buffers are free. The LRU data is written to the datafiles first. Database checkpointing may also cause DBWn to perform writes.

Log Writer (LGWR)

The *LGWR process* writes out the redo buffer to the redo logs on a commit. At specific times, all modified database buffers in the SGA are written to the datafiles by DBWn; this event is called a *checkpoint*. If the checkpoint (CKPT) process in not enabled, LGWR is responsible for signaling DBWn at checkpoints and updating all the headers of the datafiles and control files of the database to indicate the most recent checkpoint. LGWR also allows for recovery of committed data in the database buffer cache at the time of an instance failure.

System Monitor (SMON)

The *SMON process* monitors the Oracle instance and recovers temporary segment space when it is no longer needed. It coalesces contiguous areas of free space in database tablespaces, where the default storage parameter, **PCTINCREASE**, is not set to zero and recovers dead transactions skipped during crash and instance recovery because of file-read or offline errors. These transactions are eventually recovered by SMON when the tablespace or file is brought back online. If SMON dies, the instance crashes, requiring instance recovery on restart.

Process Monitor (PMON)

The *PMON process* cleans up failed transactions. This cleanup involves clearing out cache entries, releasing locks, and freeing other process resources. If MTS is being used, PMON watches for dead dispatcher and server processes and restarts them as needed. If PMON dies, the instance crashes, requiring instance recovery on startup. When an instance crashes and is restarted, PMON rolls back any uncommitted transactions, using the information in the rollback segments.

Checkpoint (CKPT)

When a *checkpoint* occurs, all modified database buffers in the SGA are written to the datafiles by DBWn. The CKPT process is enabled by setting the **CHECKPOINT_PROCESS** parameter to **TRUE** in the initialization parameter file. The CKPT process is responsible for signaling DBWn at checkpoints and updating all the headers of the datafiles and control files of the database to indicate the most recent checkpoint.

Archiver (ARCH)

The *archiver (ARCH) process* copies filled redo log files to the archive log destination. ARCH is only present if archive logging is enabled for the instance. If the archive log destination is full, ARCH will silently hang. When new users try to log on the database, they will get an archiver error. This problem is reported in the alert log. No redo log will be reused until it has been archived if archive logging is in effect for the database. The **ARCHIVE_LOG_START** parameter must be set to **TRUE** and the archive log mode must be set in the database for archive logging to be in effect. If only the archive log mode is set via the **ALTER DATABASE** command, database processing will continue until all available redo logs are filled; then Oracle will hang with an error in the alert log, indicating that all online redo logs need archiving. If ARCH abnormally terminates, the database will continue operation until all online redo logs are filled before it will hang.

Recoverer (RECO)

The *recoverer (RECO) process* recovers failed distributed transactions. The RECO process is started only if the **DISTRIBUTED_TRANSACTIONS** initialization parameter is set to a value greater than zero. If you want to disable RECO, you must explicitly set this parameter to zero in the parameter file.

Dispatcher (Dnnn) And Shared Server (Snnn)

The *dispatcher (Dnnn) processes* ("nnn" is a sequential number) distribute instance attachments to the *shared server (Snnn) processes*. Snnn takes the place of dedicated servers for user connections in MTS-enabled systems. Dnnn and Snnn are only present in MTS systems. In some Oracle versions, abnormal or forced termination of Dnnn can result in instance termination.

The **MTS_DISPATCHERS, MTS_MAX_DISPATCHERS, MTS_SERVERS,** and **MTS_MAX_SERVERS** parameters control Dnnn and Snnn. In an MTS system, the SQLNET listener process determines if user connections should be dedicated or should use Snnn. If the listener determines that a shared connection is appropriate, it gives the user process the address of a Dnnn.

Lock (LCKn)

The inter-instance locking found in the Oracle Parallel Server is handled by using the *lock processes* (LCKn). Oracle allows up to 10 lock processes named LCK0 to LCK9. LCKn coordinates requests for locks in the current instance by other instances. The number of LCKn is set by the **GC_LCK_ PROCS** initialization parameter.

Job Queue (SNPn)

Table snapshots can be refreshed automatically by up to 36 *job queue (SNP0, ..., SNP9, SNPA, ..., SNPZ) processes* in a distributed database configuration. Periodically, these processes wake up and refresh any snapshots that are scheduled to be refreshed. The processes share the task of refreshing snapshots when more than one SNPn is used. Job requests created by the **DBMS_JOB** package are executed, and queued messages are propagated to queues on other databases, by these processes.

Queue Monitor (QMNn)

The *queue monitor (QMNn) processes* are optional and monitor the message queues for Oracle Advanced Queuing (Oracle AQ).

Oracle Database Structure

This section describes what makes up an Oracle *database*. Although an Oracle database is defined technically as a set of physical structures called datafiles, redo log files, and control files, it is important to understand the logical structures used in the database. After all, the purpose of the database is to store and retrieve information. This purpose can be achieved only by using logical and physical structures together. I will discuss the logical structures first and then describe what physically makes up the logical structures on the computer. Finally, I will present a summary of how Oracle commits changes to the database. This section shows how the Oracle instance and database structures work together in the processing of changes to the database.

Logical Database Structures

Logical database structures consist of tablespaces, schema objects, segments, extents, and data blocks.

Tablespaces

Tablespaces are the logical storage divisions of an Oracle database, which group schema objects together. For example, all the tables for the **SYS** schema in Oracle are grouped together in the system tablespace. A tablespace is made up of one or more *datafiles*. The datafiles physically store the data of all logical structures in a tablespace.

Schemas And Schema Objects

Groups or sets of Oracle database objects are *schemas*. Logical arrangements that refer directly to the data are called *schema objects*. Tables, views, sequences, stored procedures, synonyms, indexes, clusters, and database links are all schema objects. No relationship exists between a tablespace and a schema. Objects associated with a schema can be in different tablespaces, and a tablespace can hold objects from different schemas.

Segments

A *segment* is a set of extents allocated for a logical structure. The different types of segments include the following:

- *Data segment*—Each table or cluster has a data segment. A table's or cluster's data segments extents hold all relevant data for the schema object.
- *Index segment*—An index segment associated with each index stores all the index data.
- *Rollback segment*—Rollback segments store database undo data, allowing noncommitted transactions to be rolled back. Undo information is used in creating read-consistent database information so that all transactions can maintain a read-consistent view of the database.
- *Temporary segment*—Oracle creates temporary segments in cases where a SQL statement requires a work area to complete execution. Temporary segments are either freed or reused by the database once the statement finishes execution.

Extents

An *extent* is made up of a specific number of contiguous data blocks. Extents are allocated in a single action and used to store a specific type of information (i.e., table or index). When extents become full, Oracle dynamically allocates more space by adding more extents. Because extents are allocated as needed, the extents of a segment are usually not contiguous on disk.

Data Blocks

An Oracle database's data is stored in *data blocks*. A data block is made up of a specific number of bytes of physical memory space on disk. A data block size is specified for each Oracle database when the database is created. A database uses and allocates database space in Oracle data blocks.

Physical Database Structures

The following section explains the physical database structures of an Oracle database, including datafiles, redo log files, and control files.

Datafiles

All Oracle's database data is stored in *datafiles* that are unique to each database. The data of logical database structures, such as tables and indexes, is physically stored in a database's datafiles. One or more datafiles make up a tablespace (see the "Tablespaces" section in this chapter).

Under normal database execution, data in a datafile is read as necessary and is stored in the instance data buffer cache. If information that is not yet in the data buffer cache for the instance is requested, that data is read from the datafiles and stored in the cache.

Modified or new data is not immediately written to a datafile. Instead, the DBWn pools data in memory and writes it to the appropriate datafiles at one time to reduce I/O and improve performance.

Redo Log Files

The *redo log files* are set up at instance creation. A minimum of two one-member groups in a single thread is required for instance startup. The redo logs hold records used for recovery purposes, and they contain information on all data modifying transactions that occur in the database, unless these transactions have been run with the **NOLOGGING** option. LGWR writes data on changes from the redo log buffers to the redo logs. A commit is not considered complete until the LGWR signals that all redo log entries have been written to disk. (Remember that the redo log buffer is a part of the SGA.) The information in a redo log file is used only to recover the database from a system or media failure that prevents database data from being written to a database's datafiles.

Control Files

The *control files* contain the names and locations of all datafiles and log files for the database and their current transaction state. These files also contain the database name and the timestamp of database creation. The control files are read to mount and open the database, and transaction numbers are recorded for each datafile. If the control files and datafiles are out of sync, the database will not start up and will report either that recovery is needed or that the datafiles are out of sync with the control files. Control files are required for database startup and recovery. The database is required to have one control file; however, Oracle recommends a minimum of two control files on separate physical disks as a protective measure against failure.

Commit Processing

When a commit happens in a transaction, it is parsed by Oracle and a commit record is placed in the redo log buffer. A system change number (SCN) is also assigned to the transaction. LGWR writes the redo log buffer to the active redo log group. The transaction process is notified that the commit was successful. All resources held by that transaction, such as locks and rollback entries, are released. Finally, DBWn writes the database blocks to disk.

The following sequence shows the order of events when a commit is issued:

1. The SCN and the commit record are placed in the redo log buffer by a server process.
2. LGWR writes the redo log buffer entries and the SCN to the redo log files. Only the minimum information is written to record the change; this is known as a *fast commit*.
3. The user is notified that the commit is complete.
4. The server process records that the transaction is complete and that the resource locks can be released.

Note: The data changes for a committed transaction, stored in the database buffers of the SGA, are not written immediately to the datafiles by the DBWn. This writing takes place when it is most efficient to do so.

Practice Questions

Question 1

Which component of the SGA records changes made to the database by the current instance?

- a. Redo log buffer
- b. Shared pool
- c. Database buffer cache
- d. Dictionary cache

Answer a is correct. All four options listed are components of the SGA. The redo log buffer stores changes before they are written to the redo log files. The shared pool contains the library cache and data dictionary cache, not database changes. The database buffer cache stores the MRU data, but not changes to the data. The dictionary cache is in the shared pool and holds the MRU data dictionary data.

Question 2

What is the last step of a transaction when a commit is issued?

- a. The redo log buffer is written to disk by LGWR.
- b. The message "Commit Complete" is sent back to the user process.
- c. Dirty buffers in the database buffer cache are flushed.
- d. The server process records that the resource locks on the data can be released.

Answer d is correct. When a commit is issued, it is processed in this order:

1. The commit record with an SCN is placed in the redo log buffer by a server process.
2. LGWR writes the redo log buffer entries with the SCN to the redo log files.
3. The user process is notified that the commit is complete.

4. The server process records that the transaction is complete and that the resource locks can be released.

Answer c is wrong because dirty buffers in the database buffer cache are flushed independantly of the commit.

Question 3

Where is parsed code for SQL statements kept in the SGA?

- ❍ a. Database buffer cache
- ❍ b. Redo log buffer
- ❍ c. Data dictionary cache
- ◉ d. Library cache

Answer d is correct. The library cache stores the parsed code for a SQL statement. If a query is re-executed before it is aged out of the library cache, the server will use the parsed code and execution plan from the library cache instead of recompiling the statement. The database buffer cache stores the MRU data. The redo log buffer stores redo information. The data dictionary cache is used to cache the data dictionary tables.

Question 4

Which component interacts with, but is not defined as part of, an Oracle instance?

- ❍ a. Background process
- ◉ b. User process
- ❍ c. Redo log buffer
- ❍ d. Shared pool

Answer b is correct. When a user attempts to connect to a database, the user creates a user process. This process interacts with a server process and provides it the username and password. In a client/server environment, the user process runs on the client and communicates with the server process over a network. The background processes are part of an Oracle instance. The redo log buffer is part of the SGA. The shared pool is part of the SGA, which in turn is part of an Oracle instance.

Question 5

Which background process manages the database buffer cache and maintains a sufficient number of free buffers for server processes to use?

- ❍ a. CKPT
- ❍ b. LGWR
- ❍ c. DBWn
- ❍ d. SMON
- ❍ e. PMON

Answer c is correct. DBWn writes to disk frequently enough to ensure that free blocks are available when a server process needs to store a block in the database buffer cache. To minimize I/O, DBWn defers writes to the datafiles until dirty buffers reach a threshold, not enough free buffers are available, or a timeout or checkpoint occurs. CKPT is responsible for signaling DBWn at checkpoints and updating all the datafiles and control files of the database to indicate the most recent checkpoint. LGWR writes redo log entries to disk. SMON performs instance recovery at instance startup. PMON performs process recovery when a user process fails.

Question 6

Which background process writes dirty buffers in the database buffer cache to the datafiles?

- ❍ a. SMON
- ❍ b. PMON
- ❍ c. CKPT
- ❍ d. LGWR
- ❍ e. DBWn

Answer e is correct. DBWn writes dirty buffers to disk to ensure that free blocks are available when a server process needs to store a block in the database buffer cache. To minimize I/O, DBWn defers writes to the datafiles until dirty buffers reach a threshold, not enough free buffers are available, or a timeout or checkpoint occurs. SMON performs instance recovery at instance startup. PMON performs process recovery when a user process fails. CKPT is responsible for signaling DBWn at checkpoints and updating all the datafiles and control files of the database to indicate the most recent checkpoint. LGWR writes redo log entries to disk.

Question 7

If a user abnormally terminates a database connection, which background process will release the locks held by the user?

- ❍ a. PMON
- ❍ b. SMON
- ❍ c. LGWR
- ❍ d. DBWn
- ❍ e. CKPT

Answer a is correct. PMON is responsible for cleaning up after a failed user process. SMON coalesces tablespaces, cleans up temporary segments, and performs instance recovery at instance startup. LGWR writes redo log entries to disk. DBWn maintains the data buffer cache. CKPT is responsible for signaling DBWn at checkpoints and updating all the datafiles and control files of the database to indicate the most recent checkpoint.

Question 8

How does Oracle accomplish a fast commit?

- ❍ a. By writing transactions immediately to the datafiles, bypassing the buffer cache.
- ❍ b. By breaking large transactions and writing more small transactions that are processed more quickly than larger ones.
- ❍ c. By writing the minimal information required to record the changes in the redo logs.
- ❍ d. By giving transactions requesting a commit a higher priority over other processing.

Trick! question

Answer c is correct. Writes to the datafiles are deferred to reduce disk contention and I/O. Oracle's fast commit allows LGWR to record only the changes and SCN in the redo log files. The size of the transaction does not affect the time required to write to the redo log files. These writes are sequential and faster than writing entire blocks to the datafiles. Writes to the datafiles occur independently of the commit. The question is tricky because Oracle always uses the same method of committing, but it does allow commits to happen very quickly. The question implies there is a special fast commit that Oracle can do—this is not the case. Answer a is incorrect because database transactions are not written directly to datafiles. Answer b pertains to parallel query. Answer d is incorrect because all Oracle processes run at the same priority.

Question 9

When transactions commit, which background process writes redo log entries to the redo log files?

- a. LGWR
- b. PMON
- c. DBWn
- d. SMON
- e. CKPT

Answer a is correct. The redo log buffer stores changes to the database in memory until LGWR can write the changes to the redo log files. LGWR flushes the redo log buffer when the buffer becomes one-third full, when a timeout occurs, before DBWn writes to disk, and when a transaction commits. LGWR writes to the redo logs sequentially so that transactions can be applied in order in the event of a failure. Once a transaction is recorded in the redo log files, the changes to the data cannot be lost. LGWR writes redo log entries to disk. PMON performs process recovery when a user process fails. DBWn writes to the datafiles. SMON performs instance recovery at instance startup. CKPT is responsible for signaling DBWn at checkpoints and updating all the datafiles and control files of the database to indicate the most recent checkpoint.

Question 10

What are free buffers in the database buffer cache?

- a. Buffers that have changed and should be flushed to disk.
- b. Buffers that are currently in use.
- c. Buffers that are being written to disk.
- d. Buffers that can be overwritten.

Answer d is correct. Only free buffers can be overwritten. Answer a is incorrect because if a buffer has not been written to disk, it can't be overwritten. Answer b is incorrect because buffers that are in use are not on the free list. Answer c is incorrect because buffers are free only after they are written to disk.

Need To Know More?

Loney, Kevin, and Marlene Theriault: *Oracle8 DBA Handbook*, Oracle Press, Berkeley, CA, 1997. ISBN 0-07882-406-0. This book is a comprehensive guide and a must have for all DBAs.

See the Oracle documentation that is provided on CD with the Oracle RDBMS software. Pertaining to this chapter are:

Fee, Joyce: *Oracle8 Administrator's Guide*, Oracle Corporation, Redwood City, CA, 1997. Complete documentation of database administration tasks.

Lane, Paul: *Oracle8 Reference Manual*, Oracle Corporation, Redwood City, CA, 1997.

Leverenz, Lefty: *Oracle8 Concepts Guide*, Oracle Corporation, Redwood City, CA, 1997. Complete documentation of Oracle concepts.

http://education.oracle.com/tbt/ocp8.html is the site from which you can order the Oracle Education CD-ROM bundle for Oracle8 Database Administration.

www.revealnet.com is the site where RevealNet Corporation provides Oracle Administration reference software.

3

Using Administration Tools

Terms you'll need to understand:

- √ Server Manager line mode
- √ Intelligent agent
- √ Oracle Enterprise Manager (OEM) console Navigator
- √ OEM Job scheduling
- √ OEM repository
- √ Backup Manager
- √ Data Manager
- √ Instance Manager
- √ Schema Manager
- √ Security Manager
- √ Storage Manager

Techniques you'll need to master:

- √ Using Server Manager line mode
- √ Using OEM console
- √ Using Backup Manager
- √ Using Data Manager
- √ Using Instance Manager
- √ Using Schema Manager
- √ Using Security Manager
- √ Using Storage Manager

Although you can use many new graphical user interface (GUI) tools, including Oracle Enterprise Manager (OEM), to manage an Oracle database, it is important for a database administrator (DBA) to be familiar with the line mode version of Server Manager. You can use *Server Manager line mode* for batch operations, such as running nightly jobs or scripts, or when a GUI device is not available. Once you understand how to manage your database with Server Manager, you will appreciate how much easier and faster OEM is to use for daily interaction with the database. Unlike Server Manager, OEM also has the capability to manage multiple databases throughout your network. These tools are essential in order to administer Oracle databases effectively.

Server Manager

GUI tools, such as OEM, are very helpful with interactive database management. Although OEM can centralize administration of databases, many DBAs prefer to automate database administration tasks such as **STARTUP**, **SHUTDOWN**, and **BACKUP** using a command interface on the local machine. All of Oracle's installation scripts, as well as the scripts for automatic startup and shutdown of the database, use Server Manager in line mode.

The syntax for starting Server Manager is platform specific and executed from the operating system (OS) prompt. On Unix platforms, the command is **svrmgrl**. On the Windows platform, the command is **svrmgrXX** (the XX is replaced with the version of Server Manager installed). The Server Manager version shipped with Oracle 8.0.5 is **svrmgr30**. Server Manager can also start in line mode and execute a script in one command, as follows:

```
Svrmgrl command=@dbstart
```

Executing Commands Using Server Manager In Line Mode

In addition to Server Manager commands like **CREATE DATABASE**, **STARTUP**, and **SHUTDOWN**, you can execute SQL statements and PL/SQL code while in line mode. Many Server Manager commands are single line commands that do not require a command line terminator. These commands can be continued to more than one line by using a backslash (\) at the end of each line.

You can enter and execute SQL statements or PL/SQL code in Server Manager just as you can in SQL*Plus. Use a semicolon (;) to terminate and execute SQL statements and a slash (/) by itself on the last line of PL/SQL code to terminate and execute PL/SQL statements. Run SQL scripts by using the @

command. To run the script dbstart.sql, for example, the command would be as follows:

```
SVRMGR> @dbstart
```

If you do not supply a file name with the @ command, Server Manager prompts for one, as follows:

```
SVRMGR> @
Name of script file:
```

Server Manager Commands

Server Manager uses a number of commands, such as @, **ARCHIVE LOG**, **CONNECT**, **RECOVER**, **SET**, **SHOW**, **STARTUP**, and **SHUTDOWN**. Although you can run most of these commands from OEM, it is more common to use Server Manager in line mode to accomplish these tasks.

The @ Command

The @ command is used to execute a script stored as an OS file. You must give the full pathname unless the file is in the current directory. You can use a double @ (@@) within an executing script to call other scripts. The use of @@ assumes that the script file is in the same directory as the calling script. Here is an example:

```
SVRMGR> @/u01/sql/begin_bk.sql
```

The **ARCHIVE LOG** Command

The **ARCHIVE LOG** command is used to control automatic archiving or redo log files. Figure 3.1 shows the **ARCHIVE LOG** syntax.

The following list explains the **ARCHIVE LOG** command options:

➤ **LIST**—Displays current archive log mode information, as follows:

```
SVRMGR> ARCHIVE LOG LIST
Database log mode              Archive mode
Archive destination            /u01/app/oracle/admin/DB1/
                               arch/log
Oldest online log sequence     33838
Next log sequence to archive   33840
Current log sequence           33840
```

➤ **STOP**—Stops automatic archiving. This does not take the database out of archive log mode. After all redo log file groups are full, database operations stop until one of the redo log files is archived.

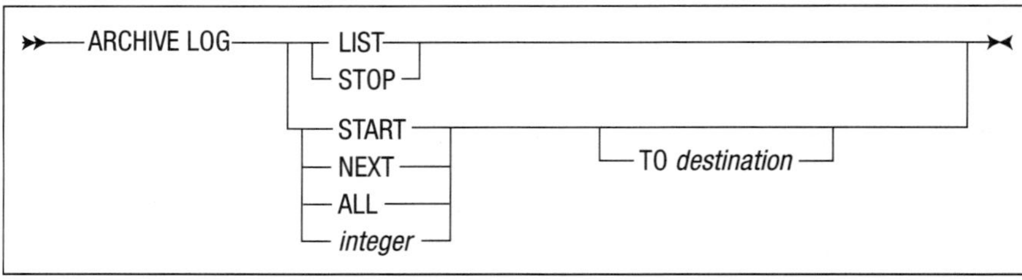

Figure 3.1 The syntax for the **ARCHIVE LOG** command.

- START—Begins automatic archiving of the database. If no location is given for the archive files, the database will use the initialization parameter **LOG_ARCHIVE_DEST**. If a location is given, it overrides the initialization parameter and starts archiving in the new location. On non-Windows NT platforms, the archiver (ARCH) background process will start. Under Windows NT, ARCH will start as a thread of the Oracle.exe process.
- NEXT—Performs a manual archive of the next online redo log file group that has been filled but not yet archived.
- ALL—Performs a manual archive of all online redo log file groups that are full but not yet archived.
- *integer*—Archives the online redo log file group with the log sequence number equal to the integer even if the log file group is not full. For example:

```
SVRMGR> ARCHIVE LOG 33840
--Archives log sequence 33840 to the current LOG_ARCHIVE_DEST
```

The **CONNECT** Command

The **CONNECT** command is used to log on a user to a local or remote database. The following are some examples of the **CONNECT** command:

```
CONNECT username/password
CONNECT username/password@instance_alias
CONNECT username/password AS (SYSOPER or SYSDBA)
CONNECT INTERNAL
CONNECT username/ AS SYSDBA
```

The **CONNECT** command has the following parameters and options:

- *username*—Includes all usernames currently defined to the database.
- *password*—Is the password for the username given.

- *instance_ alias*—Connects to a remote database.
- AS (**SYSOPER** or **SYSDBA**)—Enables users granted access to the database through OS authentication or through the Oracle password file to connect with system privileges. **SYSOPER** logs in the user with **OSOPER** database role, and **SYSDBA** logs in the user with **OSDBA** database role. **OSOPER** allows database startup, shutdown, and general maintenance, whereas **OSDBA** allows database creation as well as all the other operations.
- INTERNAL—Connects to the database as the **SYS** account.
- **Slash** (/)—Connects with OS authentication.

TIP: The **CONNECT INTERNAL** command is supported for backward compatibility only. Do not use this method of connecting to the database in your scripts, because it will be discontinued in a future version of Oracle8.

Two OS roles are used to control administrator connections when OS authentication is used: **OSOPER** and **OSDBA**. These roles are granted at the OS level and not through an Oracle grant. The method for granting these privileges is OS specific.

OSOPER allows the user to perform the following actions and grants the **RESTRICTED SESSION** privilege:

- STARTUP
- SHUTDOWN
- ALTER DATABASE
- OPEN/MOUNT
- ALTER DATABASE BACKUP
- ARCHIVE LOG
- RECOVER

OSDBA grants the user all system privileges with the **ADMIN OPTION** as well as the **OSOPER** role. A user granted the **OSDBA** role can also execute **CREATE DATABASE** and time-based recover commands.

To use password file authentication, a password file first must be created using the **ORAPWD** command. This command is executed at an OS prompt. Users are added to the password file when they are granted the **SYSDBA** or **SYSOPER** roles in Oracle. The following syntax is used for the **ORAPWD** command:

```
ORAPWD FILE=file_name PASSWORD=password \
ENTRIES=max number of users in file
```

In addition to the password file, the initialization parameter **REMOTE_LOGIN_PASSWORDFILE** must be set to one of the values described here:

- NONE—This value is the default and causes Oracle to not access user password files.
- EXCLUSIVE—This value causes the password file to be used by only one database. Any database user can be added to an exclusive password file.
- SHARED—This value causes the password file to be shared by more than one database. In this case, only the **SYS** and **INTERNAL** users can be added to the password file.

The following are some example connections:

- To connect to the database using the schema and privileges associated with the username, use the following:

  ```
  CONNECT john/doe
  ```

- To connect using a password file as user "john" but with the **SYS** schema and DBA privileges, use the following:

  ```
  CONNECT john/doe AS SYSDBA
  ```

The **RECOVER** Command

The **RECOVER** command performs media recovery on the database, tablespaces, or datafiles. To issue the **RECOVER** command, you must be connected to Oracle as **SYSDBA**, **SYSOPER**, or **INTERNAL**. Figure 3.2 shows the **RECOVER** command syntax.

The **RECOVER** command uses the following parameters:

- DATABASE—Recovers the entire database.
- UNTIL CANCEL—Indicates an incomplete recovery.
- UNTIL TIME—Indicates an incomplete point in time recovery. Use the following format:

```
'YYYY-MM-DD:HH24:MI:SS'
```

- **UNTIL CHANGE**—Specifies an incomplete, change-based recovery. It is followed by the system change number (SCN) to which you want to recover.
- **USING BACKUP CONTROL FILE**—Indicates that the backup control file will be used instead of the active control file for the recovery.
- **TABLESPACE**—Indicates that a tablespace will be recovered and is followed by the tablespace name.
- **DATAFILE**—Indicates the datafiles to be recovered and is followed by the datafile names.
- **LOGFILE**—Continues media recovery by applying the specified redo log file.

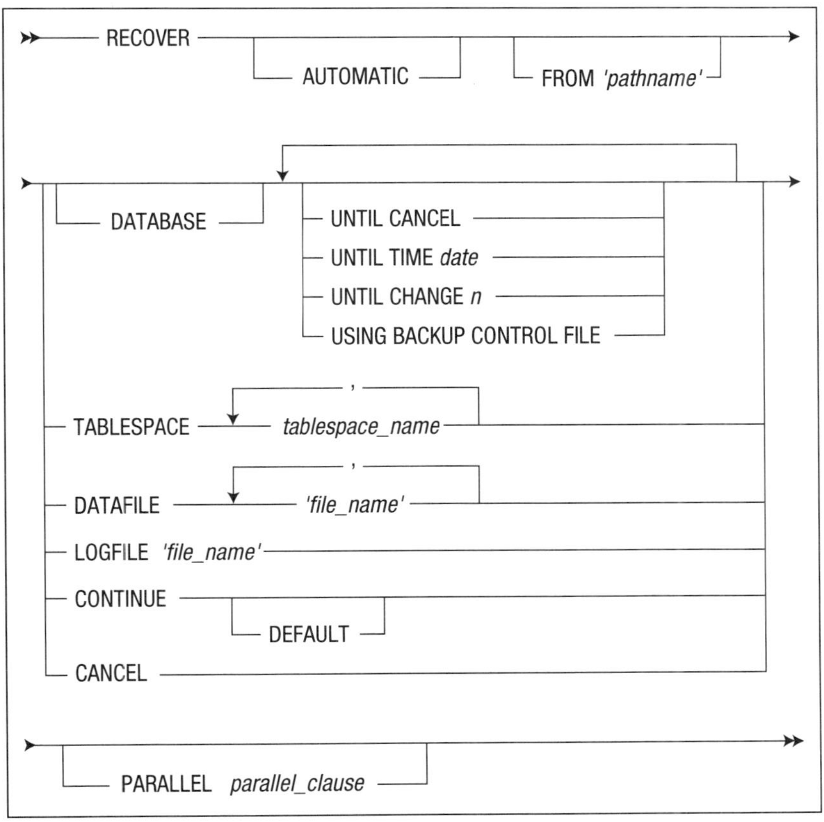

Figure 3.2 The syntax for the **RECOVER** command.

- **CONTINUE**—Continues multi-instance recovery after it has been interrupted to disable a thread.
- **CANCEL**—Terminates cancel-based recovery.
- **PARALLEL**—Sets the number of parallel recovery processes to use in applying redo entries. If you use the **DEFAULT DEGREE** clause, the recovery uses twice the number of processes as the number of datafiles being recovered.
- **NOPARALLEL**—Indicates that the recovery will be done serially.
- **INSTANCES**—Indicates how many instances will be used for parallel recovery.

The **SET** Command

The **SET** command is used in both the Server Manager and SQL*Plus to alter the sessions environment. Figure 3.3 shows the **SET** command syntax.

The **SET** command options have the following definitions:

- **AUTORECOVERY**—Setting to **ON** causes the **RECOVER** command to automatically apply archive log files during recovery. The archive log files are applied based on the initialization parameters **LOG_ARCHIVE_DEST** and **LOG_ARCHIVE_FORMAT**.
- **CHARWIDTH**—Fixes the width of the column display for **CHAR** data. The default is 80 characters.
- **COMPATIBILITY**—Changes database compatibility for the current session. Native compatibility matches the database.
- **DATEWIDTH**—Sets the column display width for **DATE** data.
- **ECHO**—Setting to **ON** echoes commands from scripts that are run.
- **INSTANCE**—Changes the default instance to which you are connected.
- **LOGSOURCE**—Sets the location from where archive logs are retrieved during recovery. This parameter overrides the initialization parameter **LOG_ARCHIVE_DEST**.
- **LONGWIDTH**—Sets the column display width for **LONG** data. The default is 80 characters.
- **MAXDATA**—Sets the maximum number of bytes a **SELECT** statement can return in a fetch. The default is 20,480 bytes.

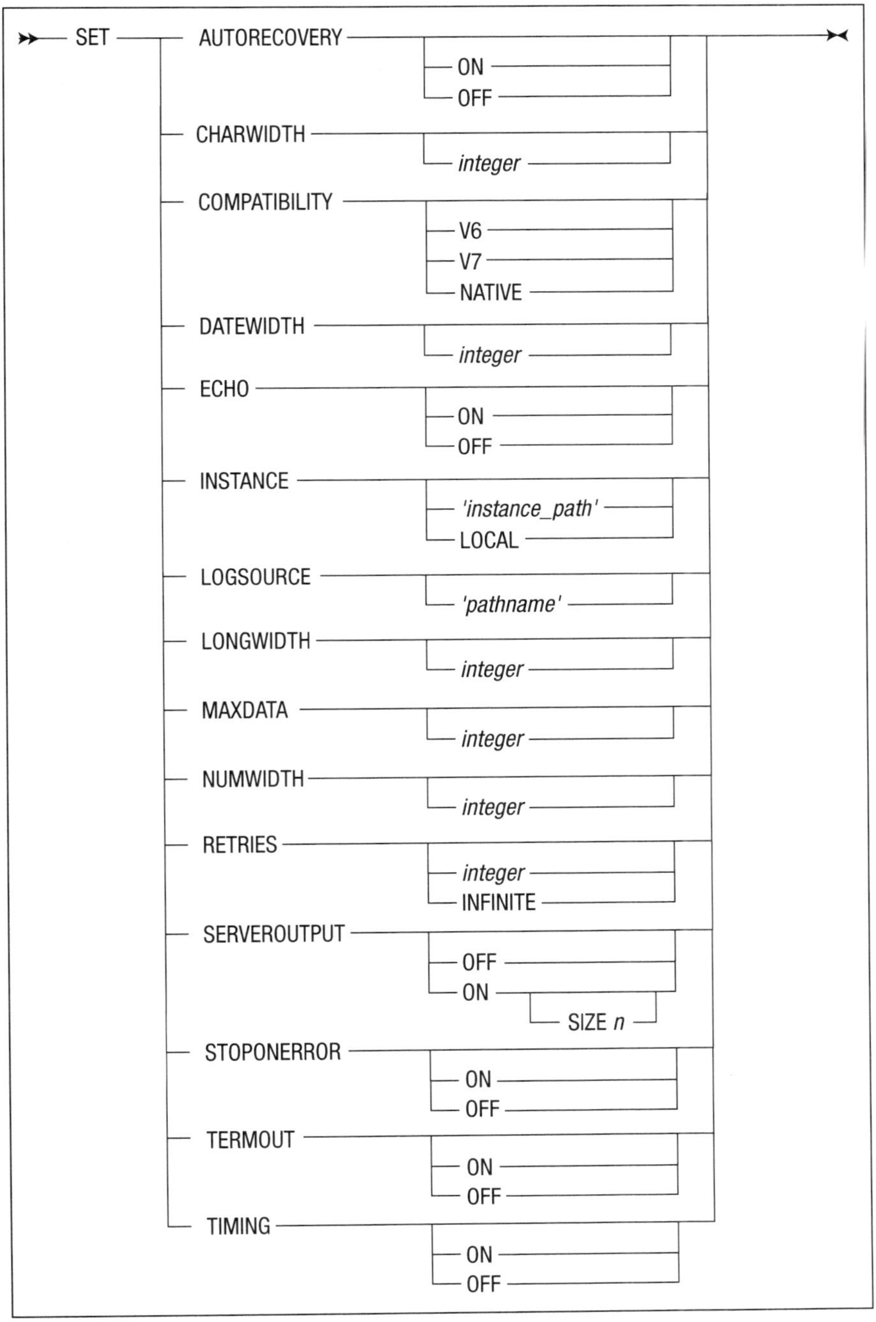

Figure 3.3 The syntax for the **SET** command.

- **NUMWIDTH**—Sets the column display width for **NUMBER** data. The default is 10 single-place numeric characters (including any decimals).
- **RETRIES**—Affects the **STARTUP** command if the **RETRY** option is used. The **STARTUP** command will retry the specified number of times. The default number of tries is infinite.
- **SERVEROUTPUT**—Setting to **ON** enables output from the **DBMS_OUTPUT** and **PUT_LINE** packages.
- **STOPONERROR**—Setting to **ON** causes command files to stop execution if an error occurs.
- **TERMOUT**—Setting to **OFF** stops output from SQL commands from coming back to the screen. The default is **ON**, which allows output to come to the terminal.
- **TIMING**—Setting to **ON** gives timing feedback on parse, execute, and fetch times.

The **SHOW** Command

The **SHOW** command is used to show the current value of each **SET** command with the addition of the **ERRORS**, **SGA**, and **SPOOL** parameters. Figure 3.4 shows the **SHOW** command syntax.

The **SHOW** command has the following three important options:

- **ERRORS**—Shows the errors from the last procedure, package, or function that was complied.
- **PARAMETERS**—Displays the value of initialization parameters.
- **SGA**—Shows the current instance's system global area (SGA). Here is an example:

```
SHOW SGA
Total Shared Global Area    32420880
Fixed Size                  38944
Variable Size               11869168
Database buffers            20480000
Redo Buffers                32768
```

The **STARTUP** Command

The **STARTUP** command starts the Oracle instance, mounts the database, and opens it for use. **STARTUP** can also be combined with any of the options discussed here to perform maintenance or other activities. When you issue a

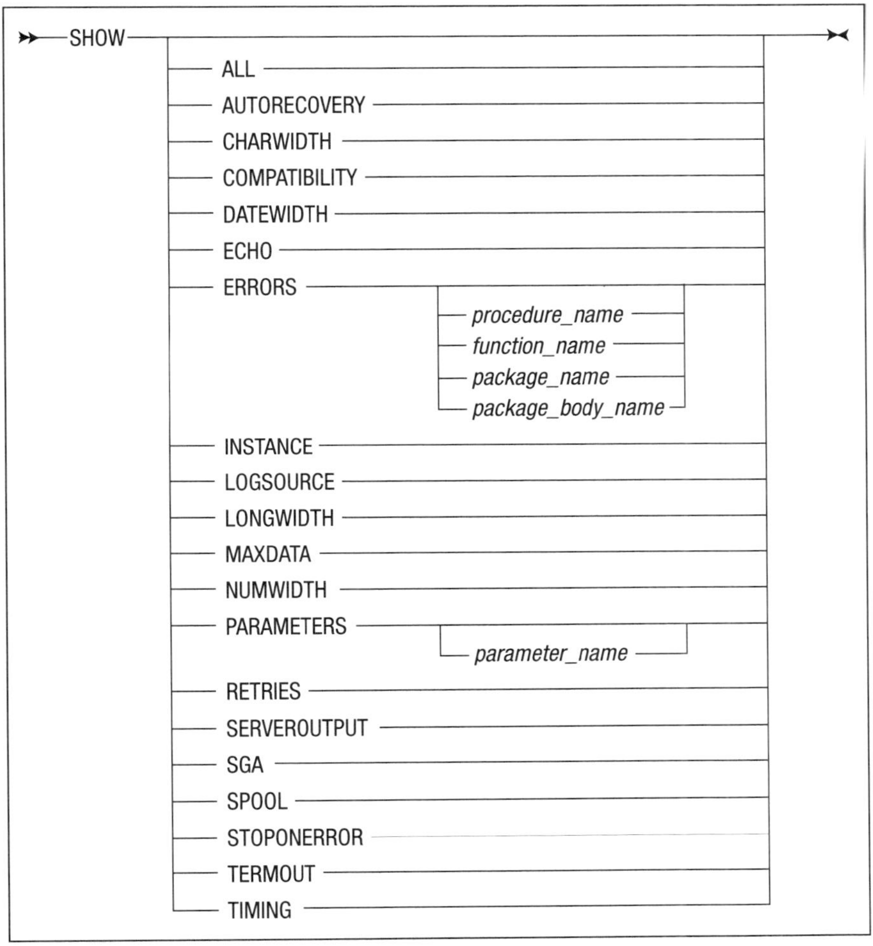

Figure 3.4 The syntax for the **SHOW** command.

STARTUP OPEN command, the database goes through **NOMOUNT** and **MOUNT** phases before being in an **OPEN** state. Figure 3.5 shows the **STARTUP** command syntax.

The **STARTUP** command has the following options:

- FORCE—Performs a **SHUTDOWN ABORT** followed by a **STARTUP OPEN**, and is used only in emergencies. This option is also used with certain undocumented initialization parameters to force open a corrupted database.
- RESTRICT—Performs a **NOMOUNT**, **MOUNT**, and **OPEN**, leaving the database in restricted user mode. The restricted user mode allows

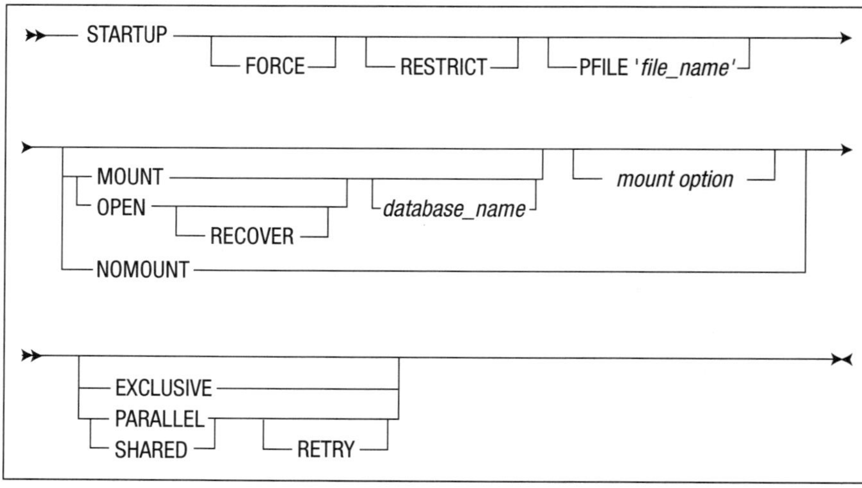

Figure 3.5 The syntax for the **STARTUP** command.

only users (usually DBAs) with the **RESTRICTED SESSION** privilege to log into the instance.

- PFILE—Specifies a parameter file with initialization parameter values to start the instance with.
- MOUNT—Used for certain maintenance operations. It performs a startup of the instance processes and mounts the database, leaving it accessible only to Server Manager connections. This option is performed automatically by **STARTUP, STARTUP OPEN, STARTUP FORCE, STARTUP RESTRICT**, and **STARTUP RECOVER** command options.
- NOMOUNT—Starts the instance but doesn't mount any database files. This option is used for creation of a database or for creating a control file, and it is performed automatically by all other options. This option cannot be used with **OPEN, MOUNT, SHARED, EXCLUSIVE**, or **PARALLEL** options.
- OPEN—Used to **NOMOUNT, MOUNT**, and **OPEN** a database, the same as issuing a **STARTUP** command with no options.
- RECOVER—Used when it is known that a database will need recovery. Note that instance recovery will be performed automatically on instance startup. This option is only needed to force media recovery.
- *database_name*—This is the database name to mount or open. If a database name is not given, **STARTUP** uses the name in the parameter file (init<*SID*>.ora).

- **EXCLUSIVE**—When opened in this mode, a database can be mounted or opened only by one Oracle instance. This parameter cannot be used with the **SHARED** or **PARALLEL** options.
- **PARALLEL**—This option is used only when mounting the database for use in a parallel server configuration (one where multiple instances use the same set of database files). This is also known as the **SHARED** option.
- **RETRY**—This option can be used only with instances in parallel mode. If the database is busy being recovered by another instance, the **RETRY** command makes Oracle attempt to open the database every five seconds. The number of attempts can be set with the **SET RETRIES** command in Server Manager.

The following examples explain when to use the **STARTUP** command:

- To start an Oracle instance, mount the database in exclusive mode and open the database using the default init<*SID*>.ora file. Enter:

  ```
  SVRMGR> STARTUP
  ```

  or:

  ```
  SVRMGR> STARTUP OPEN database_name EXCLUSIVE
  ```

- To start up the same database in parallel mode, enter:

  ```
  SVRMGR> STARTUP PARALLEL
  ```

  or:

  ```
  SVRMGR> STARTUP OPEN database_name PARALLEL
  ```

- To force the database to restart without mounting or opening, enter:

  ```
  SVRMGR> STARTUP FORCE NOMOUNT
  ```

- To start up a database using a parameter file named initdb1.ora (located in the current directory) enter:

  ```
  SVRMGR> STARTUP PFILE=initdb1.ora
  ```

The **SHUTDOWN** Command

The **SHUTDOWN** command has a similar syntax to the **STARTUP** command; however, the options are different. Figure 3.6 shows the **SHUTDOWN** command syntax.

The **SHUTDOWN** command has the following options:

- NORMAL—This is the default if the **SHUTDOWN** command is issued with no options. It is the most polite of the shutdown options because it waits patiently for all users to log off before shutting down the instance, whether they are actively engaged in transactions or just sitting idle. **NORMAL** is also the safest shutdown and the preferred approach to use prior to a cold backup. (However, I have never experienced a problem recovering from a shutdown using the next option, **IMMEDIATE**.) **SHUTDOWN NORMAL** is the slowest shutdown option. A startup from a normal shutdown is the fastest startup because no instance recovery is performed.
- IMMEDIATE—This is the next most polite shutdown option. It waits until pending transactions are complete, then it logs users off and shuts down the instance. **SHUTDOWN IMMEDIATE** is faster than **SHUTDOWN NORMAL**. Instance recovery is not required after a **SHUTDOWN IMMEDIATE**. **SHUTDOWN IMMEDIATE** provides an alternative to killing user sessions and then performing a **SHUTDOWN NORMAL**.
- ABORT—This is the rudest shutdown option. It immediately stops the Oracle processes and should be used only when all other options have failed to shut down the instance. The database is left in an inconsistent state. In this situation, a cold backup may not recover the database. **SHUTDOWN ABORT** is the fastest of all the shutdown options, but always requires instance recovery (and in some rare cases may cause database corruption that is not recoverable).

> **EXAM ALERT:** You should always follow a **SHUTDOWN ABORT** with a **STARTUP OPEN** and **SHUTDOWN NORMAL**. This puts the database in a consistent state.

Here are some examples of the **SHUTDOWN** command:

```
SVRMGR> SHUTDOWN
SVRMGR> Database closed
SVRMGR> Database dismounted
SVRMGR> Oracle instance shut down
```

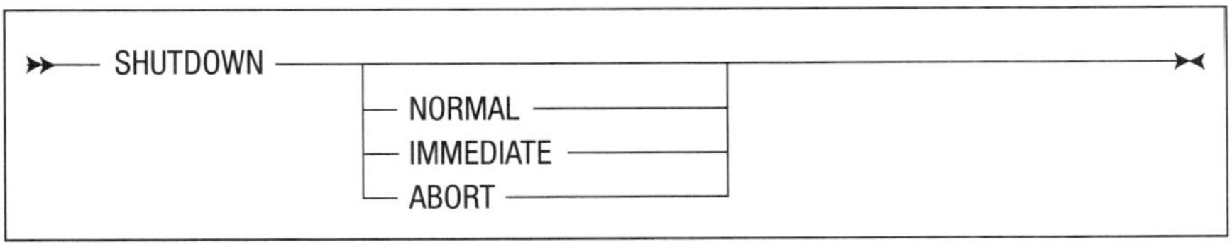

Figure 3.6 The syntax for the **SHUTDOWN** command.

Oracle Enterprise Manager

OEM is a graphical console of tools, agents, and services that help manage Oracle databases. OEM replaces the graphical version of Server Manager. It provides an integrated systems management platform in a client/server architecture. OEM can perform many useful administrative tasks, including the following:

- Manage, diagnose, and tune multiple databases.
- Distribute software to multiple servers and clients.
- Schedule jobs on multiple systems.
- Monitor and set events on multiple servers.
- Administer Oracle parallel servers.
- Integrate with third-party tools.

Agents

The *intelligent agents* are processes running on remote nodes in the network. An agent runs on the same node as the database service it supports. The intelligent agent can support more than one database service on a node. The intelligent agent is responsible for the following:

- Accepting jobs or events from the console.
- Running jobs, collecting their results and output, and queuing them for the communication daemon.
- Checking for events, and queuing the resulting event reports for the communication daemon.
- Canceling jobs or events as directed by the console or other applications.
- Handling Simple Network Management Protocol (SNMP) requests, if SNMP is supported on the agent's platform.

Console

The OEM *console* is the main interface through which all the OEM tools and utilities can be accessed or launched. Many of the OEM management utilities can also be launched on their own from the Start menu. You can also add utilities from third-party vendors. Figure 3.7 shows the OEM console.

The console's interface consists of the Navigator, Map, Job, and Event windows. You can also use toolbars and tool palettes to access OEM applications. The following sections give an overview of all the components of OEM.

Navigator

The *Navigator* discovers and displays a tree list of all the services and objects in a network, providing a direct view of objects such as databases, groups, listeners, and nodes, plus the objects that they contain. Figure 3.8 shows an expanded view of the OEM Navigator window.

Through the Navigator, you can also perform administration tasks like creating, editing, or dropping a user. The top object in the Navigator tree is the

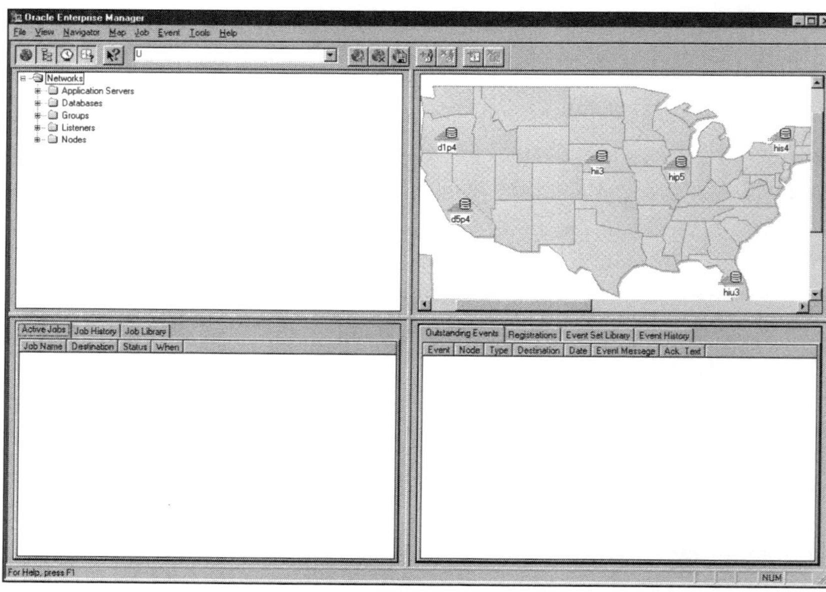

Figure 3.7 The four windows of the OEM console: Navigator, Map, Job, and Event.

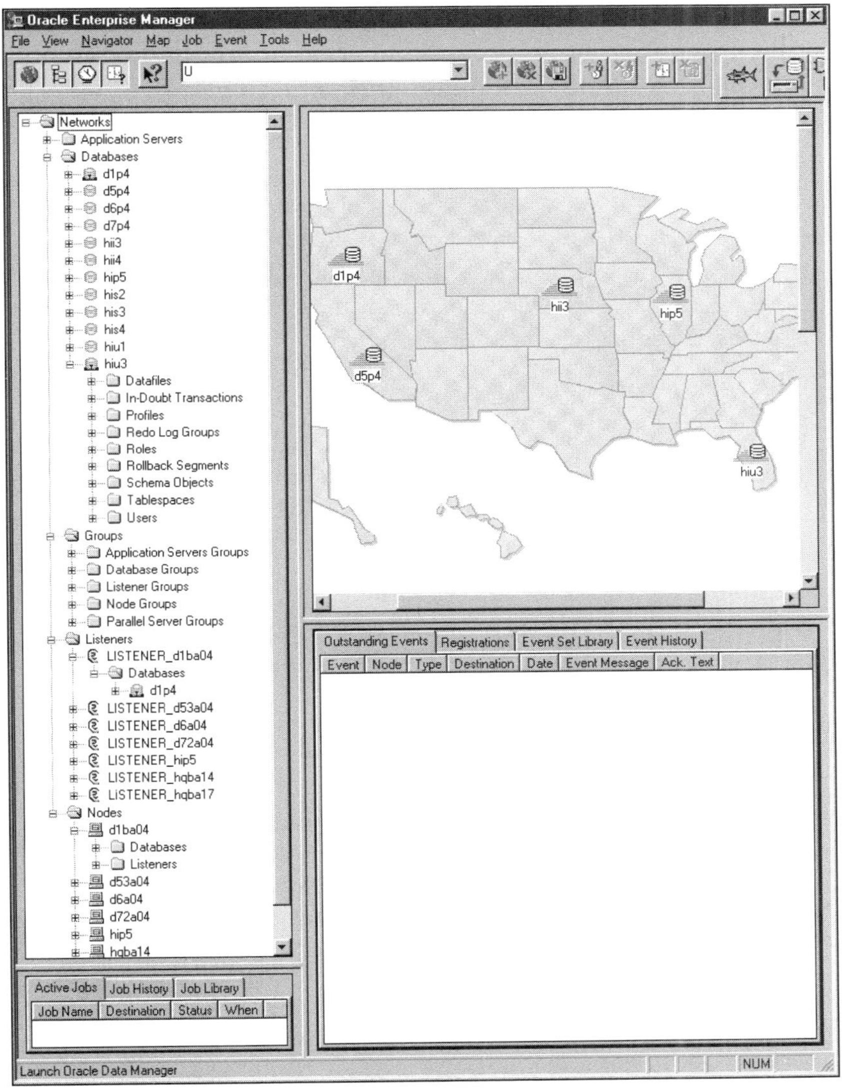

Figure 3.8 Navigator showing databases, listeners, nodes, and more.

Networks folder. The Networks folder contains these following four subfolders:

- Databases
- Groups
- Listeners
- Nodes

You can expand the Navigator tree to view the objects and drill down to other related objects. For example, you can expand a node to view the databases and listeners on that node. You can expand a database to view datafiles, in-doubt transactions, profiles, redo log groups, roles, rollback segments, schema objects, tablespaces, and users.

The Navigator menu allows you to manage objects in the Navigator window. The menu options are enabled according to the selected object in the Navigator tree. For most objects, the Create, Create Like, Quick Edit, and Remove menu options are enabled. In addition to managing objects, a selected database can be started or shut down.

Map

The *Map* system allows you to monitor network objects with a graphical display. It lets you create, save, modify, and recall views of the network. You simply drag and drop objects from the Navigator into the Map view to create groups that you want to monitor.

With the Map system you can produce customized graphic views of network objects and modify and save the maps. The Map system also allows you to create user-defined groups of network objects and organize them as map objects. Map customized views allow you to manage and monitor a subset of your system objects.

> **TIP** With the OEM, you can create a map made up of the databases, groups, listeners, and nodes that you want to monitor. You can call this map up as needed. For example, you can create a group of all production databases in your environment. Then, you can perform actions against all of these databases simply by referencing the production database group, rather than each database individually.

You can determine the status of an object on a map if the object has been registered as an event destination. The state of the event condition is graphically displayed as a colored flag. For status monitors to display on a map object, an agent must be running on the node where the object is located. The status monitor displays indicate the following:

- A green signal flag means all of the registered events are operating normally.
- A yellow signal flag means a registered event has encountered a warning or problem that needs attention.

- A red signal flag means a severe error has been encountered by a registered event and must be attended to immediately.
- A circle with a slash through it means the map object or group is unavailable.

Job Scheduling

Job scheduling allows you to manage job execution among databases, listeners, and nodes. Jobs can be scheduled at various times, such as daily or weekly, and at single or multiple destinations. The Job system allows you to automate standard and repetitive tasks, like executing SQL scripts or an OS command. Jobs can be run only on nodes where an intelligent agent is running. If you send a job to a group, the job is only scheduled on the nodes in the group where the agent is running.

The Console's daemon process sends job information to intelligent agents when you submit a job. These agents execute the job and return job status messages to the Console.

On the Job console, you submit a job to destinations (nodes, databases, listeners, and user-defined groups you have created with the Map system). It is not necessary to connect to the node on which a job is to be run to schedule the job. Figure 3.9 shows the OEM Job Schedule window.

In the Job Schedule window of the OEM console, you can view the different parts of job information by selecting the tabs. Below is a description of what is in each tab:

- *Active Jobs*—This tab contains a summary of the active jobs for the whole network. These are the jobs that are not yet completed. These jobs cannot be modified.
- *Job History*—This tab contains a list of jobs that have already executed. These jobs cannot be modified.
- *Job Library*—This tab contains a list of the jobs that you have created and saved. These jobs can be modified.

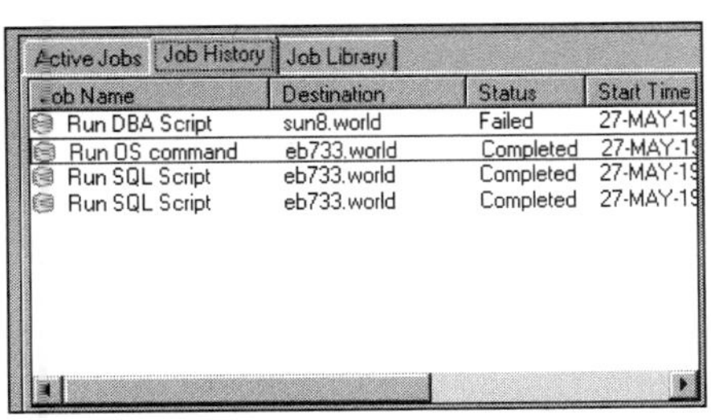

Figure 3.9 An example of the Job Schedule window.

Event Management

Event management allows you to track and display the status of events occurring on the databases, listeners, and nodes in your network system. You can also create jobs that can be run automatically to fix problems. Figure 3.10 shows the OEM Event Management window.

The Event Management window contains the following tabs of information:

- *Outstanding Events*—Displays event sets that have been applied and have occurred.
- *Event Set Library*—Displays event sets that have been created. This tab contains the following information:
    - *Registrations*—Displays event sets and their destinations that you want to monitor.
    - *Event History*—Displays a history of events that have occurred and have been acknowledged by a DBA or cleared by an agent.

The *Event Management System (EMS)* allows you to monitor specific event conditions. An example of an event would be loss of service or running out of disk space. You can place events on databases, listeners, or nodes, and then select the threshold parameters for those events. When the threshold is reached, you will be notified. In some cases, you can choose to execute a fix-it job that automatically corrects the problem. To use the EMS for configuring mail and paging services, as well as a modem, you must first set up DBAs, who interpret and correct the events as needed.

OEM Repository

The *OEM repository* is a set of tables in a schema of an Oracle database. Each OEM DBA is associated with a specific repository. The repository keeps information about tasks that the DBA has performed, including any jobs scheduled or events being monitored.

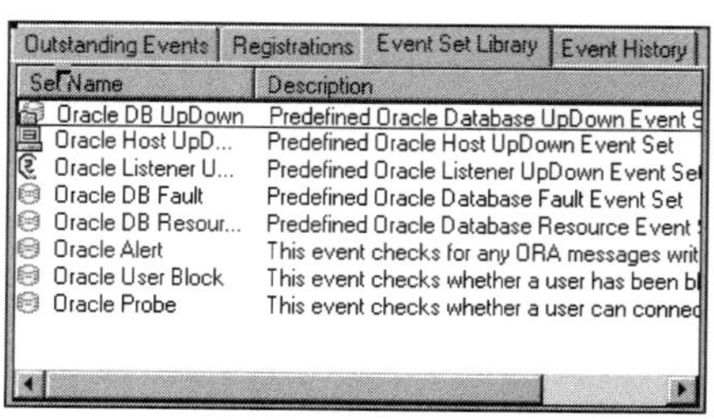

Figure 3.10 An example of the Event Management window.

The repository must be stored in a database the console can connect to. OEM will automatically create or upgrade the repository if necessary when you start the console. Because the repository is stored in the database, a DBA can log on from any computer on the network. DBAs can have their repositories in the same database or in different databases.

TIP

Remember that only one repository should be set up for each schema name. Creating multiple repositories on different databases for the same account can cause problems with agent notifications. The intelligent agents use the unique schema name when tracking jobs and events. The schema name is appended to the console location when creating a return address for notifications. When you log into the console, you must enter the connect information for the database that contains your repository.

DBA Administration Database Tools And Utilities

The database tools and utility applications provide an easy-to-use GUI to execute administrative tasks on Oracle databases. You can use these applications to perform most of your DBA administration tasks. The administration tools have several advantages over entering SQL commands in SQL*Plus:

- Use of the GUI to execute the commands—it is faster and it does not require you to look up exact syntax.
- Performance of multiple tasks at the same time in different OEM windows.
- Management of multiple databases in different OEM windows.

The application tools allow you to perform the following tasks:

- Manage instances, initialization parameters, and sessions.
- Manage schema objects.
- Manage users, privileges, and profiles.
- Manage software distribution.
- Manage storage.
- Enter and execute SQL statements, PL/SQL code, and Server Manager DBA commands.

- Back up, recover, and restore a database.
- Export/import data to/from an Oracle database.

Backup Manager

Backup Manager allows you to administer backup and recovery for Oracle databases. Figure 3.11 shows the OEM Backup Manager tool. With this tool, you can use three subsystems:

- *Oracle8 Recovery Manager*—Uses a GUI for Recovery Manager. This simplifies the command line interface with wizards to help with backup and recovery operations.
- *OS Backup*—Uses the OEM Job system to do OS backups.
- *Enterprise Backup Utility*—Provides backup and recovery functionality for Oracle7 databases only.

Data Manager

Data Manager uses a wizard to perform export, import, and SQL*Loader utilities. The export utility exports data from an Oracle database; the exported data is written to an OS file in Oracle's binary format. Export files can only be read

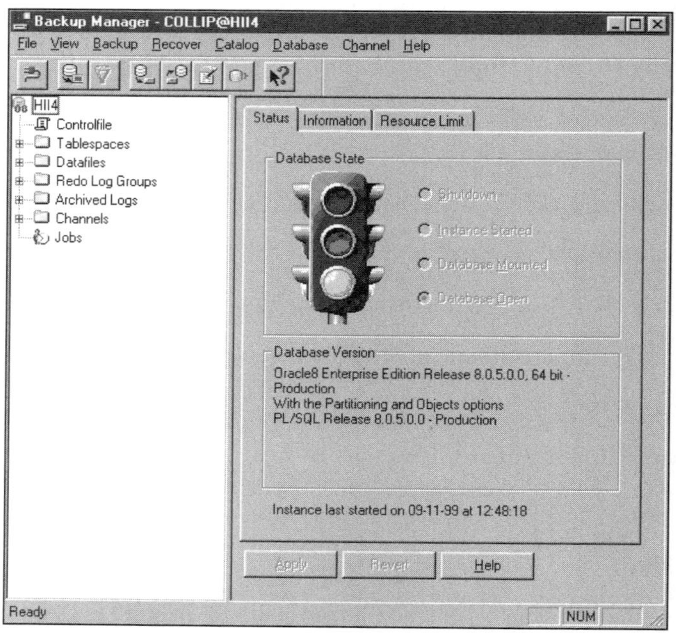

Figure 3.11 An example of the Backup Manager tool.

by the import utility. Export files can be used for backing up a database or to transfer data between databases.

The import utility imports data to an Oracle database. Only files created with the export utility can be read by the import utility.

The SQL*Loader utility is used to transfer data into Oracle tables from text files. A control file is used to specify the format of the external data and the order in which it is to be loaded. Figure 3.12 shows the OEM Data Manager tool.

Instance Manager

Instance Manager allows you to start up or shut down a database or put the database in archive log or no archive log mode. It lets you list and edit database initialization parameters, manage in-doubt transactions, and get information on user sessions. Figure 3.13 shows the OEM Instance Manager tool.

Schema Manager

Schema Manager can create, edit, and display schema objects. This schema application manages the following database objects:

- Array types
- Clusters
- Database links
- Functions and procedures

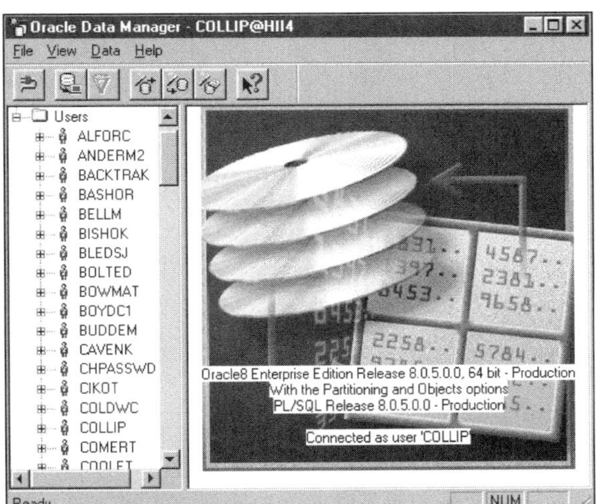

Figure 3.12 An example of the Data Manager tool.

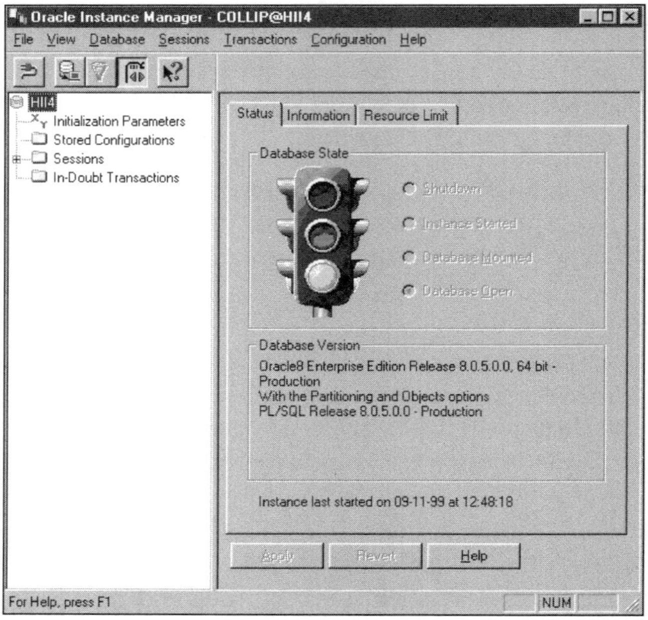

Figure 3.13 An example of the Instance Manager tool.

- Indexes
- Object types
- Packages and package bodies
- Refresh groups
- Queue tables
- Sequences
- Snapshots and snapshot logs
- Synonyms
- Tables
- Table types
- Triggers
- Views

Figure 3.14 shows an example screen from Schema Manager.

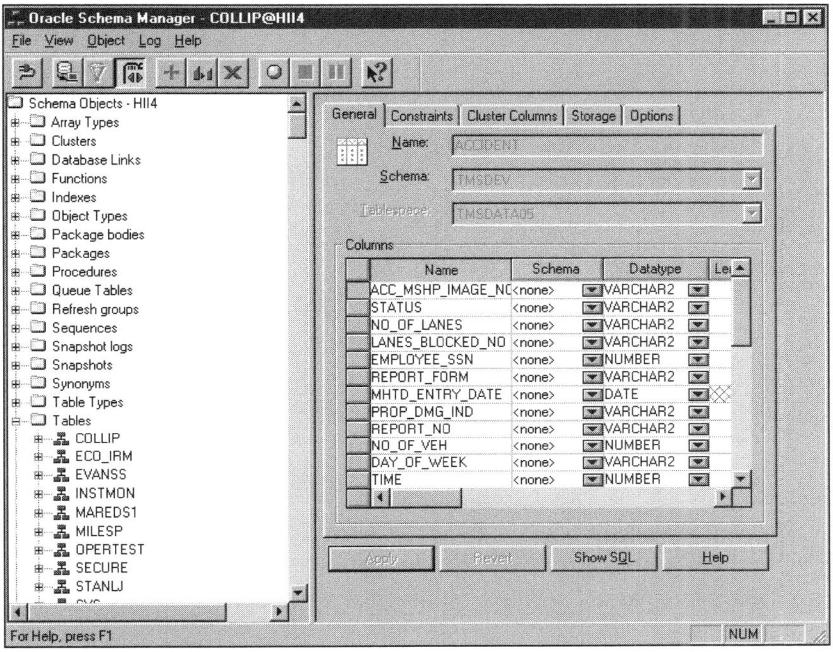

Figure 3.14 An example of the Schema Manager tool.

Security Manager

Security Manager can create, alter, and drop users, roles, and profiles. This application manages users, roles, and profiles. Figure 3.15 shows the Security Manager tool.

Storage Manager

Storage Manager allows you to perform administrative tasks affecting database storage, including creating, adding, dropping and expanding tablespaces, rollback segments, and datafiles. Figure 3.16 shows the Storage Manager tool.

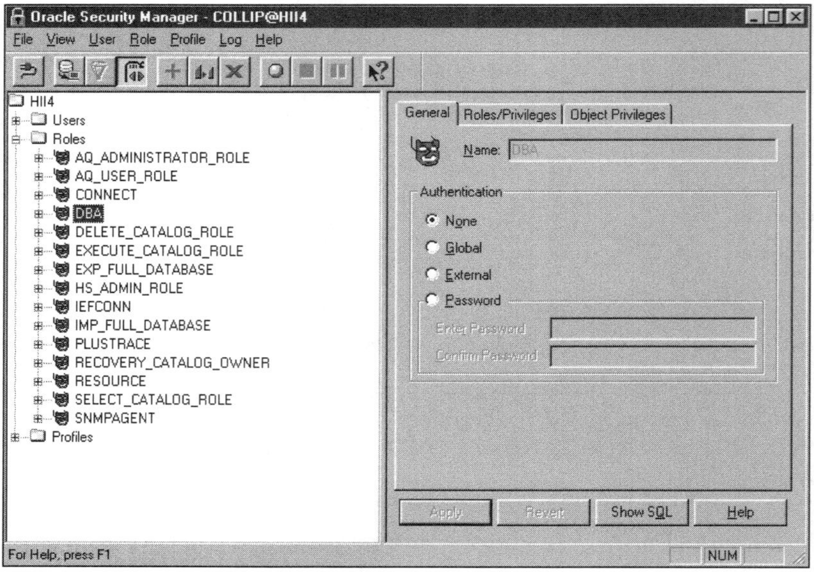

Figure 3.15 An example of the Security Manager tool.

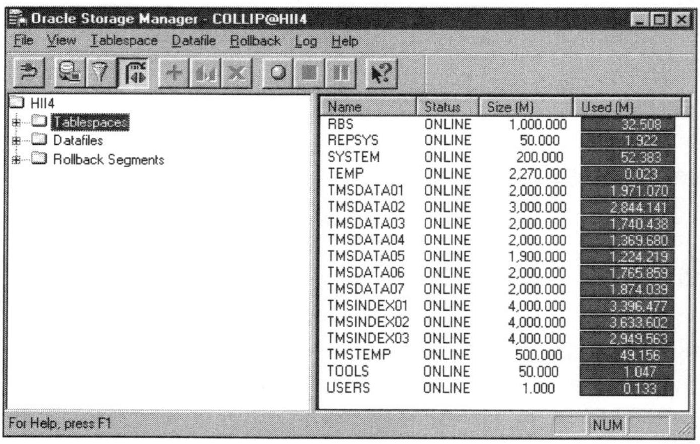

Figure 3.16 An example of the Storage Manager window.

Practice Questions

Question 1

You create a SQL script that examines database extents. Which Server Manager line mode command would you use to create the output file for the script?

- a. **DESCRIBE**
- b. **SPOOL**
- c. **EXECUTE**
- d. **SHOW**
- e. **SET**

Answer b is correct. The **SPOOL** command sends the output to a file. The **DESCRIBE** command describes tables, views, and other database objects. The **EXECUTE** command executes a PL/SQL statement. The **SHOW** command displays the current settings of the Server Manager session. The **SET** command is used to change characteristics for the Server Manager session.

Question 2

Which part of OEM would you use to schedule an OS backup of your database?

- a. OEM console Navigator
- b. OEM repository
- c. Intelligent agent
- d. OEM console Job system

Answer d is correct. The OEM console Job system allows a DBA to schedule OS backups. The OEM console Navigator allows the DBA to view the hierarchy of all the Oracle services on the network. The OEM repository is created for each OEM user and contains a set of tables that store information related to the OEM user. The intelligent agent runs on remote nodes to execute and manage the jobs and events sent out by OEM.

Question 3

Which component of OEM would you use to view the names of the databases running on your network?

- ❍ a. OEM console Job system
- ❍ b. OEM repository
- ❍ c. OEM console Navigator
- ❍ d. Intelligent agent

Answer c is correct. The OEM console Navigator allows the DBA to view the hierarchy of all the Oracle services on the network, including databases. The OEM console Job system allows the DBA to schedule and view the administration jobs. The OEM repository is created for each OEM user and contains a set of tables that store information related to the OEM user. The intelligent agent resides on remote nodes and manages the jobs and events sent by the OEM console.

Question 4

Which OEM application would you use to alter a database initialization parameter?

- ❍ a. Backup Manager
- ❍ b. Data Manager
- ❍ c. Security Manager
- ❍ d. Instance Manager
- ❍ e. Schema Manager
- ❍ f. Storage Manager

Answer d is correct. Instance Manager is used for managing instances, sessions, startup, and shutdown, and for changing initialization parameters. Backup Manager is used for backing up an Oracle database. Data Manager is used for exporting, importing, and loading data in and out of an Oracle database. Security Manager is used for setting up users and controlling security. Schema Manager is used for managing schema objects. Storage Manager is used for managing storage and rollback segments.

Question 5

Which command can you execute from Server Manager line mode without being connected to a database?

- ❍ a. **EXIT**
- ❍ b. **ARCHIVE LOG**
- ❍ c. **DESCRIBE**
- ❍ d. **SHOW PARAMETER**

Answer a is correct. This is somewhat of a trick question. You can execute Server Manager without connecting to a database. Then, you can execute the **CONNECT** command from within Server Manager. Because you can enter Server Manager without connecting, it follows that you can exit as well. **ARCHIVE LOG** commands can only be executed while connected to a database. **DESCRIBE** describes a database object, such as a table or view, and requires a database connection. **SHOW PARAMETER** shows the current instance parameters and requires a database connection.

Question 6

Which OEM application would you use to add a rollback segment to the rollback segment tablespace?

- ❍ a. Instance Manager
- ❍ b. Data Manager
- ❍ c. Storage Manager
- ❍ d. Schema Manager
- ❍ e. Security Manager

Answer c is correct. Storage Manager is used for managing storage and rollback segments. Instance Manager is used for managing instances, sessions, startup, and shutdown, and for changing initialization parameters. Data Manager is used for exporting, importing, and loading data in and out of an Oracle database. Schema Manager is used for managing schema objects. Security Manager is used for setting up users and controlling security.

Question 7

Which OEM application would you use to give a user the **CREATE PUBLIC SYNONYM** privilege?

- ❍ a. Data Manager
- ❍ b. Schema Manager
- ❍ c. Storage Manager
- ❍ d. Instance Manager
- ● e. Security Manager

Answer e is correct. Security Manager is used for setting up users, controlling security, and managing user privileges. Data Manager is used for exporting, importing, and loading data in and out of an Oracle database. Schema Manager is used for managing schema objects. Storage Manager is used for managing storage and rollback segments. Instance Manager is used for managing instances, sessions, startup, and shutdown, and for changing initialization parameters.

Question 8

You have changed some database initialization parameters and added a tablespace. You now want to restart the database so the new parameters will take effect. Which OEM applications have you used to accomplish these tasks? [Choose two]

- ❑ a. Data Manager
- ❑ b. Schema Manager
- ❑ c. Backup Manager
- ■ d. Storage Manager
- ❑ e. Security Manager
- ■ f. Instance Manager

Answers d and f are correct. Storage Manager is used for adding tablespaces and Instance Manager is used for changing initialization parameters. Data Manager is used for exporting, importing, and loading data in and out of an Oracle database. Schema Manager is used for managing schema objects. Backup Manager is used for backing up an Oracle database. Security Manager is used for setting up users, controlling security, and managing user privileges.

Question 9

Which commands can you execute in Server Manager line mode to display the size of the redo log buffer? [Choose two]

- ❑ a. **SHOW PARAMETER**
- ❑ b. **DESCRIBE**
- ❑ c. **SHOW SGA**
- ❑ d. **SET**
- ❑ e. **ARCHIVE LOG**
- ❑ f. **LIST BUFFER**

Answers a and c are correct. The **SHOW PARAMETER** command displays all the current initialization parameters, including redo log buffers. The **SHOW SGA** command displays the current setting for the database buffer cache, the redo log buffer, and the shared pool. The **DESCRIBE** command describes tables, views, and other database objects. The **SET** command is used to change characteristics for the Server Manager session. **ARCHIVE LOG** commands show the status of ARCH, not the size of the redo log buffer. **LIST BUFFER** is not a Server Manager command.

Question 10

Which OEM application would you use to add a constraint to a table?

- ❍ a. Data Manager
- ❍ b. Schema Manager
- ❍ c. Backup Manager
- ❍ d. Storage Manager
- ❍ e. Security Manager
- ❍ f. Instance Manager

Answer b is correct. Schema Manager is used for managing schema objects including tables, constraints, indexes, views, clusters, and so forth. Data Manager is used for exporting, importing, and loading data in and out of an Oracle database. Backup Manager is used for backing up an Oracle database. Storage Manager is used for managing storage and rollback segments. Security Manager is used for setting up users, controlling security, and managing user privileges. Instance Manager is used for managing instances, sessions, startup, and shutdown, and for changing initialization parameters.

Need To Know More?

Loney, Kevin, and Marlene Theriault: *Oracle8 DBA Handbook*, Oracle Press, Berkeley, CA, 1997. ISBN 0-07882-406-0. This book is a comprehensive guide and a must have for all DBAs.

See the Oracle documentation that is provided on CD with the Oracle RDBMS software. Pertaining to this chapter are:

Belden, Eric, Valerie Kane, Vrinda Kirloskar, and Harry Sun: *Oracle Server Manager User's Guide*, Oracle Corporation, Redwood City, CA, 1995. See Chapter 5, "Line Mode."

Dialeris, Connie, and Joyce Fee: *Oracle8 Backup and Recovery Guide*, Oracle Corporation, Redwood City, CA, 1997. Complete coverage of Oracle backup and recovery.

Lane, Paul: *Oracle8 SQL Reference*, Oracle Corporation, Redwood City, CA, 1997. Complete documentation of syntax for all Oracle SQL commands.

Oracle8 Enterprise Manager Administrator's Guide, Oracle Corporation, Redwood City, CA, 1998. Complete documentation of OEM concepts.

Oracle8 Enterprise Manager Concepts Guide, Oracle Corporation, Redwood City, CA, 1998. Complete documentation of OEM concepts.

http://education.oracle.com/tbt/ocp8.html is the site from which you can order the Oracle Education CD-ROM bundle for Oracle8 Database Administration.

www.revealnet.com is the site where RevealNet Corporation provides Oracle Administration reference software.

4

Managing An Oracle Instance

Terms you'll need to understand:

- √ **OSOPER**
- √ **OSDBA**
- √ **REMOTE_LOGIN_ PASSWORDFILE**
- √ **SYSDBA**
- √ **SYSOPER**
- √ **ORAPWD**
- √ **V$PWFILE_USERS**
- √ **STARTUP**
- √ **SHUTDOWN**
- √ **DB_NAME**
- √ Session identifier (SID)
- √ Session serial number
- √ **V$SESSION**
- √ Alert file
- √ **BACKGROUND_DUMP_DEST**
- √ **USER_ DUMP_DEST**
- √ **MAX_DUMP_FILE_SIZE**
- √ **SQL_TRACE**
- √ catalog.sql
- √ catproc.sql

Techniques you'll need to master:

- √ Using operating system (OS) authentication
- √ Using database authentication
- √ Using password file authentication
- √ Starting the Oracle instance and database
- √ Shutting down the Oracle database and instance
- √ Viewing session information and killing sessions
- √ Monitoring alert and trace files
- √ Building the Oracle data dictionary

Managing an Oracle instance is often confused with managing the database. Remember from Chapter 2 that the Oracle instance is made up of the system global area (SGA) and the Oracle background processes. Some Information Systems departments break the job of the database administrator (DBA) into two positions: the system DBA and the application DBA. The system DBA is responsible for installing Oracle, setting up a backup strategy, and managing the Oracle instance. The application DBA is responsible for logical database design, installing application objects (tables, indexes, triggers, packages, and more), and tuning applications. There are many variations on this division of responsibilities, but the bottom line is that all DBAs must know how to manage an Oracle instance in order to have a well-rounded understanding of how to manage the Oracle environment. This chapter concentrates on the tasks a DBA must do to effectively manage the Oracle instance. These tasks include setting up authentication, creating a parameter file, start up, shut down, and monitoring the alert and trace files.

Setting Up The Operating System And Password File Authentication

During the creation of an Oracle instance and database, several schemas and roles are set up. By default, user authentication is done by the database using passwords stored in the database. As the DBA, you must make several decisions at this point:

- What method(s) of authentication should be used for the database (operating system [OS] or database)?
- Will the database be administered locally or remotely?
- What tools will be used to administer the database (Oracle Enterprise Manager [OEM], Server Manager, or third-party software)?

User Authentication

Authentication is the process by which Oracle determines if a user should be allowed access to the database. Normal database users have three options for authentication:

- Authentication by the OS
- Authentication by the associated Oracle database
- Authentication by a network service

Normally one method of authentication is used. No reason exists, however, to preclude the use of all three methods.

Authentication By The Operating System

Oracle can use OS authentication. In this case, the user has an OS account that matches an Oracle database username. Oracle does not store a password for the username because the OS password will be used for authenticating the user. The benefits of authentication by the OS are as follows:

- Users can connect to Oracle more easily because they do not have to enter a password if they are already logged onto the OS. For example, a user can run SQL*Plus by simply entering **SQLPLUS/**.
- Control of database authorization is centralized in the OS, eliminating the need to maintain two sets of accounts and passwords. Accounts are still created in Oracle, but they match the OS accounts.
- OS trace and log files match up more easily with the database trace and log files, because the usernames are the same.

Authentication By The Oracle Database

If the OS cannot be used for authentication or if you would prefer to use the database for authentication, Oracle can authenticate users attempting to connect to a database. To use database authentication, each user is created with a password, which the user must then provide when connecting to the database. The user's password is stored in the data dictionary in encrypted format. Database authentication is the most frequently used approach.

Authentication By The Network

Oracle can accept authentication from network services if available. Some examples of third-party authentication vendors include Distributed Computing Environment (DCE), Kerberos, and Secure European System for Applications in a Multi-vendor Environment (SESAME). You must have the Oracle Secure Network Services product to use a network authentication service. This product is called the Advanced Networking option and has gone through several name changes from Oracle 7.3 to Oracle8i. In Oracle8i, it is called the Advanced Security Option. While some features have changed, the product is basically the same.

Database Administrator Authentication Methods

Because DBAs perform special tasks, such as adding files to the database or doing database recovery, they are authenticated somewhat differently than normal users. DBAs can administer databases locally on the same machine where the database resides or remotely from a client. To facilitate DBA authentication, Oracle uses *OS authentication* or *password files*.

Operating System Authentication

OS authentication for DBAs is platform specific, but on most systems, it involves putting the OS username of the DBA in a special group (on Unix systems this is the DBA group) or giving that OS username special rights on the system. After the DBA is set up with an OS account, two OS roles must be created and granted to the DBA:

- OSOPER—Allows performance of **STARTUP, SHUTDOWN, ALTER DATABASE OPEN/MOUNT, ALTER DATABASE BACKUP, ARCHIVE LOG**, and **RECOVER**, and includes the **RESTRICTED SESSION** privilege.
- OSDBA—Comprises every system privilege with **ADMIN OPTION** and the **OSOPER** role; allows both **CREATE DATABASE** and time-based recovery.

> **EXAM ALERT:** Depending on the underlying OS, **OSOPER** and **OSDBA** roles might have different names and functions.

The **OSOPER** and **OSDBA** roles are not Oracle roles. They are granted through the OS, not the database. The process of granting these privileges is OS specific. When a DBA logs on with administrator privileges and the initialization parameter **REMOTE_LOGIN_PASSWORDFILE** is set to **NONE**, Oracle communicates with the OS and attempts to enable first **OSDBA** and then, if unsuccessful, **OSOPER**. If both attempts fail, the connection fails.

To connect to the database via OS authentication, use one of the following commands:

```
CONNECT / AS SYSOPER
CONNECT / AS SYSDBA
```

> **TIP:** To connect as **SYSOPER** or **SYSDBA** using OS authentication, you do not need the **SYSOPER** or **SYSDBA** system privileges in Oracle. Instead, the server verifies that you have been granted the appropriate **OSDBA** or **OSOPER** roles at the OS level. This is controlled by the initialization parameter **REMOTE_LOGIN_PASSWORDFILE**.

Authentication Password File

When a password file is used, users can log in as themselves and use the DBA privileges associated with the **SYSDBA** and **SYSOPER** database roles. The **SYSDBA** role has the same privileges as the **OSDBA** role and the **SYSOPER** role has the same privileges as the **OSOPER** role. When a user is granted **SYSDBA** or **SYSOPER** privileges, the user's name and privilege information becomes part of the password file. In cases in which the server does not have an exclusive password file; e.g., when the initialization parameter **REMOTE_ LOGIN_PASSWORDFILE** is **NONE** or **SHARED**, Oracle sends you an error message when you try to grant these privileges. Revoked privileges are removed from the password file automatically.

The syntax for connecting is:

```
CONNECT username/password@connect_string AS SYSDBA
```

To use a password file to authenticate DBAs, you must first create the password file using the **ORAPWD** utility. Set the **REMOTE_LOGIN_PASSWORDFILE** initialization parameter to **EXCLUSIVE** and add users to the password file by using SQL to grant one or both of the **SYSDBA** and **SYSOPER** roles.

Use the following syntax to create a password file:

```
ORAPWD FILE=file_name PASSWORD=password ENTRIES=max_users
```

TIP: In Windows NT, the command is **ORAPWD80**.

The parameters for **ORAPWD** are as follows:

- FILE—This is a mandatory parameter and must specify the full pathname of the file. The password file is encrypted and can't be viewed. See your OS-specific Oracle documentation for the names and locations allowed on your platform. If you are using Oracle Parallel Server, the environment variable for each instance should point to the same password file.
- PASSWORD—This is a mandatory parameter that sets the password for **INTERNAL** and **SYS**. If the password for **SYS** is changed after connecting to the database, both the password stored in the data dictionary and the password stored in the password file are updated.
- ENTRIES—This parameter sets the maximum number of entries (users) allowed to connect to the database as **SYSDBA** or **SYSOPER**. This

parameter must be used if the **REMOTE_LOGIN_PASSWORDFILE** initialization parameter is set to **EXCLUSIVE**.

> If you ever need to exceed the **ENTRIES** limit, you must create a new password file. Use a number larger than you think you will ever need.

Use the **V$PWFILE_USERS** view to determine which users have been granted **SYSDBA** and **SYSOPER** system privileges for a database. The columns in this view are as follows:

- **USERNAME**—The names of all the users in the password file.
- **SYSDBA**—The value in this column is **TRUE** when the user has been granted the **SYSDBA** system privilege.
- **SYSOPER**—The value in this column is **TRUE** when the user has been granted the **SYSOPER** system privilege.

If the file full error (ORA-1996) is returned in response to an attempt to grant a user **SYSDBA** or **SYSOPER** system privileges, you have to create a new larger password file by increasing the **ENTRIES** parameter. All users must then be regranted the **SYSDBA** and **SYSOPER** privileges so they can be added back into the new file.

Use the following steps to replace a password file:

1. The **V$PWFILE_USERS** view allows you to see which users have **SYSDBA** and **SYSOPER** system privileges for a database.
2. Shut down the database.
3. Delete the existing password file.
4. Use the **ORAPWD** utility to create a new password file.
5. Grant **SYSOPER** or **SYSDBA** privileges to users as appropriate. Oracle will automatically add them to the password file.

If you no longer need to authenticate users via a particular password file, delete the password file and reset **REMOTE_LOGIN_PASSWORDFILE** to **NONE**. You must not remove or change the password file if there is a database or instance mounted using **REMOTE_LOGIN_PASSWORDFILE= EXCLUSIVE** or **SHARED**. Otherwise, you won't be able to use the password file to reconnect remotely. Even if you replace the file, you cannot use the new file; the timestamp and checksums will not match.

The **REMOTE_LOGIN_ PASSWORDFILE** parameter has the following three values:

- **NONE**—This is the default value for this parameter. This value causes Oracle to behave as if the password file does not exist; that is, remote DBA connections are not allowed over nonsecure connections.
- **EXCLUSIVE**—This value allows users other than **INTERNAL** and **SYS** to be added to the password file. This also means that the password file can be used only with one database. This value allows you to grant **SYSDBA** and **SYSOPER** system privileges to individual users, and then they can connect as themselves.
- **SHARED**—This value allows multiple databases to use the same password file. The only users in a **SHARED** password file are **SYS** and **INTERNAL**. You cannot add users to a **SHARED** password file. All users needing **SYSDBA** or **SYSOPER** system privileges must connect as **SYS**.

The *state* of the password file is stored in the file. When it is first created, the password file default state is **SHARED**. To change this state, set the **REMOTE_LOGIN_PASSWORDFILE** parameter to one of the values stated previously. When an instance is started up, Oracle retrieves this parameter's value from the initialization parameter file. When the database is mounted, Oracle compares this parameter's value to the value in the password file. If the values are not the same, Oracle overwrites the value stored in the file.

Creating The Parameter File

Although not considered to be a part of the database because the Oracle processes don't write to it, the *parameter file* contains the initialization parameters that instruct the Oracle instance on how to set itself up with buffers, processes, caches, and the like. The parameter file is read while starting the instance. Thus, the instance sizes all SGA components either directly through parameter values or indirectly from calculations based on parameter values specified in the parameter file. The DBA is responsible for tuning the database by using the initialization parameters. Over 200 initialization parameters exist; the exact number varies, depending on the version of Oracle and the platform you are running on. Tables 4.1 through 4.3 show parameters that can change dynamically by issuing commands in Server Manager. Table 4.4 is an abbreviated list of common parameters that can only be changed by shutting down the database and then restarting it.

Table 4.1 Initialization parameters alterable with ALTER SESSION.

Parameter Name	Default Value	Description
ALLOW_PARTIAL_SN_RESULTS	FALSE	Parallel Server parameter that allows for partial results to be returned on queries to global performance tables (GV$).
B_TREE_BITMAP_PLANS	FALSE	Enables the use of bitmap; plans for tables with only B-tree indexes.
CLOSE_CACHED_OPEN_CURSORS	FALSE	Specifies whether cursors opened and cached in memory by PL/SQL are automatically closed at each commit.
COMPLEX_VIEW_MERGING	OFF	Causes complex views or subqueries to be merged.
DB_FILE_MULTIBLOCK_READ_COUNT	8	Specifies the maximum number of blocks read in one input/output (I/O) operation during a sequential scan.
GLOBAL_NAMES	FALSE	Enforces that database links have same name as remote database.
HASH_AREA_SIZE	0	Sets the size of in-memory hash work area.
HASH_JOIN_ENABLED	TRUE	Enables/disables hash join.
HASH_MULTIBLOCK_IO_COUNT	1	Number of blocks hash join reads/writes at once.
JOB_QUEUE_PROCESSES	0	Number of job queue (SNPn) processes to start.
MAX_DUMP_FILE_SIZE	10,000	Maximum size (in blocks) of dump file.
NLS_CALENDAR	Gregorian	Specifies which calendar system is used by Oracle.
NLS_CURRENCY	Derived	National Language Support (NLS) local currency symbol.

(continued)

Table 4.1 Initialization parameters alterable with ALTER SESSION (continued).

Parameter Name	Default Value	Description
NLS_DATE_FORMAT	Derived	Default Oracle date format.
NLS_DATE_LANGUAGE	Value for **NLS_LANGUAGE**	NLS language name.
NLS_ISO_CURRENCY	Derived	NLS Organization for International Standards (ISO) currency territory name.
NLS_LANGUAGE	OS dependent	NLS language name.
NLS_NUMERIC_CHARACTERS	Derived	NLS numeric characters.
NLS_SORT	Derived	**BINARY** or valid linguistic definition name.
NLS_TERRITORY	OS dependent	NLS territory name.
OBJECT_CACHE_MAX_SIZE_PERCENT	10 percent	Cache size that the session object cache can grow past the optimal size.
OBJECT_CACHE_OPTIMAL_SIZE	100K	Size to which the session object cache is reduced when the size of the cache exceeds the maximum size.
OPS_ADMIN_GROUP	All active instances	Allows instances to be partitioned in a Parallel Server environment for monitoring or administration purposes.
OPTIMIZER_MODE	**CHOOSE**	Specifies the behavior of the optimizer.
OPTIMIZER_PERCENT_PARALLEL	0	Amount of parallelism that the optimizer uses in its cost functions.
OPTIMIZER_SEARCH_LIMIT	5	Search limit for the optimizer.
PARALLEL_ADAPTIVE_MULTI_USER	**FALSE**	Enables an adaptive algorithm designed to improve performance in multiuser environments that use PQ.

(continued)

Table 4.1 Initialization parameters alterable with ALTER SESSION (continued).

Parameter Name	Default Value	Description
PARALLEL_INSTANCE_GROUP		Uses all instances currently active as a group to be used for spawning parallel query (PQ) slaves.
PARALLEL_MIN_PERCENT	0	Minimum percent of threads required for PQ.
PARTITION_VIEW_ENABLED	FALSE	Enables/disables partitioned views.
PLSQL_V2_COMPATIBILITY	FALSE	Sets PLSQL V2 compatibility level for PL/SQL.
PUSH_JOIN_PREDICATE	FALSE	Cost-based way of improving performance in certain queries.
REMOTE_DEPENDENCIES_MODE	TIMESTAMP	Remote-procedure-call dependencies mode parameter.
SESSION_CACHED_CURSORS	OS dependent	Number of session cursors to cache.
SORT_AREA_RETAINED_SIZE	SORT_AREA SIZE	Size of in-memory sort work area retained between fetch calls.
SORT_AREA_SIZE	OS dependent	Size in memory of sort work area.
SORT_DIRECT_WRITES	AUTO	Controls whether sort data bypasses the buffer cache.
SORT_READ_FAC	OS dependent	Ratio that describes the amount of time to read a single database block divided by the block transfer rate
SORT_WRITE_BUFFER_SIZE	32,768	Size of the sort I/O buffer when the **SORT_DIRECT_WRITES** parameter is set to **TRUE**.
SORT_WRITE_BUFFERS	1	Number of sort buffers when the **SORT_DIRECT_WRITES** parameter is set to **TRUE**.
SPIN_COUNT	2,000	Number of times to spin on latch miss.

(continued)

Table 4.1 Initialization parameters alterable with ALTER SESSION (continued).

Parameter Name	Default Value	Description
STAR_TRANSFORMATION_ENABLED	FALSE	Determines whether a cost-based query transformation is applied to star queries.
TEXT_ENABLE	FALSE	Enables text searching.
TIMED_STATISTICS	FALSE	Maintains internal timing statistics.

Table 4.2 Initialization parameters alterable with ALTER SYSTEM.

Parameter Name	Default Value	Description
AQ_TM_PROCESSES	0	Specifies whether a queue monitor is created.
BACKGROUND_DUMP_DEST	OS dependent	Pathname for a directory where debugging trace files for the background processes (LGWR, DBWn, SMON, PMON, etc.) are written.
CONTROL_FILE_RECORD_KEEP_TIME	7	Specifies the minimum age (in days) that a record must be before it can be reused.
CORE_DUMP_DEST	$ORACLE_HOME/DBS/	Specifies the directory where core files are dumped.
DB_BLOCK_CHECKPOINT_BATCH	0	Number of buffers that will be added to each batch of buffers that the database writer (DBWn) process writes.
DB_BLOCK_CHECKSUM	FALSE	Stores a checksum in the cache header of every data block when writing it to disk.
DB_BLOCK_MAX_DIRTY_TARGET	All the buffers in the cache	Number of buffers that can be dirty.
DB_FILE_MULTIBLOCK_READ_COUNT	8	Specifies the maximum number of blocks read in one I/O operation during a sequential scan.

(continued)

Table 4.2 Initialization parameters alterable with ALTER SYSTEM (continued).

Parameter Name	Default Value	Description
FIXED_DATE	NULL	Constant date that SYSDATE always returns instead of the current date.
FREEZE_DB_FOR_FAST_INSTANCE_RECOVERY	Derived	Parallel Server parameter used to speed recovery.
GC_DEFER_TIME	10	Time (in 100ths of a second) that the server waits (or defers) before responding to forced write requests for hot blocks from other instances.
GLOBAL_NAMES	FALSE	Enforces that database links have same name as remote database.
HASH_MULTIBLOCK_IO_COUNT	1	Number of blocks hash join reads/writes at once.
JOB_QUEUE_PROCESSES	0	Number of SNPn to start.
LICENSE_MAX_SESSIONS	0	Maximum number of nonsystem user sessions allowed.
LICENSE_MAX_USERS	0	Maximum number of named users that can be created in the database.
LICENSE_SESSIONS_WARNING	0	Warning level for number of nonsystem user sessions.
LOG_ARCHIVE_DUPLEX_DEST	NULL	Specifies a second archive destination.
LOG_ARCHIVE_MIN_SUCCEED_DEST	1	Minimum number of archive log destinations that must succeed.
LOG_CHECKPOINT_INTERVAL	OS dependent	Indicates number of redo blocks for checkpoint threshold.
LOG_CHECKPOINT_TIMEOUT	0	Maximum time interval in seconds between check-points.
LOG_SMALL_ENTRY_MAX_SIZE	OS dependent	Redo entries larger than this will acquire the redo copy latch.

(continued)

Table 4.2 Initialization parameters alterable with ALTER SYSTEM (continued).

Parameter Name	Default Value	Description
MAX_DUMP_FILE_SIZE	10,000	Maximum size (in blocks) of dump file.
MTS_DISPATCHERS	NULL	Enable various attributes for each dispatcher.
MTS_SERVERS	0	Specifies the number of server processes.
OPS_ADMIN_GROUP	All active instances	Allows instances to be partitioned in a Parallel Server environment for monitoring or administration purposes.
PARALLEL_INSTANCE_GROUP	All instances currently active	Group to be used for spawning PQ slaves.
PARALLEL_TRANSACTION_RESOURCE_TIMEOUT	300	Parallel Server parameter that specifies the maximum amount of time a session executing a parallel operation will wait for a resource held by another session in an incompatible lock mode.
PLSQL_V2_COMPATIBILITY	FALSE	Sets PLSQL V2 compatibility level for PL/SQL.
REMOTE_DEPENDENCIES_MODE	TIMESTAMP	Remote-procedure-call dependencies mode parameter.
RESOURCE_LIMIT	FALSE	Enables/disables the enforcement of resource limits.
SPIN_COUNT	2,000	Number of times to spin on latch miss.
TEXT_ENABLE	FALSE	Enables text searching.
TIMED_OS_STATISTICS	0	Used by the system administrator to gather OS statistics.
TIMED_STATISTICS	FALSE	Maintains internal timing statistics.
USER_DUMP_DEST	OS dependent	Pathname for a directory where the server will write debugging trace files on behalf of a user process.

Table 4.3 Initialization parameters alterable with ALTER SYSTEM DEFERRED.

Parameter Name	Default Value	Description
ALLOW_PARTIAL_SN_ RESULTS	FALSE	Parallel Server parameter that allows for partial results to be returned on queries to global performance tables (GV$).
BACKUP_DISK_IO_SLAVES	0	Number of I/O slaves used by the Recovery Manager to back up, copy, or restore.
BACKUP_TAPE_IO_SLAVES	FALSE	Specifies whether I/O slaves are used by the Recovery Manager to back up, copy, or restore data to tape.
DB_FILE_DIRECT_IO_COUNT	64	Number of blocks used for I/O operations done by backup, restore, or direct path read and write functions.
OBJECT_CACHE_MAX_ SIZE_PERCENT	10 percent	Cache size that the session object cache can grow past the optimal size.
OBJECT_CACHE_OPTIMAL_ SIZE	100K	Size to which the session object cache is reduced when the size of the cache exceeds the maximum size.
SORT_AREA_RETAINED_SIZE	SORT_AREA_ SIZE	Size of in-memory sort work area retained between fetch calls.
SORT_AREA_SIZE	OS dependent	Size in memory of sort work area.
SORT_DIRECT_WRITES	AUTO	Controls whether sort data bypasses the buffer cache.
SORT_READ_FAC	OS dependent	Ratio that describes the amount of time to read a single database block divided by the block transfer rate.
SORT_WRITE_BUFFER_SIZE	32,768	Size of the sort I/O buffer when the **SORT_DIRECT_ WRITES** parameter is set to **TRUE**.

(continued)

Table 4.3 Initialization parameters alterable with ALTER SYSTEM DEFERRED (continued).

Parameter Name	Default Value	Description
SORT_WRITE_BUFFERS	1	Number of sort buffers when the **SORT_DIRECT_WRITES** parameter is set to **TRUE**.
TRANSACTION_AUDITING	TRUE	Enables/disables special redo record that contains session and user information.

Table 4.4 Other nondynamic initialization parameters.

Parameter Name	Default Value	Description
ALWAYS_ANTI_JOIN	NESTED_LOOPS	Sets the antijoin algorithm to **NESTED_LOOPS**, **MERGE**, or **HASH**.
ALWAYS_SEMI_JOIN	Standard	Sets the semijoin algorithm to **NESTED_LOOPS**, **MERGE**, or **HASH_SJ**.
ARCH_IO_SLAVES	0	Number of I/O slaves used by the archiver (ARCH) process.
AUDIT_FILE_DEST	$ORACLE_HOME/RDBMS/AUDIT	Directory where auditing files are stored.
AUDIT_TRAIL	NONE	Enables/disables writing of rows to the audit trai .
BACKGROUND_CORE_DUMP	FULL	Specifies whether the SGA is dumped as part of the generated core file.
BITMAP_MERGE_AREA_SIZE	1MB	Amount of memory used to merge bitmaps retrieved from a range scan of the index.
BUFFER_POOL_KEEP	NONE	Allows you to keep an object in the buffer cache.
BUFFER_POOL_RECYCLE	NONE	Limits the size of an object in the buffer cache.
CONTROL_FILES	OS dependent	Specifies one or more names of control files.

(continued)

Table 4.4 Other nondynamic initialization parameters (continued).

Parameter Name	Default Value	Description
DB_BLOCK_BUFFERS	200 buffers	Number of database blocks cached in memory.
DB_BLOCK_LRU_ EXTENDED_STATISTICS	0	Disables/enables compilation of statistics that measures the effects of increasing the number of buffers in the buffer cache in the SGA.
DB_BLOCK_LRU_STATISTICS	**FALSE**	Disables/enables compilation of statistics in the **V$CURRENT_BUCKET** table, which measures the effect of fewer buffers in the SGA buffer cache.
DB_BLOCK_SIZE	OS dependent	Size in bytes of Oracle database blocks.
DB_DOMAIN	**WORLD**	Extension components of a global database name.
DB_FILES	OS dependent	Maximum number of database files that can be opened for this database.
DB_FILE_SIMULTANEOUS_ WRITES	4	Maximum number of simultaneous writes that can be made to a given database file.
DB_NAME	Any valid database name	Database identifier.
DB_WRITER_PROCESSES	1	Number of DBWn for an instance.
DBWR_IO_SLAVES	0	Number of I/O slaves used by DBWn.
DISK_ASYNCH_IO	**TRUE**	Controls whether I/O to datafiles, control files, and log files are asynchronous.
DML_LOCKS	Derived (4 * **TRANSACTIONS**)	Maximum number of data manipulation language (DML) locks.

(continued)

Table 4.4 Other nondynamic initialization parameters (continued).

Parameter Name	Default Value	Description
FAST_FULL_SCAN_ENABLED	FALSE	Enables/disables fast full scans.
IFILE	Valid parameter file names	Embeds another parameter file within the current parameter file.
LARGE_POOL_MIN_ALLOC	16K	Minimum allocation size from the large pool.
LARGE_POOL_SIZE	0	Size of the large pool allocation heap.
LGWR_IO_SLAVES	0	Number of I/O slaves used by the log writer (LGWR) process.
LOG_ARCHIVE_DEST	OS dependent	Default location of the archive log files.
LOG_ARCHIVE_FORMAT	OS dependent	Default file name format when archiving redo log files.
LOG_ARCHIVE_START	FALSE	Indicates whether archiving should be automatic or manual when the instance starts up.
LOG_BUFFER	OS dependent	Memory, in bytes, that is used when buffering redo entries.
OPEN_CURSORS	50	Maximum number of open cursors (context areas) a session can have at once.
ORACLE_TRACE_ENABLE	FALSE	Enables/disables Oracle trace collections for the server.
PARALLEL_MAX_SERVERS	OS dependent	Maximum number of PQ servers or parallel recovery processes for an instance.
PARALLEL_MIN_SERVERS	0	Minimum number of query server processes for an instance.
PARALLEL_SERVER	FALSE	Enables/disables the Parallel Server option.

(continued)

Table 4.4 Other nondynamic initialization parameters (continued).

Parameter Name	Default Value	Description
PROCESSES	30	Maximum number of OS user processes that can simultaneously connect to an Oracle server.
REMOTE_LOGIN_PASSWORDFILE	NONE	Specifies whether Oracle checks for a password file.
ROLLBACK_SEGMENTS	NULL	Specifies one or more rollback segments to allocate by name to this instance.
SESSIONS	Derived (1.1 * **PROCESSES** + 5)	Total number of user and system sessions.
SHARED_POOL_SIZE	3,500,000 bytes	Size of the shared pool in bytes.
SQL_TRACE	FALSE	Disables/ enables the SQL trace facility.

TIP: To start up an instance or database using OEM, you must specify a database name and a parameter file to initialize the instance settings. The initialization parameter file and any associated files, such as a configuration file, must exist on the client machine on which you are running OEM.

Starting Up An Instance And Opening The Database

To start up an Oracle instance and open the database, use either the OEM Startup Database dialog box or the **STARTUP** command in Server Manager. To start an instance and mount a database, you must specify the name of the database that will be mounted to the instance by either using the **STARTUP** command and specifying the database name, or specifying the **DB_NAME** in the parameter file that starts the instance. You have several options when starting up an Oracle instance, which are explained in the following sections.

STARTUP NOMOUNT

There may be cases in which you want to start an instance without mounting a database, such as during database creation or when recreating a control file. You can do this by using the OEM Startup Database dialog box by selecting the Startup Nomount radio button or issue the **STARTUP** command with the **NOMOUNT** option in Server Manager.

STARTUP MOUNT

There may be cases in which you need to start an instance and mount a database without opening it to carry out certain maintenance operations. A database must be mounted, but not opened, to perform the following tasks:

- Adding, dropping, or renaming redo log files
- Enabling/disabling redo log archiving options
- Performing full database recovery
- Renaming datafiles

You can start an instance and mount a database by using the OEM Startup Database dialog box's Startup Mount radio button or by using the **STARTUP** command with the **MOUNT** option in Server Manager.

STARTUP OPEN

When an instance is started and the database is open, any valid user can connect to the database and perform typical data access operations. You can start an instance and open a database by using the OEM Startup Database dialog box and selecting the Startup Open radio button or by using the **STARTUP** command with the **OPEN** option in Server Manager.

STARTUP RESTRICTED

At times you may want to have the database open, but not allow non-DBA account access to the database. In this case, you can start the instance and mount and open a database in restricted mode so that the database is available only to DBAs. When a database is opened in restricted mode, only users with both **CREATE SESSION** and **RESTRICTED SESSION** can access the database. Typical tasks you might want to perform in restricted mode are:

- Maintaining database structure, such as adding/rebuilding indexes, altering tables, or adding triggers

- Exporting or importing database data
- Loading data with SQL*Loader

You can start an instance and mount a database by using the OEM Startup database dialog box's Restrict radio button or by using the **STARTUP** command with the **RESTRICT** option in Server Manager.

STARTUP FORCE

In rare cases, you might experience problems attempting to start a database instance. You should not force the start unless it is absolutely necessary, because it will almost always result in the need for an instance recovery. Try to determine why the instance and database will not start up normally before using this option. If you think this is the only way to start your instance, I recommend that you call Oracle support staff and get their guidance. The last thing you want to do is force a recovery that fails and be in a worse position than when you started. You can force an instance and database to start by using the OEM Startup Database dialog box's Force radio button or by using the **STARTUP** command with the **FORCE** option in Server Manager.

Starting In Exclusive Or Parallel Mode

On Oracle servers that are licensed for the Parallel Server option, you must decide whether to mount that database in parallel or exclusively. You can start an instance and database in exclusive or parallel mode by using the OEM Startup Database dialog box's Exclusive/Parallel radio button or by using the **STARTUP** command with the **EXCLUSIVE/PARALLEL** option in Server Manager.

Closing The Database And Shutting Down An Instance

As with instance and database startup, shutdown can be done by using either the OEM Shutdown dialog box or the **SHUTDOWN** command in Server Manager. You can shut down a database using three methods; each will be discussed in the following sections. While a shutdown is in progress, any user who tries to access the database will receive the following message:

```
ORA-01090: shutdown in progress connection is not permitted
```

SHUTDOWN NORMAL

When an instance and database are shut down with the **NORMAL** option, no new connections are allowed after the statement is issued. Oracle will wait for all connected users to disconnect from the database before proceeding with the database shutdown. When Oracle is shut down using the **NORMAL** option, database startup is faster because no recovery is required.

SHUTDOWN IMMEDIATE

The **SHUTDOWN IMMEDIATE** statement closes all idle connections and shuts down the database. No new connections are allowed after the statement is issued. If, however, you've submitted processes (for example, inserts, selects, or updates) that are awaiting results, the **SHUTDOWN IMMEDIATE** statement allows the processes to complete. Uncommitted transactions are rolled back prior to database shutdown. **SHUTDOWN IMMEDIATE** is normally used when the database must be shut down quickly; the most common reason is a power outage. **SHUTDOWN IMMEDIATE** usually requires an instance recovery on startup, which Oracle does automatically without action from the DBA. To begin a **SHUTDOWN IMMEDIATE**, use either the OEM Shutdown Database dialog box's Immediate radio button or the SQL command **SHUTDOWN IMMEDIATE** in Server Manager.

SHUTDOWN TRANSACTIONAL

The **SHUTDOWN TRANSACTIONAL** statement is the same as the **SHUTDOWN IMMEDIATE** statement, except that executing inserts, updates, and deletes must be committed before the database closes the connections. Using **SHUTDOWN TRANSACTIONAL** saves all changes to the database and usually does not require an instance recovery. To begin **SHUTDOWN TRANSACTIONAL**, use either the OEM Shutdown Database dialog box's Transactional radio button or the SQL command **SHUTDOWN TRANSACTIONAL** in Server Manager.

SHUTDOWN ABORT

If you must shut down the database in an emergency or when the database will not shut down using one of the previous three methods, you can use the **SHUTDOWN ABORT** option. This is also used to stop an Oracle instance that did not start up properly and must be shut down. **SHUTDOWN ABORT** stops all the Oracle background processes instantaneously; this terminates all connections, regardless of their transaction state. At the very least, instance recovery will be required (and possibly even database recovery). This method of shutdown should be avoided if possible. To begin a shutdown abort, use either the OEM Shutdown Database dialog box's Abort radio button or the SQL command **SHUTDOWN ABORT** in Server Manager.

Managing Sessions

In some situations, such as when two users are in deadlock or database maintenance is necessary, the DBA may need to stop an individual session. When a session is killed, all transactions are rolled back, and memory and locks are released. You can use Instance Manager to terminate a session, or you can use SQL*Plus. To use SQL*Plus, you will first have to query the data dictionary to find the session information necessary to kill the session.

Killing a session requires two pieces of information about the session: the *session identifier (SID)* and the *session serial number.* You can find the SID and the serial number in the **V$SESSION** view. To find all the session information for the user named "Justin", you would execute the following query:

```
SELECT sid, serial#
  FROM v$session
  WHERE username = 'JUSTIN';
  SID    SERIAL#    STATUS
  ---    -------   --------
   25         15     ACTIVE
   72       2463   INACTIVE
```

You can kill sessions when they are **ACTIVE** or **INACTIVE.** A session is **ACTIVE** when it is making an SQL call to Oracle and **INACTIVE** when it is not making an SQL call to Oracle.

To kill the active session, execute the following command in SQL*Plus:

```
ALTER SYSTEM KILL SESSION '25,15';
```

When you kill an active session, the user will receive the following message the next time he or she tries to execute a command:

```
ORA-00028: your session has been killed
```

Once a session has been killed, all attempts to issue any additional SQL commands will fail and the following message will be delivered:

```
ORA-01012: not logged on
```

Monitoring Alert And Trace Files

Each Oracle background process creates and writes its own trace file. If an Oracle process identifies an internal error, it dumps the error information to its trace file. Trace files can be used by the DBA and Oracle support staff to troubleshoot problems or tune applications and instances.

The alert file is a special trace file; it is a chronological log of messages and errors. Every message includes a timestamp. The following list shows many of the messages included in the alert file:

- All "ORA-600" errors
- Block corruption errors
- Deadlock errors
- **CREATE DATABASE, TABLESPACE**, or **ROLLBACK SEGMENT** commands
- **ALTER DATABASE, TABLESPACE**, or **ROLLBACK SEGMENT** commands
- **DROP DATABASE, TABLESPACE**, or **ROLLBACK SEGMENT** commands
- **STARTUP** commands
- **SHUTDOWN** commands
- **ARCHIVE LOG** commands
- **RECOVER** commands
- Automatic snapshot refresh messages
- All initialization parameters at instance startup

As a DBA, you should check the alert<*SID*>.log file and other trace files of an instance to see if the background processes have encountered errors. For example, when LGWR is unable to write to a log group member, an error is written to the alert file and the LGWR trace file. Also, if dynamic initialization parameters have been changed while the database was running, you could check the alert file to see what the parameters were when the database was started and again when they were changed.

Use the initialization parameters **BACKGROUND_DUMP_DEST** to set the location of trace files for background processes and **USER_DUMP_DEST** for user server process trace files. The alert file will grow continuously and must be monitored to make sure it does not run out of disk space. If the alert file has grown too large, you can just delete it. (Oracle will create a new one the next time it tries to write to the alert file and finds that it does not exist.) All other trace files have a maximum size set by the initialization parameter **MAX_DUMP_FILE_SIZE**.

Trace files can be generated for all user server processes by setting the initialization parameter **SQL_TRACE** to **TRUE**. This is not usually done for the entire database because of the drag on performance. However, you can turn on tracing for the current individual session by using the **ALTER SESSION** command or for another session by executing the **DBMS_SYSTEM** package. The following SQL statements show the syntax for the two commands, respectively:

```
ALTER SESSION SET SQL_TRACE TRUE;
EXECUTE DBMS_SYSTEM.SET_SQL_TRACE_IN_SESSION(session identifier,
session serial number, TRUE)
```

Data Dictionary

When you create a database, the associated *data dictionary* is created automatically. The data dictionary base tables are also created and must stay in the system tablespace. These tables store information about all user-defined objects in the database. The following list shows information found in the data dictionary:

- Definitions of all schema objects in the database (tables, views, indexes, clusters, synonyms, sequences, procedures, functions, packages, and triggers, plus other objects, depending on the options installed)
- Space allocation for all schema objects
- Integrity constraint information
- Oracle usernames and encrypted passwords
- Privileges and roles each user has been granted
- Auditing information if auditing is turned on
- Other general database information

Two scripts, catalog.sql and catproc.sql, are used to build the basic Oracle data dictionary. Additional scripts extend the data dictionary, depending on the options of Oracle being installed. Even though these scripts are run automatically, it is important to know what they are because you might need to run them again when upgrading to a new release of Oracle8. You must run all of these scripts when connected to the database as the user **SYS**. The following list gives a short description of each script:

- *catalog.sql*—Creates the data dictionary objects and public synonyms for many of its views, and grants public access to the synonyms.
- *catproc.sql*—Runs all the scripts required for Oracle PL/SQL.
- *catrep.sql*—Runs all scripts for the **ADVANCED REPLICATION** option.

The data dictionary is normally accessed through a set of user-accessible views. These views summarize and display the information stored in the base tables of the data dictionary, making the dictionary information much easier to understand and use. Most users are given access to the views, but not the base tables.

TIP: Altering or manipulating the data in underlying data dictionary tables can permanently and detrimentally affect the operation of a database, and this action is not supported.

Oracle uses the data dictionary to find information about users, schema objects, and storage structures. Oracle modifies the data dictionary every time that a *data definition language (DDL)* statement is executed. Any Oracle user can use the data dictionary as a read-only reference for information about the database. The data dictionary scripts create public synonyms on many data dictionary views so that users can access them easily. These views are broken down into three groups:

- **USER** views—Show all the data dictionary information for the user accessing the data dictionary.
- **ALL** views—Show the dictionary information for any objects the user owns or has access to.
- **DBA** views—Show all the information in the data dictionary. Public synonyms are not created for these views, because they should be queried only by DBAs. Oracle supplies a script called catdbsyn.sql to create private synonyms for the DBA views. Each DBA should run this script in his or her schema.

Practice Questions

Question 1

You set up password file authentication and set the **REMOTE_LOGIN_PASSWORDFILE** initialization parameter to **SHARED**. Which answers will be recognized by the password file? [Choose two]

- ❑ a. **SYSDBA**
- ❑ b. **SYS**
- ❑ c. **SYSOPER**
- ❑ d. **SYSTEM**
- ❑ e. **INTERNAL**

Answers b and e are correct. If you use the **SHARED** option, the password file only recognizes users **SYS** and **INTERNAL**. **SYSDBA** and **SYSOPER** are roles, not accounts. **SYSTEM** can be added to the password file if the **REMOTE_LOGIN_PASSWORFILE** parameter is set to exclusive.

Question 2

If you want to rename multiple datafiles, which startup mode would you use to start an instance?

- ❍ a. **OPEN**
- ❍ b. **NOMOUNT**
- ❍ c. **MOUNT**

Answer c is correct. To rename multiple datafiles, the **ALTER DATABASE** command must be used with the database in a mounted but not open state. Answers a and b are incorrect; **OPEN** opens the online datafiles and redo log files and detects if instance recovery is necessary. It is the default mode for instance startup. **NOMOUNT** starts an instance, reads the parameter file, allocates memory for the SGA, starts the background processes, and opens the alert logs and trace files.

Question 3

Which initialization parameter specifies the location of the alert file?

- ❍ a. **BACKGROUND_DUMP_DEST**
- ❍ b. **USER_DUMP_DEST**
- ❍ c. **CORE_DUMP_DEST**
- ❍ d. **LOG_ARCHIVE_DEST**

Answer a is correct. BACKGROUND_DUMP_DEST specifies the location of the alert file and the background trace files. USER_DUMP_DEST specifies the location of user trace files. CORE_DUMP_DEST specifies the directory where core files are dumped. LOG_ARCHIVE_DEST is a text string that specifies the default location of the disk file or tape device when archiving redo log files.

Question 4

What information is written to an Oracle process trace file?

- ❍ a. Sequence generator cache
- ❍ b. Initialization parameters used at instance startup
- ❍ c. Date and time of the last full backup
- ❍ d. Information about background processes

Answer d is correct. Trace files record information about the background processes. These files are useful when trying to determine the cause of a failure. The sequence generator cache is stored in the SGA. Initialization parameters are written in the alert file. Backup time is not written in the trace file and can be found in different locations depending on the backup method.

Question 5

Using Server Manager in line mode, what methods could you use to display the current locations of the control files? [Choose three]

- ❑ a. Use the **SHOW SGA** command.
- ❑ b. Query **V$CONTROLFILE**.
- ❑ c. Use the **DESCRIBE** command.
- ❑ d. Query **V$PARAMETER**.
- ❑ e. Query **V$SYSTEM_PARAMETER**.
- ❑ f. Use the **SHOW PARAMETER** command.

Answers b, d, and f are correct. **V$CONTROLFILE** displays the names and locations of the control files, and **V$PARAMETER** displays the current settings of any parameter. In Server Manager, you can view the current parameter values by using the **SHOW PARAMETER** command. The **SHOW SGA** command displays SGA information for the current instance. The **DESCRIBE** command describes tables, views, and other database objects. **V$SYSTEM_PARAMETER** displays the current system values.

Question 6

Your database is mounted and you need to make it available for normal database operations. Which Server Manager command should you use?

- ❍ a. **ALTER SYSTEM OPEN**
- ❍ b. **ALTER SESSION OPEN**
- ❍ c. **ALTER DATABASE NOMOUNT**
- ❍ d. **ALTER SESSION MOUNT**
- ❍ e. **ALTER DATABASE OPEN**

Answer e is correct. To change the state of the database from **MOUNT** to **OPEN**, use the **ALTER DATABASE OPEN** command. **ALTER SYSTEM OPEN**, **ALTER SESSION OPEN**, **ALTER DATABASE NOMOUNT**, and **ALTER SESSION MOUNT** are invalid commands.

Question 7

Which shutdown mode only shuts down the instance, but does not dismount the database?

- ❍ a. **IMMEDIATE**
- ❍ b. **NORMAL**
- ◉ c. **ABORT**
- ❍ d. **TRANSACTIONAL**

Answer c is correct. Aborting the database stops all processes immediately. The database does not perform a checkpoint or close files. An instance recovery will be required on **STARTUP**. **SHUTDOWN IMMEDIATE** rolls back uncommitted transactions and dismounts the database. **SHUTDOWN NORMAL** waits for processes to disconnect and dismount the database. **SHUTDOWN TRANSACTIONAL** waits for current transactions to finish before dismounting the database.

Question 8

Why would you set the **REMOTE_LOGIN_PASSWORDFILE** initialization parameter to **NONE**?

- ◉ a. To use OS authentication
- ❍ b. To use a password file for remote login
- ❍ c. To enforce the Oracle server to verify a user's object privileges
- ❍ d. To enforce the Oracle server to verify a user's system privileges

Answer a is correct. To allow users to connect to the database using OS authentication, set the **REMOTE_LOGIN_PASSWORDFILE** parameter to **NONE**. Answer b is incorrect because Oracle will not use a password file when **REMOTE_LOGIN_PASSWORDFILE** is set to **NONE**. The Oracle server will always verify a user's object or system privileges.

Question 9

What is the effect of this Server Manager command:

```
ALTER SYSTEM SET SORT_AREA_SIZE=327680 DEFERRED;
```

- a. **SORT_AREA_SIZE** will be altered immediately.
- b. **SORT_AREA_SIZE** will be set to 327680 when the next sort operation occurs.
- c. **SORT_AREA_SIZE** will be altered for all future instances.
- d. **SORT_AREA_SIZE** will be set to 327680 for all future sessions.

Trick! question

Answer d is correct. The **DEFERRED** option will change the **SORT_AREA_SIZE** for all future sessions. Answer a is incorrect because the new **SORT_AREA_SIZE** will only affect future sessions. An immediate change would affect current sessions. You could be tricked into answer b because if the next sort operation is done by a new session, it would use the new value 327680. Answer c is wrong because this command only affects the current instance.

Question 10

Which shutdown mode waits for all current users to disconnect before shutting down the instance?

- a. **NORMAL**
- b. **ABORT**
- c. **IMMEDIATE**
- d. **TRANSACTIONAL**

Answer a is correct. **SHUTDOWN NORMAL** waits for processes to disconnect while not allowing new connections. Once all connections are disconnected, the database will shut down. **NORMAL** is the default shutdown mode. Aborting the database (answer b) stops all processes immediately; the database does not perform a checkpoint or close files. An instance recovery will be required on **STARTUP**. **SHUTDOWN IMMEDIATE** rolls back uncommitted transactions and dismounts the database. **SHUTDOWN TRANSACTIONAL** waits for current transactions to finish before dismounting the database.

Need To Know More?

Loney, Kevin, and Marlene Theriault: *Oracle8 DBA Handbook*, Oracle Press, Berkeley, CA, 1997. ISBN 0-07882-406-0. This book is a comprehensive guide and a must have for all DBAs.

See the Oracle documentation that is provided on CD with the Oracle RDBMS software. Pertaining to this chapter are:

Belden, Eric, Valerie Kane, Vrinda Kirloskar, and Harry Sun: *Oracle Server Manager User's Guide*, Oracle Corporation, Redwood City, CA, 1995. See Chapter 5, "Line Mode."

Fee, Joyce: *Oracle8 Administrator's Guide*, Oracle Corporation, Redwood City, CA, 1997. Complete documentation of database administration tasks.

Lane, Paul. *Oracle8 Reference Manual*, Oracle Corporation, Redwood City, CA, 1997. See Chapter 1, "Initialization Parameters."

Leverenz, Lefty: *Oracle8 Concepts Guide*, Oracle Corporation, Redwood City, CA, 1997. Complete documentation of Oracle concepts.

http://education.oracle.com/tbt/ocp8.html is the site from which you can order the Oracle Education CD-ROM bundle for Oracle8 Database Administration.

www.revealnet.com is the site where RevealNet Corporation provides Oracle Administration reference software.

5

Creating A Database

Terms you'll need to understand:

- √ DB_NAME
- √ DB_DOMAIN
- √ CONTROL_FILES
- √ DB_BLOCK_SIZE
- √ DB_BLOCK_BUFFERS
- √ PROCESSES
- √ ROLLBACK_SEGMENTS
- √ DATAFILE
- √ LOGFILE
- √ MAXLOGFILES
- √ MAXDATAFILES
- √ MAXINSTANCES
- √ ARCHIVELOG
- √ NOARCHIVELOG
- √ MAXLOGMEMBERS
- √ MAXLOGHISTORY
- √ CHARACTER SET
- √ NATIONAL CHARACTER SET

Techniques you'll need to master:

- √ Planning properly for creating a database
- √ Using the **CREATE DATABASE** command
- √ Creating rollback segments
- √ Creating tablespaces
- √ Altering users
- √ Dropping a database

Creating a database is one of the most important tasks a database administrator (DBA) can perform. Certain database parameters can be set only at database creation time, requiring prior planning before the database itself is created. Creating a database can also be a destructive command, because files from previous or current databases can be overwritten. Review this chapter before you create your next database and make sure you have thought through the process and considered all your options.

Before You Create A Database

Before you create a database, you must make several decisions. First, what character set will you use? After a database is created, you cannot change the character set choices without recreating the database. Second, what is your backup and recovery strategy? Third, what are the estimated space requirements for the database, including all system requirements, as well as database tables, indexes, clusters, and so forth?

Once you answer these questions, you are ready to create a database. Make sure you have the operating system (OS) privileges outlined in the platform installation guide and sufficient disk storage based on the planned size of the database. Enough memory must also be available for the Oracle instance to start.

Creating A Database

To create a new database and make it available for use, follow these steps:

1. If one or more databases already exist on the system, as a precaution you should perform a backup of each one before you create a new database. Although this is not mandatory, if you make a mistake when creating a database, you could wipe out an existing one.

2. Create an initialization parameter file with any database-specific parameters for the new database. You should always change the following parameters for the specific needs of each database:

   - DB_NAME—Required when the database is first created. Normally, the **DB_NAME** is the same as the instance name.

   - DB_DOMAIN—Specifies the extension components of a global database name. The **DB_DOMAIN** combined with **DB_NAME** should have a unique string for every database. For example, this parameter allows one department to create a database without worrying that it might have the same name as a database created by another department. If one sales department's **DB_DOMAIN** =

"UK.MYCO.COM," then their "SALES" database (SALES.UK.MYCO.COM) is uniquely identified from another database with **DB_NAME** = "SALES", but with **DB_DOMAIN** = "US.MYCO.COM".

- **CONTROL_FILES**—Specifies one or more names of control files, including a full directory path. Oracle recommends using multiple files on different devices or mirroring the file at the OS level for redundancy.
- **DB_BLOCK_SIZE**—Specifies the size in bytes of Oracle database blocks. This parameter should be set to a multiple of OS file blocks. The default value is 2K. **DB_BLOCK_SIZE** can only be specified when the database is first created.
- **DB_BLOCK_BUFFERS**—Specifies the number of database buffers available in the buffer cache. **DB_BLOCK_BUFFERS** is one of the primary parameters, which determines the total memory requirements of the system global area (SGA) for an instance. The **DB_BLOCK_BUFFERS** parameter with the **DB_ BLOCK_ SIZE** parameter determines the total size of the buffer cache.
- **PROCESSES**—Specifies the maximum number of OS user processes that can simultaneously connect to an Oracle server. This includes all background processes, job queue (SNPn) processes, and parallel query processes.
- **ROLLBACK_SEGMENTS**—Specifies one or more rollback segments to allocate to this instance. (This parameter is added to the initialization file after the database is created and rollback segments are created in the database.)

3. Start an Oracle instance. You can use the Startup Database dialog box of Oracle Enterprise Manager (OEM) or use Server Manager in line mode on the server. Use the **STARTUP NOMOUNT** command. Now the Oracle instance (SGA and background processes) is started, but no database exists yet.
4. Create the database. Use the SQL command **CREATE DATABASE**. When you execute a **CREATE DATABASE** statement, Oracle does the following operations:
   - Creates the control files for the database.
   - Creates the redo log files for the database.

- Creates the **SYSTEM** tablespace and datafiles.
- Creates the users **SYS** and **SYSTEM**.
- Creates the **SYSTEM** rollback segment.
- Creates the data dictionary.
- Specifies the character set that stores data in the database.
- Mounts and opens the database for use.

5. Back up the database. Once the database is created, you are in an unrecoverable state if you suffer a media failure. You should make a full OS backup of the database to ensure recoverability.

The CREATE DATABASE Command

When invoked with the **REUSE** options, **CREATE DATABASE** erases all data in designated datafiles to prepare them for use in the new database. Figure 5.1 shows the syntax of the **CREATE DATABASE** command.

The **CREATE DATABASE** command uses the following parameters:

- *database_name*—Designates the name of the database (up to eight bytes long) that you are creating. Oracle writes the database name into the control file. If you omit the database name from a **CREATE DATABASE** statement, Oracle uses the name specified by the initialization parameter **DB_NAME**.
- **CONTROLFILE REUSE**—Reuses extant control files distinguised by the **CONTROL_FILES** initialization parameter, overwriting any information the files contain. You cannot use this option if you also specify a parameter value that changes the size of the control file. These parameters are **MAXLOGFILES**, **MAXDATAFILES**, **MAXINSTANCES**, **MAXLOGMEMBERS**, and **MAXLOGHISTORY**.
- **DATAFILE**—Designates one or multiple files as datafiles, all of which become part of the **SYSTEM** tablespace.
- **LOGFILE**—Designates one or multiple files as redo log files, each of whose file specification designates a redo log file group with one or more redo log file members.
- **GROUP**—Uniquely identifies a redo log file group and can range from one to the value of the **MAXLOGFILES** parameter. You cannot specify multiple redo log file groups having the same **GROUP** value. If you

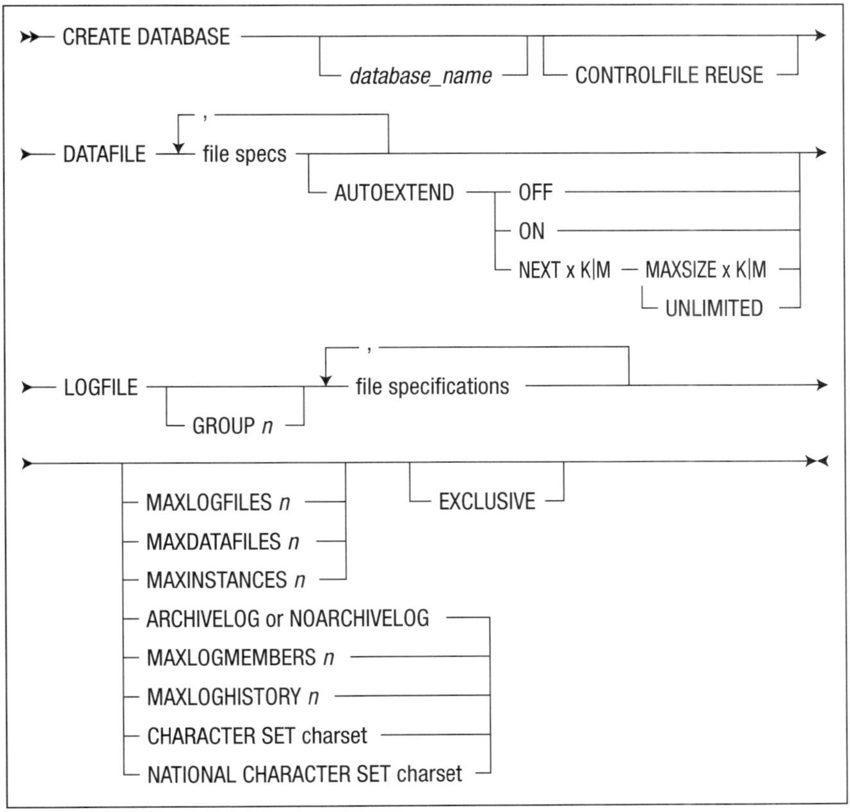

Figure 5.1 The syntax for the **CREATE DATABASE** command.

omit this parameter, Oracle generates its value automatically. If you omit the **LOGFILE** clause, Oracle creates two redo log file groups by default.

- **MAXLOGFILES**—Designates the maximum number of redo log file groups you can create for the database. This value sets the amount of control file space to allocate for redo log files names.
- **MAXDATAFILES**—Designates initial size of the control file's datafiles section when you use **CREATE DATABASE** or **CREATE CONTROL FILE**.
- **MAXINSTANCES**—Designates the maximum number of instances that can have the database mounted and open concurrently. This parameter is useful only if you are using Oracle with the Parallel Server option in parallel mode.

- **ARCHIVELOG**—Starts the database in archive log mode for redo log file groups. In this mode, the contents of a redo log file group must be archived before the group can be reused.
- **NOARCHIVELOG**—Starts the database in no archive log mode for redo log file groups. In this mode, the contents of a redo log file group need not be archived before the group can be reused. After creating the database, you can change between archive log mode and no archive log mode with the **ALTER DATABASE** command. No archive log mode is the default mode.
- **MAXLOGMEMBERS**—Specifies the maximum number of members, or copies, for a redo log file group. Oracle uses this value to determine how much space in the control file to allocate for the names of redo log files.
- **MAXLOGHISTORY**—Specifies the maximum number of archived redo log files for automatic media recovery of Oracle with the Parallel Server option.
- **CHARACTER SET**—Designates the character set the database will use in storing data. The setting cannot be changed after you create the database.
- **NATIONAL CHARACTER SET**—Specifies the national character set used to store data in columns specifically defined as **NCHAR**, **NCLOB**, or **NVARCHAR2**. You cannot change the national character set after creating the database.

The following statement is an example of the **CREATE DATABASE** command:

```
CREATE DATABASE mydb
     DATAFILE '/u01/oracle/mydb/system.dbf' SIZE 10M
     LOGFILE GROUP 1 ('mydb_log1a', 'mydb_log1b') SIZE 5M,
     GROUP 2 ('mydb_log2a', 'mydb_log2b') SIZE 5M;
```

The values of the **MAXLOGFILES**, **MAXDATAFILES**, **MAX INSTANCES**, **MAXLOGMEMBERS**, and **MAXLOGHISTORY** options in this example will use OS-dependent defaults. The database is mounted in the no archive log and exclusive default modes and then opened.

If your database creation fails, you must shut the instance down and delete all files that the **CREATE DATABASE** statement created before you try to create the database again—including control files, log files, and datafiles. After correcting the error that caused the failure of the database creation, rerun the **CREATE DATABASE** command.

Creating A Unique Database Name

A database's global database name is created by setting both the **DB_NAME** and **DB_DOMAIN** parameters before database creation. Once a database is created, the database name cannot be changed easily. The **DB_NAME** parameter assigns the local part of the database's name, whereas the **DB_DOMAIN** parameter is the domain (logical location) within a network structure. The combination of these two parameters should form a database name that is unique within a network. For example, to create a database with a global database name of MYDB.US.MYCO.COM, edit the parameters of the new parameter file as follows:

```
DB_NAME = MYDB
DB_DOMAIN = US.MYCO.COM
```

DB_NAME can be a string of up to eight ASCII characters. During database creation, the name provided for **DB_NAME** is recorded in the datafiles, redo log files, and control file of the database. If during database instance startup the value of the **DB_NAME** parameter (of the parameter file) and the database name in the control file are not the same, the instance will start, but the database will not mount.

Database-Specific Parameters

The following set of database parameters is normally specific to each database and is set when the database is created. Some of the parameters can't be changed once the database is created; others can be changed and are used to tune the database for better performance.

CONTROL_FILES

You should include the **CONTROL_FILES** parameter in the new parameter file with its value set to a list of control file names for use by the new database. Oracle can create new control files. Also, if you want Oracle to reuse or overwrite existing files, you can use the **REUSE** option when specifying the control files in the **CREATE DATABASE** command. If no file names are listed for the **CONTROL_FILES** parameter, Oracle uses a default file name. Oracle strongly recommends that you use at least two control files stored on separate physical disk drives for each database. Always use the full pathname when specifying the control files in your **CREATE DATABASE** command.

EXAM ALERT: Be careful when setting the **CONTROL_FILES** option. If you mistakenly designate a file and execute the **CREATE DATABASE** statement, the contents of that file will be overwritten.

DB_BLOCK_SIZE

The default data block size for every Oracle server is OS specific, but is normally 2K or 4K. Each database's block size is set during database creation by the initialization parameter **DB_BLOCK_SIZE**. The block size cannot be changed after database creation except by recreating the database.

If a database's block size is different from the OS's block size, make the data block size a multiple of the OS's block size. For example, if your OS's block size is 512 bytes, the following setting for the **DB_BLOCK_SIZE** initialization parameter would be valid:

```
DB_BLOCK_SIZE=8192
```

DB_BLOCK_SIZE is also a factor in determining the size of the database buffer cache of the SGA.

DB_BLOCK_BUFFERS

The number of buffers in the buffer cache in the SGA is determined by the **DB_BLOCK_BUFFERS** parameter. You can improve the performance of the cache by increasing the number of buffer blocks. Be careful that you do not increase the buffer cache to the point that the SGA begins to page and swap out of memory. **DB_BLOCK_BUFFERS** multiplied by the **DB_BLOCK_SIZE** is the size of the database buffer cache. For example, a **DB_BLOCK_SIZE** of 2K times 2000 **DB_BLOCK_BUFFERS** would create a buffer cache of 4MB. This parameter can be changed after the database is created.

PROCESSES

The **PROCESSES** parameter sets the maximum number of OS processes that can be simultaneously connected to Oracle. The value of this parameter will include the background processes as well as the user processes. This parameter can be changed after the database is created.

Actions After Creating The Database

Once the database is created, several actions are required to really make the database operational. The first step is to install the data dictionary views by executing the catalog.sql script:

```
@$ORACLE_HOME/rdbms/admin/catalog.sql
```

Create Additional Rollback Segments

After you execute the **CREATE DATABASE** command, connect to the database as **SYS** and create a rollback segment in the **SYSTEM** tablespace. Do this before you create additional rollback segments and schema objects in other tablespaces. Next, create a tablespace for rollback segments. The following code example shows the syntax for this action:

```
create rollback segment r0 tablespace system;
alter rollback segment r0 online;
create tablespace rbs01 datafile
        '/u52/oradata/HIP5/rbs01.dbf' size 1000M
default storage (
        initial         1M
        next            1M
        pctincrease     0
        minextents      8
);
```

Once the rollback tablespace is created, you can create additional rollback segments. Remember to put the rollback segments in the parameter file or they will not be available when the database is restarted. Once the additional rollback segments are created and brought online, you no longer need the second rollback segment in the **SYSTEM** tablespace. It should be altered offline and dropped:

```
create rollback segment r01 tablespace rbs01
    storage (optimal 8M maxextents 1000);
alter rollback segment r01 online;
create rollback segment r02 tablespace rbs01
    storage (optimal 8M maxextents 1000);
alter rollback segment r02 online;
create rollback segment r03 tablespace rbs01
    storage (optimal 8M maxextents 1000);
alter rollback segment r03 online;
```

Create A Tablespace For Temporary Segments

Every database should have one or more tablespaces dedicated for temporary segments created by the database. If applications that access the data in a very large table perform large sorts that can't be done in memory, Oracle will use the temporary tablespace assigned to a user. Oracle recommends that you create temporary tablespaces specifically for this task. Here is an example:

```
CREATE TABLESPACE TEMP
    DATAFILE '/u26/oradata/mydb/temp01.dbf'
```

```
SIZE 1000M AUTOEXTEND OFF
LOGGING
DEFAULT STORAGE(INITIAL 5M
                NEXT 5M
                MINEXTENTS 1
                MAXEXTENTS UNLIMITED
                PCTINCREASE 0)
ONLINE
TEMPORARY;
```

Create Tablespaces For Applications And Users

Do not use the **SYSTEM** tablespace for any schema objects other than the ones owned by the **SYS** or **SYSTEM** accounts. Create additional tablespaces on multiple disk drives so as to spread out input/output (I/O) contention. At a minimum, you should create a tablespace for tables and a tablespace for indexes on separate disk drives. This will allow Oracle to access indexes and table simultaneously without I/O contention. Obviously the larger and more active the database, the more tablespace and disk drives you will need to maintain adequate I/O performance.

Alter SYS And SYSTEM Users

You should alter the default passwords for **SYS** and **SYSTEM** once the database is created. The default password for **SYS** is "change_on_install" and for **SYSTEM**, it is "manager". They should also have the temporary tablespace set to the **TEMP** tablespace:

```
alter user sys temporary tablespace temp;
alter user sys identified by password;
alter user system temporary tablespace temp;
alter user system identified by password;
```

Create The Necessary Packages

Now the database is ready to run the additional catalog scripts. For an explanation of each script, you can look in the *Oracle8 Administrator's Guide* or in the file itself—they are all documented within the file. These are the scripts that are run if you use the installer to create an initial database:

```
@$ORACLE_HOME/rdbms/admin/catproc.sql
@$ORACLE_HOME/rdbms/admin/cat8000s.sql
@$ORACLE_HOME/rdbms/admin/caths.sql
@$ORACLE_HOME/rdbms/admin/cathsoci.sql
```

```
@$ORACLE_HOME/rdbms/admin/otrcsvr.sql
@$ORACLE_HOME/rdbms/admin/catblock.sql
@$ORACLE_HOME/rdbms/admin/dbmspool.sql
@$ORACLE_HOME/rdbms/admin/prvtpool.plb
@$ORACLE_HOME/rdbms/admin/dbmsjob.sql
@$ORACLE_HOME/rdbms/admin/prvtjob.plb
@$ORACLE_HOME/rdbms/admin/catjobq.sql
@$ORACLE_HOME/rdbms/admin/catperf.sql
@$ORACLE_HOME/rdbms/admin/utlchain.sql
```

If you are licensed for the Oracle Replication option, execute the following script:

```
@$ORACLE_HOME/rdbms/admin/catrep.sql
```

Backup The Database

After you finish creating the database, you should shut down the database and do a complete OS backup of all the files associated with the new database. Once you have made your complete backup, you can start the database up and continue operations. It is always a good idea to make a backup of the database whenever you perform a significant amount of structural changes. This action will save a lot of time if you have to do a recovery.

Dropping A Database

To drop a database, shut it down and remove its datafiles, redo log files, and all other associated files (control files, parameter files, and archived log files). To view the names of the database's datafiles and redo log files, query the data dictionary views **V$DATAFILE** and **V$LOGFILE**.

Practice Questions

Question 1

What is the minimum recommended control file configuration?

- ❍ a. One file
- ❍ b. Two files on the system disk
- ❍ c. Two files on separate disks
- ❍ d. Three files placed on the same disk as the system tablespace
- ❍ e. Three files placed on separate disks

Answer c is correct. Oracle recommends that you have at least two copies on separate disks, even though only one control file is required to create a database. To mirror the control file, alter the **CONTROL_FILES** initialization parameter. Maintaining more than two control files can be done, but it is not the *minimum* that Oracle recommends. Keeping extra copies of control files on separate disks guards against the loss of the control file during media failure.

Question 2

Why does the control file need to be recreated when the **MAXDATAFILES** parameter is changed?

- ❍ a. To update it with the new datafiles
- ❍ b. To reallocate the space needed for the parameter
- ❍ c. To update it with the current version of the parameter file
- ❍ d. To update it with any changes made to any of the initialization parameters

Answer b is correct. Oracle allocates space within the control file for MAXDATAFILES. The control file must be recreated, because more space must be allocate within it, when you change the following parameters:

- MAXLOGFILES
- MAXDATAFILES
- MAXINSTANCES

- MAXLOGMEMBERS
- MAXLOGHISTORY

Because space in the control file is preallocated, no reason exists to recreate the file to update changes made to the database structure, as in answers a, c, and d.

Question 3

You issue a **CREATE DATABASE** command that fails because you attempted to create log files that already existed. Which answers will solve the problem so you can reissue the command? [Choose two]

- ❑ a. Change the **REUSE** options in the **LOGFILE** parameter of the **CREATE DATABASE** command.
- ❑ b. Shut down the instance and change the **SIZE** option to **REUSE** in the **LOGFILE** parameter of the **CREATE DATABASE** command.
- ❑ c. Issue the **DROP DATABASE** command and change the **SIZE** option to **REUSE** in the **LOGFILE** parameter of the **CREATE DATABASE** command.
- ❑ d. Shut down the instance, delete any files created by the **CREATE DATABASE** command, and change the **SIZE** option to **REUSE** in the **LOGFILE** parameter of the **CREATE DATABASE** command.
- ❑ e. Shut down the instance, delete any files created by the **CREATE DATABASE** command, and delete the log files that failed to create.

Trick! question

Answers d and e are correct. In the case of d, the log files already existed, so the CREATE DATABASE command must not have used the REUSE option in the file SIZE clause. By using the REUSE option in the size clause, the create error can be avoided. Alternatively, deleting the files as in answer e will also eliminate the error. When you issue a CREATE DATABASE command that fails, you should do the following:

1. Shut down the instance.
2. Delete any files created by the failed CREATE DATABASE command.
3. Correct the error in the CREATE DATABASE command.
4. Restart the instance.

The other answers are incorrect because they do not follow this sequence. Also, there is no DROP DATABASE command. This is a trick question because the answers are mutually exclusive, which might throw you off.

Question 4

What should a DBA do before using the **CREATE DATABASE** command? [Choose three]

- ☐ a. Connect as **SYSDBA**.
- ☐ b. Create a control file.
- ☐ c. Start up an instance.
- ☐ d. Create a database user.
- ☐ e. Create a parameter file.
- ☐ f. Start an instance and **MOUNT** the database.

Answers a, c, and e are correct. Before using the **CREATE DATABASE** command, the DBA should have created an initialization parameter file, connected as **SYSDBA**, and started up an instance in no mount mode. The control file is created as a result of running the **CREATE DATABASE** command, as are database users. The database is mounted after it is created.

Question 5

When planning your database configuration, how should you organize the data storage?

- ○ a. Group objects with different backup requirements.
- ○ b. Group objects together with competing I/O requirements.
- ○ c. Separate tables and indexes on different disks.

Answer c is correct. When planning your database configuration, you should try to distribute I/O. One of the basic methods recommended is to put tables and their associated indexes on different disk drives. Grouping objects according to their backup requirements may hurt online performance and is probably not a good trade off. Putting objects together that compete for I/O would degrade performance.

Question 6

What must be true for the following **CREATE DATABASE** command to be successful?

```
CREATE DATABASE mydb
   CONTROLFILE REUSE
   MAXLOGFILES 5
   MAXLOGMEMBERS 5
   MAXDATAFILES 75
   MAXLOGHISTORY 75
DATAFILE '/u03/oracle/mydb/system.dbf'
SIZE 10M
LOGFILE
GROUP 1 '/u01/oracle/mydb/log1a.rdo',
'/u02/oracle/mydb/log1b.rdo' SIZE 10M,
GROUP 2 '/u01/oracle/mydb/log2a.rdo',
'/u02/oracle/mydb/log2b.rdo' SIZE 10M;
```

- ❍ a. The datafile must exist and be 10MB in size.
- ❍ b. The log files must exist.
- ❍ c. **/u03** must be able to hold **MAXDATAFILES**.
- ❍ d. The control files specified in the parameter file must exist.
- ❍ e. The user must have **SYSOPER** privileges to create the log files and datafiles.

Answer d is correct. Because the **CREATE DATABASE** command uses the **CONTROLFILE REUSE** option, the control files listed in the parameter file will be reused and must exist. The datafile should not exist because the **REUSE** option is not used. The log files do not need to exist. **MAX DATAFILES** is a parameter that sets a limit of datafiles for the database. No requirement exists that the datafiles reside on any particular disk. The Oracle account is normally used to create databases, so there is no need for the **SYSOPER** role.

Question 7

Which parameter specifies the names of the redo log files in a **CREATE DATABASE** command?

- a. **LOGFILE**
- b. **MAXLOGFILES**
- c. **MAXLOGMEMBERS**
- d. **MAXLOGHISTORY**
- e. **CONTROLFILE REUSE**

Answer a is correct. In the **CREATE DATABASE** command, the **LOGFILE** parameter specifies the number for the **LOGFILE** groups and the names and locations of the redo log files in each group. The **MAXLOGFILES** parameter determines the maximum number of groups of online redo log files per database. The **MAXLOGMEMBERS** parameter determines the maximum number of members per group. **MAXLOGHISTORY** specifies the maximum number of archived redo log files for automatic media recovery of Oracle with the Parallel Server option. The **CONTROLFILE REUSE** clause names a control file to overwrite and reuse.

Question 8

What happens if the database name in the parameter file does not match the name in the control file?

- a. An instance would start and the database would go into recovery mode.
- b. An instance would start, but the database would not be mounted.
- c. The instance would not start.
- d. An instance would start and the database would be mounted, but would not be opened.

Answer b is correct. When a database is created, the database name is specified in the **CREATE DATABASE** command and it must match the **DB_NAME** parameter in the parameter file. The database will not mount if the database name recorded in the control file does not match the database name in the **STARTUP** command or parameter file. Because the instance did not attempt to mount the database, it is not necessary to go into recovery mode. The instance would start but the database would not mount because of the database name mismatch.

Need To Know More?

Loney, Kevin, and Marlene Theriault: *Oracle8 DBA Handbook*, Oracle Press, Berkeley, CA, 1997. ISBN 0-07882-406-0. This book is a comprehensive guide and a must have for all DBAs.

See the Oracle documentation that is provided on CD with the Oracle RDBMS software. Pertaining to this chapter are:

Fee, Joyce: *Oracle8 Administrator's Guide*, Oracle Corporation, Redwood City, CA, 1997. Complete documentation of database administration tasks.

Lane, Paul: *Oracle8 Reference Manual*, Oracle Corporation, Redwood City, CA, 1997. See Chapter 1, "Initialization Parameters."

Lane, Paul: *Oracle8 SQL Reference*, Oracle Corporation, Redwood City, CA, 1997. Complete documentation of syntax for all Oracle SQL commands.

Leverenz, Lefty: *Oracle8 Concepts Guide*, Oracle Corporation, Redwood City, CA, 1997. Complete documentation of Oracle concepts.

http://education.oracle.com/tbt/ocp8.html is the site from which you can order the Oracle Education CD-ROM bundle for Oracle8 Database Administration.

www.revealnet.com is the site where RevealNet Corporation provides Oracle Administration reference software.

6

Data Dictionary Views And Standard Packages

Terms you'll need to understand:

- √ Standard packages
- √ catalog.sql
- √ **USER_*** dictionary views
- √ **ALL_*** dictionary views
- √ **DBA_*** dictionary views
- √ catproc.sql

Techniques you'll need to master:

- √ Understanding which Oracle script creates the data dictionary views
- √ Understanding which Oracle script enables the procedural features and creates the standard packages
- √ Understanding what a .plb file is

The *data dictionary* is a set of tables created when the database is created. These tables are owned by the **SYS** account and stored in the **SYSTEM** tablespace. The data in these tables is encoded and almost impossible to understand; that is why three categories of data dictionary views are built in the **SYS**. These views interpret and display the information in the data dictionary for users and database administrators (DBAs) in a format that is much easier to understand. This chapter explains what the three categories of views are, how they are used, and what Oracle script creates them.

In addition to the data dictionary views, Oracle creates a set of *standard packages* when the procedural code is installed. Installing the procedural code is what enables PL/SQL to work. Therefore, you need to know which Oracle script enables the procedural features and what standard packages are created.

Data Dictionary Views

Running the catalog.sql in the ORACLE_HOME/rdbms/admin directory creates the data dictionary views. The catalog.sql script executes many other SQL scripts, each starting with "cat.", with the exception of the standard package. Most of the data dictionary views fall into one of three categories of views: *user views*, *all views*, and *dba views*. These views use the following naming conventions:

- USER_*
- ALL_*
- DBA_*

> *Note: The asterisk (*) is a wild card for the actual view names.*

The **USER_*** views contain information about all objects owned by the current user. The **ALL_*** views contain information about all objects accessible to the current user; this includes objects granted to the user as well as object owned by the user. The **DBA_*** views contain information about all objects in the database.

The database automatically updates the data dictionary anytime changes are made to a schema in the database. Public synonyms are created for the USER_* and ALL_* views so that users without DBA privileges can see them. Only users with DBA privileges can see the **DBA_*** views, unless they have been granted specific select privileges on them or have the **SELECT ANY TABLE** privilege.

The data dictionary views are owned by the **SYS** account and should never be modified, except by an upgrade script provided by Oracle.

A full list of all the views can be queried from the **DICTIONARY** view. The **DICTIONARY** view is accessible to all users. Use the following query to see all the views and their corresponding description:

```
SELECT * FROM dictionary ORDBY BY table_name;
```

Oracle Standard Packages

The database user **SYS** owns all of the supplied packages. Public synonyms are created with the packages so they can be referenced without using the "sys." prefix. The same script that creates the standard packages installs the PL/SQL procedural features. This script is called *catproc.sql* and can be found in the ORACLE_HOME/rdbms/admin directory. (The catproc.sql is a controlling program that just executes other SQL scripts.) Each standard package is created from an individual script in the ORACLE_HOME/rdbms/admin directory.

If you are interested in finding out more about the functionality of the packages, the programs are fairly well documented in the package header file, which you can identify by its .sql extension. The package body is in a wrapped format, identified by a .plb extension, so it can't be modified. The scripts that create the standard packages start with "**DBMS**". Table 6.1 has a list of the standard packages with a brief description of each.

Table 6.1 Oracle standard packages.

Package Name	Description
DBMS_ALERT	Asynchronous inter-session communication.
DBMS_APPLICATION_INFO	Allows registering of an application for tracing purposes.
DBMS_AQ	Lets you add a message to a queue or dequeue a message.
DBMS_AQADM	Lets you perform administrative functions on a queue or queue table.
DBMS_DDL	Allows PL/SQL to execute DDL.

(continued)

Table 6.1 Oracle standard packages (continued).

Package Name	Description
DBMS_DEFER/ DBMS_DEFER_ SYS/ DBMS_DEFER_QUERY	Lets you build and administer deferred remote procedure calls.
DBMS_DESCRIBE	Describes stored subprograms.
DBMS_JOB	Allows scheduling stored procedures.
DBMS_LOB	Manipulates Oracle8 large objects (LOBs).
DBMS_LOCK	Allows users to request, convert, release locks.
DBMS_OUTPUT	Provides screen output for PL/SQL programs.
DBMS_PIPE	Allows messaging between sessions.
DBMS_REFRESH	Allows management of snapshots.
DBMS_REPCAT	Manages symmetric replication facility.
DBMS_REPCAT_ADMIN	Manages symmetric replication facility.
DBMS_REPCAT_AUTH	Manages symmetric replication facility.
DBMS_ROWID	Converts ROWID to V7 format.
DBMS_SESSION	Allows alter session in PL/SQL.
DBMS_SHARED_POOL	Controls the shared pool.
DBMS_SNAPSHOT	Allows management of snapshots.
DBMS_SPACE	Provides segment space information.
DBMS_SQL	Allows dynamic PL/SQL.
DBMS_SYSTEM	Provides system level utilities.
DBMS_TRANSACTION	Transaction management commands.
DBMS_UTILITY	Additional utility procedures.
UTL_FILE	Provides file input/output (I/O).

Practice Questions

Question 1

Which script creates a standard package body?

❍ a. cat*.sql

❍ b. utl*.sql

❍ c. prvt*.plb

❍ d. dbms*.sql

Answer c is correct. The prvt*.plb script provides wrapped package body code. The cat*.sql script provides catalog and data dictionary information. The utl*.sql script creates views and tables for database utilities. The dbms*.sql script defines the database package specification.

Question 2

Which table or view contains the names of all the data dictionary views?

❍ a. **DB_NAME**

❍ b. **DBA_VIEWS**

❍ c. **DICTIONARY**

❍ d. **DBA_DATA_FILES**

Answer c is correct. The **DICTIONARY** view contains the name of each data dictionary view and a comment field describing the purpose of that view. **DB_NAME** is the name assigned to the database. The **DBA_VIEWS** view contains the text of all views in the database, not just data dictionary views. **DBA_DATA_FILES** contains information about database files.

Question 3

Which category of scripts contains database package specifications and is usually run during the execution of catproc.sql?

- a. prvt*.plb
- b. utl*.sql
- c. cat*.sql
- d. dbms*.sql

Answer d is correct. The dbms*.sql script defines the database package header specification. The prvt*.plb script provides wrapped package code. The utl*.sql script creates views and tables for database utilities. The cat*.sql script provides catalog and data dictionary information.

Question 4

Which data dictionary category would a user with the **SELECT ANY TABLE** privilege query to find the owner of the **PRODUCT1** table?

- a. **ALL_**
- b. **DBA_**
- c. **USER_**

Trick! question

Answer b is correct. DBA_ is accessible to the DBA or anyone with the SELECT ANY TABLE privilege, providing information on all the objects in the database. It has an owner column. ALL_ is accessible to all users and each view has an owner column, providing information on objects accessible by the user. Because ALL_ has an owner column, you might choose Answer a incorrectly—making this question tricky. This is wrong because ALL_ does not show all the tables in the database; it shows only the ones accessible by the user doing the query. USER_ is accessible to all users, providing information on objects owned by the user.

Question 5

You have been asked to troubleshoot a new database that is not working properly. You check the packages and notice that the package named **STANDARD** is invalid. Which script creates the **STANDARD** package?

- ❍ a. dbmsutil.sql
- ❍ b. catalog.sql
- ❍ c. catproc.sql
- ❍ d. sql.bsq

Answer b is correct. The catalog.sql script creates data dictionary views and the package named STANDARD. Answer a, the dbmsutil.sql script, creates the DBMS_TRANSACTION, TRANSACTION COMMANDS, DBMS_SESSION, DBMS_DDL, DBMS_UTILITY, DBMS_APPLICATION_INFO, DBMS_SYSTEM, PRVTUTIL.SQL, DBMS_SPACE, and DBMS_ROWID packages. Answer c, the catproc.sql script, creates the other standard packages. Answer d, the sql.bsq script, creates the base tables of Oracle.

Question 6

Which data dictionary view does not have an owner column in it?

- ❍ a. **ALL_**
- ❍ b. **DBA_**
- ❍ c. **USER_**

Answer c is correct. USER_ is accessible to all users, providing information on objects owned by the user. ALL_ is accessible to all users and each view has an owner column, providing information on objects accessible by the user. DBA_ is accessible to the DBA or anyone with the SELECT ANY TABLE privilege, providing information on all the objects in the database. It has an owner column.

Question 7

Which data dictionary view should you update when you drop a table?

- ❍ a. **USER_DATA**
- ❍ b. **DBA_OBJECTS**
- ❍ c. **DBA_SEGMENTS**
- ❍ d. **USER_SEGMENTS**
- ◉ e. None

Answer e is correct. You should never attempt to update the data dictionary. This is done automatically by Oracle. **USER_DATA** is not a valid view. **DBA_OBJECTS**, **DBA_SEGMENTS**, and **USER_SEGMENTS** are valid data dictionary views, but you should never attempt to update or modify them.

Question 8

During database creation, which script creates the base data dictionary tables?

- ◉ a. sql.bsq
- ❍ b. catexp.sql
- ❍ c. cataudit.sql
- ❍ d. catproc.sql
- ❍ e. utlxplan.sql

Answer a is correct. The sql.bsq script creates the base data dictionary tables. Because most of the information in these tables is encoded, most database users do not directly access these tables. The catexp.sql script is executed from the catalog.sql script and creates the export views. The cataudit.sql script creates the audit views. The catproc.sql script runs all the SQL scripts for the procedural features. The utlxplan.sql script creates the execution plan table.

Question 9

Which script is used to create the data dictionary views?

- ❍ a. sql.bsq
- ❍ b. catproc.sql
- ❍ c. dbmsutil.sql
- ❍ d. catalog.sql

Answer d is correct. The catalog.sql script creates the data dictionary views to decode and summarize the data in the base tables. Synonyms are created on the views by the script to allow users easy access to the views. User **SYS** owns the data dictionary views. The sql.bsq script creates the base data dictionary tables. The catproc.sql script runs all the SQL scripts for the procedural features. The dbmsutil.sql script creates the **DBMS_TRANSACTION**, **TRANSACTION COMMANDS**, **DBMS_SESSION**, **DBMS_DDL**, **DBMS_UTILITY**, **DBMS_APPLICATION_INFO**, **DBMS_SYSTEM**, **PRVTUTIL.SQL**, **DBMS_SPACE**, and **DBMS_ROWID** packages.

Question 10

Which script provides standard package header information?

- ❍ a. cat*.sql
- ❍ b. utl*.sql
- ❍ c. prvt*.plb
- ❍ d. dbms*.sql

Answer d is correct. The dbms*.sql script defines the standard package header specification. The cat*.sql script provides catalog and data dictionary information. The utl*.sql script creates views and tables for database utilities. The prvt*.plb script provides wrapped package body code.

Need To Know More?

Loney, Kevin, and Marlene Theriault: *Oracle8 DBA Handbook*, Oracle Press, Berkeley, CA, 1997. ISBN 0-07882-406-0. This book is a comprehensive guide and a must have for all DBAs.

Scott, Urman: *Oracle8 PL/SQL Programming*, Oracle Press, Berkeley, CA, 1997. ISBN 0-07882-305-6. See Appendix B, "Guide to Supplied Packages."

See the Oracle documentation that is provided on CD with the Oracle RDBMS software. Pertaining to this chapter are:

Lane, Paul: *Oracle8 Reference Manual*, Oracle Corporation, Redwood City, CA, 1997. See Chapter 2, "Static Data Dictionary Views."

Leverenz, Lefty: *Oracle8 Concepts Guide*, Oracle Corporation, Redwood City, CA, 1997. See Chapter 4, "The Data Dictionary."

http://education.oracle.com/tbt/ocp8.html is the site from which you can order the Oracle Education CD-ROM bundle for Oracle8 Database Administration.

www.revealnet.com is the site where RevealNet Corporation provides Oracle Administration reference software.

7

Maintaining Control Files And Redo Log Files

Terms you'll need to understand:

- Control file
- **MAXLOGFILES**
- **MAXLOGMEMBERS**
- **MAXLOGHISTORY**
- **MAXDATAFILES**
- **MAXINSTANCES**
- **V$PARAMETER**
- **V$CONTROLFILE**
- **V$CONTROLFILE_RECORD_SECTION**
- Redo log
- Checkpoint
- **LOG_CHECKPOINT_INTERVAL**
- **LOG_CHECKPOINT_TIMEOUT**
- Log switch
- Fast checkpoint
- **V$LOG**
- **V$LOGFILE**
- **V$THREAD**
- Thread

Techniques you'll need to master:

- Recreating control files
- Relocating control files
- Querying information about control files
- Creating redo log file groups
- Creating redo log file members
- Dropping redo log groups
- Dropping, moving, or renaming redo log files
- Clearing redo log files
- Querying information about redo log groups

Because control files and redo log files are created when the **CREATE DATABASE** command is executed and are automatically maintained by Oracle, many database administrators (DBAs) tend to forget about them after they create a database. Understanding how to manage these files is a crucial task that DBAs must be proficient at. Making a mistake while making changes to control files or redo log files has the potential to make the database unusable and in need of recovery. If proper backups are not performed, you could even find yourself with a database that is not recoverable. Therefore, you must know what these files are used for, which configuration Oracle recommends, and how to recreate or move them.

Control Files

The physical structure of a database is recorded in its *control file*. The file also maintains change information that keeps consistency between all the database files. When a database needs recovery, the control file is used to guide the recovery operation. The following list outlines some of the information kept in the control file:

- Database name
- Date/timestamp of database creation
- Names and locations of all datafiles
- Names and locations of online redo log files
- Tablespace information (online, offline, etc.)
- Log switch history
- Archive log information
- Backup information
- Current log sequence number
- Checkpoint information

Recommended Configuration

Every database should have at least two control files stored on different disk drives. This guards against loss of the control file with a single media failure. The initial control files are created during database creation via the initialization parameter **CONTROL_FILES**. Use the complete pathname when specifying control files, as in the following example:

```
CONTROL_FILES = (/u53/oradata/HIP5/control01.ctl,
                 /u54/oradata/HIP5/control02.ctl,
                 /u55/oradata/HIP5/control03.ctl)
```

TIP You can specify a maximum of eight control files in the **CONTROL_FILES** parameter.

If the location and name of the control file are not specified, Oracle creates a file with a default name and location; these are platform specific and can be found in the platform installation guide. If you are recreating a database and want to reuse the existing control files, the **CONTROLFILE_REUSE** parameter must be used in the **CREATE DATABASE** command and the control file for the new database must be the same size as the old one, or you will get errors. Changing **MAXLOGFILES**, **MAXLOGMEMBERS**, **MAXLOG HISTORY**, **MAXDATAFILES**, or **MAXINSTANCES** affects the control file size.

One strategy for control file location is to store a control file on the same drive with redo log group members. This ensures that you have a valid copy of the control file with every set of online redo log files.

EXAM ALERT Even though you specify multiple control files to keep Oracle in sync, the Oracle server only reads from the first file in the list. If any of the control files cannot be written to, the instance will become inoperable and should be aborted. Once the instance is aborted, the control file locations can be edited in the parameter file and valid copies moved to those locations. The instance is then ready to restart.

Moving, Copying, And Renaming Control Files

When working with control files, it is important to remember that when an instance is started, it reads the control files when it mounts the database. Therefore, if the instance is started with the **NOMOUNT** option, the control files have not been read yet.

The control files are binary files and maintained by Oracle, so direct editing of the control files is not supported. The process for adding, copying, and renaming control files is generally the same:

1. To make sure the control files do not change during the process, shut down the database. (If your next step is going to be renaming or moving the file without leaving a valid copy, make sure you have backed up the existing files.)
2. Now you can use operating system (OS) commands to copy, move, or rename the control files.
3. Edit the **CONTROL_FILES** parameter in the parameter file according to the new names and/or locations of the control files.
4. Restart the database.

You can verify that the database is using the correct control files in three ways. The first way is to query the **V$PARAMETER** view:

```
select name, value from v$parameter where name='control_files';
NAME
-------------------------------------------------------------
VALUE
-------------------------------------------------------------
control_files
/u53/oradata/HIP5/control01.ctl, /u54/oradata/HIP5/control02.ctl,
/u55/oradata/HIP5/control03.ctl
```

The second verification method is to query the **V$CONTROLFILE** view:

```
select name from v$controlfile;
NAME
-------------------------------
/u53/oradata/HIP5/control01.ctl
/u54/oradata/HIP5/control02.ctl
/u55/oradata/HIP5/control03.ctl
```

The third way to verify that the database is using the correct control files is to use the Server Manager command **SHOW PARAMETER**:

```
SVRMGR> show parameter control_files
NAME                 TYPE     VALUE
-------------        ------   -------------------------------
control_files        string   /u53/oradata/HIP5/control01.ctl
```

Note: The SHOW PARAMETER command shows only the first control file and not the copies.

If you want to look at the contents of the control file, use the view **V$CONTROLFILE_RECORD_SECTION**. For example, if you no longer had a copy of the **CREATE DATABASE** command and you wanted to find out what the value of **MAXDATAFILES** is, you could execute the following query:

```
select * from v$controlfile_record_section where type='DATAFILE';

         RECORD RECORDS RECORDS FIRST LAST  LAST
TYPE     SIZE   TOTAL   USED    INDEX INDEX RECID
----     ------ ------- ------- ----- ----- -----
DATAFILE    428    1022      30     0     0    30
```

The **MAXDATAFILES** value is 1022, with only 30 data files used.

Creating New Control Files

In a couple of cases, you may need to create a new control file for a database. One case occurs when all the control files for a database are unusable and no backup copies exist. The second happens if you need to change {"permanent parameter that was set in the **CREATE DATABASE** command. For example, if you did not specify the **MAXDATAFILES** parameter when you created the database, it would have a default value of 32 on most systems. If your database now needs to grow beyond 32 files, you must recreate the control file. Use the following steps to do so:

1. Put together a list of all the database datafiles and online redo log files (be sure to have complete pathnames). Any files not included on this list will be unrecoverable when the new control file is created.
2. Shut down the database. Begin this by trying to do a **SHUTDOWN NORMAL**. If that fails to shut down the database, cancel the **SHUTDOWN NORMAL** and try a **SHUTDOWN IMMEDIATE**. If the database still does not shut down, execute a **SHUTDOWN ABORT**. If you are forced to do a **SHUTDOWN ABORT**, you should then perform a **STARTUP RESTRICTED** and then a **SHUTDOWN NORMAL** to make sure you have the database shut down in a consistent state.
3. Back up all datafiles and online redo log files associated with the database.
4. Start up the instance, but do not mount the database.
5. Use the **CREATE CONTROLFILE** command to create a new control file. The following command uses the **NORESTLOGS** option to just

increase the value of the **MAXDATAFILES** parameter. If you are changing the database name or had lost any of the online redo log files, you should use the **RESETLOGS** option:

```
CREATE CONTROLFILE
SET DATABASE MYDB
LOGFILE GROUP 1 ('/u50/oradata/MYDB/redo01a.dbf',
                 '/u51/oradata/MYDB/redo01b.dbf') size 100M,
        GROUP 2 ('/u50/oradata/MYDB/redo02a.dbf',
                 '/u51/oradata/MYDB/redo02b.dbf') size 100M,
NORESETLOGS
DATAFILE '/u51/oradata/HIP5/system01.dbf' SIZE 50M,
         '/u52/oradata/HIP5/rbs01.dbf' SIZE 1000M,
         '/u51/oradata/HIP5/temp01.dbf' SIZE 1000M,
         ' /u51/oradata/HIP5/users01.dbf' SIZE 1000M
MAXLOGFILES 50
MAXLOGMEMBERS 3
MAXDATAFILES 200
MAXINSTANCES 6
ARCHIVELOG;
```

6. Make a backup of the new control file.
7. Edit the parameter file for the database, reflecting the new name and location of the control file.
8. Open the database. (If you are recreating the control file as part of a recovery, you would do the recovery first and then open the database.)

Another alternative is to use the **BACKUP CONTROLFILE TO TRACE** command, which will produce a trace file you can edit and run to create a new control file.

Redo Log Files

The *redo log* is made up of two or more online redo log files that record all committed changes made to the database. When transactions are committed, the redo entries stored in redo log buffers are written to the online redo log files by the background log writer (LGWR) process. The online redo log files are used only to recover the database from a system or media failure where data can't be written to datafiles.

The online redo log files are used in a circular fashion. Figure 7.1 illustrates how redo log files are used and then reused. This case has four redo log files.

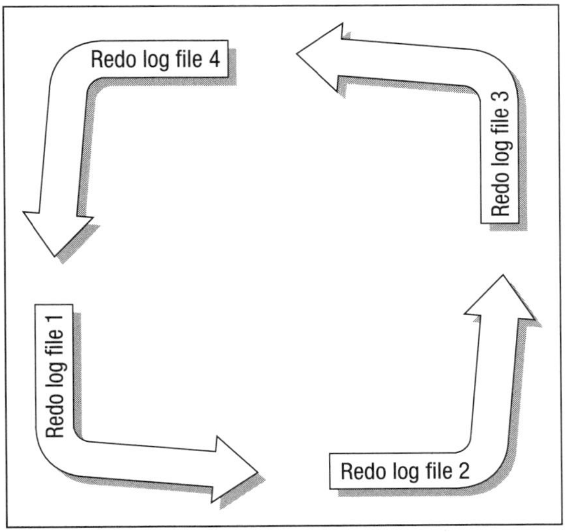

Figure 7.1 Redo log file usage.

Assuming that redo log file 1 is the active redo log file, when it is full, the database performs a log switch to using redo log file 2. If the database is in archive mode, redo log 1 is copied to an archive file by the database background archiver (ARCH) process. When redo log file 2 is full, the database switches to redo log file 3. This continues until the last redo log file is used, at which point the database reuses redo log file 1. If the database is in archive mode, redo log file 1 must finish being archived before the database will reuse it. Each time a redo log file is filled, it is assigned a log sequence number to identify the set of redo entries.

As with control files, multiple copies of a redo log file can be maintained by the database to avoid a single point of failure. The following example of the **CREATE DATABASE** command shows four redo log groups being created with two members per group. By placing the members of a redo log group on different disks, the group is protected from a single point of failure. Changes made to one member of a group are made to all members:

```
create database "MYDB"
    maxinstances 8
    maxlogfiles  32
    maxlogmembers 5
    maxdatafiles 1022
    maxloghistory 800
    character set "US7ASCII"
    national character set "US7ASCII"
```

```
datafile
   '/u15/oradata/MYDB/system01.dbf' size   100M
logfile group 1 ('/u50/oradata/MYDB/redo01a.dbf',
                 '/u51/oradata/MYDB/redo01b.dbf') size 100M,
        group 2 ('/u50/oradata/MYDB/redo02a.dbf',
                 '/u51/oradata/MYDB/redo02b.dbf') size 100M,
        group 3 ('/u50/oradata/MYDB/redo03a.dbf',
                 '/u51/oradata/MYDB/redo03b.dbf') size 100M,
        group 4 ('/u50/oradata/MYDB/redo04a.dbf',
                 '/u51/oradata/MYDB/redo04b.dbf') size 100M;
```

If a disk that contains an online redo log file fails, Oracle automatically uses the other member of the group on a different disk. The redo log file error will be recorded in the alert log file and the LGWR trace file.

Recommended Configuration

No recommended number of redo log file groups exists, because the needs of each database vary. A minimum configuration to protect against a single point of failure is two log file groups, each with two members; this requires two disk drives. One file from each group is placed on each drive, as Figure 7.2 shows.

Two permanent log file parameters, **MAXLOGFILES** and **MAXLOG MEMBERS**, are used in the **CREATE DATABASE** command. They can only be changed by recreating the database or by recreating the control file. **MAXLOGFILES** stipulates the maximum number of online redo log file groups for each database. **MAXLOGMEMBERS** stipulates the maximum number of members for each log group. Be sure these parameters are large enough for any planned database growth, which might require additional redo log file groups or members. In addition to the permanent parameters, one dynamic parameter, **LOG_FILES**, can limit the number of online redo log groups. This dynamic parameter cannot be used to increase the number of redo log file groups above **MAXLOGFILES**.

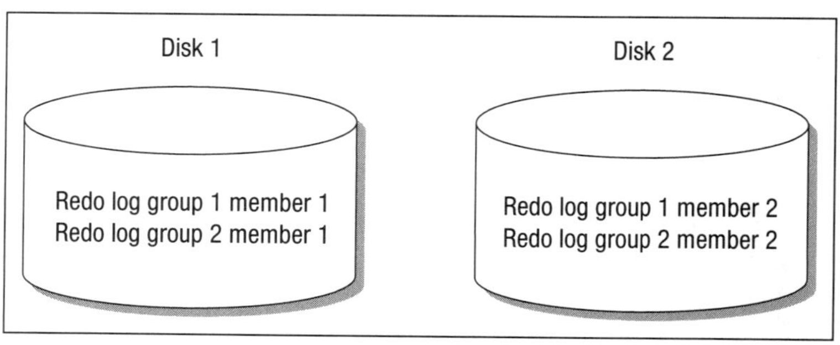

Figure 7.2 Redo log file disk layout.

Creating, Moving, Or Renaming Redo Log Groups And Members

After the database is created, you can create new log groups or log members, as well as drop or relocate them if you have the **ALTER DATABASE** system privilege. To add a new log file group, use the following command:

```
SVRMRG> alter database
        add  logfile group 5 ('/u50/oradata/MYDB/redo05a.dbf')
        size 100M;
```

> *Note: Always use complete pathnames; otherwise, the redo log files will be created in the platform-specific default directory.*

To add a log member to a log group, use the following command:

```
SVRMRG> alter database
        add logfile member '/u51/oradata/MYDB/redo05b.dbf'
        to group 5;
```

The size of the new log member will be the same as the other one. You incur no benefit by varying the sizes of the redo log groups, so they should all be the same size. Syntax varies somewhat for these commands; consult the *Oracle8 Database Administrator's Guide* for more details.

If you want to change the location of any redo log files or change the name of a redo log file, do the following:

1. Make a complete backup of the database.
2. Close the database so it is mounted to, but not opened by, the instance.
3. Copy the online redo log files to the new location or rename them using OS commands.
4. Use the **ALTER DATABASE RENAME FILE** command to record the changes in the control file. Remember that the files must exist in their new locations before you execute this command:

```
SVRMRG> alter database
      rename file '/u50/oradata/MYDB/redo05a.dbf',
      '/u51/oradata/MYDB/redo05b.dbf' to
      '/u55/oradata/MYDB/redo05a.dbf',
      '/u55/oradata/MYDB/redo05b.dbf';
```

5. Open the database for normal use.
6. Back up the control file.

Dropping Online Redo Log Groups Or Members

If you need to drop a redo log group or a redo log member, the following criteria must first be satisfied:

- At least two redo log file groups must be online always and each group must have at least one member.
- The redo log group must be inactive, because active redo log groups can't be dropped. If the redo log group is active, use the **ALTER SYSTEM SWITCH LOGFILE** command to force a log switch.
- If the database is in archive log mode, make sure the redo log group has been archived. You can use the **ARCHIVE LOG LIST** command in Server Manager to see if the log file to be dropped has been archived.

The following code example shows the command for dropping a log member first and then a log group:

```
SVRMGR> alter database
         drop logfile member '/u55/oradata/MYDB/redo05b.db';
SVRMGR> alter database drop logfile group 5;
```

Dropping a log group member or a log group in Server Manager does not physically delete the file; it only records the change in the database. You must use an OS command to actually delete the file. A log member that is the last log member of a log group can't be dropped by the **DROP LOGFILE MEMBER** command; you must use the **DROP LOGFILE GROUP** command.

Checkpoints And Log Switches

During a checkpoint, the database writer (DBWn) process writes all modified data buffers to the database datafiles. Checkpoints help reduce the time it takes a database to do an instance recovery. Because a well-organized and -configured database should not need frequent instance recovery, most DBAs try to minimize the number of checkpoints that occur.

At a minimum, a checkpoint will occur at every log switch. To minimize checkpoints, set the **LOG_CHECKPOINT_INTERVAL** parameter larger than the size of the online redo log files and the **LOG_CHECKPOINT_TIMEOUT** parameter to 0. If you have very large redo log files, you may want to checkpoint more often. In this case, set the parameter **LOG_CHECKPOINT_INTERVAL** to a smaller value. Remember the **LOG_CHECKPOINT_INTERVAL** is measured in OS blocks and not Oracle data blocks. If you would like to have the checkpoints happen on a time interval instead, set the **LOG_CHECKPOINT_TIMEOUT** parameter to the number of seconds you would like to pass between checkpoints. A checkpoint will still occur at every log switch.

If you are using very large redo log files, sometimes a checkpoint without a log switch might be useful. This is called a *fast checkpoint*, because it does not include the overhead of a log switch. This could be helpful, for example, when you abort the database and bring it back up as fast as possible. Because an abort causes an automatic instance recovery, forcing a checkpoint before aborting the database would speed up the startup process. The following command forces a checkpoint:

```
SVRMGR> alter system checkpoint;
```

If you find that LGWR is frequently waiting for checkpoints to complete and checkpointing has been minimized, add additional redo log groups until LGWR no longer waits for checkpoints.

Troubleshooting Online Redo Log Files

When archiving is enabled and Oracle encounters a corrupted redo log member while trying to archive it, Oracle tries to use one of the other members of the group. If all members of the group are corrupted, archiving stops. When all the redo log groups are full, the database hangs. If this happens, use the command **ALTER DATABASE CLEAR UNARCHIVED LOGFILE** to clear the redo log files (even though they were not archived). While this solves the log file corruption problem, you now have a database that cannot recover any changes in the cleared log file. The best course of action is to begin a backup as soon as possible.

Use the **V$LOG**, **V$LOGFILE**, and **V$THREAD** views to query information about the online redo log groups. Tables 7.1, 7.2, and 7.3 describe the columns of each view. The status field in the **V$LOG** view is very important to understanding what the current state of a redo log group is. The following list describes the meaning of each status:

- **UNUSED**—Indicates that the online redo log has never been written to. A redo log has this status if it was just added or just after a command with **RESETLOGS** is used when it is not the current redo log.
- **CURRENT**—Indicates that this is the current redo log and that it is active.

- ACTIVE—Indicates that the log is active, but that it is not the current log. This would normally happen if this log were being used for recovery.
- CLEARING—Indicates that the log is being recreated as an empty log after an **ALTER DATABASE CLEAR LOGFILE** command. After the log is cleared, the status changes to **UNUSED**.
- CLEARING_CURRENT—Indicates that the current log is being cleared of a closed thread. The log can stay in this status if some failure occurs in the switch, such as an input/output (I/O) error writing the new log header.
- INACTIVE—Indicates that the log is no longer needed for instance recovery.

Table 7.1 V$LOG view.

Column	Description
Archived	Archive status: **YES**, **NO**
Bytes	Size of the log in bytes
First_change#	Lowest system change number (SCN) in the log
First_time	Time of first SCN in the log
Group#	Log group number
Members	Number of members in the log group
Thread#	Log thread number
Sequence#	Log sequence number
Status	Log status: **UNUSED**, **CURRENT**, **ACTIVE**, **CLEARING**, **CLEARING_CURRENT**, **INACTIVE**

Table 7.2 V$LOGFILE view.

Column	Description
Group#	Log group number
Member	Redo log member name
Status	Log status: **INVALID**, **STALE**, **DELETED**

Table 7.3 V$THREAD view.

Column	Description
Checkpoint_change#	SCN at last checkpoint
Checkpoint_time	Time of last checkpoint
Current_group#	Current log group
Disable_change#	SCN when thread was disabled
Disable_time	Time when thread was disabled
Enable_time	Time when thread was enabled
Enabled	Status: **DISABLED**, **PRIVATE** (enabled), or **PUBLIC** (enabled)
Enabled_change#	SCN when thread was enabled
Groups	Number of log groups assigned to this thread
Instance	Instance name
Open_time	Last time the thread was opened
Sequence#	Sequence number of current log
Status	Thread status: **OPEN**, **CLOSED**
Thread#	Thread number

Practice Questions

Question 1

What is the maximum number of control files that you can specify in the **CONTROL_FILES** parameter?

❍ a. 2

❍ b. 4

❍ c. 8

❍ d. 12

❍ e. 16

❍ f. Unlimited

Answer c is correct. You can specify a maximum of eight control files for a database. Oracle recommends a minimum of two control files.

Question 2

If you rename the control file for your database without updating the parameter file, what happens when you attempt to start up an instance for the database?

❍ a. The database opens after creating a new control file with the default name.

❍ b. The database opens and prompts for the new control file location.

❍ c. The database is mounted, but does not open.

❍ d. The database is not mounted.

Answer d is correct. When the control file name or location is changed, the **CONTROL_FILES** initialization parameter must be altered to specify the current control file name and location. The default name is used only if the control file is not specified in the **CREATE DATABASE** command. The database does not prompt for the new control file. The database cannot mount, because that would require reading the control file.

Question 3

You notice in review of a client's database that it has only one control file. What are the proper steps to multiplex a control file for an existing database?

- ❍ a. Shut down the database, copy the existing control file using OS commands, edit the **CONTROL_FILES** initialization parameter, and restart the instance.
- ❍ b. Use the **ALTER DATABASE COPY CONTROLFILE** command to copy the existing control file and update the parameter file.
- ❍ c. Use the **ALTER SYSTEM COPY CONTROLFILE** command to copy the existing control file and update the parameter file.
- ❍ d. Shut down the database, copy the existing control file using OS commands, restart the instance, and update the **V$PARAMETER** view.

Answer a is correct. Following the process in Answer a will allow you to make as many copies of the control as needed. The command **ALTER DATABASE COPY CONTROLFILE** and **ALTER SYSTEM COPY CONTROLFILE** are invalid commands. **V$PARAMETER** is a view for viewing parameters and you can't update them.

Question 4

When you start an instance, at what stage is the control file read?

- ❍ a. **NOMOUNT**
- ❍ b. **MOUNT**
- ❍ c. **OPEN**

Answer b is correct. Because the control file records the database structure, the control file is read when a database is mounted by an instance. The **NOMOUNT** state is used for recreating control files and recovery operations. When the database is opened, the instance must have already read the control file.

Question 5

Which view would you query to display the name and location of the control files? [Choose two]

- ❑ a. **V$OPTION**
- ❑ b. **V$SESSION**
- ❑ c. **V$INSTANCE**
- ❑ d. **V$PARAMETER**
- ❑ e. **V$CONTROLFILE_RECORD_SECTION**
- ❑ f. **V$CONTROLFILE**

Answers d and f are correct. **V$PARAMETER** displays the information about the initialization parameters. **V$CONTROLFILE** displays the name and location of each control file. The **V$OPTION** view lists options that are installed with the Oracle server. The **V$SESSION** view lists session information for each current session. The **V$INSTANCE** view displays the state of the current instance. The **V$CONTROLFILE_RECORD_SECTION** view displays information about the records contained in the control file.

Question 6

If your database has four redo log groups with three members in each group, how many disks does Oracle recommend to maintain the redo log files?

- ❍ a. 8
- ❍ b. 4
- ❍ c. 6
- ❍ d. 3
- ❍ e. 12

Answer d is correct. Oracle recommends each member should be placed on a different disk, so three members require three disks, four members would require four disks, and so forth.

Question 7

You are tuning the database and need to know the sequence number of the current redo log group. Which view would you query to display the sequence number of online redo log groups?

- ❍ a. **V$DATABASE**
- ❍ b. **V$LOGFILE**
- ❍ c. **V$THREAD**
- ❍ d. **V$INSTANCE**

Answer c is correct. **V$THREAD** displays the current redo log group, the number of online redo log groups, and the current sequence number. **V$DATABASE** does not show redo log information. **V$LOGILE** does not show the log sequence number. **V$INSTANCE** does not show redo log information.

Question 8

Which of the following files are only read from during recovery operations?

- ❍ a. Data
- ❍ b. Trace
- ❍ c. Control
- ❍ d. Redo log
- ❍ e. Parameter

Answer d is correct. If an instance failure occurs, the redo log files are used to recover committed data not yet written to the datafiles. Datafiles are used to store user data, not for recovery. Trace files are used to troubleshoot database or user process problems, not for recovery. Control files are used in recovery operations, but the control file is also read by the instance when it mounts a database. Parameter files are read during startup.

Question 9

Assuming the instance is shut down, how would you move an online redo log file to a new location?

❍ a. Use OS commands to move the file, mount the database, and issue the **ALTER DATABASE RENAME FILE** command.

❍ b. Mount the database and issue the **ALTER DATABASE MOVE FILE** command to move the file and update the control file.

❍ c Mount the database, use OS commands to move the file, and issue the **ALTER DATBASE RENAME FILE** command.

❍ d. Copy the existing control file using OS commands, restart the instance, and use the **ALTER SYSTEM** command to update the parameter file.

Answer a is correct. Use OS commands to move the file, mount the database, and issue the ALTER DATABSE RENAME FILE command to update the control file. Answer b is incorrect, because ALTER DATABASE MOVE FILE is an invalid command. Answer c seems to be correct, making the question tricky, but the question stated that the instance is shut down and the database cannot be mounted to an instance that is shut down. Answer d is incorrect, because copying the control file does not move the redo log file.

Question 10

What would you do if your database has two redo log groups and group 2 becomes corrupted?

❍ a. Drop group 2 and add a new group.

❍ b. Drop all the groups and issue the **ALTER DATABASE ADD LOGFILE** command.

❍ c. Reinitialize the log files in group 2 with the **ALTER DATABASE CLEAR LOGFILE** command.

❍ d. Clear group 2 by issuing the **ALTER DATABASE CLEAR LOGFILE** command, drop the group, and create a new group.

Answer c is correct. You can clear a group if all its members become corrupt by issuing the ALTER DATABASE CLEAR LOGFILE command. Answers a, b, and d are incorrect, because you must have at least two log groups at all times.

Need To Know More?

Loney, Kevin, and Marlene Theriault: *Oracle8 DBA Handbook*, Oracle Press, Berkeley, CA, 1997. ISBN 0-07882-406-0. This book is a comprehensive guide and a must have for all DBAs.

See the Oracle documentation that is provided on CD with the Oracle RDBMS software. Pertaining to this chapter is:

Fee, Joyce: *Oracle8 Administrator's Guide*, Oracle Corporation, Redwood City, CA, 1997. See Chapter 5, "Managing the Online Redo Log," and Chapter 6, "Managing Control Files." These chapters have complete and detailed discussions of these topics.

Lane, Paul: *Oracle8 Reference Manual*, Oracle Corporation, Redwood City, CA, 1997. See Chapter 3, "Dynamic Performance (V$) Views."

http://education.oracle.com/tbt/ocp8.html is the site from which you can order the Oracle Education CD-ROM bundle for Oracle8 Database Administration.

www.revealnet.com is the site where RevealNet Corporation provides Oracle Administration reference software.

8

Loading And Reorganizing Data

Terms you'll need to understand:

- √ SQL*Loader
- √ Conventional path load
- √ Direct path load
- √ Control file
- √ Bad file
- √ Discard file
- √ Table mode export
- √ User mode export
- √ Full database mode export
- √ Table mode import
- √ User mode import
- √ Full database mode import
- √ Direct-load insert

Techniques you'll need to master:

- √ Using conventional path data loading
- √ Using direct path data loading
- √ Exporting databases
- √ Importing databases
- √ Knowing when to use direct-load insert

This chapter discusses the SQL*Loader, import, and export database utilities, as well as a new feature of Oracle8 called *direct-load insert*. These are the primary tools used by the database administrator (DBA) to load and reorganize data. With the proliferation of data warehousing, understanding how to effectively use these tools has become even more important. Unlike online transaction processing systems, data warehouses receive bulk loads of new data on a regular basis; thus, they can grow very quickly. This chapter explains how and when you should use these tools.

SQL*Loader

*SQL*Loader* loads data into an Oracle database from external files and is the only way you can load data created in another DBMS into Oracle without creating a third-generation (3gl) program or using an Oracle gateway product. Alternative methods of loading data are coding load programs in a third-generation language such as C++ or using direct file reads using the **UTL_FILE** set of stored procedures.

SQL*Loader can do the following:

- Load data from multiple files.
- Load delimited, fixed-length, and variable-length data.
- Use SQL functions on data before inserting it into Oracle.
- Load many data types that are not native to Oracle by converting them to Oracle data types.
- Combine more than one physical record into a single logical record.
- Break a single physical record into multiple logical records.
- Generate unique keys via a sequence generator.
- Load from disk or tape drives.
- Load data directly into Oracle for faster loads.

Conventional Path Load

The *conventional path load* uses the same method as all other Oracle tools for inserting data. Conventional path load does a SQL insert with a bind array buffer. In addition, conventional path loads look for and try to fill partially filled blocks. While under normal database operations, this helps performance of the database; moreover, the search for partially filled blocks slows downloads.

Direct Path Load

Direct path loads are much faster than conventional path loads, because they write directly to the database files, bypassing the overhead of the database. Consequently, they do not compete for database resources with other user processes.

EXAM ALERT: To use the direct path load, tables must not be clustered and they cannot have any active transactions.

SQL*Loader Files

SQL*Loader can have up to five file types associated with a load:

- Control file
- Log file
- Bad file
- Discard file
- Data file

Control File

The *control file* contains the SQL*Loader data definition language (DDL) definitions that show the format of the data, the location of the data file, and the Oracle table that the file will be loaded to. The control file is normally created with a text editor and can also contain the data to be loaded, instead of using a separate data file.

The keywords used with SQL*Loader control files are:

- LOAD DATA—Must be the first line of the control file.
- INFILE *file_name*—Denotes when data is not in the control file. INFILE * is used if the data is in the control file.
- INTO TABLE *table_name*—Oracle table to load into.
- WHEN—Rejects data based on special criteria.
- BEGINDATA—Denotes the beginning of data in the control file.
- POSITION—Defines column positions; used with fixed-length data.

- **FIELDS TERMINATED BY ','**—Defines the delimiting character in a delimited file.
- **APPEND**—Loads data into Oracle tables, even if they are not empty.
- **REPLACE**—Deletes the data before starting the load if data is in the Oracle table.
- **SEQUENCE**—Generates unique numbers sequentially for the load.
- **DISCARDFILE *file_name.dsc***—File for records discarded by SQL*Loader.
- **DISCARDMAX**—Denotes the maximum number of discards allowed before stopping the load.
- **BADFILE *file_name.bad***—File for bad records.

Log File

When you start SQL*Loader, the utility creates a *log file.* This log file contains detailed information about the load, including the number of records loaded, number of records not loaded, error messages, and so on. If SQL*Loader cannot create a log file, the program aborts.

Bad File

The *bad file* contains records that Oracle rejects. Oracle may reject a record because it is missing data for a **NOT NULL** field or perhaps because of a duplicate key in a unique index. The bad file is in the same format as the original data file. After the data is corrected, the same control file can be used to load the bad file. The infile file name is changed to the bad file name.

Discard File

The *discard file* is created only if any discarded records are present. Records in the discard file are discarded by SQL*Loader because they do not match the record selection criteria of the control file. The discard file is also written in the same format as the original data file, so the same control file can be used to load it.

Data File

The *data file* contains the data to be loaded. The data can be fixed-length records or comma (or some other character) delimited. The data file can even be in EBCDIC (IBM) format. For small amounts of data, the control and data portions can be combined into a single file.

SQL*Loader Command Line

You can start SQL*Loader from the operating system (OS) command line. Parameters given on the command line override the parameters in the control file. On Unix systems, the command is:

```
sqlldr "command line parameters"
```

On Windows systems running Oracle8, the command is:

```
Sqlldr80 "command line parameters"
```

The command line parameters for the command line (or loaded into a parameter file) are:

- USERID—Oracle username/password.
- CONTROL—Control file name.
- LOG—Log file name.
- BAD—Bad file name.
- DATA—Data file name.
- DISCARD—Discard file name.
- DISCARDMAX—Maximum number of discards allowed (default is infinite).
- SKIP—Number of records to skip in the data file (default is 0).
- LOAD—Number of records to load (default is all).
- ERRORS—Number of errors allowed before the load is terminated (default is 50).
- ROWS—Number of rows in the conventional path bind array or between saves in direct path.
- BINDSIZE—Size, in bytes, of the conventional path bind array.
- SILENT—No terminal feedback is generated during load.
- DIRECT—Use direct path load.
- PARFILE—Name of a file that holds parameters for the load.
- PARALLEL—Performs a parallel load (default is false).

- **FILE**—Database file from which to allocate extents. This is used only with a **PARALLEL** load.

Here is an example of a SQL*Loader command line:

```
sqlldr userid=john/doe control=testload.ctl log=testload.log
```

Export

An *export* is a logical backup of a database. The export utility copies the data and database definitions to a binary OS file. Export can be used only against an open database. Because export copies one table at a time, it can guarantee read consistency only for *individual* tables unless you specify **CONSISTENT=Y** (which will ensure that the data seen by export is consistent to a single point in time and does not change during the execution of the **EXPORT** command).

Exports can be used to supplement OS backups. They have several advantages:

- Unlike an OS backup, export reads each Oracle data block and lists an error if it discovers a bad block. This warns you so that you can try to correct the problem before users try to access the bad data.
- You can use export backups to move databases between computers. Because exports are contained in a binary file, they can be sent to tape or disk and moved by hand or through file transfer protocol (FTP) on a network. Exports can also move a database from one OS to another, such as from Unix to Windows NT.
- It is much easier to replace a table that was inadvertently dropped with an import than by performing an incomplete recovery.
- Exports can provide more granularity to your backup scheme by backing up individual tables, schemas, and entire databases.
- The export utility can perform a complete, an incremental, or a cumulative export.

> *Note: Remember that exports are not alternatives to OS backups. You should perform physical OS backups and also use exports to add flexibility to recovery. For example, you should recover a lost datafile using the OS backup. In the case of a dropped table, importing the table is quicker than a point-in-time recovery (as long as the table has not changed or has changed very little since the last export).*

You can run multiple exports simultaneously to improve performance; for example, you could do multiple user mode exports at the same time instead of performing one long, running, full database export. You can also use the **DIRECT** parameter to significantly speed up exports.

Export Modes

Three export modes determine which parts of the database can be exported. All database users have the authority to export in table mode or user mode on their own tables or schema without any additional privileges being granted.

Table Mode

In *table mode*, a list of tables is exported. The table definitions, data, grants, indexes, constraints, and triggers are exported with the table. Cluster definitions are not included in the export; import can therefore be used to uncluster tables. DBAs can export tables belonging to any schema.

User Mode

In *user mode*, all the objects belonging to a schema are exported. These include clusters, database links, views, private synonyms, sequences, snapshots, snapshot logs, and stored procedures. DBAs can export any schema in the database.

Full Database Mode

In *full database mode*, only users with the **EXP_FULL_DATABASE** role can export using the **FULL=Y** option. This role is included in the DBA role and does not need to be granted to DBA users. All objects in the database are exported, except the ones owned by **SYS**. In addition to tables and indexes, a full export includes roles, public and private synonyms, system privileges, tablespace definitions, tablespace quotas, rollback segment definitions, system audit options, all triggers, and profiles. A full database export can be complete, incremental, or cumulative, as follows:

- *Complete*—Establishes the starting point for cumulative and incremental exports. A complete export exports all objects and updates the data dictionary tables that record incremental and cumulative exports. A complete export is done when the **INCTYPE=COMPLETE** parameter is used. Incremental exports or cumulative exports can be taken by using the **INCTYPE=INCREMENTAL** and **INCTYPE=CUMULATIVE** parameters, respectively.
- *Incremental*—Exports all the tables changed or created since the last incremental, cumulative, or complete export. Because incremental exports back up only the new or changed tables, they perform much faster than an export that backs up all the unchanged tables. The resulting export files are smaller as well because they have fewer tables contained in the export.

Note: A single row change in a multimillion row table will result in the whole table being exported.

- *Cumulative*—Exports those tables that have been changed since the last cumulative or complete export. Cumulative exports are a way to roll up many incremental exports into one file. Once the cumulative export is done, the incrementals done between the last cumulative or complete export and the current cumulative export can be removed.

The following is an example of a full database export schedule using incremental and cumulative export:

- Full complete exports every four weeks on Sunday
- Cumulative exports every seven days on Sunday
- Incremental exports every night

To restore the data on Wednesday of the third week, restore the system information from the last incremental, then import the data from the last complete export. Next, import the second and third week cumulative exports. Finally, import the incremental data from Monday, Tuesday, and Wednesday.

Oracle keeps track of complete, incremental, and cumulative exports by updating the following **SYS** tables:

- INCFL—Tracks the incremental and cumulative exports and assigns a unique identifier to each.
- INCEXP—Maintains which objects were exported in specific exports.
- INCVID—Contains one column for the **EXPID** of the last valid export. This information determines the **EXPID** of the next export.

When an incremental or cumulative export is done, a row is also added to the **SYS.INCFIL** to identify the export file and the user doing the export. When a complete export is done, all the previous entries are deleted from the **SYS.INCFIL**, and a new row is added, specifying an *x* in the **EXPTYPE** column.

Partition-Level Export

Unless otherwise specified, all of a table's partitions are exported when the table is exported. In a *partition-level export*, you can export one or more specified partitions of a table. Because the full database and user mode exports get all the objects for a database or user respectively, they do not support partition-level exports. Partitioned data is exported in a format so that the partitions can be selectively imported.

Export Parameters

The sections that follow describe the export utility parameters and how to use them to write data from an Oracle database into an OS file in binary format. For a more detailed description, see the *Oracle8 Utilities*.

BUFFER

BUFFER is the number of bytes used to fetch data rows. This determines the number of rows fetched at a time. The formula for **BUFFER** is buffer size = (rows in array) * (maximum row size). The default is OS dependent.

COMPRESS

COMPRESS causes export to resize the initial extents for all tables so that they will import into one initial extent. The default value is **YES**.

CONSISTENT

If **CONSISTENT** is set to **YES**, export makes the export consistent to a single point in time. A rollback segment is retained for the duration of the export. The default value is **NO**. Setting this value to **YES** could cause rollback segments to grow very large if many changes are occurring to the database.

CONSTRAINTS

If **CONSTRAINTS** is set to **YES**, constraints are exported. The default value is **YES**.

DIRECT

Setting **DIRECT=YES** causes export to read data directly without using the public buffer cache or the SQL command processing layer. The default value is **NO**.

FEEDBACK

When **FEEDBACK** is set to a number other than zero, export displays a dot every time the number of exported rows equals that number. The default value is zero, which provides no feedback.

FILE

The **FILE** parameter is the name of the export file you want to create. The default value is **EXPDAT.DMP**.

FULL

If **FULL** is set to **YES**, a full database export is performed. The default value is **NO**. Only users with the **EXP_FULL_DATABASE** role enabled can use this parameter.

GRANTS

If **GRANTS** is set to **YES**, grants are exported with database objects. The default value is **YES**.

HELP

HELP=Y displays the export parameters on screen with a brief explanation. The default value is **NO**.

INCTYPE

INCTYPE determines whether the export is a complete, incremental, or cumulative. It has no default value. If **INCTYPE** is left out, the export cannot be used as part of an incremental backup scheme.

INDEXES

INDEXES specifies whether indexes are exported with the tables. The default value is **YES**.

LOG

LOG specifies the file name to which to record the screen output and error messages. By default, no log file is created.

OWNER

OWNER specifies one or more usernames whose objects are exported in user mode. There is no default value.

RECORD

If **RECORD** is set to **YES**, an incremental or cumulative export updates the **SYS.INCVID**, **SYS.INCFIL**, and **SYS.INCEXP** tables. The default value is **YES**.

ROWS

ROWS determines whether rows of data or only the object definitions are exported. The default value is **YES**.

STATISTICS

STATISTICS can be set to **ESTIMATE**, **COMPUTE**, or **NONE**, which does not generate any statistics for the optimizer. The other parameters work the same as in the **ANALYZE** command. The default value for this parameter is ESTIMATE.

TABLES

TABLES specifies a list of tables to export in table mode. It has no default value.

USERID

To connect with the database and use the export utility, you must use a valid username and password. The correct usage of **USERID** is **USERID**=*username/password*.

Things To Remember About Exports

If the database continues to be updated during exports, sequence numbers can be skipped. Also, because sequence numbers are normally cached, the exported value for the sequence is the next number after the last cached value. Sequence numbers that are in cache but not used are lost when the sequence is imported.

LONG data types require contiguous memory when exporting and importing. This can cause problems, because an Oracle **LONG** can be 2GB in length. Export can export **LONG** data types, but system resources could restrict this function.

Direct path exports cannot be used to import to an Oracle7.2 or an earlier release database.

Export Examples

The following are some examples of how to export:

- To execute an incremental, cumulative, or complete export:

```
exp username/password inctype=incremental file=export_file_name
                              cumulative
                              complete
```

- To execute a table mode export:

```
exp username/password tables=table1,table2 ... file=file_name
```

- To execute a user mode export:

```
exp username/password owner=... file=export_file_name
```

➤ To export a partition:

```
exp username/password tables=emp:m rows=Y
```

Import

The import utility is used to create and populate objects from an export file to an Oracle database. Import only reads files created by the export utility. The export and import utilities make it easy to move data from one schema to another or from one database to another.

TIP: Export and import can also be used to start replication between two databases if you are using the advanced replication features of Oracle. For more information, look up offline instantiation in the *Oracle8 Replication Guide*.

Import reads the export file and loads data in the following order:

1. Table definitions
2. Table data
3. Table indexes
4. Integrity constraints, triggers, and bitmap indexes

Tables are loaded in alphabetical order; using this order avoids referential integrity problems. If, however, you are loading into existing tables where referential integrity constraints might cause valid records to be rejected because of the order in which they are imported, you should disable referential constraints prior to importing.

Import Modes

Three import modes control the objects the import utility can import. The import option is also limited by the export options used to create the export file. For example, a full database import cannot be done if the export file was created as a full database export. Only users with the **IMP_FULL_DATABASE** role can perform a full database import. The following sections describe the three modes of import

Table Mode

This mode allows you to import a list of tables into your schema. DBAs or privileged users can also import tables from any schema by specifying the schema that contains them in the table list. DBAs can also use this mode to move tables from one schema to another. The default is to import all tables in the schema of the user doing the import.

User Mode

This mode allows you to import all objects that belong to you. A DBA or privileged user importing in user mode can import all objects for a list of schemas.

Full Database Mode

Only users with the **IMP_FULL_DATABASE** role can import in this mode, which imports a full database export file.

Partition-Level Import

Partition-level imports only import data from the specified source partitions. If the table does not exist, and if the exported table was partitioned, a table mode import creates a partitioned table. Importing by partition lets you selectively retrieve data from partitions in an export file. You can only do importing by partition during a table mode import. Export and import can also be used to merge partitions.

Import Parameters

The sections that follow describe the import utility parameters and how to use them to import to an Oracle database. For a more detailed description, see the *Oracle8 Utilities*.

ANALYZE

When **ANALYZE** is set to **YES**, import executes **ANALYZE** statements in the export file. The default value is **YES**.

BUFFER

BUFFER specifies the size, in bytes, of the buffer used to move records from the import file to the database. The default is OS dependent.

COMMIT

If the **COMMIT** option is set to **YES**, import commits after every array insert. The default value for **COMMIT** is **NO**, which means import commits after it has finished inserting into a table.

DESTROY

When set to **YES**, the **DESTROY** option will make import overwrite any of the datafiles used by objects that are being imported. All existing information in those datafiles will be lost. The default value is **NO**. Be very careful when using this option. As the name implies, this can be a very destructive command.

FEEDBACK

When **FEEDBACK** is set to a non-zero number, export displays a dot every time that that many rows are exported. The default value is zero, which gives no feedback.

FILE

The **FILE** parameter is the name of the export file you want to import. The default value is **EXPDAT.DMP**.

FROMUSER

The **FROMUSER** option lets you list the schemas you wish to import objects from. It has no default value.

FULL

FULL specifies whether to import the entire export file. The default value is NO.

GRANTS

GRANTS specifies whether to import object grants. The default value is **YES**.

HELP

HELP=Y displays the import parameters on screen with a brief explanation. The default value is **NO**.

IGNORE

If **IGNORE=N**, import reports an error stating that the object already exists and skips to the next object. If **IGNORE=Y**, import inserts data into any existing objects and does not report an error. The default value is **NO**.

INCTYPE

INCTYPE specifies the type of incremental import. The default is no specified type (undefined).

INDEXES

If **INDEXES=Y**, indexes are created during the import. The default value for this parameter is **YES**.

INDEXFILE

The INDEXFILE=*file_name* parameter creates a file with all the create table and index statements from the export file. The create table statements are preceded with a **REMARK** (**REM**) clause so they will not execute. If constraints are defined for the table using the **ALTER TABLE** statements, the constraints will also be in the file, but specially designated so they will not execute. This file can be used to create indexes from SQL*Plus instead of creating indexes during import. This option has no default.

Import Examples

This section gives some examples of import commands:

- Importing selected tables for a specific user:

```
imp system/manager file=expdat.dmp fromuser=scott tables=dept,emp
```

- Importing tables exported by another user:

```
imp system/manager fromuser=jones touser=scott file=jones.dmp
   tables=emp,dept
```

- Importing tables from one user to another:

```
imp system/manager file=scott.dmp fromuser=scott touser=jones
```

Direct-Load Insert

Direct-load insert improves performance when inserting data from one table to another by writing directly to Oracle datafiles and bypassing the buffer cache. When direct-load insert is used, the data is appended to the table. Free space in the table is not used. Other users can continue to update other rows in the table, because no table level lock is acquired for a direct-load insert. When you use the direct-load insert, you can avoid logging redo or undo entries, which speeds up the insert considerably.

Practice Questions

Question 1

Which SQL*Loader file specifies the database tables to be loaded?

- ❍ a. Log
- ❍ b. Loader
- ❍ c. Control
- ❍ d. Parameter

Answer c is correct. The control file specifies the table to be loaded. The log file generated by SQL*Loader stores information about the load. Loader is not a valid SQL*Loader file. The parameter normally refers to the database initialization file.

Question 2

In which sequence is the import file loaded?

- ❍ a. Table data, integrity constraints, triggers, and bitmap indexes, indexes on the table, and table definitions
- ❍ b. Table definitions, table data, indexes on the table, integrity constraints, triggers, and bitmap indexes
- ❍ c. Indexes on the table, integrity constraints, triggers, bitmap indexes, table definitions, and table data
- ❍ d. Table definitions, table data, integrity constraints, triggers, bitmap indexes, and indexes on the table
- ❍ e. Table definitions, integrity constraints, triggers, bitmap indexes, indexes on the table, and table data

Answer d is correct. The correct order of import is table definitions, table data, integrity constraints, triggers, bitmap indexes, and indexes on the table.

Question 3

Which SQL*Loader parameter specifies the number of logical records to load?

❍ a. **LOG**

❍ b. **ROWS**

❍ c. **LOAD**

❍ d. **BINDSIZE**

Answer c is correct. The **LOAD** parameter in the SQL*Loader command specifies the number of records to load. **LOG** specifies the log file name. **ROWS** specifies the number of rows in the conventional path bind array or between saves in direct path. **BINDSIZE** is the size, in bytes, of the conventional path bind array.

Question 4

Which method would you use to move the ownership of tables and their data between two users?

❍ a. Direct-load insert

❍ b. SQL*Loader direct path

❍ c. Export/import utilities

❍ d. SQL*Loader conventional path

Answer c is correct. Export/import utilities can be used to move tables from one schema to another. Direct-load insert moves data, but does not change ownership. SQL*Loader does not change ownership of tables.

Question 5

Which export parameter ensures that when the data is imported, the initial extent will be equal to the current size of the table?

- ❍ a. **FULL**
- ❍ b. **DIRECT**
- ❍ c. **GRANTS**
- ❍ d. **COMPRESS**
- ❍ e. **CONSTRAINTS**

Answer d is correct. Setting the **COMPRESS** export parameter to **YES** creates an initial extent the size of the current segment when the data is imported. The **FULL** option does a full database export. The **DIRECT** option exports the data directly from the datafiles without going through the SQL layer. The **GRANTS** option determines if **GRANTS** are exported. The **CONSTRAINTS** option determines if **CONSTRAINTS** are exported.

Question 6

Which SQL*Loader file holds detailed information about the load?

- ❍ a. Bad
- ❍ b. Log
- ❍ c. Discard
- ❍ d. Control

Answer b is correct. The log file generated by SQL*Loader stores information about the load. The bad file is used to hold records that are rejected by Oracle. The discard file is used to hold records discarded by SQL*Loader, because they do not match the record selection criteria of the control file. The control file contains the SQL*Loader DDL definitions that show the format of the data and the Oracle table that they will be loaded to.

Question 7

What utility would you use to create a test database from your production database?

- ❍ a. Direct-load insert
- ❍ b. SQL*Loader direct path
- ❍ c. Export/import utilities
- ❍ d. SQL*Loader conventional path

Answer c is correct. Use a full database export/import to move the whole database to a new system for testing. Direct-load insert only moves data from one table to another; it does not build all schema objects. SQL*Loader can't unload data and move it to another database.

Question 8

Which SQL*Loader file holds rejected records?

- ❍ a. Bad
- ❍ b. Log
- ❍ c. Discard
- ❍ d. Control
- ❍ e. Datafile

Answer a is correct. The bad file holds the rejected records. The log file generated by SQL*Loader stores information about the load. The discard file is used to hold records discarded by SQL*Loader, because they do not match the record selection criteria of the control file. The control file contains the SQL*Loader DDL definitions that show the format of the data and the Oracle table that they will be loaded to. A datafile is not a SQL*Loader file.

Question 9

For which two reasons would you use direct-load inserts when loading data into a table? [Choose two]

- ❑ a. Redo is generated in case of failure.
- ❑ b. Indexes are dropped to speed the data load.
- ❑ c. Loads data below the high water mark reclaim disk space.
- ❑ d. Other rows in the same table can be concurrently modified by other users.
- ❑ e. Data can be quickly copied from one table into another within the same database, because it bypasses the buffer cache.

Answers d and e are correct. During a direct-load insert, users can be concurrently modifying existing data in the table. In addition, the buffer cache is bypassed to speed the insert. Answer a is wrong because redo information would slow down the load. Direct-load insert does not drop indexes (answer b). Answer c is wrong because data is loaded above the high water mark.

Question 10

Which export utility keyword exports triggers?

- ❍ a. **ROWS**
- ❍ b. **DIRECT**
- ❍ c. **TABLES**
- ❍ d. **CONSISTENT**
- ❍ e. **TRIGGERS**

Answer c is correct. When a table is exported in table mode, the table definition, data, indexes, triggers, constraints, and grants on the table are included. This is a trick question, because no trigger keyword exists for export. Triggers just follow the table they are associated with. The **ROWS** parameter determines whether rows of data or only the object definitions are exported. Setting **DIRECT=YES** causes export to read data directly without using the public buffer cache or the SQL command processing layer. If **CONSISTENT** is set to **YES**, export makes the export consistent to a single point in time. **TRIGGERS** is not a valid keyword.

Need To Know More?

Ault, Mike: *Oracle8 Administration and Management*, John Wiley & Sons, Inc., New York, NY, 1998. ISBN 0-471-19234-1. See Chapter 17, "Backup and Recovery Procedures for Oracle."

Loney, Kevin, and Marlene Theriault: *Oracle8 DBA Handbook*, Oracle Press, Berkeley, CA, 1997. ISBN 0-07882-406-0. This book is a comprehensive guide and a must have for all DBAs.

See the Oracle documentation that is provided on CD with the Oracle RDBMS software. Pertaining to this chapter are:

Bobrowski, Steve, and Gordon Smith: *Oracle8 Replication Guide*, Oracle Corporation, Redwood City, CA, 1997. See Chapter 7, "Advanced Techniques."

Durbin, Jason: *Oracle8 Utilities*, Oracle Corporation, Redwood City, CA, 1997. See Chapter 1, "Export," Chapter 2, "Import," and Chapter 3, "SQL*Loader Concepts."

Leverenz, Lefty: *Oracle8 Concepts Guide*, Oracle Corporation, Redwood City, CA, 1997. See Chapter 21, "Direct-Load Insert."

http://education.oracle.com/tbt/ocp8.html is the site from which you can order the Oracle Education CD-ROM bundle for Oracle8 Database Administration.

www.revealnet.com is the site where RevealNet Corporation provides Oracle Administration reference software.

9

Managing Tablespaces And Datafiles

Terms you'll need to understand:

- √ Tablespaces
- √ Datafiles
- √ **MINIMIM EXTENT**
- √ **AUTOEXTEND**
- √ Online tablespaces
- √ Offline tablespaces
- √ Temporary tablespaces
- √ **COALESCE**
- √ Read-only tablespaces
- √ Online datafiles
- √ Offline datafiles

Techniques you'll need to master:

- √ Planning a database layout to optimize input/output (I/O) performance
- √ Creating tablespaces
- √ Creating temporary tablespaces
- √ Altering tablespaces
- √ Coalescing tablespaces
- √ Bringing tablespaces online and offline
- √ Altering tablespace default storage
- √ Making tablespaces read-only
- √ Dropping tablespaces
- √ Adding datafiles to a tablespace
- √ Changing datafile size
- √ Bringing datafiles online and offline
- √ Renaming and relocating datafiles

As discussed in Chapter 2, a *tablespace* is a logical structure for storing permanent data segments or for temporary storage to facilitate sorting, grouping, and summarizing data. Tablespaces are physically made up of datafiles located on disk. In this chapter, I first discuss how to effectively manage tablespaces and then how to manage the datafiles. Tablespace and datafile management skills are critical to keeping the data stored in the database intact and available for your users.

These data dictionary views furnish information about database tablespaces:

- DBA_DATA_FILES
- DBA_FREE_SPACE_COALESCED
- DBA_TABLESPACES
- DBA_TS_QUOTAS
- DBA_USERS
- USER_EXTENTS, DBA_EXTENTS
- USER_FREE_SPACE, DBA_FREE_SPACE
- USER_SEGMENTS, DBA_SEGMENTS
- USER_TABLESPACES
- V$DATAFILE

Managing Tablespaces

Although only the SYSTEM tablespace is required to create an Oracle database, you should consider some standard tablespace conventions when planning your database. By following these simple guidelines, you will have a database that is easier to manage and performs better.

Creating Multiple Tablespaces

The SYSTEM tablespace should only store objects owned by SYS and SYSTEM. Don't create any additional objects in the SYSTEM tablespace. If you have a utility that must be run as SYSTEM and it creates additional tables, indexes, and so forth, alter the SYSTEM account to have a default tablespace other than SYSTEM before you install the product. This reduces fragmentation, improves performance, and makes upgrades easier. If the SYSTEM tablespace becomes fragmented, the only way to defragment it is to recreate the database. Obviously, this is reason enough to make sure unnecessary data, rollback, or sort segments are never created in the SYSTEM tablespace.

Rollback Tablespaces

Separate rollback segment data from user data, which prevents a single disk failure from causing permanent loss of data. Depending on the size and transaction activity of your database, you should have one or more tablespaces dedicated to rollback segments. One common philosophy is to have one tablespace where you create small transactional rollback segments and one tablespace that holds one large rollback segment to handle long running transactions.

Temporary Tablespaces

Create one or more tablespaces for temporary segment storage. Oracle creates temporary segments dynamically, as they are needed. By creating a dedicated tablespace for temporary segments, you can optimize the segment size for the best performance. Prior to Oracle8, when Oracle completed the execution of a statement requiring a temporary segment, Oracle automatically dropped the temporary segment and returned the extents allocated for that segment to the associated tablespace. In Oracle8, temporary segments do not always go away when a statement is finished.

When multiple sorts are required, Oracle allocates the segments for sort operations only once and then retains the segments for future multiple sort operations. This saves the overhead of recreating the temporary segments. These aspects make it desirable to create special tablespaces for temporary segments.

Data And Index Tablespaces

Using multiple tablespaces for data and indexes has many advantages. By grouping application data and indexes into different tablespaces, you can do the following:

- Take individual tablespaces offline and affect only specific applications within the database system.
- Improve performance by putting tables and indexes in separate tablespaces. By placing the tables and indexes in different tablespaces on separate disk drives, less input/output (I/O) contention and queries are read from both the indexes and tables simultaneously, providing better response time.
- Tailor backup and recovery more specifically to application requirements.
- Create tablespaces for special use, such as high update activity or read-only activity.
- Put tables in different tablespaces on separate disk drives to optimize join performance.

Creating Tablespaces

Once you've done proper analysis and know how many tablespaces you are going to create, where their datafiles will be placed on disk, and what objects will be placed in them, it's time to create more tablespaces.

> In order to insert data into tablespaces other than **SYSTEM**, first you must create an additional rollback segment other than the **SYSTEM** rollback segment (which is created when you create the database). Once both rollback segments are online, you will be able to insert data into other tablespaces.

A new tablespace is created by using either the SQL command **CREATE TABLESPACE** or the Create Tablespace property sheet of the Oracle Enterprise Manager (OEM). The **CREATE TABLESPACE** system privilege is required to create a tablespace.

Keywords And Parameters

The following list describes the keywords and parameters of the **CREATE TABLESPACE** command:

- *Tablespace*—The name of the tablespace to be created.
- DATAFILE—The datafile or files that comprise the tablespace (give complete pathnames).
- MINIMIM EXTENT—An integer value that controls free space fragmentation in the tablespace by ensuring that every extent size in a tablespace is at least as large as, and is a multiple of, the integer value.
- AUTOEXTEND—Enables or disables the automatic extension of a datafile.
  - ON—Enables autoextend.
  - NEXT—Specifies the disk space to allocate to the datafile when more extents are required.
  - MAXSIZE—Specifies the maximum disk space allowed for allocation to the datafile.
  - UNLIMITED—Sets no limit on allocating disk space to the datafile.
  - OFF—Disables autoextend if it is turned on. **OFF** is the default value.

- LOGGING/NOLOGGING—Specifies the default logging attributes of all tables, indexes, and partitions within the tablespace. LOGGING is the default.
- DEFAULT STORAGE—Specifies the default storage parameters for all objects created in the tablespace.
- ONLINE—Makes the tablespace available immediately after creation to users who have been granted access to the tablespace. ONLINE is the default value.
- OFFLINE—Makes the tablespace unavailable immediately after creation.
- PERMANENT—Specifies that the tablespace will be used to hold permanent objects. This is the default.
- TEMPORARY—Specifies that the tablespace will only be used to hold temporary objects, for example, segments used by implicit sorts to handle ORDER BY clauses.

The data of the new tablespace is contained in a single datafile, which is 100MB in size. The default storage parameters for any segments created in this tablespace are explicitly set. After the tablespace is created, it is left offline. The following statement creates the tablespace RBS:

```
CREATE TABLESPACE rbs
    DATAFILE '/u01/oradata/hqt2/rbs.dbf' SIZE 100M
    DEFAULT STORAGE (
      INITIAL 1M
      NEXT 1M
      MINEXTENTS 2
      MAXEXTENTS 50
      PCTINCREASE 0)
    OFFLINE;
```

If you do not specify file names fully when creating tablespaces, the corresponding datafiles are created in the current directory of the database server. If you want to create a temporary tablespace, add the TEMPORARY keyword after the tablespace name, as follows:

```
CREATE TABLESPACE tablespace_name TEMPORARY;
```

Using The **ALTER TABLESPACE** Command

Once a tablespace is created, the ALTER TABLESPACE command is used to change the default storage parameters, prepare for backup, or alter the availability of the tablespace. To alter a tablespace, use either the Alter Tablespace property sheet of OEM or the SQL command **ALTER TABLESPACE**. To use the **ALTER TABLESPACE** command, you must have the **ALTER TABLESPACE** system privilege.

Temporary Tablespace

To alter a tablespace from permanent to temporary or from temporary to permanent, use the following commands:

```
ALTER TABLESPACE tablespace_name TEMPORARY;
ALTER TABLESPACE tablespace_name PERMANENT
```

Coalesce Tablespace

Coalescing is the process of combining adjacent extents of free space into one large extent. The system monitor (SMON) process does this as the database operates. SMON will not coalesce tablespaces where the **PCTINCREASE** storage parameter is set to 0. You can coalesce all contiguous free space in a tablespace manually by using the **ALTER TABLESPACE COALESCE** command.

```
ALTER TABLESPACE tablespace_name COALESCE;
```

Online And Offline Tablespaces

You can bring an offline tablespace online to make the schema objects within the tablespace available to database users. Alternatively, you can take an online tablespace offline while the database is open, so that this portion of the database is temporarily unavailable for general use, but the rest is available.

The **SYSTEM** tablespace must always be online, because the data dictionary must always be available to Oracle. To bring an offline tablespace online while the database is open, use either the Place Online menu item of OEM or the SQL command **ALTER TABLESPACE**. You must have the **MANAGE TABLESPACE** system privilege to bring a tablespace online.

> **TIP:** Media recovery must be performed on a tablespace before bringing it online if it was not taken offline using the **NORMAL** option of the **ALTER TABLESPACE OFFLINE** command. Otherwise, an error will be returned and the tablespace will remain offline.

You may wish to take a tablespace offline for any of the following reasons:

- To make a part of the database unavailable while allowing normal access to the rest of the database.
- To perform an offline (cold) tablespace backup.
- To make an application and its group of tables temporarily unavailable while updating or maintaining the application programs.

To take an online tablespace offline while the database is open, use either the Take Offline menu item of OEM or the SQL command **ALTER TABLESPACE**. You must have the **MANAGE TABLESPACE** system privilege to take a tablespace offline.

You can specify any of the following priorities when taking a tablespace offline:

- **OFFLINE NORMAL**—You can take a tablespace offline normally when there are no error conditions for any of that tablespace's datafiles. Oracle takes a checkpoint for all the tablespace's datafiles before taking them offline. **OFFLINE NORMAL** is the default priority, so you don't need to specify it on the command line.
- **OFFLINE TEMPORARY**—You can take a tablespace offline temporarily, even when there are error conditions for one or more tablespace datafiles. Oracle takes checkpoints on all online datafiles before taking them offline. Recovery is necessary on any datafile that is in an error state when taken offline before it can be brought back online.
- **OFFLINE IMMEDIATE**—If you choose to take a tablespace offline immediately, Oracle does not take a checkpoint on any datafiles. Tablespace media recovery is necessary before bringing the tablespace back online. You cannot use this option for databases running in no archive log mode mode.

The following statements bring the **USERS** tablespace online and offline, respectively. Notice that when bringing a tablespace offline, it is not necessary to use the **NORMAL** keyword, because that is the default:

```
ALTER TABLESPACE users ONLINE;
ALTER TABLESPACE users OFFLINE;
```

Tablespace Storage

New values for the default storage parameters of a tablespace affect only future extents allocated for the segments within the tablespace. You can change tablespace storage parameters all at once or one at a time. The code example shows the entire storage clause being changed first, and then just a single parameter being changed:

```
ALTER TABLESPACE users
     DEFAULT STORAGE (
       INITIAL 50K
       NEXT 50K
       MINEXTENTS 2
       MAXEXTENTS 20
       PCTINCREASE 50);

ALTER TABLESPACE users DEFAULT STORAGE(INITIAL 1M);
```

Read-Only Tablespaces

Making a tablespace read-only prevents further write operations on the datafiles in the tablespace. Any tablespace you intend to make read-only must meet these conditions.

- It must be online.
- The entire database must not have any active transactions. This guarantees that the tablespace does not require the application of undo information.
- The tablespace must not contain active rollback segments.
- The tablespace cannot be part of a current online backup, because backup completion updates the header file of all datafiles contained in the tablespace.

TIP: You cannot rename or resize datafiles belonging to a read-only tablespace.

Use the SQL command **ALTER TABLESPACE** to change a tablespace to read-only. You must have the **ALTER TABLESPACE** system privilege to make a tablespace read-only. Altering a tablespace to read-only will result in a change to the control file. It is always a good idea to perform a backup anytime the control file is changed. Once a tablespace has been changed to read-only and has been backed up, you can take it out of your backup procedures until it is made writeable again.

The following statement makes the **DATAMART** tablespace read-only:

```
ALTER TABLESPACE datamart READ ONLY;
```

Making a read-only tablespace writeable updates the control file for the datafiles, so that you can use the read-only version of the datafiles as a starting point for recovery. To make a read-only tablespace writeable, all the datafiles in the tablespace must be online.

To change a read-only tablespace back to a read-write tablespace, use the SQL command **ALTER TABLESPACE**. You must have the **ALTER TABLESPACE** system privilege to do so. The following command makes the **DATAMART** tablespace writeable:

```
ALTER TABLESPACE datamart READ WRITE;
```

Dropping Tablespaces

A tablespace and its contents can be dropped from the database if the tablespace and its contents are no longer needed. Any tablespace in an Oracle database can be dropped with the exception of the **SYSTEM** tablespace. To execute the **DROP TABLESPACE** command, you must be granted the **DROP TABLESPACE** system privilege.

Dropping a tablespace actually results in dropping only the file pointers in the database's control files. The physical datafiles that make up the tablespace continue to exist. To free up the disk space, delete the datafiles of the dropped tablespace using operating system (OS) commands.

You cannot drop a tablespace that contains any active segments, such as a table in the tablespace that is currently being used or a tablespace that contains an active rollback segment. For this reason, it is a good practice to take the tablespace offline before dropping it.

Once you drop a tablespace, that tablespace's entry stays in the data dictionary and the tablespace status is changed to **INVALID**.

The **INCLUDING CONTENTS** option is not needed if the tablespace is empty. If the tablespace contains any tables with primary keys referenced by foreign keys of tables in other tablespaces and you want to cascade the drop of the foreign key constraints of the child tables, use the **CASCADE CONSTRAINTS** option.

A tablespace can be dropped by using either the SQL command **DROP TABLESPACE** or the Drop Tablespace menu item of OEM. The following command drops the **TOOLS** tablespace, including the objects in the tablespace and any foreign key constraints of child tables in other tablespaces, with the following statement:

```
DROP TABLESPACE tools INCLUDING CONTENTS CASCADE CONSTRAINTS;
```

Managing Datafiles

At least one datafile is required for the **SYSTEM** tablespace of a database. Every datafile has two associated file numbers: an absolute file number and a relative file number.

Each database datafile is uniquely identified by an *absolute file number*. Prior to the advent of Oracle8, this number was called *file number*.

Each tablespace datafile is uniquely identified by a *relative file number*. Except in large databases (more than 1,023 datafiles), relative file numbers are usually the same as the absolute file numbers. Relative file numbers are referenced in many of the data dictionary views.

These data dictionary views furnish information about a database's datafiles:

- DBA_DATA_FILES
- DBA_TS_QUOTAS
- DBA_USERS
- USER_EXTENTS, DBA_EXTENTS
- USER_FREE_SPACE, DBA_FREE_SPACE
- USER_SEGMENTS, DBA_SEGMENTS
- USER_TABLESPACES, DBA_TABLESPACES
- V$DATAFILE

Understanding the limits of the system you are working on can save you from having to do major reorganizations of the database. Be sure you understand the following limitations:

- *OS limit*—Each OS has a limit on the maximum number of open files per process. Once this limit is reached, more datafiles cannot be created.
- *Oracle system limit*—Oracle imposes a maximum limit on the number of datafiles for any Oracle database opened by any instance. This limit is platform specific, but for most platforms it is 65,533 files.

- *Control file size*—If the control file size is exceeded by adding more datafiles, the control file can be recreated with a larger **MAXDATAFILES** parameter.
- *Instance or system global area (SGA) limit*—When starting an Oracle8 instance, the database's parameter file indicates the amount of SGA space to reserve for datafile information. This is controlled by the **DB_FILES** parameter. This limit applies only for the life of the instance.

Datafile Placement

The placement of datafiles is very important for performance reasons. Your goal in file placement should be to have I/O evenly spread across the available disk drives to minimize simultaneous access to each disk. The **V$FILESTAT** view provides statistical information on physical reads (**PHYRDS**) and writes (**PHYWRTS**) by file number.

For example, if several disk drives are available to store the database, it might be helpful to store table data in a tablespace on one disk drive and index data in a tablespace on another disk drive. This way, when users query table information, both disk drives can work simultaneously, retrieving table and index data at the same time.

If enough drives are available, datafiles should not be stored on the same disk drive that stores the database's redo log files. If the datafiles and redo log files are stored on the same disk drive and that disk drive fails, the files cannot be used in your database recovery procedures.

Adding Datafiles To A Tablespace

You can increase a tablespace's total amount of allocated disk space by adding datafiles to the tablespace. To do this, use either the OEM's Add Datafile dialog box or the SQL command **ALTER TABLESPACE**. If you do not have the **ALTER TABLESPACE** system privilige, you cannot add datafiles to a tablespace.

The following statement creates a new datafile for the RBS tablespace:

```
ALTER TABLESPACE rbs
   ADD DATAFILE '/u01/oradata/hqt4/rbs02.dbf' SIZE 100M;
```

Alternatively, you can reuse an existing datafile. The **REUSE** option allows Oracle to reuse an existing file. If the file already exists, Oracle verifies that its size matches the value of the **SIZE** parameter and overwrites the contents of the file. If the file does not exist, Oracle creates it.

Changing A Datafile's Size

You can alter existing datafiles so that they automatically increase in size when more space is needed in the database. The files increase in specified increments up to a specified maximum. By letting datafiles automatically increase in size, you reduce the need for immediate attention by a database administrator (DBA) when a tablespace runs out of space. This also means that applications will not stop working because of failures to allocate extents.

You can specify the **AUTOEXTEND** keyword for file extension when you create datafiles with the **CREATE DATABASE**, **CREATE TABLESPACE**, or **ALTER TABLESPACE** commands.

You can enable or disable automatic file extensions for existing datafiles, or manually resize datafiles, by using the SQL command **ALTER DATABASE**.

The following example enables automatic extension for a datafile, added to the **USERS** tablespace:

```
ALTER TABLESPACE users
    ADD DATAFILE '/u01/oradata/hqt4/users2.dbf' SIZE 10M
      AUTOEXTEND ON
      NEXT 512K
      MAXSIZE 250M
```

The **NEXT** parameter sets how much space will be added to the datafile when it extends. **MAXSIZE** is the maximum size a datafile can automatically extend to.

To turn automatic extension off for the datafile, use the **ALTER DATABASE** command, as in the following example:

```
ALTER DATABASE DATAFILE '/u01/oradata/hqt4/users2.dbf'
    AUTOEXTEND OFF
```

The **ALTER DATABASE** command can also manually increase or decrease the size of a datafile. Manually reducing the size of a datafile allows you to reclaim unused space for use by the database. Manually increasing the size of a datafile gives the DBA more control over the growth of datafiles. It may not be possible to reduce the size of a datafile, depending on where in the file extents are being used. Resizing a datafile does not reorganize or consolidate the data segments in the datafile. Oracle reclaims space starting at the end of the file and moving towards the beginning of the file until it finds an extent in use. At this point, Oracle can't reduce the size of the file any further.

In this example, assume that the datafile users2.dbf has extended up to 500MB. However, several large schemas have been dropped so that the datafile can be reduced in size. The following command decreases the size of datafile users2.dbf:

```
ALTER DATABASE DATAFILE '/u01/oradata/hqt4/users2.dbf'
   RESIZE 100M
```

Online And Offline Datafiles

In rare situations, you might need to bring specific datafiles online or take specific files offline. Normally this only happens when Oracle has a problem writing to a datafile. You might need to take the datafile offline or bring the damaged datafile online manually for recovery purposes. Once the datafile is offline, it cannot be accessed.

You must have the **ALTER DATABASE** system privilege to bring a datafile online or take it offline.

To bring a datafile online, issue the SQL command **ALTER DATABASE** and include the **DATAFILE** parameter. The following statement brings the specified datafile online:

```
ALTER DATABASE DATAFILE 'file_name' ONLINE;
```

When the database is in no archive log mode, use the **OFFLINE DROP** option to take a datafile offline. This option drops the datafile immediately when taking the datafile offline, because it is likely to be unusable. The following statement brings the specified datafile offline:

```
ALTER DATABASE DATAFILE 'file_name' OFFLINE DROP;
```

Renaming And Relocating Datafiles

You can use the **ALTER TABLESPACE RENAME DATAFILE** command to rename datafiles or change their locations. It is possible to use this command to rename and relocate datafiles for a single tablespace or for multiple tablespaces simultaneously. Remember that the Oracle commands only change the pointers to the datafiles, as recorded in the database's control file; they do not physically rename any OS files, nor do they copy files at the OS level. Files must be renamed or relocated using OS commands. Before making any structural changes to a database, such as renaming and relocating the datafiles of one or more tablespaces, always perform a complete backup of the database. You must have the **ALTER TABLESPACE** system privilege to rename or relocate datafiles.

Follow these steps to rename or relocate datafiles from a single tablespace:

1. Take offline the non-**SYSTEM** tablespace containing the datafiles.
2. Use the OS to copy datafiles to new locations or new names. It is very important that the new, fully specified file names differ from the original file names.
3. Change the file names within the database using the OEM or the SQL command **ALTER TABLESPACE** with the **RENAME DATAFILE** option. The following example renames the datafiles *file_name_1* and *file_name_2* to *file_name_3* and *file_name_4*, respectively:

```
ALTER TABLESPACE users
  RENAME DATAFILE 'file_name_1', 'file_name_2'
    TO 'file_name_3', 'file_name_4';
```

Always provide complete file names, including their paths, to properly identify the old and new datafiles. You can query the **DBA_DATA_FILES** view to get all the Oracle datafile names.

The SQL command **ALTER DATABASE** with the **RENAME FILE** option allows you to rename and relocate datafiles of multiple tablespaces. This option is the only choice if you want to rename or relocate datafiles of several tablespaces in one operation, or if you want to rename or relocate datafiles on the **SYSTEM** tablespace. The **ALTER DATABASE** system privilege is required to rename datafiles of several tablespaces in one operation or to rename datafiles of the **SYSTEM** tablespace.

Follow these steps to rename or relocate datafiles from multiple tablespaces:

1. Make sure that the database is mounted and closed.
2. Use OS commands to copy the datafiles you are renaming to their new locations or new names. Make sure the new copies of the datafiles have different, fully specified file names from the datafiles currently in use.
3. Rename the file pointers in the database's control file using the SQL command **ALTER DATABASE**. The following example renames the datafiles *file_name_1* and *file_name_2* to *file_name_3* and *file_name_4*, respectively:

```
ALTER DATABASE
  RENAME FILE 'file_name_1', 'file_name_2'
    TO 'file_name_3', 'file_name_4';
```

Practice Questions

Question 1

When moving datafiles, what do the **ALTER DATABASE RENAME FILE** and **ALTER TABLESPACE RENAME DATAFILE** commands do?

- ❍ a. Move datafiles.
- ❍ b. Rename datafiles.
- ❍ c. Copy datafiles.
- ❍ d. Reset internal file pointers in the control file.

Answer d is correct. ALTER DATABASE RENAME FILE and ALTER TABLESPACE RENAME DATAFILE only update the control file. When moving, renaming, or copying a datafile, you must use OS commands.

Question 2

When moving datafiles, when would you use the **ALTER DATABASE** command rather than **ALTER TABLESPACE** command?

- ❍ a. When the tablespace is offline
- ❍ b. When the tablespace is the **SYSTEM** tablespace
- ❍ c. When the tablespace does not contain active rollback segments
- ❍ d. When the tablespace does not contain active temporary segments

Answer b is correct. The ALTER DATABASE command must be used when datafiles for the SYSTEM tablespace are being renamed or moved. Answer a is incorrect because the ALTER TABLESPACE command can be used on an offline tablespace. Rollback and temporary segments have no bearing on which command you would use to move datafiles.

Question 3

Which condition will prevent the DATA01 tablespace from being dropped in the following command?

```
DROP TABLESPACE data01;
```

❍ a. It is online.

❍ b. It is offline.

❍ c. It is read-only.

❍ d. It contains objects.

Answer d is correct. To drop a tablespace with objects, you must use the **INCLUDING CONTENTS** option in the **DROP TABLESPACE** command. Although it is a better practice to put tablespaces offline before dropping them, no requirement exists to do so. Read-only tablespaces can be dropped like any other tablespace.

Question 4

What happens when a tablespace is taken offline normally?

❍ a. A checkpoint occurs.

❍ b. Recovery is needed before the tablespace can be brought online.

❍ c. Users can query objects in the tablespace, but cannot alter the objects.

❍ d. Users can create new objects in the tablespace, but cannot query any objects.

Answer a is correct. Before the datafiles associated with the tablespace are taken offline, a checkpoint occurs. When a tablespace is taken offline normally, recovery is not needed. When a tablespace is taken offline, it cannot be queried. New objects cannot be created in an offline tablespace.

Question 5

The USERS1 tablespace is offline and contains the EMP table. The USERS2 tablespace is online and contains the DEPT table. Which three SQL statements will return an error due to the respective tablespace's online/offline status? [Choose three]

- ❑ a. **TRUNCATE TABLE emp;**
- ❑ b. **ALTER TABLESPACE user_data01 READ ONLY;**
- ❑ c. **ALTER INDEX dept_idx DEALLOCATE UNUSED;**
- ❑ d. **ANALYZE TABLE dept COMPUTE STATISTICS;**
- ❑ e. **ALTER TABLE emp STORAGE (MINEXTENTS 5);**
- ❑ f. **ALTER TABLESPACE users1**
  RENAME DATAFILE '/disk2/data/old.dbf'
  TO '/disk2/data/new.dbf';

Answers a, b, and e are correct. When a tablespace is offline, SQL statements cannot be issued against any of the tablespace objects. Answers c and d will succeed because they are being executed against an online tablespace. Answer f will succeed based on the online/offline status. This is tricky because you must assume the datafile has been copied already using OS commands.

Question 6

You created a tablespace with **MAXEXTENTS** equal to 500. How could you increase the setting?

- ❍ a. Alter the **MAXEXTENTS** initialization parameter.
- ❍ b. Issue the **ALTER DATABASE** command with the **AUTOEXTEND** option.
- ❍ c. Issue the **ALTER TABLESPACE** command with the **AUTOEXTEND** option.
- ❍ d. Issue the **ALTER TABLESPACE** command with the **DEFAULT STORAGE** option.

Answer d is correct. Use the ALTER TABLESPACE command with the DEFAULT STORAGE clause to change the MAXEXTENTS value. MAXEXTENTS is not an initialization parameter. The AUTOEXTEND option allows datafiles to expand, but has no effect on extents.

Question 7

Which command would you use to change the size of the minimum extent allocated to the **USERS** tablespace from 2MB to 3MB?

❍ a. **ALTER SYSTEM**

❍ b. **ALTER DATABASE DATAFILE**

❍ c. **ALTER TABLESPACE MINIMUM EXTENT**

❍ d. **ALTER TABLESPACE DEFAULT STORAGE**

Answer c is correct. Use the **ALTER TABLESPACE** command to change the **MINIMIM EXTENT** value for a tablespace. The **ALTER SYSTEM** command does not affect tablespace storage parameters. The **ALTER DATABASE DATAFILE** command is used to rename or relocate datafiles. The **DEFAULT STORAGE** clause changes the storage parameters for objects created in a tablespace, but cannot change **MINIMUM EXTENT.**

Question 8

The **USERS** tablespace has never been used, but new information about the contents of the tablespace makes you want to change its size. What will be the size of users.dbf if it was 150MB when the datafile was created after the following command is executed?

```
ALTER DATABASE prod
  DATAFILE '/u01/oradata/hqt4/users.dbf'
  RESIZE 50M;
```

❍ a. 50MB

❍ b. 100MB

❍ c. 150MB

❍ d. 200MB

Answer a is correct. Use the **ALTER DATABASE DATAFILE** command to manually resize a datafile.

Question 9

Why will this statement fail?

```
CREATE TABLESPACE user_data
   DATAFILE '/disk2/us_data01.dbf' SIZE 10M
   MINIMIM EXTENT 500K
   DEFAULT STORAGE
      (INITIAL 100K NEXT 100K
       MAXEXTENTS 500 PCTINCREASE 0);
```

❍ a. **MAXEXTENTS** is set too high.

❍ b. **MINMUM EXTENT** cannot be set at the tablespace level.

❍ c. **INITIAL** and **NEXT** should be a multiple of **MINIMUM EXTENT**.

❍ d. The datafile is too large for the default storage parameters.

Answer c is correct. When MINIMUM EXTENT is specified, every extent allocated in the tablespace should be a multiple of MINIMUM EXTENT. MAXEXTENTS is not too high and could be set to unlimited because Oracle8 has no limit to extents. MINIMUM EXTENT is a valid tablespace parameter. The default storage parameters affect the objects that are created in a tablespace without a storage clause of their own. A datafile can be too small for the default storage parameters, but not too large.

Question 10

Which is the correct sequence of steps to move datafiles in the **USERS** tablespace?

- ❍ a. Take the tablespace offline, issue the **ALTER TABLESPACE** command, move the files using OS commands, and bring the tablespace back online.
- ❍ b. Issue the **ALTER TABLESPACE** command, take the tablespace offline, move the files using OS commands, and bring the tablespace back online.
- ❍ c. Take the tablespace offline, move the files using OS commands, bring the tablespace back online, and issue the **ALTER TABLESPACE** command.
- ❍ d. Take the tablespace offline, move the files using OS commands, issue the **ALTER TABLESPACE** command, and bring the tablespace back online.

Answer d is correct. The correct sequence of steps to move a datafile that is not in the SYSTEM tablespace is this: Take the tablespace offline, move the files using OS commands, issue the ALTER TABLESPACE command, and bring the tablespace back online. Answers a and b are incorrect because the files must exist before the ALTER TABLESPACE command is used. Answer c is incorrect because you must execute the ALTER TABLESPACE command before the files are brought back online.

Need To Know More?

Ault, Mike: *Oracle8 Administration and Management*, John Wiley & Sons, Inc., New York, NY, 1998. ISBN 0-471-19234-1. See Chapter 3, "Tablespace Administration."

Loney, Kevin, and Marlene Theriault: *Oracle8 DBA Handbook*, Oracle Press, Berkeley, CA, 1997. ISBN 0-07882-406-0. This book is a comprehensive guide and a must have for all DBAs.

See the Oracle documentation that is provided on CD with the Oracle RDBMS software. Pertaining to this chapter are:

Fee, Joyce: *Oracle8 Administrator's Guide*, Oracle Corporation, Redwood City, CA, 1997. See Chapter 8, "Managing Tablespaces" and Chapter 9, "Managing Datafiles."

Lorentz, Diana: *Oracle8 SQL Reference*, Oracle Corporation, Redwood City, CA, 1997. See Chapter 4, "Commands."

http://education.oracle.com/tbt/ocp8.html is the site from which you can order the Oracle Education CD-ROM bundle for Oracle8 Database Administration.

www.revealnet.com is the site where RevealNet Corporation provides Oracle Administration reference software.

10

Storage Structure And Relationships

Terms you'll need to understand:

- √ Data block
- √ Extent
- √ Segment
- √ Data block header
- √ Table directory
- √ Row directory
- √ Row data
- √ Free space
- √ **PCTFREE**
- √ **PCTUSED**
- √ Free list
- √ Data segment
- √ Index segment
- √ Temporary segment
- √ Rollback segment

Techniques you'll need to master:

- √ Understanding the relationship between data blocks, extents, and segments
- √ Knowing what **PCTFREE** and **PCTUSED** are used for
- √ Understanding how blocks get put on the free list
- √ Understanding how data blocks become fragmented
- √ Understanding how row chaining and migration occurs
- √ Understanding how extents are allocated
- √ Knowing what the different types of segments are used for
- √ Knowing which views to query to list information about extents and segments

In previous chapters, we briefly discussed how Oracle stores data. In this chapter, we will get down to the bit and bytes, or more specifically, data blocks, extents, and segments. These are the basic storage elements of Oracle. Understanding these elements and how they are allocated is important to many database designs and tuning concepts. Misunderstanding these concepts can cause incorrect data type usage, resulting in poor performance and misallocation of database space. So if it has been a while since you have looked over this material, take the time now to review it again. You will be glad you did.

Data Blocks, Extents, And Segments

Oracle stores all information in the database by using storage structures called data blocks, extents, and segments. The smallest unit of storage, called the *data block*, represents physical space on a disk drive. The next unit of storage, a logical one called an *extent*, is a specific number of adjacent data blocks apportioned for storing information belonging to segment. The next logical unit, a *segment*, is a group of extents apportioned for a logical data structure, such as rollback, temporary, table, or index. Oracle adds space to segments one extent at a time when all existing extents for the database object are full. So although extents are contiguous storage units, segments are not. Finally, segments for a particular object can exist in only one tablespace, whereas the associated extents can exist in more than one datafile. However, a single extent cannot span multiple datafiles.

Data Blocks

Because database block size can't be changed once the database is created, you should give this parameter careful consideration. Oracle block size should not be confused with the operating system (OS) block size. Most file systems also have a block size that is used by the OS to actually retrieve data from disks. Because Oracle always makes requests for data in Oracle blocks that are then translated into requests by the OS using OS blocks, Oracle block size should always be a multiple of the OS block size. This avoids unnecessary input/output (I/O).

Oracle data block format is the same, no matter what the data block contains—table, index, or clustered data. The following list describes the parts of an Oracle data block:

- *Data block header*—Contains block information (i.e., block address and segment type).

- *Table directory*—Contains data about tables that have rows in this block.
- *Row directory*—Contains the address of each row piece in the block. Row directory space is not released when rows are deleted. The space is reused when new rows are inserted into the block.
- *Row data*—Contains table or index data.
- *Free space*—Consists of free space for new rows or updates to rows that require additional space. The use of free space is controlled by the space management parameter **PCTFREE**, which is explained in the following section. Free space is also used for transaction entries. Each transaction that updates a block requires a transaction entry in the block. The size of a transaction entry depends on your OS, but is normally around 23 bytes.

The data block header, table directory, and row directory are referred to as *overhead*. On average, the fixed and variable portions of data block overhead total 84 to 107 bytes.

PCTFREE

PCTFREE represents the percentage of each data block that is reserved as free space. This space is used when rows that already exist in that block are updated and grow in length. The value of **PCTFREE** must be between 0 and 99. A value of 0 allows the entire block to be filled by inserts of new rows. The default value is 10. This reserves 10 percent of each block for updates to existing rows and allows inserts of new rows to fill a maximum of 90 percent of each block. The proper **PCTFREE** should be determined for each segment (i.e., table, index, or rollback).

> TIP: The **PCTFREE** parameter is inapplicable to large object (**LOB**) datatypes (**BLOB**, **CLOB**, **NCLOB**, and **BFILE**), as these do not use this storage parameter or free lists.

PCTUSED

PCTUSED defines the amount of space available within a block. It represents the percentage of block space used that a block must fall to after reaching the row limit determined by **PCTFREE**. (This probably seems confusing; hopefully the following example will clear things up.)

A table is created with a **PCTFREE** of 20 percent and a percent used of 40 percent. As discussed in the "PCTFREE" section of this chapter, 20 percent of each block for this table remains free for growth of existing rows. Blocks remain available for insertion until they reach 80 percent full, at which point they are taken off the free list and can no longer have new rows inserted. If rows are now deleted, the block remains off the free list until usage of the block falls below the **PCTUSED** value of 40 percent. Oracle then places the block back on the free list and new rows can be inserted into the block again.

Free Lists

Oracle maintains at least one *free list* for each data and index segment. These are lists of all data blocks apportioned for that segment's extents and are available for inserts. When you issue an **INSERT** statement, Oracle checks a free list of the table for the first available data block and uses it if possible. If there is not enough free space in that block for the row to be inserted and the block is at least **PCTUSED**, Oracle takes the block off the free list. If your system is going to have concurrent inserts to the same table, you can have Oracle maintain multiple free lists to reduce contention.

Transactions that delete from or update a segment, causing a block to fall below **PCTUSED** and go back on the free list, always reuse the same blocks for inserts until a commit is executed, completing the transaction. Once a transaction commits, free space in the block becomes available for other transactions.

Data Block Fragmentation

Repeated inserts, updates, and deletes can fragment the free space of an Oracle block. When space is freed by a transaction, only that transaction can reuse that free space until the transaction completes making the space available to other transactions. When a transaction issues an **INSERT** or **UPDATE** command, Oracle coalesces free space in the block if it can't find enough contiguous free space. If enough free space for row expansion still does not exist, the row is migrated to another block.

Row Chaining And Migration

Row chaining or *row migration* happens in two situations. The first occurs when a row is too large to be inserted into a single data block and Oracle stores the row in multiple blocks. The second occurs when a row that originally fit into one data block is updated so that the row length increases and not enough free space exists for the update in the current block. When this happens, Oracle migrates the entire row's data to a new data block. A pointer is maintained in the original row piece of the migrated row to point to the new block containing the migrated row. Thus, the **ROWID** of the migrated row remains unchanged. Row chaining or migration can cause I/O performance problems, because Oracle must scan more than one data block to retrieve the information for a single row.

Extents

An extent is a logical storage unit that consists of a number of adjacent data blocks. Segments are made up of one or more extents. When a segment uses all the space in its currently assigned extents, Oracle allocates a new extent for the segment. There is a directory of the extents in a segment in the header block of that segment. Rollback segments are always created with at least two extents.

For example, when you create a table, you specify a value for the initial extent size of the table's data segment. When the data blocks of the initial extent become full and more space is needed, Oracle allocates another extent whose size is based on the **NEXT** parameter of the storage clause. All subsequent extents will be the same size or larger than the second extent based on the **PCTINCREASE** value of the storage clause.

When you create indexes and tables in parallel, each server process allocates a new extent and fills the extent with the table or index's data. Thus, if you create an index with a degree of parallelism of three, that index initially has at least three extents.

With a few exceptions, once an extent is allocated to a segment, it is not returned to the tablespace for reuse until the object using the segment is dropped. Extents allocated to an index segment are never freed until the index is dropped or the table/cluster the index is associated with is dropped. The exceptions to this include the following:

- The table or cluster is truncated with the **DROP STORAGE** statement.
- The extent is part of a rollback segment that has an **OPTIMAL** size specified.
- A database administrator (DBA) deallocates the unused extents of a table above the high watermark using the following SQL statement:

```
ALTER TABLE table_name DEALLOCATE UNUSED;
```

When extents are freed by dropping an object or by one of the exceptions listed previously, the data dictionary is updated to show the extents as available space. Although the data in the extents is no longer available, Oracle does not clear the data blocks for performance reasons until they are reused.

Extents that are allocated to temporary segments are freed when the temporary segments are dropped. If the temporary segments are part of a multiple sort, however, the segments are maintained by the instance for reuse and the extents are not freed at the end of the sort operation. These segments and their associated extents are freed when the instance is restarted.

You can query the **DBA_EXTENTS** view to examine the extents comprising all the segments in the database. The following list explains the meaning of each column in the view:

- BLOCK_ID—The starting block number for an extent.
- BLOCKS—The size of an extent in Oracle blocks.
- BYTES—The size of an extent in bytes.
- EXTENT_ID—The extent number in a segment.
- FILE_ID—The name of the file an extent is in.
- OWNER—The schema name of the segment owner associated with an extent.
- PARTITION_NAME—The segment partition name, which is null for nonpartitioned objects.
- RELATIVE_FNO—The relative file number of a first extent block.
- SEGMENT_NAME—The name of an extent's associated segment.
- SEGMENT_TYPE—This can be the index partition, table partition, table, cluster, index, rollback, deferred rollback, or temporary.
- TABLESPACE_NAME—The name of an extent's tablespace.

The **DBA_FREE_SPACE** view lists the free extents in each tablespace. The following list explains the meaning of each column in the view:

- BLOCK_ID—The starting block number for an extent.
- BLOCKS—The size of an extent in Oracle blocks.
- BYTES—The size of an extent in bytes.
- FILE_ID—The ID number of the file an extent is in.
- RELATIVE_FNO—The relative file number of a first extent block.
- TABLESPACE_NAME—The name of the tablespace an extent is in.

Segments

A segment is made up of extents and contains all the data for a logical structure in a tablespace, such as a table or index. Tables are associated with data segments, and indexes are associated with index segments; two other segment types are temporary segments and rollback segments. The following sections describe each type of segment.

Data Segments

All tables, partitions, and clusters have a single *data segment* that holds all of the data for that object. All the characteristics of a segment (size, number of extents, growth rate, tablespace, etc.) are specified in the **CREATE** command. All the storage parameters, except the initial extent size, can be changed with the **ALTER** command.

The storage parameters for data segments affect performance and should be tailored to the requirements of each segment for best performance. For example, if your application never expands the size of a row, minimize wasted space in a data segment by tuning the **PCTFREE** parameter to a low value of one or two percent. Remember not to set the value to zero if you have concurrent updates of the segment. Performance degrades if not enough room exists for the transaction entries in the free space.

Index Segments

Using the **CREATE INDEX** command, *index segments* are created separately from the data segments. They do not have to, and should not, share the same tablespace as the data segment they are indexing. They should be separated into different tablespaces on different disk drives for improved performance.

The storage parameters for index segments affect performance the same way they do in data segments and should be tailored to the requirements of each segment for best performance. If you find that an index segment is wasting space that you want to reclaim, you can drop and recreate the index or you can use the **ALTER INDEX REBUILD** command to rebuild the index from the existing index. During the rebuild process, however, the new index is created as a temporary segment until the operation is complete and then the original index is dropped and the temporary segment is renamed to the original index name. Therefore, you must have enough space to store both the temporary segment that will become the new index and the old index; otherwise, the command will fail.

Temporary Segments

Temporary segments store temporary data during sorting operations, such as large sorting queries, index creations, and unions. Temporary segments use the default storage parameters for the tablespace they are created in. Once a temporary segment is created, changing the default storage parameters for the tablespace cannot alter its storage parameters.

Temporary segments extend themselves as necessary, and are dropped when the operation completes or has an error. Because of this, they could exceed the maximum number of extents or run out of space in the tablespace. Therefore, the size of large sorting queries or large table index creation operations should be taken into consideration when sizing the temporary tablespace.

Temporary segment operations perform better if a dedicated temporary tablespace is used. To dedicate a tablespace for temporary segments, specify the **TEMPORARY** clause of the **CREATE TABLESPACE** or **ALTER TABLESPACE** command. If you try to alter a tablespace to be temporary and any permanent segments exist, the **ALTER** statement will fail.

The temporary tablespace is fragmented because of the way it is used. Temporary segments are constantly created, extended, and then dropped. To maximize the efficiency of the temporary tablespace, choose an extent size that will give the best overall performance for the type of temporary operations on your system and set the **PCTINCREASE** parameter to 0. The result will be segments made up of identically sized extents. When these segments are dropped, the next temporary segment to be formed will be able to reuse the dropped extents. This saves the cost of coalescing data blocks and forming new extents. Remember, if the temporary segments are part of a multiple sort operation, the segments are maintained by the instance for reuse and the extents are not freed at the end of the sort operation. These segments and their associated extents are freed when the instance is restarted.

Rollback Segments

Rollback segments act as before-image journals and are critical for undoing data changes as well as during instance and database recovery. Also, when Oracle needs to provide a read-consistent set of results for a query, it can use information in rollback segments to create a set of data consistent with respect to a single point in time. They can be either private (recommended) or public. Private rollback segments must be specified in the initialization file (using the initialization parameter **ROLLBACK_SEGMENTS**) to be brought automatically online at startup. Public rollback segments remain offline until the calculation:

```
CEIL(TRANSACTIONS/TRANSACTIONS_PER_ROLLBACK_SEGMENT)
```

tells the Oracle server to bring another online. **CEIL** is a SQL function that returns the smallest integer greater than or equal to the numeric input. So if **TRANSACTIONS** equals 155 and **TRANSACTIONS_PER_ROLLBACK_ SEGMENT** equals 10, the instance will try to acquire at least 16 rollback segments.

> The **TRANSACTIONS_PER_ROLLBACK_SEGMENT** parameter does not limit the number of transactions that can use a rollback segment. This parameter determines the number of rollback segments an instance attempts to acquire when opening a database.

Only Oracle can access or read rollback segments and only Oracle can write to them. They are owned by the user **SYS**, no matter which user creates them. Rollback segments are usually stored in their own tablespace (other than the single **SYSTEM** rollback segment, which is in the **SYSTEM** tablespace) for two reasons. First, a tablespace cannot be taken offline if it contains even a single online rollback segment. Second, rollback segments grow and shrink as needed (assuming that the **OPTIMAL** setting is used) and with dynamic table extension, this could result in severe tablespace fragmentation.

Rollback segments are created using the **CREATE ROLLBACK SEGMENT** command. This command has an optional **STORAGE** clause. If this clause is not specified in the **CREATE** command, the default storage for the rollback segment tablespace is used instead. **MINEXTENTS** for all rollback segments must be set to a minimum of 2. The **OPTIMAL** parameter sets the size to which the rollback segment will shrink if it grows beyond **OPTIMAL** in size (it should be set to at least **MINEXTENTS * DB_BLOCK_SIZE**; otherwise, it will be ignored).

A transaction is assigned to a rollback segment in one of two ways. First, Oracle can assign a transaction automatically to the next available rollback segment. Transactions are only assigned if they issue a **DML** or **DDL** statement in the transaction. Read-only transactions are never assigned to a rollback segment. Second, a transaction can be explicitly assigned to a specific rollback segment using the **SET TRANSACTION USE ROLLBACK SEGMENT** ***rollback_segment_name*** statement; this allows the selection of a large or small rollback segment, as appropriate for the transaction. For the duration of a transaction, the associated process writes rollback information only to the assigned rollback segment.

When a transaction is committed, Oracle releases the rollback information, but does not immediately destroy it. The information remains in the rollback segment to create read-consistent views for queries that started before the transaction committed. To guarantee that rollback data is available for as long as possible, Oracle writes the extents of rollback segments sequentially. When the last extent of the rollback segment becomes full, Oracle continues writing rollback data by wrapping around to the first extent in the segment.

When a database is created, Oracle creates an initial rollback segment called **SYSTEM** in the **SYSTEM** tablespace. The **SYSTEM** rollback segment cannot be dropped. If multiple rollback segments are present, Oracle uses the **SYSTEM** rollback segment only for data dictionary updates and distributes user transactions among other rollback segments.

You can query the **DBA_SEGMENTS** view to examine information about storage allocated for all database segments. The following list explains the meaning of each column in the view:

- BLOCKS—Size of the segment in Oracle blocks.
- BUFFER_POOL—Name of the default buffer pool for the appropriate object.
- BYTES—Size of the segment in bytes.
- EXTENTS—Number of extents allocated to the segment.
- FREELIST_GROUPS—Number of free list groups allocated to this segment.
- FREELISTS—Number of process free lists allocated to this segment.
- HEADER_BLOCK—ID of the block containing the segment header.
- HEADER_FILE—ID of the file containing the segment header.
- INITIAL_EXTENT—Size of the initial extent of the segment in bytes.
- MAX_EXTENTS—Maximum number of extents allowed in the segment.
- MIN_EXTENTS—Minimum number of extents allowed in the segment.
- NEXT_EXTENT—Size, in bytes, of the next extent to be allocated to the segment.
- OWNER—Username of the segment owner.
- PARTITION_NAME—Segment partition name, null for nonpartitioned objects.
- PCT_INCREASE—Percent by which to increase the size of the next extent to be allocated.
- RELATIVE_FNO—Relative file number of the segment header.
- SEGMENT_NAME—Name of the segment.

- **SEGMENT_TYPE**—Type of segment: index partition, table partition, table cluster, index, rollback, deferred rollback, or temporary.
- **TABLESPACE_NAME**—Name of the tablespace containing the segment.

Practice Questions

Question 1

Which view would you use to find the size of the first extent allocated to a table?

- ❍ a. **DBA_EXTENTS**
- ● b. **DBA_SEGMENTS**
- ❍ c. **DBA_DATAFILES**
- ❍ d. **DBA_TABLESPACES**

Answer b is correct. **DBA_SEGMENTS** displays the size and storage settings for all the segments in the database. **DBA_EXTENTS** lists the extents comprising all segments in the database, but does not show the size of the storage settings for segments. **DBA_DATAFILES** shows information on the datafiles that make up tablespaces. **DBA_TABLESPACES** lists information about tablespaces, not data segments.

Question 2

Which type of segment is the most common segment used in a database?

- ● a. Data
- ❍ b. Index
- ❍ c. Library
- ❍ d. Rollback
- ❍ e. Temporary

Answer a is correct. Data segments are the most common segment in a database. In most databases, less space is used for indexing than for data. Library is not a valid segment type. Rollback segments shrink back to an optimal size and make up a very small portion of overall data space. Most temporary segments are transient and go away after the transaction is completed.

Question 3

Which parameter specifies the percentage of space in each data block reserved for updates?

- ❍ a. **MAXTRANS**
- ❍ b. **PCTUSED**
- ❍ c. **IINTRANS**
- ● d. **PCTFREE**

Answer d is correct. **PCTFREE** determines the percentage of space in each block that will be reserved for updates. **MAXTRANS** is the limit of concurrent transactions allowed in a data block. **PCTUSED** is the amount of space available for insert that the Oracle server maintains in each data block. **INITRANS** is the initial number of transaction blocks in a data block.

Question 4

When a row is inserted into a table, which portion of a database block holds the row data?

- ❍ a. Header
- ● b. Data space
- ❍ c. Free space
- ❍ d. Row directory
- ❍ e. Table directory

Answer b is correct. The data space holds row data. The header contains general block information, such as the block address and the type of segment. Free space holds no data. The row directory contains information about the actual rows in the block. The table directory contains information about the tables having rows in this block.

Question 5

What is the result of extents being frequently deallocated from a segment?

- ❍ a. Fragmented blocks
- ❍ b. Truncated segments
- ❍ c. Fragmented tablespace
- ❍ d. Nonincremental extents

Answer c is correct. Fragmentation in a tablespace is caused by frequent allocation and deallocation of extents to objects in the tablespace. Fragmented blocks are caused by frequent insert, update, and delete activity associated with a data block. Truncated segments are the result of the **TRUNCATE** command. Answer d, nonincremental extents, is not a valid answer.

Question 6

Which type of segment speeds data retrieval?

- ❍ a. Table
- ❍ b. Rollback
- ❍ c. Temporary
- ❍ d. Hash cluster
- ❍ e. Index

Answer e is correct. An index segment can decrease the amount of time required for queries. A table is not a segment type and is made up of a data segment and is searched via a full scan of the data unless an index is available. Rollback segments are used for rollback and read-consistency. Temporary segments are used for sorting. A hash cluster is not a segment type.

Question 7

Why would you query **DBA_EXTENTS**?

- ❍ a. To display the **PCTINCREASE** value of a given extent
- ● b. To determine the number of extents allocated to a table
- ❍ c. To determine the number of extents available in a database
- ❍ d. To display the value of the next extent to be allocated to a table

Answer b is correct. **DBA_EXTENTS** displays the owner, segment name, extent ID, and the size of each extent in the database. **DBA_EXTENTS** does not show storage parameters. **DBA_EXTENTS** does not show available extents or the next extent to be allocated.

Question 8

What happens when a segment needs more space?

- ❍ a. The segment is truncated.
- ● b. Extents are allocated to the segment.
- ❍ c. Extents are deallocated within the segment.
- ❍ d. Extents are compressed within the segment.

Answer b is correct. As a segment grows and requires more space, extents are added to the segment. Oracle does not truncate segments automatically. Extents are deallocated when segments are dropped. Extents are not compressed within a segment.

Question 9

Which type of segment is used to store a read-consistent state as of a certain point in time?

- ❍ a. Data
- ❍ b. Index
- ❍ c. Rollback
- ❍ d. Temporary

Answer c is correct. Rollback segments are used for read-consistency. Data segments store table data. Index segments store index data. Temporary segments are used for sort operations.

Question 10

What is the minimum number of extents for a segment?

- ❍ a. 0
- ❍ b. 1
- ❍ c. 2
- ❍ d. 5
- ❍ e. 15

Trick! question

Answer b is correct. When a segment is created, it is allocated at least one extent as specified by the initial extent parameter at the segment or the tablespace level. This is a trick question, because rollback segments must have a minimum of two extents. If you read the question quickly, you might choose answer c instead.

Need To Know More?

Ault, Mike: *Oracle8 Administration and Management*, John Wiley & Sons, Inc., New York, NY, 1998. ISBN 0-471-19234-1. An easy-to-understand book that explains how to set up Oracle for optimal performance.

Loney, Kevin, and Marlene Theriault: *Oracle8 DBA Handbook*, Oracle Press, Berkeley, CA, 1997. ISBN 0-07882-406-0. See Chapter 4, "Physical Database Layouts."

See the Oracle documentation that is provided on CD with the Oracle RDBMS software. Pertaining to this chapter are:

Fee, Joyce: *Oracle8 Administration Guide*, Oracle Corporation, Redwood City, CA, 1997. See Chapter 8, "Managing Tablespaces," Chapter 10, "Guidelines for Managing Schema Objects," and Chapter 18, "Managing Rollback Segments."

Lane, Paul: *Oracle8 Reference Manual*, Oracle Corporation, Redwood City, CA, 1997. See Chapter 2, "Static Data Dictionary Views."

Leverenz, Lefty: *Oracle8 Concepts Guide*, Oracle Corporation, Redwood City, CA, 1997. See Chapter 2, "Data Blocks, Extents, and Segments."

http://education.oracle.com/tbt/ocp8.html is the site from which you can order the Oracle Education CD-ROM bundle for Oracle8 Database Administration.

www.revealnet.com is the site where RevealNet Corporation provides Oracle Administration reference software.

11

Managing Rollback And Temporary Segments

Terms you'll need to understand:

- √ Rollback segment
- √ Optimal
- √ Shrink
- √ Offline
- √ Online
- √ Transaction
- √ "Snapshot too old" error
- √ High watermark (HWM)
- √ **DBA_SEGMENTS**
- √ **SORT_AREA_SIZE**
- √ Temporary segment
- √ **V$SORT_SEGMENT**
- √ **V$SORT_USAGE**

Techniques you'll need to master:

- √ Creating rollback segments
- √ Shrinking rollback segments
- √ Resolving "snapshot too old" errors
- √ Querying **DBA_SEGMENTS**
- √ Sizing rollback segments
- √ Assigning transactions to rollback segments
- √ Assigning temporary tablespaces to users
- √ Using temporary tablespaces
- √ Monitoring temporary segments

Every Oracle database contains one or more *rollback segments*, which provide read-consistency, transaction rollback, and database recovery. The rollback segment records changes for multiple transactions. Each transaction is assigned to a single rollback segment extent. The most costly statement in terms of rollback segment space usage is an update because it must capture both the before and the after image. The least expensive statement is a delete because the rollback captures the deleted **ROWID**s only.

When Oracle can't perform a sort in memory, it must allocate some temporary workspace. This is not unlike an operating system (OS) that must swap processes out of memory when memory is at a high level of utilization. While memory has become less expensive, few systems operate completely in memory. Oracle uses temporary segments allocated in tablespaces to complete queries that require large sorts that can't complete in memory.

Managing Rollback Segments

Rollback segments store system undo data, allowing noncommitted transactions to be rolled back. They can be likened to before-image logs or journals in other database systems. Rollback segments store the before images of changed data. Large transaction failures are often caused by rollback-related problems. Public rollback segments are most often used in parallel server configurations when more than one Oracle instance is accessing the database and you want the rollback segments to be available to all instances. Private rollback segments can be used only by one instance and are acquired during database startup. Before you can create or manage rollback segments, you must be granted the **CREATE ROLLBACK SEGMENT** or **ALTER ROLLBACK SEGMENT** system privileges.

Creating, Altering, And Dropping Rollback Segments

The first rollback segment is the **SYSTEM** rollback segment that is created in the **SYSTEM** tablespace during database creation. You can find an example of the **CREATE DATABASE** command in Chapter 5. In order to create additional tablespaces, an additional rollback segment must be created in the **SYSTEM** tablespace. Normally a tablespace for rollback segments is created next. After additional rollback segments are created in the rollback tablespace, the second rollback segment in the **SYSTEM** tablespace should be taken offline or dropped so free space in the **SYSTEM** tablespace is not used for nonsystem transactions. After additional rollback segments are created, Oracle only uses the **SYSTEM** rollback segment for changes made to the data dictionary tables or other system-level transactions. All private rollback segments are owned by the **SYS** account, regardless of who creates them. Public rollback segments are owned by the **PUBLIC** schema.

The following statements create a private rollback segment named R05 in the RBS tablespace and bring it online:

```
CREATE ROLLBACK SEGMENT R05
TABLESPACE rbs
STORAGE
( INITIAL 1M
  NEXT 1M
  OPTIMAL 2M
  MINEXTENTS 2
  MAXEXTENTS 500);
ALTER ROLLBACK SEGMENT R05 ONLINE;
```

The **PCTINCREASE** option of the storage clause is not permitted with **CREATE ROLLBACK SEGMENT**.

The **OPTIMAL** storage parameter applies only to rollback segments. For a discussion of the optimal storage parameter, see Chapter 10. To shrink a rollback segment, use the following command:

```
ALTER ROLLBACK SEGMENT R05 SHRINK;
```

The **ALTER ROLLBACK SEGMENT** command with the **SHRINK** option shrinks a rollback segment if it has extended into additional extents. If no value is specified (as in the previous command), Oracle attempts to shrink to the **OPTIMAL** value. Use the **SHRINK TO** clause to shrink the rollback segment to a particular size.

Private rollback segments will only be brought online when the database is started if they are listed in the parameter file, like this:

```
ROLLBACK_SEGMENTS = (R01, R02, R03, R04, R05)
```

Once a rollback segment is online, you can take it offline with the **ALTER ROLLBACK SEGMENT OFFLINE** command. When a rollback segment is taken offline, all the extents allocated to the rollback remain part of the rollback segment. Rollback segments that are offline cannot be shrunk back to their optimal size until they are brought back online.

To defragment or move a rollback segment, simply drop and recreate it. Make sure the rollback segment is offline before you attempt to drop it. See the "Monitoring Rollback Segments" section of this chapter to see how to view the status of rollback segments and what each status is. To drop a rollback segment (and thus free up the space it is using), you must have the **DROP ROLLBACK SEGMENT** system privilege.

Use the **DROP ROLLBACK SEGMENT** command as in the following example:

```
DROP ROLLBACK SEGMENT R05;
```

> Remember to edit the **ROLLBACK_SEGMENTS** parameter in the initialization file and remove any rollback segments that were dropped or you will get errors the next time the instance is started. Also remember the **SYSTEM** rollback segment cannot be dropped.

Space Usage Within Rollback Segments

When a transaction starts, Oracle makes a rollback segment entry in a rollback segment. A rollback entry can expand only within the rollback segment in which it is started. Only one transaction can exist per block in a rollback segment. A rollback segment extent is made up of many blocks and can therefore have more than one transaction associated with it.

When a transaction can no longer acquire space in its current extent, the rollback segment looks for another extent to begin writing the rollback entry information. If no more extents are available, the transaction extends into the first extent of the rollback segment. If that is still in use, the rollback segment tries to extend into a new extent.

When a transaction is complete, its data is not deleted from the rollback segment. It remains there to service the queries and transactions that began executing before it was committed. Even though the data is not deleted, it can be overwritten by an active transaction and cause the all too familiar error:

```
ORA-1555: snapshot too old (rollback segment too small)
```

Causes Of And Solutions For The "Snapshot Too Old" Error

A "snapshot too old" error happens when the database cannot create a read-consistent image of the data when a query is executing. The three common causes for the "snapshot too old" error are:

- Long running queries running simultaneously with updates to the same data.
- Inserts below the table's high watermark (HWM) while a query is running.
- Fetching across commits.

Oracle tries to keep a read-consistent view of the database at the start of a query. When blocks that have been updated since the start of a query are read, the rollback segments are used to create a view of the data, as it was when the query started. The problem arises when the updates are committed and the rollback segment is released and available for reuse. If this rollback segment is overwritten before a long running query tries to use it to construct a read-consistent view of the data, the query will receive the "snapshot too old" error because the rollback segment no longer has the information necessary to maintain a read-consistent view.

It may seem strange but inserts can cause the "snapshot too old" error as well. To understand this you must first know what a table's HWM is and how Oracle performs a full table scan. A table's HWM is the point between used and unused space in a table's segment. As a block is used, the HWM is moved to the next unused block in the segment. Even if all the rows in a table are deleted, the HWM continues to point to the unused block beyond the last block used. When a query performs a full table scan, Oracle always reads to where the HWM was when the query began. The "snapshot too old" problem arises when there are blocks on the free list below the HWM. When new rows are inserted into these blocks after a full table scan is initiated, the rollback segments are used to create a read-consistent view as these blocks are scanned. As the inserts are committed and rollback segments are reused, the same problem occurs as with updates and long running queries.

When a procedural language like PL/SQL or C++ is used, programmers can cause the "snapshot too old" error by fetching across commits. *Fetching across commits* refers to when a program opens a cursor and continues to read, update, and commit the same set of data in some sort of looping operation without closing the cursor. Oracle will try to maintain a read-consistent view of the data from the time the cursor was opened. Because the updates inside the cursor are being committed and the program is refetching the data without closing the cursor, the rollback information needed to maintain a consistent view could be overwritten causing the "snapshot too old" error. Even though this programming technique is not supported by the ANSI standard, Oracle allows it because the performance of a program can be greatly improved due to the overhead of continuously opening and closing cursors. When programmers use this technique, they must understand the ramifications of the "snapshot too old" error.

You can use the following guidelines to try and avoid the "snapshot too old" error:

- Do not run long running queries and updates on the same tables at the same time.
- Create larger rollback segments.
- Add more rollback segments.
- Commit less often.
- Tune long running queries to run faster.
- Use snapshots to perform queries against a read-only snapshot of the original table and updates against the original table.
- Do not use the **DELETE** command to remove all the rows from a table; instead, use the **TRUNCATE** command. The **TRUNCATE** command will move the HWM based on the **MINEXTENTS** value for the table if the **DROP STORAGE** option is used.
- If you have a program fetching across commits, rewrite the program so it does not fetch across commits or add an **ORDER BY 1** statement to the query. A temporary segment is created to hold the results of the order by clause and does not require a consistent read.

Monitoring Rollback Segments

You can use data dictionary views or the Oracle Enterprise Manager (OEM) to monitor rollback segments. How to use the data dictionary views to monitor rollback segments is explained here because not all sites use OEM.

The **DBA_ROLLBACK_SEGS** data dictionary view stores the rollback segment name, tablespace name, and other storage information about the rollback segment. For example, if you wanted to find out the status of each rollback segment and the value of **MIN_EXTENTS**, you might use the following query:

```
SELECT segment_name, tablespace_name, status, min_extents
       FROM sys.dba_rollback_segs;

SEGMENT_NAME  TABLESPACE_NAME  STATUS      MIN_EXTENTS
------------  ---------------  ------      -----------
SYSTEM        SYSTEM           ONLINE                2
R01           RBS              ONLINE                2
```

```
R02            RBS           OFFLINE            2
R03            RBS           ONLINE             2
R04            RBS           ONLINE             2
```

The **STATUS** field can have the following values:

- **AVAILABLE**—The rollback segment has been created, but has not been brought online.
- **INVALID**—The rollback segment has been dropped.
- **NEEDS RECOVERY**—The rollback segment contains data that cannot be rolled back or is corrupted.
- **OFFLINE**—The rollback segment has not been brought online by an instance.
- **ONLINE**—The rollback segment has been brought online by an instance.
- **PARTLY AVAILABLE**—The rollback segment contains data from an unresolved transaction involving a distributed database.

In addition, the **USER_SEGMENTS** and **DBA_SEGMENTS** data dictionary views contain information about all segments of a database. To retrieve information about rollback segments, issue a select where the **SEGMENT_TYPE** column is equal to '**ROLLBACK**'. Although much of the information in these views is the same as in the **DBA_ROLLBACK_SEGS** view, you cannot use the **DBA_ROLLBACK_SEGS** view to find the size of a segment as in the following query:

```
SELECT segment_name, tablespace_name, bytes, blocks, extents
        FROM sys.dba_segments
   WHERE segment_type = 'ROLLBACK';

SEGMENT_NAME TABLESPACE_NAME BYTES   BLOCKS EXTENTS
------------ --------------- ------- ------ -------
SYSTEM       SYSTEM           409600     50       5
R0           SYSTEM            65536      8       2
R01          RBS01           8519680   1040      20
R02          RBS01           8519680   1040      20
R03          RBS01           8519680   1040      20
R04          RBS01           8519680   1040      20
R05          RBS01           8519680   1040      20
R06          RBS01           8519680   1040      20
R07          RBS01           8519680   1040      20
R08          RBS01           8519680   1040      20
```

When you take a rollback segment offline, it goes offline only if all active transactions in it have completed. You cannot tell a rollback segment is waiting for transactions to complete before it goes offline by looking at the **DBA_ROLLBACK_SEGS** view. This view does not have a pending offline status. You must join the **V$ROLLNAME** and **V$ROLLSTAT** views to find rollback segments that are waiting to go offline. By joining these views on the rollback segment number (USN), you can find the rollback segment name from **V$ROLLNAME** and the status and number of active transactions from **V$ROLLSTAT**. The following query joins these views and selects where the **STATUS** column is equal to **'PENDING OFFLINE'** so only rollback segments waiting to go offline will be reported:

```
SELECT name, xacts 'ACTIVE TRANSACTIONS'
      FROM v$rollname, v$rollstat
WHERE status = 'PENDING OFFLINE'
      AND v$rollname.usn = v$rollstat.usn;

NAME         ACTIVE TRANSACTIONS
----        --------------------
R02                            3
```

Sizing Rollback Segments

Rollback segments should be sized according to the needs of an average transaction with the goal of using only a single extent. An average transaction can vary greatly depending on the use of the database. Online transaction processing (OLTP) systems tend to execute short transactions requiring many small rollback segments. Data warehousing systems tend to have long-running batch operations for loading and purging data. This type of system works better with larger rollback segments. Unfortunately, many systems do not fall into either category. They have a diverse mix of short and long running transactions. The database administrator (DBA) must study the way a database is used and set up rollback segments accordingly.

One common scenario is a database that has short transactions during the day and long-running batch transactions at night. One strategy to overcome this issue is to create many small transactional rollback segments and a few large rollback segments. Leave the large rollback segments offline until the evening when the large batch jobs are run. At that time, put the large rollback segments online and take the small rollback segments offline. Once the batch jobs are done, put the small rollback segments back online and place the large rollback segments offline again.

If you mix long and short transactions at the same time, you could use one of two other strategies. First, you create small rollback segments for the short transactions and large rollback segments for the large transactions and tell programmers which rollback segments to assign to their long running transactions. The short transactions would rotate between all the available rollback segments. Second, create all your rollback segments to handle the average transaction and use the **OPTIMAL** parameter in the **CREATE ROLLBACK SEGMENT** command. This allows the rollback segments to grow for large transactions and then return to their **OPTIMAL** size the next time the rollback segment is used.

> *Note: Rollback segments do not automatically return to their* **OPTIMAL** *size when the transaction is finished. They will shrink back to their* **OPTIMAL** *size the next time they are accessed after they have expanded.*

Rollback segments should be created so that all extents are the same size with **MINEXTENTS** of 10 to 20. Because all extents are the same size, it should be easy to calculate the maximum number of extents that fit in the rollback segments tablespace. It is not a good idea to set the rollback tablespace to autoextend and the rollback segment's **MAXEXTENTS** to **UNLIMITED**. This could allow a buggy program to use up all available disk space and then fragment or, even worse, run the **SYSTEM** tablespace out of space trying to track all the extents being allocated.

Assigning Transactions To Rollback Segments

To assign a transaction to a rollback segment, the **SET TRANSACTION USE ROLLBACK SEGMENT** statement must be the first statement of the transaction. For example, during a nightly batch run you could assign the transaction to a large rollback segment by issuing the following command:

```
SET TRANSACTION USE ROLLBACK SEGMENT big_rbs1;
```

When the transaction is committed, the large rollback segment is released and the **SET TRANSACTION** command must be used again for each transaction that requires the large rollback segment.

Managing Temporary Segments

In this section, I present the commands that assign temporary tablespaces to users and to make or change a tablespace to hold temporary segments only. Also, you'll see how the data dictionary views are used to monitor temporary segments. For discussion of temporary segments and their allocation, see Chapter 10.

Assigning Users To Temporary Tablespaces

Every user has a temporary tablespace specified for temporary segments when the account is created via the **CREATE USER** or **ALTER USER** commands. If a user is created without specifying the temporary tablespace, the **SYSTEM** tablespace will be used for that user's temporary segments. You should never let users point to the **SYSTEM** tablespace for temporary segments, because this fragments the **SYSTEM** tablespace and possibly fills up all available space with temporary segments. To create a new user with a temporary tablespace, use the following command:

```
CREATE USER jdoe IDENTIFIED BY blue
DEFAULT TABLESPACE USERS
TEMPORARY TABLESPACE temp;
```

To alter an existing user's temporary tablespace, use the following command:

```
ALTER USER jdoe TEMPORARY TABLESPACE temp2;
```

Using Temporary Tablespaces

Although you can let users use any tablespace for temporary segments, it is recommended that you set up dedicated tablespaces for Oracle to use when creating temporary segments. Unlike permanent tablespaces, which can hold any type of segment, temporary tablespaces can hold temporary segments only. To dedicate a tablespace for temporary segments, specify the **TEMPORARY** clause of the **CREATE TABLESPACE** command, as shown in the following example:

```
CREATE TABLESPACE temp
    DATAFILE '/u51/oradata/MYDB/temp01.dbf'
    SIZE 1024000K AUTOEXTEND OFF
    LOGGING
    DEFAULT STORAGE(INITIAL 10M
                    NEXT 10M
                    MINEXTENTS 1
                    MAXEXTENTS UNLIMITED
                    PCTINCREASE 0)
    ONLINE
    TEMPORARY;
```

Or, you can use the **ALTER TABLESPACE** command, as shown in the following example:

```
ALTER TABLESPACE temp TEMPORARY;
```

In the previous **ALTER TABLESPACE** command, the statement would fail if the TEMP tablespace contained any tables or indexes. Temporary segments use the default storage parameters for the tablespace. Because temporary tablespaces are fragmented naturally, it is advantageous to maximize the reuse of extents. To do this, make the **INITIAL** and **NEXT** extent sizes equal and set **PCTINCREASE** equal to 0. The **INITIAL** and **NEXT** parameters should be a multiple of **SORT_AREA_SIZE**, which should be a multiple of **DB_BLOCK_SIZE** as well. This makes all the extents in the temporary tablespace the exact same size. When the sort segments are dropped, the next temporary segment will be able to just reuse the dropped extents without having to do any space management.

To make a temporary tablespace permanent, use the **ALTER TABLESPACE** command as follows:

```
ALTER TABLESPACE temp PERMANENT;
```

You can determine if a tablespace is permanent or temporary by selecting from the **DBA_TABLESPACES** data dictionary view with the following query:

```
SELECT tablespace_name, contents FROM dba_tablespaces;

TABLESPACE_NAME                  CONTENTS
---------------                  ---------
SYSTEM                           PERMANENT
RBS01                            PERMANENT
TEMP                             TEMPORARY
TOOLS                            PERMANENT
USERS                            PERMANENT
REPSYS                           PERMANENT
```

Monitoring Temporary Segments

You can use the **V$SORT_SEGMENT**, **V$SORT_USAGE**, and **V$SESSION** data dictionary views to monitor temporary segments. The **V$SORT_SEGMENT** view shown in Table 11.1 displays aggregated sort extent information for an instance. Table 11.2 shows individual sort information by session.

V$SESSION and **V$SORT_USAGE** can be joined to determine the number of extents being used by an active sort with the following query:

```
SELECT username, tablespace, contents, extents
FROM v$session, v$sort_usage
WHERE user = username and
 session_num = serial#
```

Table 11.1 The V$SORT_SEGMENT view contains aggregated information about all sort segments for an instance.

Column	Description
TABLESPACE_NAME	Name of tablespace
SEGMENT_FILE	File number of the first extent
SEGMENT_BLOCK	Block number of the first extent
EXTENT_SIZE	Extent size in Oracle blocks
CURRENT_USERS	Number of active users of the segment
TOTAL_EXTENTS	Total number of extents in the segment
TOTAL_BLOCKS	Total number of blocks in the segment
RELATIVE_FNO	Relative file number of the sort segment header
USED_EXTENTS	Extents allocated to active sorts
USED_BLOCKS	Blocks allocated to active sorts
FREE_EXTENTS	Extents not allocated to any sort
FREE_BLOCKS	Blocks not allocated to any sort
ADDED_EXTENTS	Number of extent allocations
EXTENT_HITS	Number of times an unused extent was found in the pool
FREED_EXTENTS	Number of deallocated extents
FREE_REQUESTS	Number of requests to deallocate
MAX_SIZE	Maximum number of extents ever used
MAX_BLOCKS	Maximum number of blocks ever used
MAX_USED_SIZE	Maximum number of extents used by all sorts
MAX_USED_BLOCKS	Maximum number of blocks used by all sorts
MAX_SORT_SIZE	Maximum number of extents used by an individual sort
MAX_SORT_BLOCKS	Maximum number of blocks used by an individual sort

Table 11.2 The V$SORT_USAGE view describes sort usage by session.

Column	Description
USER	User who requested temporary space
SESSION_ADDR	Address of shared SQL cursor
SESSION_NUM	Serial number of session
SQLADDR	Address of SQL statement
SQLHASH	Hash value of SQL statement
TABLESPACE	Tablespace in which space is allocated
CONTENTS	Indication of tablespace as **TEMPORARY** or **PERMANENT**
SEGFILE#	File number of initial extent
SEGBLK#	Block number of the initial extent
EXTENTS	Extents allocated to the sort
BLOCKS	Blocks allocated to the sort
SEGRFNO#	Relative file number of initial extent

Practice Questions

Question 1

In which tablespace will the R01 rollback segment be created?

```
CREATE ROLLBACK SEGMENT R01
 STORAGE (INITIAL 200K NEXT 200K OPTIMAL 2M
     MINEXTENTS 20 MAXEXTENTS 100);
```

- ❍ a. RBS
- ❍ b. TEMP
- ❍ c. DATA
- ❍ d. INDEX
- ◉ e. **SYSTEM**

Trick! question

Answer e is correct. In a **CREATE ROLLBACK SEGMENT** command, the tablespace clause is optional. If it is not included, the rollback segment will be created in the **SYSTEM** tablespace. This is a trick question, because all other objects would be created in the user's default tablespace. Answers a, b, c, and d are incorrect because they are not mandatory tablespace names.

Question 2

How would you find out if a rollback segment is online?

- ❍ a. Query the **DBA_OBJECTS** data dictionary view.
- ❍ b. Query the **DBA_SEGMENTS** data dictionary view.
- ❍ c. Query the **DBA_TABLESPACES** data dictionary view.
- ◉ d. Query the **DBA_ROLLBACK_SEGS** data dictionary view.

Answer d is correct. The **DBA_ROLLBACK_SEGS** view shows the status of all rollback segments for an instance. The **DBA_OBJECTS** view lists information about database objects, but it does not contain any information on rollback segments. The **DBA_SEGMENTS** view shows storage information on all segments including rollback segments; however, it does not include status information. The **DBA_TABLESPACES** view contains the status of tablespaces, but not the status of rollback segments.

Question 3

If an instance fails, which type of segment is used to recover uncommitted transactions?

- ❍ a. Table
- ❍ b. Index
- ❍ c. Rollback
- ❍ d. Temporary

Answer c is correct. Transaction recovery occurs after an instance failure. All uncommitted transactions are rolled back using the redo log files and the before images stored in rollback segments. Table is a data segment and is not used in recovery. Index is an index segment and is not used in recovery either. Temporary segments are used for sorting, not for recovery.

Question 4

During a long running transaction, you receive an error stating that insufficient space exists in the R04 rollback segment. The error leads you to believe the storage parameters for the rollback segment should be changed. Which storage parameter would you increase to solve this problem?

- ❍ a. **NEXT**
- ❍ b. **INITIAL**
- ❍ c. **OPTIMAL**
- ❍ d. **MAXENTENTS**
- ❍ e. **MINEXTENTS**

Answer d is correct. Increase the **MAXEXTENTS** value. The long running transaction has reached the **MAXEXTENTS** value for the rollback segment. Increasing this value will allow the rollback segment to acquire more extents. The **NEXT** parameter only controls the size of the extent after the initial extent. **INITIAL** is the first extent for a database object. **OPTIMAL** is the size rollback segments shrink to. **MINEXTENTS** specifies the minimum extents that will be created with the database object.

Question 5

Which dynamic performance views would you join to display the current size of the R03 rollback segment? [Choose two]

- ❑ a. **V$SESSION**
- ❑ b. **V$ROLLNAME**
- ❑ c. **V$ROLLSTAT**
- ❑ d. **V$PARAMETER**
- ❑ e. **V$DATAFILE**
- ❑ f. **V$TRANSACTION**
- ❑ g. **V$DATAFILE_HEADER**

Answers b and c are correct. **V$ROLLNAME** displays the name and USN of each rollback segment. **V$ROLLSTAT** displays the USN, status, optimal size, current size, HWM, and the current and active extent of each rollback segment. Answers a, d, e, f, and g do not show any rollback size information.

Question 6

What size should **INITIAL** and **NEXT** be when defining **DEFAULT STORAGE** for a temporary tablespace?

- ❍ a. The same as **PCTFREE** and **PCTUSED**, respectively
- ❍ b. **OPTIMAL** *(multiple of **SORT_AREA_SIZE**)
- ❍ c. **MAXEXTENTS** *(**DB_BLOCK_SIZE / PCTINCREASE**)
- ❍ d. multiple of **SORT_AREA_SIZE**

Answer d is correct. For the temporary tablespace, **INITIAL** and **NEXT** should be equal to each other and a multiple of **SORT_AREA_SIZE**. **PCTFREE** and **PCTUSED** are block-level storage parameters. **OPTIMAL** is a rollback parameter. **DB_BLOCK_SIZE** divided by **PCTINCREASE** does not make sense because there is no relationship between them.

Question 7

Why would a temporary segment be created in a permanent tablespace?

- ❍ a. A user issues a statement that requires sort space and specifies a permanent tablespace in the query.
- ❍ b. A user issues more than one statement requiring sort space filling up his or her primary temporary tablespace.
- ❍ c. A user assigned a permanent tablespace for creating database objects issues a query with a **GROUP BY** clause.
- ❍ d. A user assigned a permanent tablespace for sorting executes a statement that can't be sorted in memory and requires additional sort space.

Answer d is correct. Temporary segments will be created in whatever temporary tablespace the user requesting the temporary segment is assigned. You can't specify temporary sorting area in SQL. Users only have one temporary tablespace, thus there is no secondary area. The **GROUP BY** clause has no impact on where temporary segments are created.

Question 8

When extents are allocated to a temporary segment in a temporary tablespace, which default storage parameter determines the size of the additional extents allocated?

- ❍ a. **NEXT**
- ❍ b. **INITIAL**
- ❍ c. **MAXEXTENTS**
- ❍ d. **PCTINCREASE**

Answer a is correct. Temporary segments are based on the default storage parameters of the tablespace. Consequently, the **NEXT** storage parameter controls the size of the first extent after the initial extent. **INITIAL** controls the size of the first extent. **MAXEXTENTS** controls the number of possible extents. **PCTINCREASE** controls the growth of all extents after the **NEXT** extent.

Question 9

Why does the Oracle server create temporary segments?

- ◉ a. Sorting needs cannot be performed in memory.
- ❍ b. To allow updates to be written temporarily.
- ❍ c. To store data when users fill up their default tablespace.
- ❍ d. A user requests additional sorting space to speed up a transaction.

Answer a is correct. The Oracle server creates temporary segments when sorting cannot be done in memory. Updates are not written in temporary segments. Temporary tablespaces do not store data. Temporary segments are allocated by Oracle and are not requested in queries.

Need To Know More?

Ault, Mike: *Oracle8 Administration and Management*, John Wiley & Sons, Inc., New York, NY, 1998. ISBN 0-471-19234-1. An easy-to-understand book that explains how to set up Oracle for optimal performance.

Loney, Kevin, and Marlene Theriault: *Oracle8 DBA Handbook*, Oracle Press, Berkeley, CA, 1997. ISBN 0-07882-406-0. See Chapter 4, "Physical Database Layouts."

See the Oracle documentation that is provided on CD with the Oracle RDBMS software. Pertaining to this chapter are:

Fee, Joyce: *Oracle8 Administrator's Guide*, Oracle Corporation, Redwood City, CA, 1997. See Chapter 18, "Managing Rollback Segments."

Lane, Paul: *Oracle8 Reference Manual*, Oracle Corporation, Redwood City, CA, 1997. See Chapter 2, "Static Data Dictionary Views."

Leverenz, Lefty: *Oracle8 Concepts Guide*, Oracle Corporation, Redwood City, CA, 1997. See Chapter 2, "Data Blocks, Extents, and Segments."

http://education.oracle.com/tbt/ocp8.html is the site from which you can order the Oracle Education CD-ROM bundle for Oracle8 Database Administration.

www.revealnet.com is the site where RevealNet Corporation provides Oracle Administration reference software.

12

Managing Tables And Indexes

Terms you'll need to understand:

- √ **CHAR** datatype
- √ **VARCHAR2** datatype
- √ **LONG** datatype
- √ **NUMBER** datatype
- √ **DATE** datatype
- √ **BLOB** datatype
- √ **CLOB** and **NCLOB** datatypes
- √ **BFILE** datatype
- √ **RAW** and **LONG RAW** datatypes
- √ **ROWID** datatype
- √ Composite (concatenated) index
- √ Reverse key indexes
- √ Bitmap index

Techniques you'll need to master:

- √ Using the **CREATE TABLE** command
- √ Using the **ALTER TABLE** command
- √ Using the **DROP TABLE** command
- √ Using the **TRUNCATE TABLE** command
- √ Using the **ANALYZE** command
- √ Viewing table and index statistics
- √ Validating tables, indexes, and clusters
- √ Showing chained rows
- √ Using the **CREATE INDEX** command
- √ Creating indexes via the **CONSTRAINT** clause
- √ Using the **ALTER INDEX** command
- √ Using the **DROP INDEX** command

Some Information Systems shops separate the database tasks into *System Database Administrator (DBA)* tasks and *Application DBA* tasks. Managing both tables and indexes falls under the domain of the Application DBA, whereas installation, database creation, and backup and recovery fall under the domain of the System DBA. In either case, all DBAs need to know and understand how to manage tables and indexes. Even System DBAs install tools that create tables and indexes that need management.

Managing Tables

A little bit of planning when you are creating tables can save a lot of grief down the road. Today's graphical user interface (GUI) tools make it very easy to just start creating tables with very little forethought. Even though this might sound more like a development issue, you must remember that the most difficult problems to correct are design problems. So, take your time and look once more.

Normalization

It is always a good idea to check the basic database design. In online transaction processing (OLTP) and most other types of database systems, the tables are often normalized into *third normal form*. That is to say, if an attribute or attributes do not contribute to a description of the key, move them to a separate table. If the tables are not in third normal form, they will have repeating groups of data or redundant data within them. All rules have exceptions, and many exist here. Data warehouses use a different method of organizing tables for analysis and query performance called a *star schema design*. Even this design has a variation called the *snowflake design*. Rather than get into a full discussion on design methodologies, let's just say that whatever design rules you are supposed to be following, make sure that the new tables follow those rules.

Datatypes

Make sure that each table attribute is of the proper datatype. Misdatatyping columns in a table can cause programming problems due to the different comparison rules used with each datatype and datatype conversion.

CHAR Datatype

The **CHAR** datatype stores fixed-length character strings. A column in a table defined as **CHAR** can hold up to 2,000 characters. Columns defined as **CHAR** are blank and padded to the full length of the column. For example, if a column is defined as **CHAR(25)** and you insert the word PAUL, the column will hold 25 characters, and 21 of them will be blank.

VARCHAR2 Datatype

The **VARCHAR2** datatype stores variable-length character strings. Columns defined as **VARCHAR2** can hold up to 4,000 characters of information. Because a benefit is rarely derived in defining columns as **CHAR**, you should almost always use **VARCHAR2**. The few exceptions to this occur when you need to interface with legacy systems that are using fixed-length fields and you want to stay consistent. **VARCHAR2** and **VARCHAR** are functionally synonymous.

LONG Datatype

The **LONG** datatype is a character datatype that stores variable-length character data. A column in a table defined as **LONG** can hold up to 2GB. The **LONG** datatype is maintained for backward compatibility. In new applications, you should use the new character datatypes **CLOB** and **NCLOB**.

NUMBER Datatype

The **NUMBER** datatype is a numeric datatype that stores both fixed and floating-point numbers. Oracle can store numbers up to 38 digits of precision. Because Oracle stores and interprets numbers the same way on all systems, numbers in Oracle are completely portable between any two Oracle databases, no matter what platform they are running on.

You can specify numeric columns in the following ways:

```
column_name NUMBER (any valid number)
column_name NUMBER (precision, scale)
column_name NUMBER (*, scale)
```

The *precision* is the total number of digits, and the *scale* is the number of digits to the right of the decimal point. An asterisk (*) in place of the precision automatically has a precision of 38.

DATE Datatype

The **DATE** datatype combines date and time into one datatype. It always stores a four-digit year with the month, day, hours, minutes, and seconds. Oracle's **DATE** datatype can easily be used in date arithmetic with functions like **ADD_MONTHS** and **MONTHS_BETWEEN**. You can also add or subtract days from an Oracle date by just using integers. For example, to set the date in a column to a week from now, you would simply use **SYSDATE+7**.

BLOB Datatype

The **BLOB** datatype is a binary datatype that stores variable-length binary data. A column defined as **BLOB** can hold up to 4GB of binary data.

CLOB And **NCLOB** Datatypes

The **CLOB** and **NCLOB** datatypes are character datatypes that store fixed-length character data. A column defined as **CLOB** or **NCLOB** can hold up to 4GB of character data. The "N" in **NCLOB** stands for *national character set*. Use the **NCLOB** if your database is being used to store data with a multibyte national character set.

BFILE Datatype

The **BFILE** datatype is a binary datatype that stores binary data in an operating system (OS) file outside the database. A **BFILE** column stores a pointer to the OS file and can store up to 4GB of binary data, providing the OS file size limitation is at least 4GB.

RAW And **LONG RAW** Datatypes

The **RAW** and **LONG RAW** datatypes are binary datatypes. A column defined as **RAW** stores binary data in whatever form the host computer stores it. **RAW** columns can store up to 4,000 characters of data. A column defined as **LONG RAW** stores raw binary data and has a storage limit of 2GB. These datatypes are maintained for backward compatibility. New applications should use the **BLOB** and **BFILE** datatypes.

ROWID Datatype

The **ROWID** datatype is a special datatype used by Oracle in every table or object. The **ROWID** is a hidden column automatically maintained by Oracle, which stores the row address. In Oracle8, objects have been introduced that cause a change in the **ROWID** format. The new extended **ROWID** format is 10 bytes long, versus the 6 bytes used in Oracle7. The extended **ROWID** is displayed as a **VARCHAR2** representing a base-64 number. Here's an example of what a **ROWID** means using AAAGfOAAaAAAAReAAO:

- AAAGfO is the data object number.
- AAa is the relative file number.
- AAAARe is the block number.
- AAO is the row in the block.

The **DBMS_ROWID** package is provided by Oracle to facilitate working with the **ROWID** datatype. The functions in this package let you get all the information you need about any **ROWID**. The **DBMS_ROWID** package is created by the dbmsutil.sql script, which is automatically run by the catproc.sql script when you create a database. Table 12.1 shows a summary of the **DBMS_ROWID** functions.

Table 12.1 DBMS_ROWID functions.

Function Name	Description
ROWID_BLOCK_NUMBER	Returns the block number of a **ROWID**.
ROWID_CREATE	Creates a **ROWID** for testing only.
ROWID_INFO	Returns the type and components of a **ROWID**.
ROWID_OBJECT	Returns the object number of the extended **ROWID**.
ROWID_RELATIVE_FNO	Returns the file number of a **ROWID**.
ROWID_ROW_NUMBER	Returns the row number.
ROWID_TO_ABSOLUTE_FNO	Returns the absolute file number associated with the **ROWID** for a row in a specific table.
ROWID_TO_EXTENDED	Converts a **ROWID** from restricted to extended format.
ROWID_TO_RESTRICTED	Converts an extended **ROWID** to restricted format.
ROWID_TYPE	Returns the **ROWID** type. 0 is restricted; 1 is extended.
ROWID_VERIFY	Checks if a **ROWID** can be correctly extended by the **ROWID_TO_EXTENDED** function.

Storage And Location Information

Make sure you know the storage requirements of the tables. For example, how many rows will be in the table initially? By what percentage will the table grow per week, per month, and per year? What will be the average row size, and will rows expand much after they are initially loaded? After you have your table size and growth information, you can properly set the PCTFREE and PCTUSED parameters to maximize space utilization within the data blocks. (See Chapter 10 for more information about PCTFREE and PCTUSED.) Sometimes, this information is difficult to get, but it can save major database reorganizations and improve performance.

Table Location

Table location can have a dramatic effect on database performance and administration. If an application's tables are stored in various tablespaces mixed in with many other application tables, backup and recovery can become more complex. Tables should be placed in a manner that reduces input/output (I/O) contention. One common strategy is to put tables and indexes in different tablespaces on different drives. Nothing is inherently wrong with having data and index segments on the same drive; this is just an organizational way of spreading I/O to multiple drives. Tables that relate closely and are frequently joined also benefit from being in different tablespaces on different disks. Make sure that the tablespaces where you have large tables can expand for future growth. Also, make sure that you have enough temporary space for creating indexes and doing sorts on your large tables.

Creating Tables

Normally, when creating tables in production for application systems, the DBA runs the data definition language (**DDL**) that creates all the application objects, including tables. The DBA is responsible for optimizing performance of the database and will make adjustments to the storage and location of tables for these purposes.

To create a table in your own schema, you must have the **CREATE TABLE** system privilege. DBAs normally create tables in other users' schemas. For you to do so, you must have the **CREATE ANY TABLE** system privilege. In order to use types in a table, you must be granted the **EXECUTE** privilege on any types used in the table or have the **EXECUTE ANY TYPE** system privilege. The following is an example of the relational **CREATE TABLE** command:

```
CREATE TABLE sign
(   SIGN_ID             NUMBER(9)     NOT NULL,
    INSTALLATION_DATE   DATE DEFAULT SYSDATE,
    DEACTIVATION_DATE   DATE                ,
    ORG_UNIT_CODE       VARCHAR2(3)         ,
    BUILDING            VARCHAR2(20)        ,
    MAS_NAME            VARCHAR2(20)        ,
    MAS_RADIO_CALL_NO   VARCHAR2(4)         ,
    PROJECT_CODE        VARCHAR2(13)        NOT NULL,
    LOCATION_ID      NUMBER(9)              NULL,
    CONSTRAINT I0001153 PRIMARY KEY (SIGN_ID)
        USING INDEX PCTFREE 10
                    INITRANS 2
                    MAXTRANS 255
                    TABLESPACE TMSINDEX01
                    STORAGE(INITIAL 11400K
                            NEXT 5680K
                            MINEXTENTS 1
                            MAXEXTENTS 505
                            PCTINCREASE 50)
)
TABLESPACE TMSDATA05
```

```
LOGGING
PCTFREE 2
PCTUSED 75
INITRANS 1
MAXTRANS 255
STORAGE(INITIAL 65280K
        NEXT 17280K
        MINEXTENTS 1
        MAXEXTENTS 505
        PCTINCREASE 50
        FREELISTS 1
        FREELIST GROUPS 1
        BUFFER_POOL DEFAULT)
NOPARALLEL
NOCACHE;
```

Figure 12.1 shows the syntax for creating a standard relational table. Figure 12.2 shows the syntax for creating a table of type object. This list describes the keywords and parameters used in the **CREATE TABLE** command:

- *schema*—Stipulates the schema in which the table will be created. In the absence of the schema, Oracle creates the table in the schema of the user executing the **CREATE TABLE** command.
- *table_name*—Designates the name of the table that is to be created.
- OF *object_type*—Explicitly creates an object table of type *object_type*. In the absence of the schema, Oracle creates the table in the schema executing the **CREATE TABLE** command.
- *column*—Designates the name of a column of the table. A table can have up to 1,000 columns.
- *datatype*—Designates a column's datatype. If the column is part of a referential integrity constraint, the datatype can be omitted. Oracle will assign the datatype of the referenced column.
- *column_constraint*—Defines an integrity constraint as part of the column definition.
- *table_constraint*—Defines an integrity constraint as part of the table definition.
- *attribute*—Designates the qualified column name of an object's item.
- DEFAULT—Designates a value to be inserted into the column if an **INSERT** statement does not provide a value.

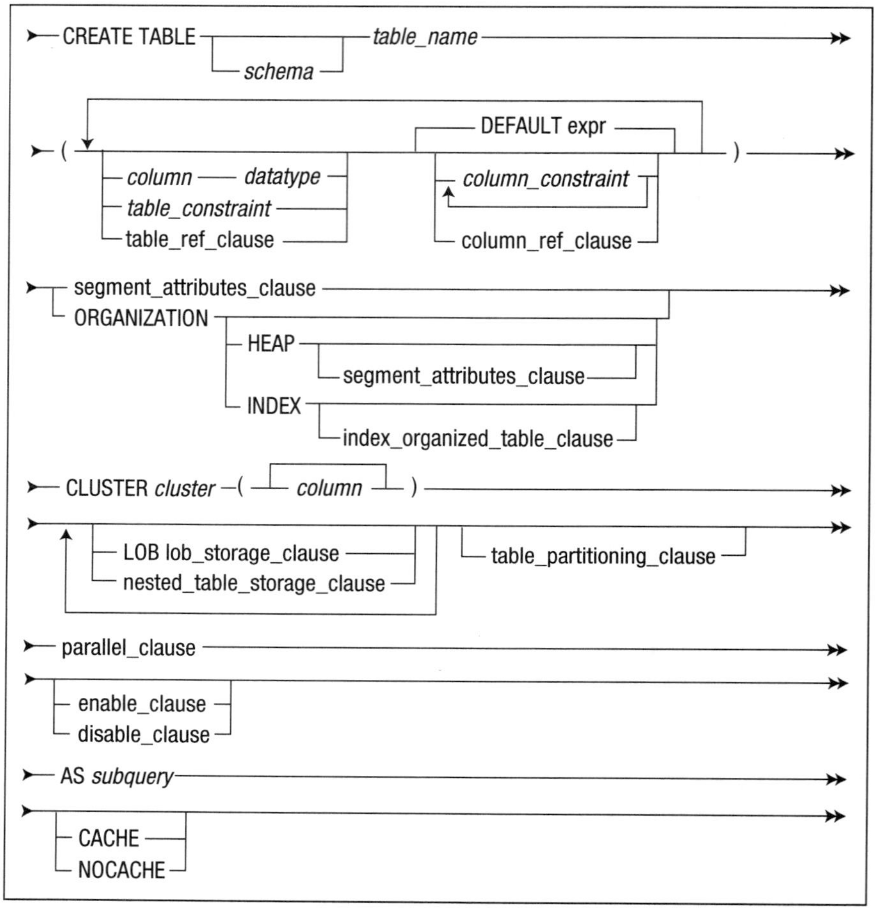

Figure 12.1 The syntax for the relational **CREATE TABLE** command.

- **ORGANIZATION HEAP**—Designates that a table's data rows are stored in no particular order. This is the default.
- **ORGANIZATION INDEX**—Designates that a table is an index-organized table, in which the data rows are held in an index defined on the table's primary key.
- **CLUSTER**—Designates that the table is to be part of the cluster. The columns listed in the **CLUSTER** clause are table columns that correspond to the cluster's columns. Object tables cannot be part of a cluster.
- **enable_clause**—Enables an integrity constraint.
- **disable_clause**—Disables an integrity constraint.

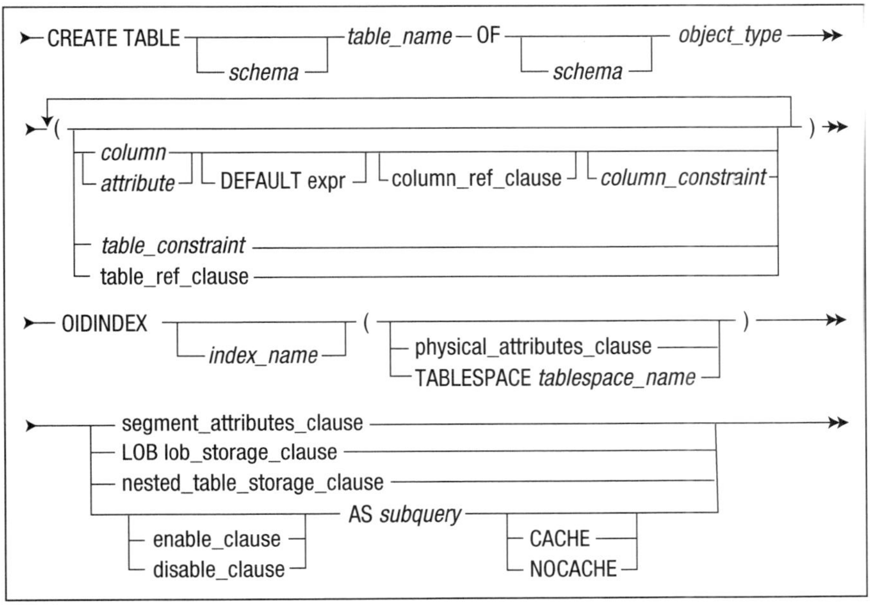

Figure 12.2 The syntax for creating a table of type object.

- AS *subquery*—Inserts the rows that the subquery returns to the table when it is created. You cannot use this option when creating an index-organized table with overflow.
    - CACHE—Stipulates that the retrieved blocks for this table are placed at the most recently used (MRU) end of the least recently used (LRU) list in the buffer cache when a full-table scan is performed. As a parameter in the **LOB** storage clause, **CACHE** specifies that Oracle preallocates and retains **LOB** data values in memory for faster access.
    - NOCACHE—Stipulates that the blocks retrieved for this table are placed at the LRU end of the LRU list in the buffer cache when a full-table scan is performed. This is the default.
- OIDINDEX—Designates an index on the hidden object identifier (OID) column and/or the index storage specification.
    - *index_name*—Indicates the name of the index in the hidden OID column. If you do not specify a name, Oracle generates one.

Various clauses are used with the **CREATE TABLE** command. The same clauses are used in the **ALTER TABLE, CREATE INDEX,** and **ALTER**

INDEX commands. The syntax for these clauses does not change, so the following clauses are explained here and referenced throughout the chapter:

- column and table reference
- parallel
- segment attribute
- physical attributes
- storage
- index-organized table
- LOB
- nested table storage
- table partition

Column And Table Reference Clauses

Figure 12.3 shows the syntax for the column and table reference clauses. The columns in the column reference clause must come from the table specified in the table reference clause. The table reference clause limits the columns in the column reference clause. The following keywords are used with the table and column reference clauses:

- **WITH ROWID**—Stores **ROWID** and **REF** value in the column. Storing a **REF** value with a **ROWID** can improve the performance of dereferencing operations, but it uses more space. The default storage for a **REF** value is without **ROWID**.
- **SCOPE IS** *scope_table_name*—Confines the scope of column **REF** values to *scope_table_name*. The column **REF** values must come from **REF** values obtained from the object table specified in the clause. You can specify only one scope table per **REF** column. The *scope_table_name* is the name of the object table in which object instances of the same type as the **REF** column are stored. The values in the **REF** column point to objects in the scope table.
- **SCOPE FOR** ***ref_column_name*** **IS** ***scope_table_name***—Confines the scope of **REF** values in ***ref_column*** or ***ref_attribute*** to ***scope_table_name***. The column or attribute **REF** values must come from **REF** values obtained from the object table specified in the clause. The ***ref_column*** is the name of a **REF** column in an object table or an embedded **REF** attribute within a relational table's object column. The values in the **REF** column or attribute point to objects in the scope table.

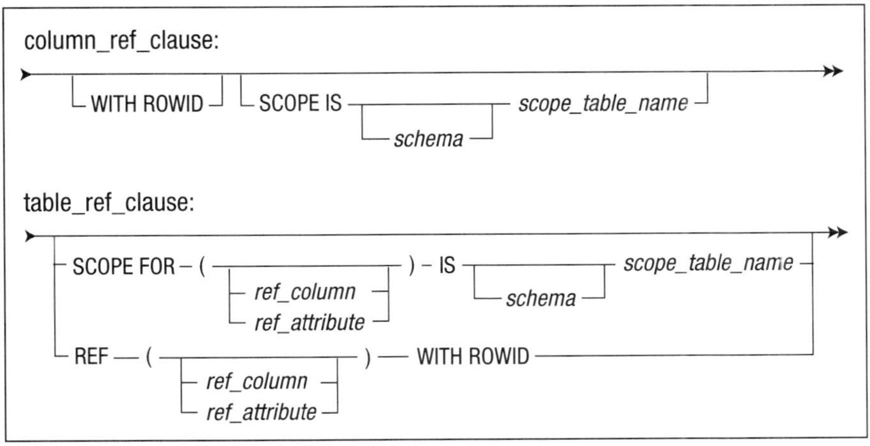

Figure 12.3 The syntax for the column and table reference clauses.

- **REF**—References a row in an object table. You can specify either an object's or relational table's **REF** column name, ***ref_column***, or an embedded **REF** attribute within an object column's ***ref_attribute***.

Parallel Clause

Figure 12.4 shows the syntax for the parallel clause. When you use the parallel clause to create tables, the database will try to use a parallel query when accessing the tables. The parallel clause can be used to create indexes in parallel, which greatly reduces the time it takes to build indexes. The parallel clause specifies the degree of parallelism for creating the table and the default degree of parallelism for queries on the table.

Segment Attribute Clause

The segment attribute clause contains the physical attributes clause as well as the tablespace name the table will be created in and the logging status of the table. Figure 12.5 shows the syntax for this clause. The following list describes the keywords and parameters used in the segment attribute clause:

- **TABLESPACE**—Designates the tablespace in which the table, object table **OIDINDEX**, partition, **LOB** storage, **LOB** index segment, or

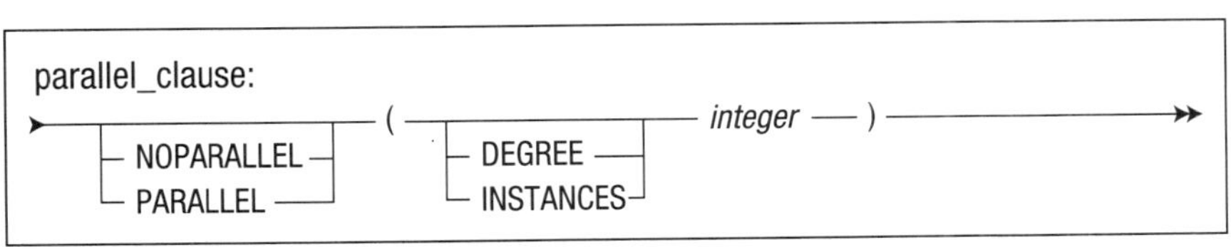

Figure 12.4 The syntax for the parallel clause.

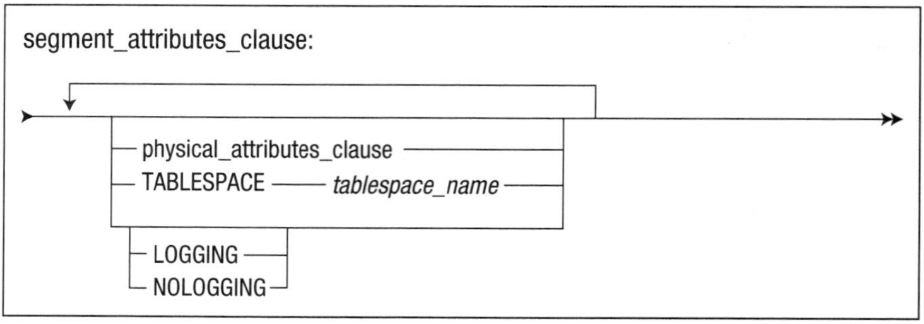

Figure 12.5 The syntax for the segment attribute clause.

index-organized table overflow data segment are created. In the absence of this option, Oracle creates the item in the default tablespace of the owner of the schema that contains the table.

- LOGGING/NOLOGGING—Stipulates whether the creation of the table and any indexes required because of constraint, partition, or **LOB** storage characteristics will be logged in the redo log file.

Physical Attributes Clause

Figure 12.6 shows the syntax for the physical attributes clause. These parameters control how Oracle stores data within Oracle data blocks as well as the number of concurrent transactions that can execute on the records in a data block. The keywords and parameters used in the physical attributes clause are as follows:

- PCTFREE *integer*—Stipulates how much space to leave in each Oracle block for future updates to rows of a table. The default value is 10 percent. The sum of **PCTFREE** and **PCTUSED** must be less than 100 percent.
- PCTUSED *integer*—Stipulates the minimum amount of space to reserve for inserts. The **PCTUSED** default value is 40 percent. If a block's storage falls below **PCTUSED**, it becomes a candidate for updates. The sum of **PCTFREE** and **PCTUSED** must be less than 100 percent.
- INITRANS *integer*—Specifies the initial number of active transactions that are allocated within each block. A large value reduces the amount of space available for data in a block. A change to this parameter affects only blocks added after the change.
- MAXTRANS *integer*—Stipulates the maximum number of concurrent transactions that can update a data block.
- STORAGE—Stipulates storage characteristics for the table, partition, object table **OIDINDEX**, **LOB** storage, **LOB** index segment, or index-organized table overflow data segment.

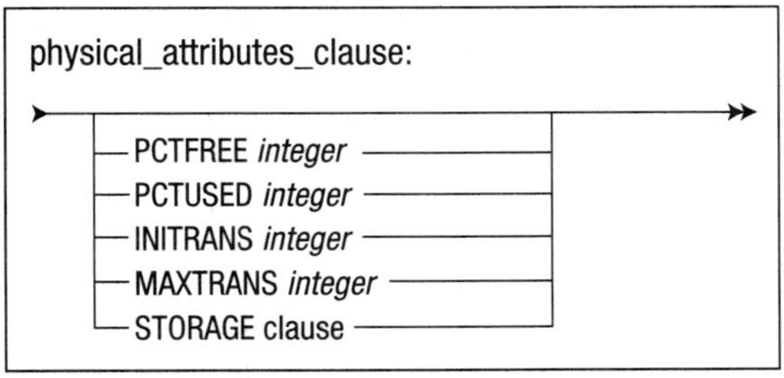

Figure 12.6 The syntax for the physical attributes clause.

Storage Clause

The storage clause specifies how extents will be allocated for tables, indexes, clusters, rollback segments, and tablespaces. Figure 12.7 shows the syntax for the storage clause. The **OPTIMAL** parameter applies only to rollback segments. The storage clause can also be used to assign tables to individual buffer caches. The keywords and parameters used in the storage clause are as follows:

- INITIAL *integer*—Specifies the size of the initial extent of the object segment. Kilobytes or megabytes are represented by "K" or "M" after the integer.
- NEXT *integer*—Specifies size for next extent after **INITIAL** is used. This value is used for each new extent if **PCTINCREASE** is set to 0.
- MINEXTENTS *integer*—Indicates the number of initial extents for the object. Generally, except for rollback segments, it is set to 1. If a large amount of space is required and not enough contiguous space is available for the table setting, using a smaller extent size and specifying several extents might solve the problem.
- MAXEXTENTS—Specifies the largest number of extents allowed for the object. The default is dependent on the Oracle block size. This can be set to an integer value or to unlimited.
- PCTINCREASE *integer*—Tells Oracle how much to grow each extent after the **INITIAL** and **NEXT** extents are used. A specification of 50 will grow each extent after **NEXT** by 50 percent for each subsequent extent. This means that for a table created with one initial and a next extent, all further extents will increase in size by 50 percent over their predecessor. A tablespace with a default storage setting for **PCTINCREASE** of 0 will not be automatically coalesced.
- FREELISTS *integer*—Designates the number of freelists for objects, other than tablespaces, for each of the freelist groups for the table, partition, index, or cluster.

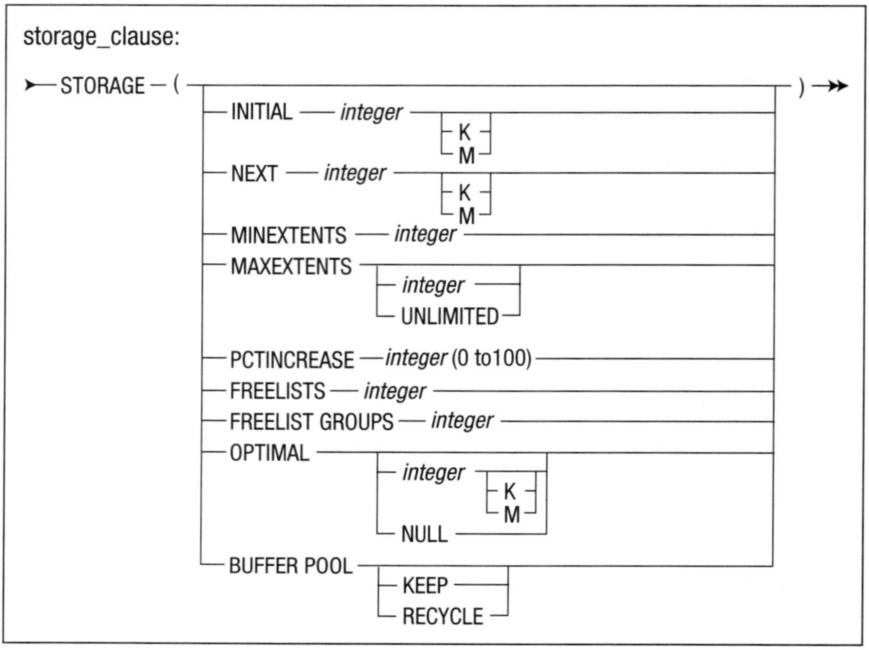

Figure 12.7 The syntax for the storage clause.

- **FREELIST GROUPS** *integer*—Stipulates the number of freelist groups to maintain for a table, partition, cluster, or index. This is used only in Parallel Server environments.
- **OPTIMAL** *integer*—Specifies the value to which a rollback segment will shrink after extending. This is used only for rollback segments.
- **BUFFER_POOL**—Allows assignment of a cache for schema objects with the exception of rollback segments. Because tablespaces are not schema objects, the **BUFFER POOL** parameter is invalid in **CREATE** and **ALTER** commands for tablespaces.
  - **KEEP**—Tries to keep all blocks of the schema object in memory.
  - **RECYCLE**—Flushes data blocks belonging to an object from the cache when they are no longer needed.

Index-Organized Table Clause

The index-organized table clause causes the table to be stored as a B-tree index. Figure 12.8 shows the syntax. This clause applies only to the **CREATE TABLE** command. The following describes the keywords and parameters used in the index-organized table clause:

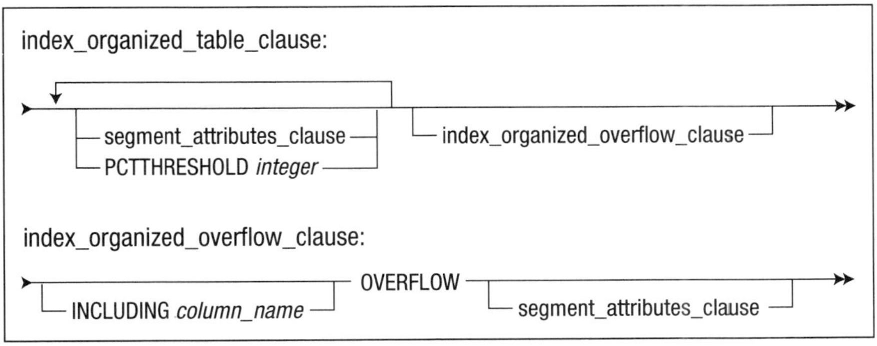

Figure 12.8 The syntax for the index-organized clauses.

- **PCTTHRESHOLD** ***integer***—Designates the percentage of space reserved in the index block for an index-organized table row. **PCTTHRESHOLD** must have a value from 0 through 50.
- **OVERFLOW**—Stipulates that index-organized table data rows exceeding the specified threshold will be placed in the data segment listed in this clause. If a clause is not specified, Oracle rejects rows exceeding the **PCTTHRESHOLD** limit.
- **INCLUDING** ***column_name***—Designates a column at which to split an index-organized table row into index and overflow portions. All columns following ***column_name*** are stored in the overflow data segment. A ***column_name*** is the name of either the last primary key column or any nonprimary key column.

LOB Clauses

The three **LOB** clauses (**lob_storage_clause**, **lob_parameters clause**, and **lob_index_clause**) specify the **LOB** storage characteristics as well as the index segment for the **LOB**. Figure 12.9 shows the syntax for the **LOB** clauses. The keywords and parameters used in the **lob_storage_clause**, **lob_parameters clause**, and the **lob_index_clause** are as follows:

- **LOB** ***lob_item***—Designates the **LOB** object attribute or **LOB** column name for which you are explicitly defining storage and tablespace characteristics different from those of the table.
- **STORE AS** ***lob_seg_name***—Designates the name of the **LOB** data segment. If you specify more than one ***lob_item***, you cannot use ***lob_seg_name***.
  - **ENABLE STORAGE IN ROW**—Stipulates that the **LOB** value is to be stored in the row if its length is less than approximately 4,000 bytes less system control information. This is the default.

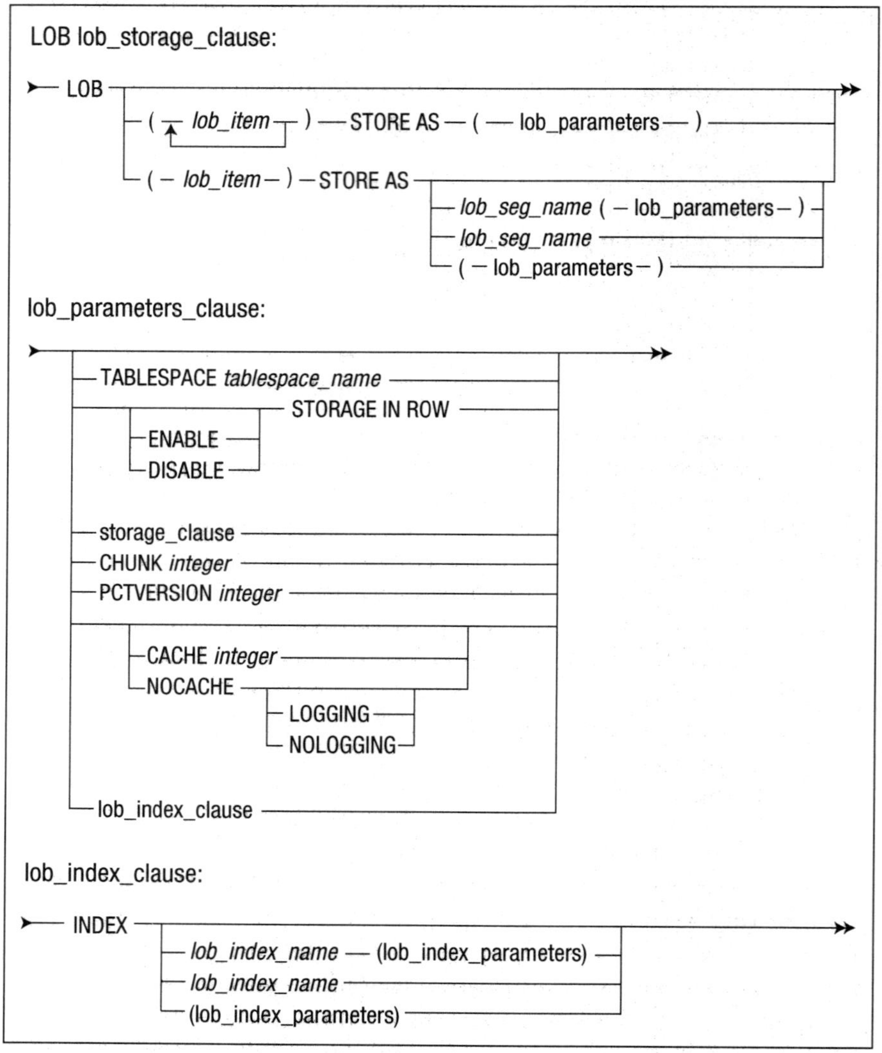

Figure 12.9 The syntax for the **LOB** clauses.

- **DISABLE STORAGE IN ROW**—Stipulates that the **LOB** value (regardless of length) is stored outside of the row.
- **CHUNK** ***integer***—Stipulates the number of bytes to be allocated for **LOB** manipulation. The maximum value is 32,768 (32K), which is the largest Oracle block size allowed. The value of **CHUNK** must be less than or equal to the values of both **INITIAL** and **NEXT**.
- **PCTVERSION** ***integer***—Stipulates the maximum percentage of overall **LOB** storage space that is to be used in creating new versions

of the **LOB**. The default value is 10; Oracle does not overwrite older versions of the **LOB** data until 10 percent of the overall **LOB** storage space is used.

- INDEX *lob_index_name*—Specifies the name of the **LOB** index segment. You cannot specify ***lob_index_name*** if you specify more than one ***lob_item*** in the associated ***lob_ item*** list.

Nested Table Storage Clause

The nested table storage clause names the table where nested item rows are found. Figure 12.10 shows the syntax for this clause. The keywords and parameters used in the nested table storage clause are as described:

- NESTED TABLE *nested_item* STORE AS *storage_table*—Designates *storage_table* as the name of the storage table in which the rows contain all ***nested_item*** values. This clause is required when creating a table with columns or column attributes with a nested table type.
  - *nested_item*—Designates the name of a column or a column-qualified attribute with the nested table type.
  - *storage_table*—Designates the storage table's name. The storage table is created in the same schema and the same tablespace as the parent table.

Table Partition Clauses

The table partition clauses specify the storage characteristics of partitions and the method of partitioning. Figure 12.11 shows the syntax for the table partition clauses. The following keywords and parameters are used in the table partition clauses:

- PARTITION BY RANGE—Stipulates that the table is partitioned on ranges of values contained in a column list.
  - *column_list*—Designates an ordered list of columns to be used in determining the partition to which a row belongs. A column list cannot have more than 16 columns.
  - PARTITION *partition_name*—Designates the physical partition clause.

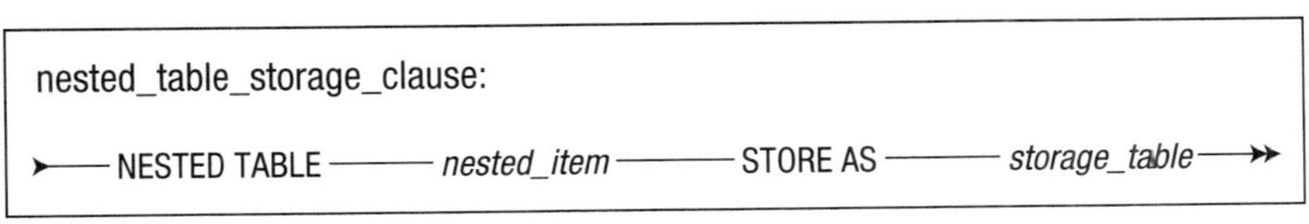

Figure 12.10 The syntax for the nested table storage clause.

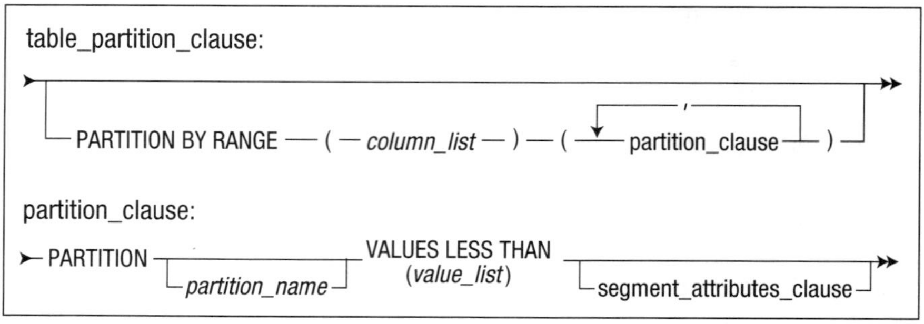

Figure 12.11 The syntax for the table partition clauses.

- **VALUES LESS THAN**—Stipulates the current partition's noninclusive upper bound.
- *value_list*—Specifies an ordered list of literal values corresponding to the column list in the **PARTITION BY RANGE** clause. You can substitute the keyword **MAXVALUE** for any literal in the value list. **MAXVALUE** specifies a maximum value that will always sort higher than any other value, including **NULL**.

Altering Tables

You can alter tables to add columns; change column types and lengths; or add, change, or drop column or table constraints. You can't alter tables to rename a column. In Oracle8.1.5, you will be able to drop a column, but not in release 8. You can also alter a table's storage characteristics. To alter a table, you must either have the table in your schema or have been granted the **ALTER TABLE** system privilege on the table. DBAs are normally granted the **ALTER ANY TABLE** system privilege, which allows them to alter tables without being granted privileges on individual tables.

When you modify a column, the size of the column cannot decrease unless the table has no rows. **CHAR** datatypes are blank padded, so an increase in size can have a dramatic effect on the amount of space used by the table. If a new column is added to a table, the column is initially null.

Changes to **PCTFREE**, **PCTUSED**, and **MAXTRANS** apply to all blocks in a table. This does not cause Oracle to recalculate **PCTFREE** and **PCTUSED** in all the table blocks when a change is made. As blocks are accessed, they use the new values. On the other hand, altering **INITRANS** affects only blocks added to the table after the parameter is changed. If you alter the **NEXT** or **PCTINCREASE** parameters, all future extent allocations will use the new values. Two parameters that cannot be altered are **INITIAL** and **MINEXTENTS**.

The following is a list and description of the keywords and parameters used in the **ALTER TABLE** command:

- *schema*—Designates the schema that contains the table. In the absence of the schema, Oracle assumes the table is in the schema of the user executing the **ALTER TABLE** command.
- *table_name*—Designates the name of the table to be altered.
- **ADD**—Adds a column or integrity constraint to the table. If the table is an index-organized table, this keyword is invalid.
- **MODIFY**—Changes an existing column's definition. You cannot modify the column definitions of an index-organized table.
  - *column*—Designates the name of the column to be added or modified.
  - *datatype*—Designates a new datatype for an existing column or a datatype for a new column.
  - **DEFAULT**—Stipulates a new default for an existing column or a default value for a new column. If you add a new column to the table and specify a default value, Oracle inserts the default column value into all rows of the table.
  - *column_constraint*—Adds or eliminates a **NOT NULL** constraint to or from an existing column.
  - *table_constraint*—Adds an integrity constraint to the table.
- **MODIFY PARTITION**—Stipulates new values for a partitioned table's default attributes.
  - **physical_attributes_clause**—Stipulates a new value for one or all of **PCTFREE**, **PCTUSED**, **INITRANS**, and **MAXTRANS** parameters for the table, partition, the overflow data segment, or the default characteristics of a partitioned table. (See Figure 12.6.)
  - **storage_clause**—Stipulates new values for storage characteristics of a partitioned table's partition, table, overflow data segment, or the default characteristics. (See Figure 12.7.)
- **OVERFLOW**—Designates the physical storage attributes of an overflow data segment for an index-organized table.
- **ADD OVERFLOW**—Adds an overflow data segment to the designated index-organized table.

- **PCTTHRESHOLD**—Stipulates the amount of space reserved in the index block for an index-organized table row. Any portion of the row that exceeds the specified threshold is stored in the overflow area. If **OVERFLOW** is not specified, Oracle rejects rows exceeding the threshold limit. **PCTTHRESHOLD** must be a value from 0 through 50 percent.
- **INCLUDING** ***column_name***—Designates a column at which to split an index-organized table row into index and overflow portions. All columns following ***column_name*** are stored in the overflow data segment.

- ***lob_item***—Designates the **LOB** object attribute or **LOB** column name for which you are explicitly defining tablespace and storage characteristics different from those of the table.
- **STORE AS** ***lob_seg_name***—Specifies the name of the **LOB** data segment. (See Figure 12.9.)
  - **ENABLE STORAGE IN ROW**—Stipulates that if the length of the **LOB** value is less than approximately 4,000 bytes minus system control information, it is stored in the row by default.
  - **DISABLE STORAGE IN ROW**—Designates that the **LOB** value (regardless of length) is stored outside of the row. You cannot change **STORAGE IN ROW** once it is set.
  - **CHUNK** ***integer***—Stipulates the number of bytes allocated for **LOB** manipulation. The maximum value is 32K, which is the largest Oracle block size allowed.
  - **PCTVERSION** ***integer***—Stipulates the maximum amount of overall **LOB** storage space to be used when creating new versions of the **LOB**. The default value is 10 percent. This means older versions of the **LOB** data are not overwritten until 10 percent of the overall **LOB** storage space is used.
  - **INDEX** ***lob_index_name***—Designates the name of the **LOB** index segment. If you specify more than one **LOB** item, you cannot use ***lob_index_name***.
- **MODIFY LOB (*lob_item*)**—Modifies the physical attributes of the **LOB** attribute ***lob_item*** or **LOB** object attribute.
- **NESTED TABLE** ***nested_item*** **STORE AS** ***storage_table***—Designates ***storage_table*** as the name of the storage table containing the rows of all

nested_item values. This is a required clause when you are modifying a table with columns or column attributes whose type is a nested table. The nested item is the name of a column or a column-qualified attribute whose type is a nested table. The storage table is the name of the storage table. The storage table is modified in the same schema and the same tablespace as the parent table.

- **drop_clause**—Eliminates an integrity constraint.
- ALLOCATE EXTENT—Allocates a new extent for the table, partition, overflow data segment, **LOB** data segment, or **LOB** index.
  - SIZE—Stipulates the extent's size in bytes: K (kilobytes) or M (megabytes). If this parameter is absent, Oracle determines the size based on the values of the table's overflow data segment's or **LOB** index's storage parameters.
  - DATAFILE—Specifies one of the datafiles in the table's tablespace, overflow data segment, **LOB** data tablespace, or **LOB** index to hold the new extent. If you omit this parameter, Oracle chooses the datafile.
  - INSTANCE—Makes the new extent available to the freelist group associated with the specified instance. You only use this parameter if you are using Oracle with the Parallel Server option in parallel mode. An instance is identified by the value of its initialization parameter INSTANCE_NUMBER.
- DEALLOCATE UNUSED—Expressly deallocates unused space at the end of a partition, table, **LOB** data segment, overflow data segment, or **LOB** index, making the space accessible to other segments. You can free only unused space above the high watermark (HWM). If **KEEP** is omitted, Oracle frees all unused space.
  - KEEP—Stipulates the number of bytes above HWM to be allocated to a table, overflow data segment, **LOB** data segment, or **LOB** index after deallocation. If the number of remaining extents is less than **MINEXTENTS**, **MINEXTENTS** is set to the current number of extents. If the initial extent becomes smaller than **INITIAL**, **INITIAL** is set to the value of the current initial extent.
- **enable_clause**—Enables an integrity constraint or all triggers associated with the table.

- **CACHE**—Stipulates that retrieved data blocks are placed at the MRU end of the LRU list in the buffer cache when a full-table scan is performed. **CACHE** cannot be used for index-organized tables.
- **NOCACHE**—Specifies that the blocks retrieved for a table are placed at the LRU end of the LRU list in the buffer cache when a full-table scan is performed. This option is the default for tables. **NOCACHE** is not a valid keyword for index-organized tables.
- **LOGGING/NOLOGGING**—Specifies whether subsequent SQL+ Loader and direct-load insert operations against a nonpartitioned table, table partition, or all partitions of a partitioned table will be logged in the redo log file. The **LOGGING/NOLOGGING** option also specifies whether **ALTER TABLE...MOVE** and **ALTER TABLE...SPLIT** operations will be logged or not logged. **NOLOGGING** is not a valid keyword for altering index-organized tables.
- **RENAME TO**—Designates a new name for a table.
- **MODIFY PARTITION**—Changes a table partition's physical attributes. You can change the physical attributes for **PCTFREE, PCTUSED, INITRANS, MAXTRANS**, or storage parameters.
- **RENAME PARTITION**—Designates new name for table partition.
- **MOVE PARTITION**—Transfers a table partition to another segment. Moving partitions can be useful in reducing fragmentation.
- **ADD PARTITION**—Adds a new partition to a partitioned table. You can specify new attributes for the partition, including **LOGGING/ NOLOGGING, PCTFREE, PCTUSED, INITRANS, MAXTRANS** or storage parameters.
    - **VALUES LESS THAN** *value_list*—Specifies the upper bound for the new partition.
- **DROP PARTITION**—Eliminates a partition and the data it contains from a partitioned table.
- **TRUNCATE PARTITION**—Eliminates all rows from a table's partition.
    - **DROP STORAGE**—Stipulates that space from the truncated rows is to be deallocated and made available to other tablespace schema objects.
    - **REUSE STORAGE**—Stipulates that space from truncated rows will remain allocated to the partition.

- SPLIT PARTITION—Creates two new partitions, each with a new segment, new physical attributes, and initial extents. Oracle drops the original partition.
    - AT *value_list*—Specifies the new noninclusive upper bound for **split_partition_1**. The *value_list* must be less than the presplit partition bound for the old partition and greater than the partition bound for the next lowest partition (if one exists).
    - INTO—Defines two partitions resulting from a split.
- EXCHANGE PARTITION—Changes a partition into a nonpartitioned table, and a nonpartitioned table into a partition of a partitioned table by exchanging data and index segments.
    - WITH TABLE—Designates the table with which to exchange the partition.
    - INCLUDING INDEXES—Stipulates the exchange of local index partitions with the corresponding regular indexes.
    - EXCLUDING INDEXES—Stipulates that all the local index partitions corresponding to the partition and all the regular indexes on the exchanged table are marked unusable.
    - WITH VALIDATION—Stipulates returning an error when rows in the exchanged table do not collate correctly.
    - WITHOUT VALIDATION—Stipulates that the proper collation of rows in the exchanged table is not verified.
- *parallel_clause*—Designates the table's degree of parallelism. (See Figure 12.4.) You cannot use the parallel clause for index-organized tables.

Figures 12.12 through 12.14 show the **ALTER TABLE** command syntax. Figure 12.15 shows the **MODIFY LOB** command.

DROP TABLE

The only way to drop an object is to use the **DROP TABLE** command. It is used for tables, indexes, clusters, tablespaces, sequences, stored objects, and synonyms. A **DROP TABLE** command is a **DDL** command and can't be rolled back. Any dropped object must be re-created if the **DROP TABLE** command was issued in error. The **DROP TABLE** command removes the table and all related objects and segments from the database. If foreign key constraints to other tables exist on the table, a **DROP** command fails. You must remove the constraints from the table or add the **CASCADE** clause

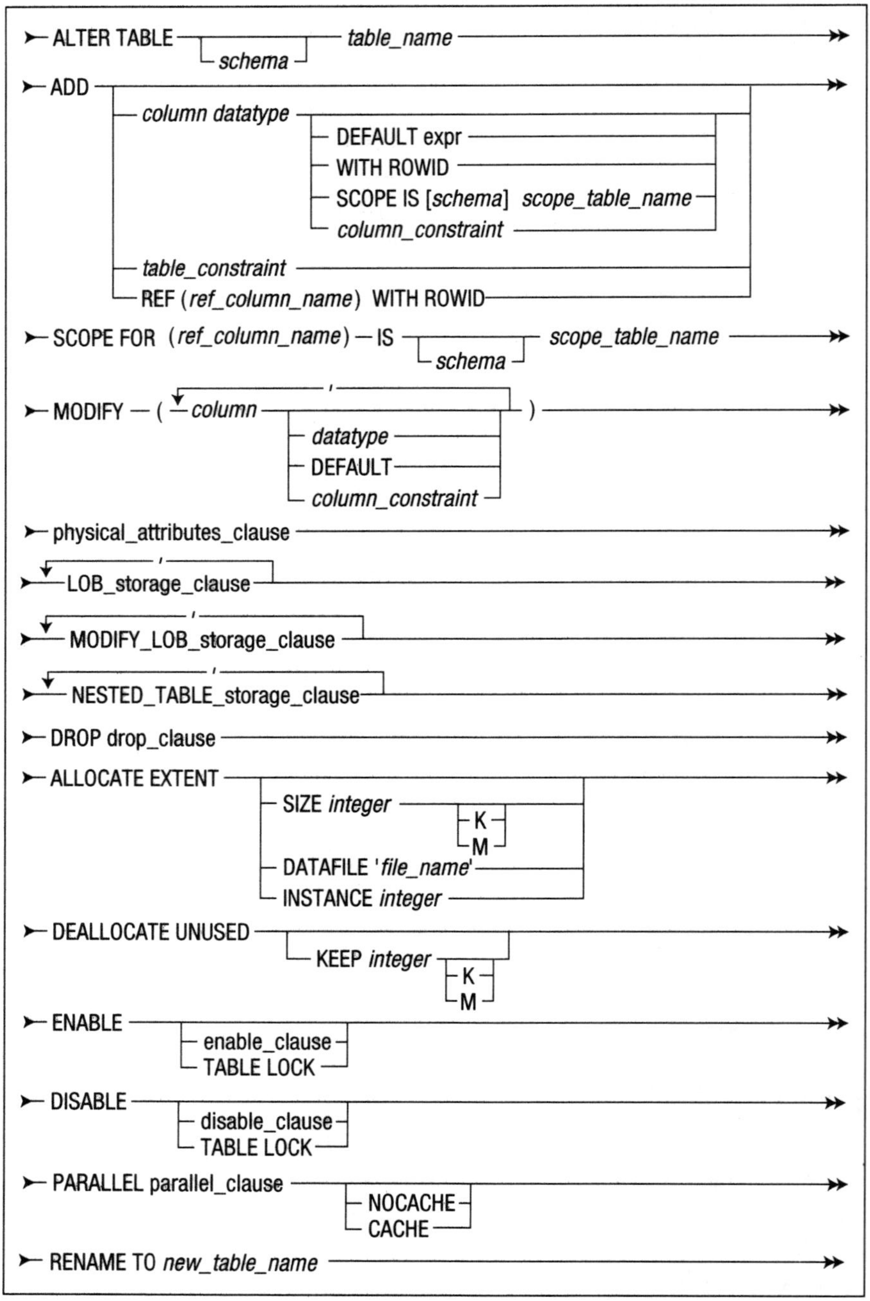

Figure 12.12 The syntax for the **ALTER TABLE** command.

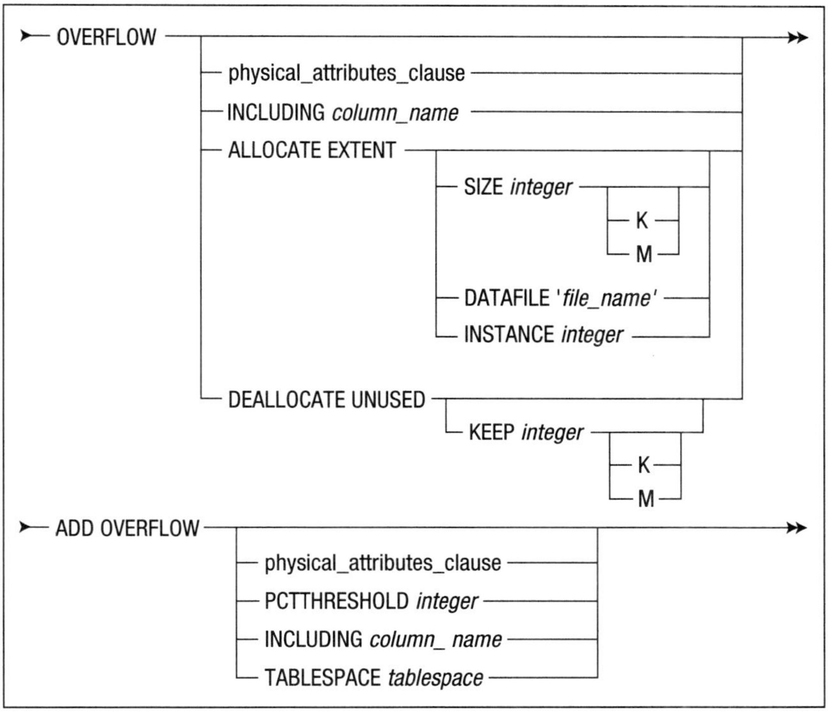

Figure 12.13 The syntax for the **OVERFLOW** clauses of the **ALTER TABLE** command.

to the **DROP TABLE** command to remove the table and any related data. DBAs normally have the **DROP ANY TABLE** privilege that allows them to drop tables, no matter who owns them. Otherwise, a table must be in your own schema to drop it. Figure 12.16 shows the **DROP TABLE** command syntax.

The following statement drops the **CUSTOMER** table:

```
DROP TABLE customer;
```

The following example shows how to use the **DROP** command to drop a table with unique or foreign key constraints:

```
DROP TABLE emp CASCADE CONSTRAINTS;
```

The following list describes the keywords and parameters used in the **DROP TABLE** command:

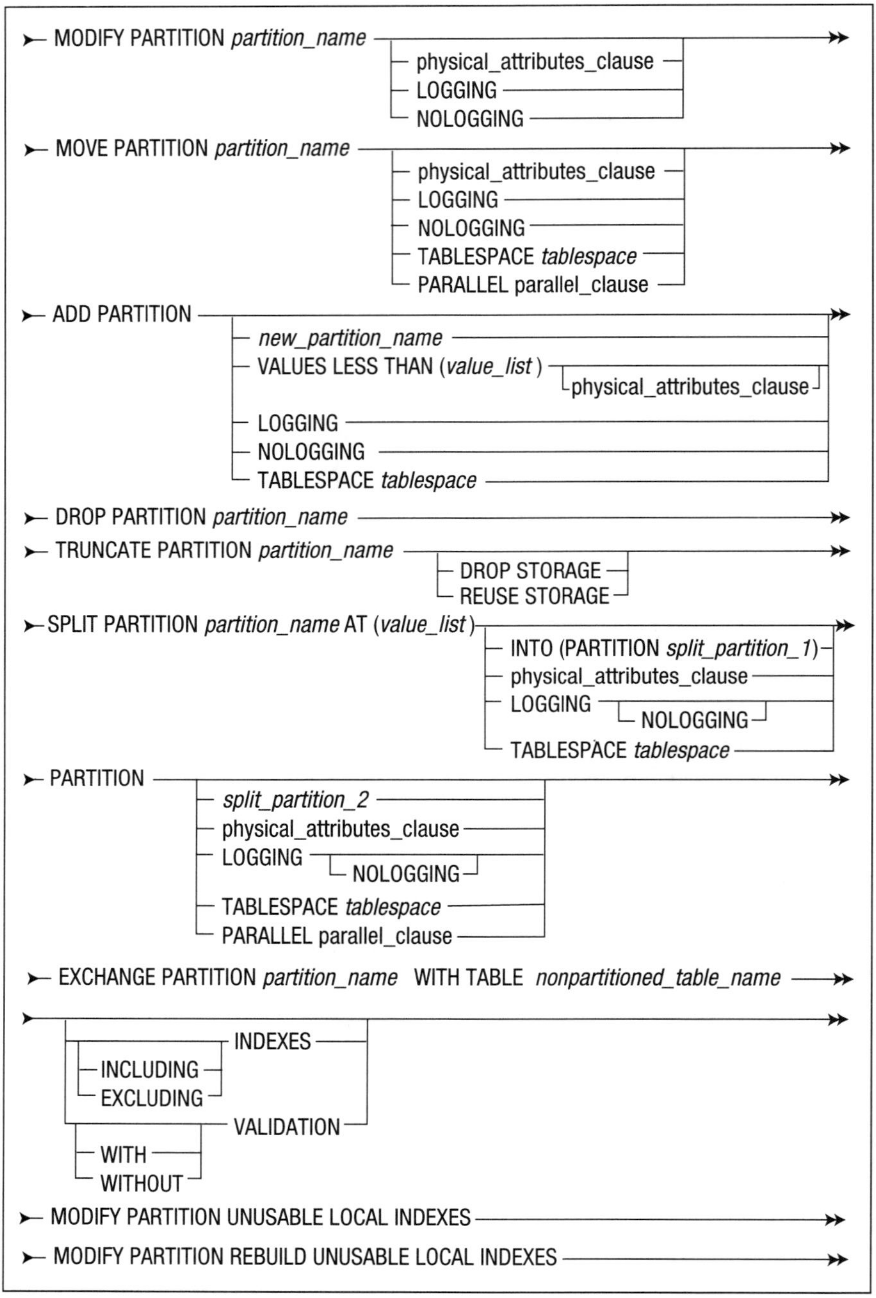

Figure 12.14 The syntax for the **PARTITION** clauses of the **ALTER TABLE** command.

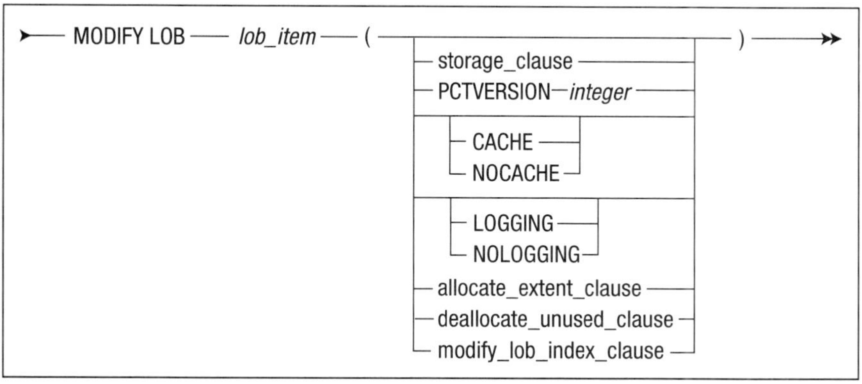

Figure 12.15 The syntax for the **MODIFY LOB** clause of the **ALTER TABLE** command.

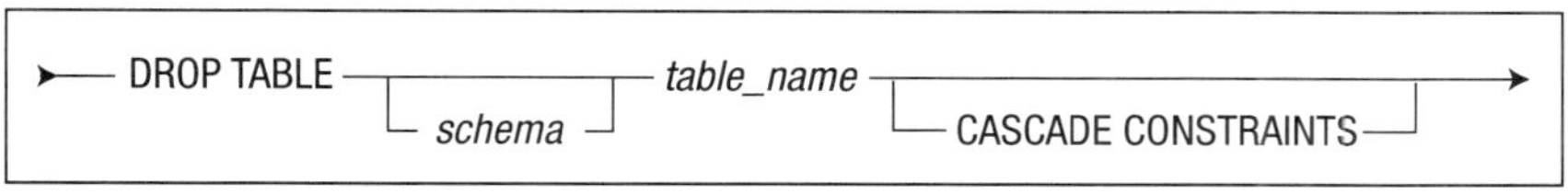

Figure 12.16 The syntax for the **DROP TABLE** command.

- *schema*—Designates the schema containing the table. If you omit the schema keyword, Oracle assumes that the table is in the schema of the user executing the DROP TABLE command.
- *table_name*—Designates the name of the table, object table, or index-organized table to be dropped.
- CASCADE CONSTRAINTS—Eliminates all referential integrity constraints referring to unique and primary keys in the dropped table.

TRUNCATE

The TRUNCATE command is very useful if you need to delete all the rows in a table or cluster. Unlike the DML DELETE command, the TRUNCATE command is a DDL command. As with all the other DDL commands, the TRUNCATE command cannot be rolled back, because it does not generate any rollback information. This makes the TRUNCATE command very fast and efficient for certain types of operations. Unlike the DELETE command, TRUNCATE does not have a WHERE clause. TRUNCATE always removes all the rows from a table. At the same time, all indexes that are associated with the table being truncated will be truncated as well. One other difference between the DELETE and the TRUNCATE commands is that the TRUNCATE command does not fire any table delete triggers. You must manually handle any constraints being enforced through triggers. You must also disable all referencing foreign keys or the **TRUNCATE** command will fail.

The default action for the **TRUNCATE** command is to drop all the extents added to the table down to **MINEXTENTS**. These freed extents can then be used by the tablespace for reallocation to other objects in the tablespace as needed. Alternatively, the **REUSE STORAGE** option maintains all extents allocated to the table and just removes the rows. This can be very useful if you are reloading tables and want to keep the current extent allocation for the table. It saves the overhead of reallocating extents to the table. The **DROP STORAGE** and **REUSE STORAGE** commands affect the extent allocation of indexes in the same way they affect the table.

All users can **TRUNCATE** their own tables. In order to truncate tables in another schema, you must be granted the **DROP ANY TABLE** system privilege. Remember, the **TRUNCATE** command cannot be rolled back, so be careful when granting this system privilege. Figure 12.17 shows the **TRUNCATE TABLE** command syntax.

The following lists the keywords and parameters used in the **TRUNCATE TABLE** command:

- *schema*—Designates the schema containing the table. If you omit the *schema* keyword, Oracle assumes the table is in the same schema as the one executing the command.
- *table_name*—Stipulates the name of the table to be truncated.
- SNAPSHOT LOG—Stipulates whether a snapshot log defined on a table will be preserved or purged when the table is truncated.
  - PRESERVE—Stipulates preservation of any snapshot log when the master table is truncated. This is the default.
  - PURGE—Specifies any snapshot log that should be purged when the master table is truncated.
- CLUSTER—Designates the name of the cluster to be truncated. Hash clusters cannot be truncated.
- DROP STORAGE—Gives the space freed by deleted rows back to the tablespace for use by other objects in the tablespace. This is the default.
- REUSE STORAGE—Retains the space from the deleted rows for the table or cluster.

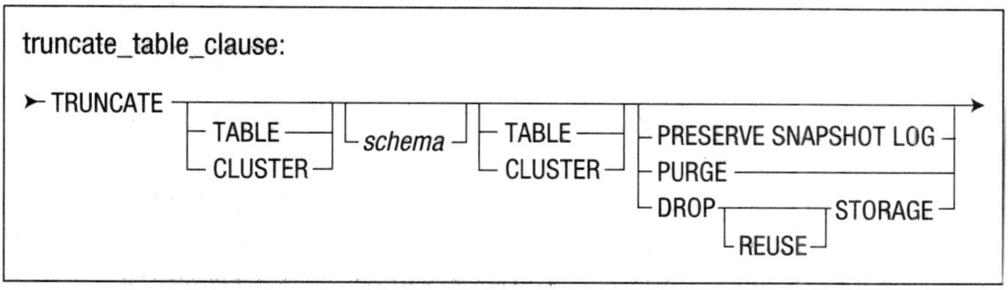

Figure 12.17 The syntax for the **TRUNCATE TABLE** command.

The following statement deletes all rows from the **CUSTOMER** table and returns the freed space to the tablespace containing **CUSTOMER**:

```
TRUNCATE TABLE customer;
```

The previous statement also deletes all data from all indexes on **CUSTOMER** and returns the freed space to the tablespaces containing them.

The following statement deletes all rows from all tables in the **CUST** cluster, but leaves the freed space allocated to the tables:

```
TRUNCATE CLUSTER cust
    REUSE STORAGE
```

The previous statement also deletes all data from all indexes on the tables in **CUST**, but leaves the freed space allocated to the tables.

The following statement is an example of a **TRUNCATE** statement that preserves a snapshot log:

```
TRUNCATE TABLE customer PRESERVE SNAPSHOT LOG;
```

Analyzing Tables, Indexes, And Clusters

The **ANALYZE** command is used to gather statistics on any object in the data dictionary tables. These statistics are then used by the cost-based optimizer to determine the optimal execution path for your SQL statements. You can also use the **ANALYZE** command to verify the validity of an object's storage format. It is possible in rare cases for indexes to become corrupt. By using the **ANALYZE** command to validate an index's structure, you can verify that every index entry points to the correct row of the associated table. To correct a corrupted index, simply drop the index and re-create it. All users can analyze tables, indexes, or clusters on their own, but, in order to analyze objects in other schemas, they must be granted the **ANALYZE ANY** system privilege. Figure 12.18 shows the **ANALYZE** command syntax.

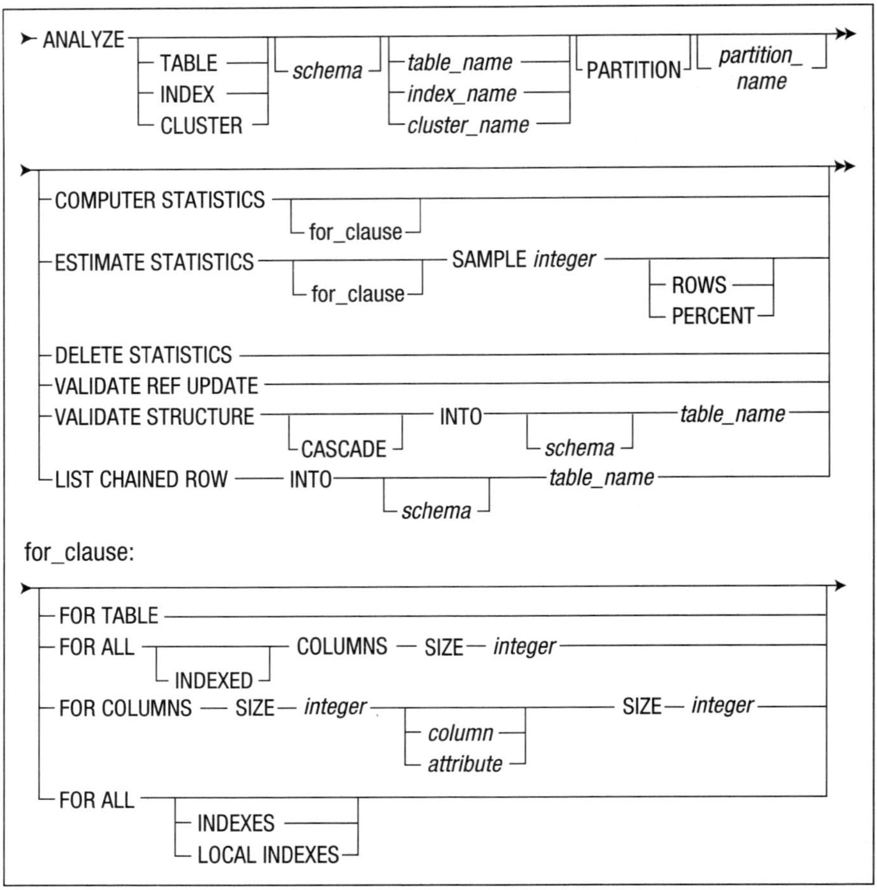

Figure 12.18 The syntax for the **ANALYZE** command.

The following list describes the keywords and parameters used in the ANALYZE command:

- *schema*—Designates the schema containing the index, table, or cluster. If you omit *schema*, Oracle assumes the index, table, or cluster is in your own schema.
- *table_name*—Identifies the table to be analyzed. Oracle automatically collects the statistics for each of the table's indexes by default.
- *index_name*—Designates an index to be analyzed.
- *cluster_name*—Designates a cluster to be analyzed. By default, Oracle automatically collects the statistics for the cluster's tables and their indexes, including the cluster index.

- PARTITION—Stipulates that statistics will be gathered for the partition named. You cannot use this option when analyzing clusters.
- COMPUTE STATISTICS—Computes exact statistics about the analyzed object and stores the information in the data dictionary.
- ESTIMATE STATISTICS—Makes statistical estimates about the analyzed object and stores the information in the data dictionary.
    - SAMPLE *integer*—Stipulates how much of the data to sample from the analyzed object for estimating statistics. Oracle samples 1,064 rows if you do not specify a sample size. If you specify more than half of the data, Oracle reads all the data and computes statistics.
    - ROWS—Instructs Oracle to sample a specific number of rows of the table, cluster, or index. The integer supplied for **ROWS** must be at least 1.
    - PERCENT—Instructs Oracle to sample a percentage of the rows from the table, cluster, or index entries. The percentage can range from 1 through 99.
- DELETE STATISTICS—Deletes statistics on an analyzed object from the data dictionary.
- VALIDATE REF UPDATE—Verifies each **REF** in the specified table. Oracle examines the **ROWID** portion in each **REF**, compares that with the true **ROWID**, and makes any necessary corrections.
- VALIDATE STRUCTURE—Verifies the structure of the analyzed object. For partitioned tables, Oracle verifies that the row belongs to the correct partition.
    - INTO—Designates a table into which Oracle is to insert each **ROWID** of partitions whose rows do not collate properly. If you don't specify a schema, Oracle uses the current schema. If you don't specify a table name, Oracle assumes that the table is named **INVALID_ROWS**. The SQL script used to create this table is utlvalid.sql.
    - CASCADE—Verifies the structure of the indexes associated with a table or cluster. If you use **CASCADE** when validating a table or cluster, the indexes are also validated.
- LIST CHAINED ROW—Lists the analyzed table's or cluster's migrated and chained rows. You cannot use this option when analyzing an index.

- INTO—Designates a table into which to insert the list of migrated and chained rows.
- FOR TABLE—Collects a table's statistics.
- FOR ALL COLUMNS—Gathers column statistics for all scalar object attributes and columns.
- INDEXED—Gathers column statistics for a table's indexed columns.
- FOR COLUMNS—Gathers column statistics for specified scalar object attributes and columns.
- *attribute*—Designates the qualified column name of an item in an object.
- FOR ALL INDEXES—Analyzes all indexes associated with a table.
- FOR ALL LOCAL INDEXES—Stipulates that all local index partitions are analyzed.

Another use for the **ANALYZE** command is to collect information about chained rows of a table or cluster. This information is useful in determining whether you have set the **PCTFREE** parameter correctly. Because chained rows can significantly impact performance, the **ANALYZE** command can be used to identify tables that should be dropped and rebuilt with new storage criteria, to improve performance.

The **ANALYZE** command can compute statistics, estimate statistics, or delete statistics. Computing statistics scans an entire object and stores the information about the object in the data dictionary. This option gives Oracle the most accurate information about the object but takes the longest to accomplish, due to the required full scan. The **ANALYZE** command can also estimate statistics by gathering sample information from portions of an object. The accuracy of the estimated statistics depends on how representative the sampling is of the actual table. This option allows statistics to be generated faster, because only a portion of the object is scanned. The sample can be specified by the number of rows or the percentage of rows to use in estimating the statistics.

When Oracle scans a table or cluster, enough temporary space must be present to hold and sort the scanned rows. Because using the **COMPUTE** option does a full-table scan, enough temporary space must exist to hold the entire table if you use this option. Indexes, on the other hand, do not require any temporary space when they are analyzed. Unless the **FOR** clause is used, all associated indexes are also analyzed when you analyze a table or cluster.

Note: Do not use the ANALYZE command to collect statistics on data dictionary tables.

Viewing Statistics

Oracle creates data dictionary views for querying statistics on tables. The listed **ALL**, **USER**, and **DBA** views use the same columns for storing statistics. The statistics can be queried using the following data dictionary views:

- ALL_INDEXES
- ALL_TAB_COL_STATISTICS
- ALL_TABLES
- DBA_INDEXES
- DBA_TAB_COL_STATISTICS
- DBA_TABLES
- USER_INDEXES
- USER_TAB_COL_STATISTICS
- USER_TABLES

Table Statistics

The following list shows the statistics that can be gathered on a table and the column that holds each statistic:

- Average available free space (**AVG_SPACE**)
- Average row length (**AVG_ROW_LEN**)
- Number of blocks never used (**EMPTY_BLOCKS**)
- Number of blocks that have been used (**BLOCKS**)
- Number of chained rows (**CHAIN_CNT**)
- Number of distinct values per column (**NUM_DISTINCT**)
- Number of rows (**NUM_ROWS**)
- Sample size used to analyze the table (**SAMPLE_SIZE**)
- Second largest value per column (**HIGH VALUE**)
- Second smallest value per column (**LOW_VALUE**)

Index Statistics

The following list shows the statistics that can be gathered on an index and the column that holds each statistic:

- Average number of data blocks/key (**AVG_DATA_BLOCKS_PER_KEY**)
- Average number of leaf blocks/key (**AVG_LEAF_BLOCKS_PER_KEY**)
- Clustering factor (**CLUSTERING_FACTOR**)
- Index level (**BLEVEL**)
- Number of distinct keys (**DISTINCT_KEYS**)
- Number of leaf blocks (**LEAF_BLOCKS**)
- Number of rows in the index (**NUM_ROWS**)
- Sample size used to analyze the index (**SAMPLE_SIZE**)

Cluster Statistics

When Oracle analyzes a cluster, it generates statistics for all associated tables, indexes, and cluster indexes. The only statistic stored in the cluster data dictionary views is the average number of blocks containing a row with a cluster key. This statistic is stored in the **AVG_BLOCKS_PER_KEY** column.

Computing Statistics

The following statements show how to compute statistics, estimate statistics, and remove statistics:

```
ANALYZE TABLE mytable COMPUTE STATISTICS;

ANALYZE TABLE mytable ESTIMATE STATISTICS;
```

The previous query estimates statistics on the MYTABLE table, using the default statistical sample of 1,064 rows.

```
ANALYZE TABLE mytable
   ESTIMATE STATISTICS
      SAMPLE 25000 ROWS;

ANALYZE TABLE mytable
   ESTIMATE STATISTICS
      SAMPLE 25 PERCENT;
```

> *Note: If you specify a percentage greater than 50 or a number of rows or index values that is greater than 50 percent of those in the object, Oracle computes the exact statistics, rather than estimates them.*

```
ANALYZE TABLE mytable DELETE STATISTICS;
```

You do not have to delete statistics in order to recompute them. Just re-execute the **ANALYZE** command and the statistics will be replaced by the newly calculated statistics. When you use the **DELETE STATISTICS** option on a table, Oracle also automatically removes statistics for all the table's indexes. You can delete statistics on objects to force Oracle to use the rule-based optimizer instead of the cost-based optimizer. Oracle will not use cost-based optimization if there are no statistics on the objects being queried, unless you add hints to your SQL, which influences Oracle to use the cost-based optimizer.

Oracle provides two built-in package procedures you can call to analyze objects as well. You can call the following procedures:

```
DBMS_UTILITY.ANALYZE_SCHEMA()

DBMS_DDL.ANALYZE_OBJECTS()
```

The first procedure takes two arguments: the name of a schema and an analysis method (**COMPUTE**, **ESTIMATE**, or **DELETE**). It gathers statistics on all the objects in the schema. The second procedure takes four arguments: the type of an object (**CLUSTER**, **TABLE**, or **INDEX**), the schema of the object, the name of the object, and an analysis method (**COMPUTE**, **ESTIMATE**, or **DELETE**).

Effects On The Shared Pool

When a table, cluster, or index is analyzed, any shared SQL statements in the shared pool that are associated with the analyzed object are flushed from the shared pool. When a statement using the newly analyzed object is executed, it will be added to the shared pool with an execution plan based on the new statistics.

Validating Tables, Indexes, And Clusters

You can use the **ANALYZE** command with the **VALIDATE STRUCTURE** clause to check the structural integrity of tables, indexes, and clusters. These integrity problems normally occur due to hardware or software problems. Analyzing the structure of objects before they cause some type of system failure can save a lot of time. Normally, the object in question can just be dropped and re-created. Use the following command to validate the structure of a table:

```
ANALYZE TABLE mytable VALIDATE STRUCTURE;
```

To analyze all related objects, include the **CASCADE** option, as follows:

```
ANALYZE TABLE mytable VALIDATE STRUCTURE CASCADE;
```

Showing Chained Rows

To use the **ANALYZE** command to list chained and migrated rows of a table or cluster, use the **LIST CHAINED ROWS** option. The results of this command are stored in a table created explicitly for storing the output from the **LIST CHAINED ROWS** option of the **ANALYZE** command. The utlchain.sql script provided with Oracle creates a table named **CHAINED_ROWS** in the schema of the user executing the script. You can edit the utlchain.sql script and change the table name to a different name if you prefer. This allows you to store the chained row information in multiple tables if needed. The following is the **CREATE TABLE** command from the utlchain.sql script:

```
create table CHAINED_ROWS (
  owner_name        varchar2(30),
  table_name        varchar2(30),
  cluster_name      varchar2(30),
  partition_name    varchar2(30),
  head_rowid        rowid,
  analyze_timestamp        date
);
```

The following command inserts rows containing information about a table's chained rows into the **CHAINED_ROWS** table:

```
ANALYZE TABLE mytable LIST CHAINED ROWS INTO chained_rows;
```

To store the chained rows information for an index-organized table, you need to run the dbmsiotc.sql script supplied by Oracle. This creates a package **DBMS_IOT** that has two procedures: **build_chain_rows_table** and **build_exceptions_table.** Use the **build_chain_rows_table** procedure to create the **IOT_CHAINED_ROWS** table. The **build_chain_rows_table** procedure has three parameters:

- **chainrow_table_name**—Name of the chained rows table to create. The default value is **IOT_CHAINED_ROWS**.

- **iot_name**—Index-organized table name.
- **owner**—Owner of the index-organized table. The default is the schema executing the procedure.

Create a separate chained rows table for each index-organized table for which you want to list chained rows.

Managing Indexes

Data is stored in tables and clusters and is uniquely identified with a hidden column called **ROWID**. The fastest way to access an Oracle table row is through the **ROWID**, which labels each row by tablespace file, block within the file, and row within the block. The use of indexes can improve performance or increase the time necessary for a SQL statement to execute. The correct use of indexes allows the optimizer to choose an efficient path and avoid unnecessary full-table scans. An index scan retrieves data on the basis of the value in one or more indexed columns. The index stores the value of the column or columns specified for the index and the **ROWID** for a row in the table. A full-table scan searches every row of the table.

Composite Indexes

A *composite index* is an index that consists of more than one column. The column order in the index is very important. If a column in the **WHERE** clause references the first column in the index, it will be able to use the index. If the column references only the column in the second position in the index, the index cannot be used. If the **WHERE** clause references columns at the beginning of the index, it is said to reference the leading edge of the index. Composite indexes should be considered when two or more columns are frequently used together in the **WHERE** clause. The first column in the composite index should be the column most frequently referenced in the **WHERE** clause. If all the columns are equally used, consider ordering the columns from the most selective to the least selective.

Reverse Key Indexes

In Oracle8, indexes can be created in *reverse order*. This means that the data is reversed before it is stored in the index. The reversing is done at the byte level, but conceptually the number 1959 becomes 9591. This keeps the data sorted better in the index and improves queries that use equivalence operations. Queries that search ranges of data might not perform as well.

Bitmapped Indexes

Bitmapped indexes are often used for a decision support system (DSS) environment or for data warehouses. They work best on large tables with values of low cardinality for the bitmapped columns. When bitmapped indexes are used properly, they result in excellent performance and an indexing scheme that requires much less storage space than the traditional B-tree index structure. A bitmap is created for each value with an entry for each row. Bitmapped indexes are especially useful when used in conjunction with other bitmapped indexes. Bitmapped indexes do not work well for columns in which additional values use a bitmapped index.

When And How To Use Indexes

The type of work that end users are performing is a key element in determining when to create an index. For applications that are insert, update, and delete intensive, indexes add additional overhead by requiring values to be added and/or changed in the index as well as in the table. For applications that are highly query intensive, more indexes are usually required. Many data warehouses are very query intensive during the day and updated with large batch jobs at night. In this hybrid situation, it might be advisable to drop the indexes before executing the batch job and to re-create the indexes after the batch job completes. When a table has no index, Oracle must read every row of the table to determine which rows meet the requirements of the SQL statement. In some cases, a full-table scan is the best way to access a table. A full-table scan is preferable in the following situations:

- When tables are small and have very few values.
- When SQL statements will change or fetch a large portion of the rows.

An index scan is preferable in the following situations:

- When selected rows are uniformly located throughout the blocks associated with the table and the number of rows to be selected is less than 4 percent.
- When selected rows are randomly located throughout the blocks associated with the table and the number of rows to be selected is less than 25 percent.

Just like tables, indexes use the **PCTFREE** parameter to control the use of space in the index data blocks. When an index is created, data blocks of the index are filled up to **PCTFREE**. Indexes do not use the **PCTUSED** parameter, because indexes (unlike tables) do not release unused space when rows are deleted. The data can be deleted, but the leaves of the B-tree index remain. When you create a unique or primary key constraint on a column or columns, a *unique index* is generated to ensure uniqueness. You don't need to create a separate unique index for columns already used in a unique or primary key constraint. If you have already created a unique index and later alter the table to add a unique or primary key constraint, the unique index will be used by the unique or primary key constraint if an exact match exists. The referenced columns must be the same and must be in the same order. Rather than creating unique indexes, you should consider creating unique or primary constraints for the indexed column or columns.

A *nonunique index* is an index created on a column or columns that can have multiple rows with the same values.

Both unique and nonunique indexes are usually stored using a B-tree index. Over time, the addition and deletion of data can fragment a B-tree index. The index will grow in width, and the SQL code using the index will degrade in performance. Dropping and re-creating or rebuilding the index will resolve this problem.

Creating Indexes

To create an index, use the **CREATE INDEX** command. You must own the table or cluster for the index, have the **INDEX** privilege on the table or cluster, or have the **CREATE ANY INDEX** system privilege. **LONG** and **LONG RAW** columns cannot be indexed. The following statement creates a concatenated index named customer_idx1 for the **NAME** and **PHONE_NUM** columns of the customer table:

```
CREATE INDEX customer_idx1 ON customer(name,phone_num)
      TABLESPACE users
      STORAGE (INITIAL 200k
      NEXT 200k
      PCTINCREASE 75)
      PCTFREE 5;
```

As with other objects created in a tablespace, if you do not specify storage options for an index, the default storage options of the tablespace are automatically used.

You can set the storage options for the indexes associated with unique key and primary key constraints using the **ENABLE** clause with the **USING INDEX** option. The following statement defines a primary key constraint and specifies the associated index's storage option:

```
CREATE TABLE DISTRICT
(
    DISTRICT_NO        NUMBER(2)          NOT NULL,
    DISTRICT_NAME      VARCHAR2 (20)      NULL,
    STREET_ADDR        VARCHAR2 (25)      NULL,
    CITY_NAME          VARCHAR2 (25)      NULL,
    STATE_ABBR         VARCHAR2 (2)       NULL,
    ZIP_CODE_15        VARCHAR2 (15)      NULL,
    CONSTRAINT DISTRICT_PK PRIMARY KEY (DISTRICT_NO)
        USING INDEX PCTFREE 0
              TABLESPACE INDEX01
              STORAGE(INITIAL 40K NEXT 40K MINEXTENTS 1
                       MAXEXTENTS UNLIMITED PCTINCREASE 50)
)
TABLESPACE ORADATA04
PCTFREE 2 PCTUSED 75
STORAGE(INITIAL 160K NEXT 160K MINEXTENTS 1 MAXEXTENTS UNLIMITED
        PCTINCREASE 50);
```

The following is a list and description of the keywords and parameters used in the **CREATE INDEX** command:

- **BITMAP**—Stipulates that the index will be created as a bitmap rather than a B-tree. You cannot use this keyword when creating a global partitioned index. You cannot create a unique bitmap index.
- **UNIQUE**—Stipulates that the value of the column or combination of columns in the table is unique. If not, the **CREATE** statement will fail.
- *schema*—Designates the schema to contain the index. If you omit *schema*, Oracle creates the index in the current schema.
- *index_name*—Designates the name of the index to be created. An index can contain several partitions if it is not associated with a cluster.
- *table_name*—Designates the name of the table on which the index will be created. If you do not qualify the table with a schema, Oracle assumes the table is contained in the current schema.
- *column*—Designates the name(s) of column(s) in the table to be indexed. An index can have up to 32 columns. A column of an index cannot be of datatype **LONG** or **LONG RAW**.
- **ASC/DESC**—Allows for DB2 syntax compatibility, although indexes are always created in ascending order.

- **CLUSTER**—Designates the cluster for which a cluster index is to be created. If you do not qualify the cluster with a schema, Oracle assumes the cluster is contained in the current schema. You cannot create a cluster index for a hash cluster.
- **physical_attributes_clause**—Sets the values for the **INITRANS**, **MAXTRANS**, and **PCTFREE** parameters and storage characteristics. (See Figure 12.6.)
- **LOGGING/NOLOGGING**—Designates whether the creation of the index will be logged in the redo log file. It also designates whether subsequent direct SQL*Loader and direct-load insert operations against the index are logged or not logged. **LOGGING** is the default when creating indexes. The logging attribute of the index is independent of that of its base table.
- **TABLESPACE**—Specifies the name of the tablespace to hold the index or index partition. If you omit this option, Oracle creates the index in the default tablespace of the owner of the schema containing the index.
- **NOSORT**—Instructs Oracle that rows are stored in the database in ascending order, so Oracle does not have to sort the rows when creating the index. You cannot specify **REVERSE** with this option.
- **REVERSE**—Stores the bytes of the index block in reverse order, excluding the **ROWID**. You cannot specify **NOSORT** with this option. You cannot reverse a bitmap index.
- **GLOBAL**—Stipulates that the partitioning of the index is user-defined. By default, nonpartitioned indexes are global indexes.
- **PARTITION BY RANGE**—Stipulates that a global index is partitioned on the ranges of values from the columns designated in the column list. You cannot specify **PARTITION BY RANGE** for a **LOCAL** index.
  - ***(column_list)***—Designates the name(s) of the table's column(s) on which the index is partitioned. The column list must specify a left prefix of the index column list. You cannot specify more than 32 columns in a column list, and the columns cannot contain the **ROWID** pseudocolumn or a column of type **ROWID**.
  - **LOCAL**—Stipulates that the index is range-partitioned on the same columns, with the same number of partitions and the same partition bounds as the table. Oracle automatically maintains **LOCAL** index partitioning for the repartitioned table.

    - PARTITION *partition_name*—Names the individual partitions. The number of clauses fixes the number of partitions.
    - VALUES LESS THAN (*value_list*)—Stipulates the upper bound for the current partition in a global index. The value list is an ordered, comma-delimited list of literal values corresponding to the column list in the **PARTITION BY RANGE** clause. You must always specify **MAXVALUE** as the value list of the last partition. You cannot specify this clause for a local index.
- **parallel_clause**—Stipulates degree of parallelism when index is created.
- **storage_clause**—Set the values of **INITIAL**, **NEXT**, **MINEXTENTS**, **MAXEXTENTS** and **PCTINCREASE** for the index. (See Figure 12.7.)

Figure 12.19 shows the **CREATE INDEX** command syntax.

Parallel Index Creation

Oracle can use multiple processes working in parallel to create indexes. This works best on a multiprocessor computer where multiple processes work together to create the index much faster than if a single server process creates the index sequentially. Each process in the parallel create uses the storage parameters to create one or more extents for the index. For example, an index created with an **INITIAL** of 5M and a **PARALLEL DEGREE** of 10 at a minimum will have 10 extents of 5M for a total of 50M of storage. This happens because each process creates an initial extent of 5M.

Altering Indexes

After an index exists on a table or cluster, you can modify the index with the **ALTER INDEX** command to modify storage parameters or to reduce fragmentation. The index must be in your schema, or you must have the **ALTER ANY INDEX** system privilege. You cannot change the column structure of an index with the **ALTER** command. The following statement alters the mytable_idx1 index:

```
ALTER INDEX mytable_idx1
      INITRANS 2
      MAXTRANS 255
      STORAGE (PCTINCREASE 50);
```

A new setting for **INITRANS** applies only to index data blocks allocated after the **ALTER** statement, while a new setting for **MAXTRANS** applies to all index data blocks of an index.

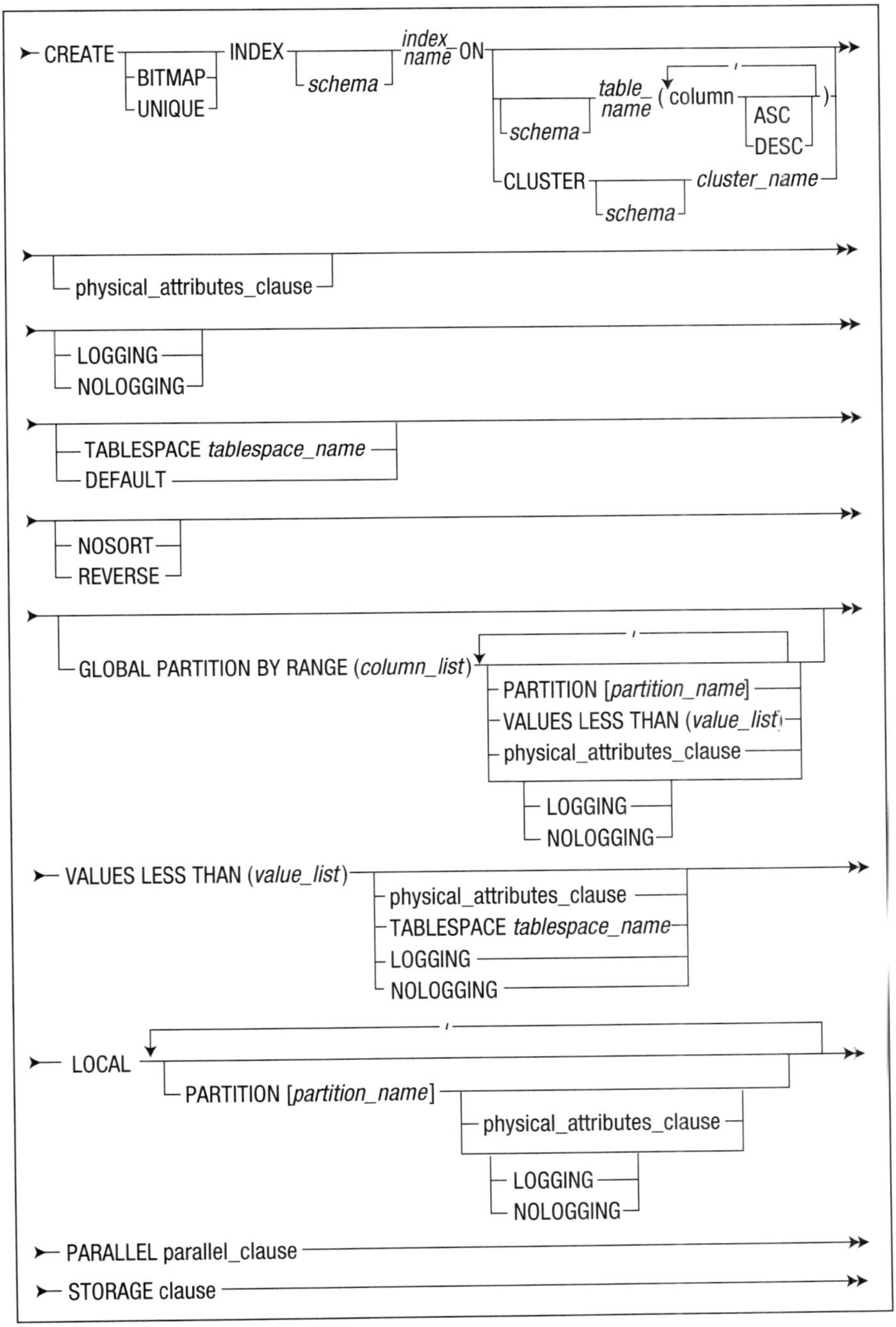

Figure 12.19 The syntax for the **CREATE INDEX** command.

You can change the storage parameters, with the exception of the **INITIAL** and **MINEXTENTS**, with the **ALTER** command. New settings for storage parameters affect only extents subsequently allocated for the index.

You can also change storage parameters for integrity constraint indexes by using the **ALTER TABLE** statement with the **ENABLE** clause and **USING INDEX** option. The following statement changes the storage options of the index defined as a primary key:

```
ALTER TABLE mytable
     ENABLE PRIMARY KEY USING INDEX
     PCTFREE 10
     STORAGE (PCTINCREASE 25);
```

The **REBUILD** clause of the **ALTER INDEX** command allows you to re-create an index from an existing index instead of using the table. You can re-create your indexes much faster using the **REBUILD** clause as well as move the index to a different tablespace. The one caveat to this is that you must have enough space to hold the existing index as well as the re-created index, because the original is not deleted until the rebuild is complete. This option is most often used when indexes have become fragmented and need to be rebuilt as quickly as possible. Issue the following command to re-create an existing index:

```
ALTER INDEX index_name REBUILD;
```

Figures 12.20 and 12.21 show the **ALTER INDEX** command syntax. These are the keywords and parameters used in this command:

- ***schema***—Designates the schema that contains the index. If you omit ***schema***, Oracle creates the index in the current schema.
- ***index_name***—Designates the name of the index that is to be altered.
- REBUILD—Rebuilds an index from an existing index.
  - **parallel_clause**—Stipulates that rebuilding the index or some queries against the index or the index partition are to be executed either serially or in parallel.
  - LOGGING/NOLOGGING—Stipulates whether **ALTER INDEX...REBUILD** and **ALTER INDEX...SPLIT** operations will be logged.
  - REVERSE—Stores the index block bytes in reverse order, excluding the **ROWID**, when the index is rebuilt.

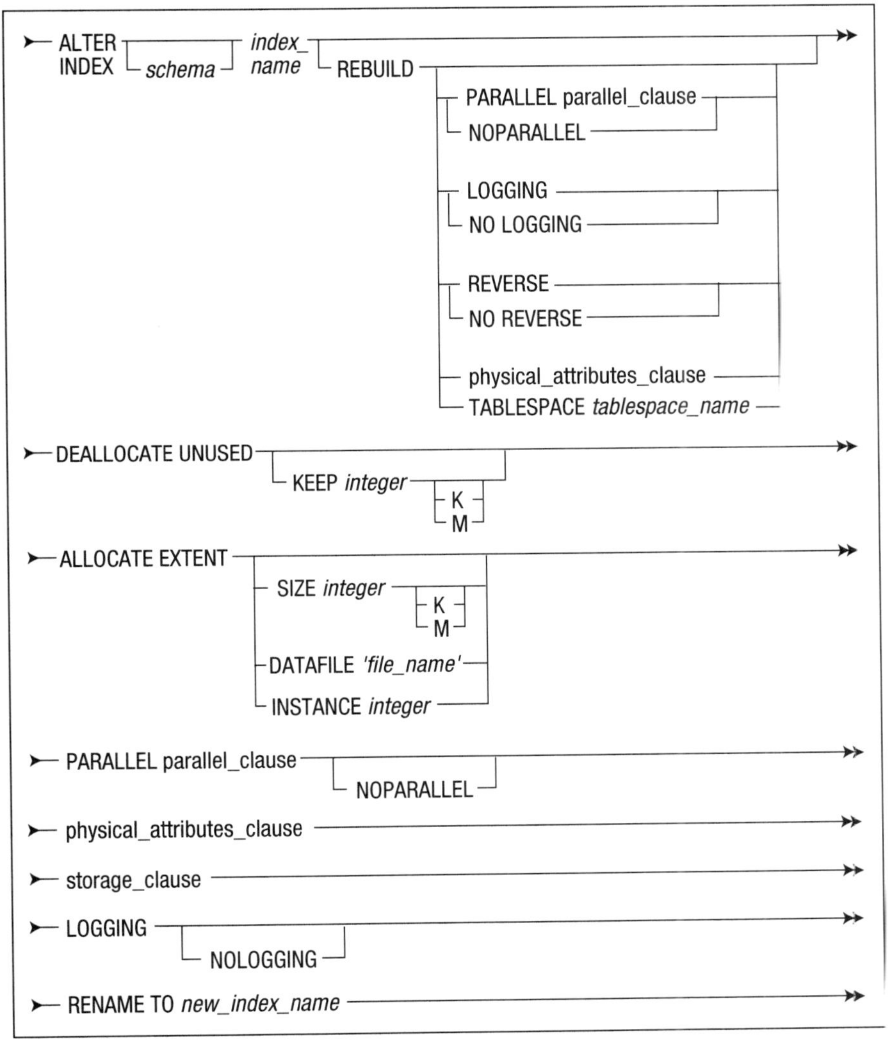

Figure 12.20 The syntax for the **ALTER INDEX** command.

- **NOREVERSE**—Stores the index block bytes without reversing the order when the index is rebuilt. Rebuilding a **REVERSE** index without the **NOREVERSE** keyword produces a rebuilt, reverse-keyed index.
- **TABLESPACE**—Designates the tablespace in which the rebuilt index or index partition is to be stored. The default is the default tablespace belonging to the user issuing the command.

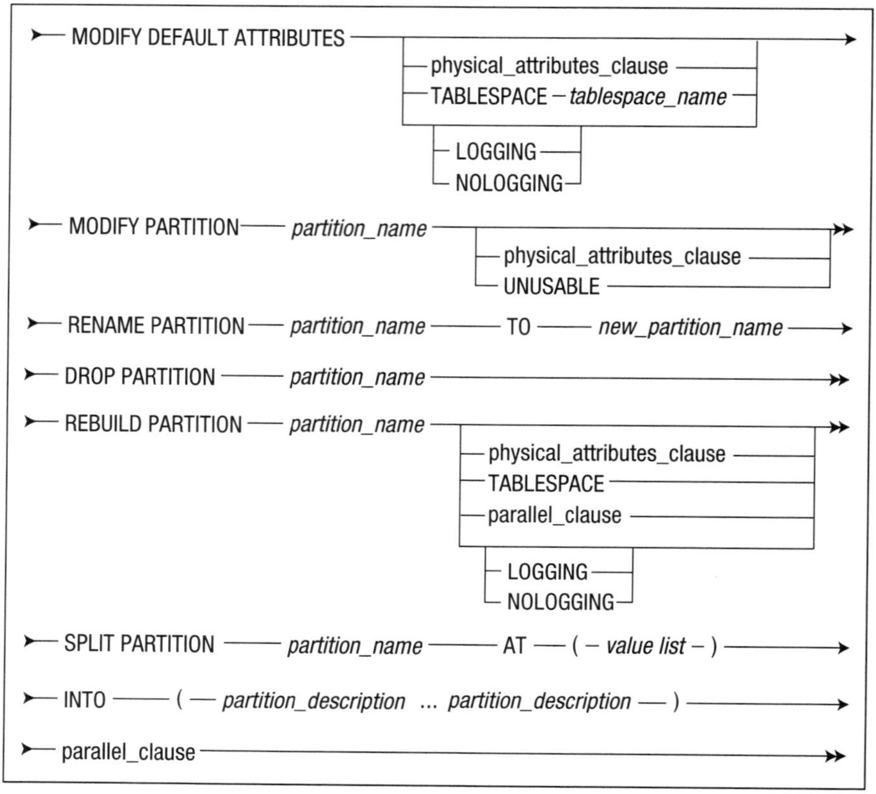

Figure 12.21 The syntax for the partition clauses of the **ALTER INDEX** command.

- **DEALLOCATE UNUSED**—Deallocates unused space at the end of the index and makes freed space accessible to other segments. Only unused space above HWM can be freed. If **KEEP** is omitted, all unused space is freed.
  - **KEEP**—Stipulates the number of bytes above HWM that will be allocated to the index after deallocation.
- **ALLOCATE EXTENT**—Allocates a new extent for index.
  - **SIZE**—Stipulates extent size in bytes. Use K to specify the extent size in kilobytes or M to specify the extent size in megabytes. If you omit this parameter, Oracle determines the size based on the index's **STORAGE** parameters.
  - **DATAFILE**—Designates the datafiles in an index's tablespace that is to contain new extent. If you omit this parameter, Oracle chooses the datafile.

- INSTANCE—Makes the new extent accessible by the specified instance. In the absence of this parameter, the extent is available to all instances. This parameter is only valid if you are using the Parallel Server option in parallel mode.

- **physical_attributes_clause**—Modifies **PCTFREE, INITRANS,** and **MAXTRANS** parameter values.
- **storage_clause**—Modifies index storage parameters.
- LOGGING/NOLOGGING—Stipulates whether subsequent direct SQL*Loader and direct-load insert operations will be logged in the redo log file.
- RENAME TO—Changes the name of an index.
  - TABLESPACE—Stipulates a partitioned index default tablespace. The default is the default tablespace of the user issuing the command.
  - LOGGING/NOLOGGING—Specifies the default logging attribute of a partitioned index.
- MODIFY DEFAULT ATTRIBUTES—Stipulates new values for the default attributes of a partitioned index.
- MODIFY PARTITION—Changes an index partition's real physical attributes, logging options, or storage characteristics.
- UNUSABLE—Designates index or index partition(s) unusable. An unusable index must be rebuilt, or dropped and re-created. If one partition of an index is unusable, queries can still execute and use the index, as long as they do not access the unusable partition.
- RENAME PARTITION—Changes the name of an index partition.
- DROP PARTITION—Eliminates a partition and the data it contains from a partitioned global index and marks the index's next partition as unusable. You cannot drop the highest partition of a global index.
- REBUILD PARTITION—Rebuilds one partition of an index.
- SPLIT PARTITION—Divides a global partitioned index into two partitions. Splitting a partition marked as unusable creates two unusable partitions. The partitions must be rebuilt before you can use them.
  - AT (*value_list*)—Stipulates the new noninclusive upper bound for **split_partition_1**. The *value_list* must be less than the original partition bound for the old partition and greater than the partition bound for the next lowest partition, if there is one.

- INTO—Designates the two partitions resulting from the split.
- *partition_description, partition_description*—Designates names and physical attributes of the two partitions resulting from a split.

Dropping Indexes

You can remove an index with the **DROP INDEX** command. No data will be affected by this command. When an index is dropped, all the space allocated to the index is freed and available to be used by other objects in the tablespace that contained the index. When a table is dropped, all associated indexes are dropped automatically. To drop an index, the index must be in your schema, or you must have the **DROP ANY INDEX** system privilege. The following is an example of the **DROP INDEX** command:

```
DROP INDEX mytable_idx1;
```

Use the **ALTER TABLE** with the **DISABLE** or **DROP CONSTRAINT** command to remove indexes that are associated with unique or primary key constraints.

Practice Questions

Question 1

Which datatype stores values as fixed-length strings?

- a. **CHAR**
- b. **LONG**
- c. **TABLE**
- d. **VARRAY**
- e. **VARCHAR2**

Answer a is correct. The CHAR datatype stores values as fixed-length strings with padded blanks. LONG stores character data of variable length up to 2GB. TABLE is not a datatype. VARRAY is an ordered set of data elements and is not a fixed-length string. VARCHAR2 stores character values as variable-length strings.

Question 2

When you create a table using the **NOLOGGING** option and perform a direct-load insert, what effect does **NOLOGGING** have on the speed of the direct-load insert?

- a. It is slower, because data is inserted.
- b. It is faster, because a direct-load insert forces the table into logging mode.
- c. It is faster, because no redo information is generated.
- d. It is slower, because the statement is recorded in the redo log.
- e. None.

Answer c is correct. When a table is created with the NOLOGGING option, the direct-load insert is faster because it is not recorded in the redo logs. Answer a is incorrect; the insert will be faster because no redo information is generated. Answer b is incorrect, because direct-load insert does not force logging. Answer d is incorrect, because the statement will not be recorded in the redo log.

Question 3

Which function in the **DBMS_ROWID** package converts **ROWID** values into the block number in the relative file?

- ❍ a. **ROWID_OBJECT**
- ❍ b. **ROWID_CREATE**
- ❍ c. **ROWID_BLOCK_NUMBER**
- ❍ d. **ROWID_ABSOLUTE_FNO**
- ❍ e. **ROWID_RELATIVE_FNO**
- ❍ f. **ROWID_TO_RESTRICTED**

Answer c is correct. The **ROWID_BLOCK_NUMBER** function in the **DBMS_ROWID** package returns the block number stored in the row in the relative file. **ROWID_OBJECT** returns the object number of the extended **ROWID**. **ROWID_CREATE** creates a **ROWID** for testing purposes only. **ROWID_TO_ABSOLUTE_FNO** returns the absolute file number associated with the **ROWID** for a row in a specific table. **ROWID_RELATIVE_FNO** returns the file number of a **ROWID**. **ROWID_TO_RESTRICTED** converts an extended **ROWID** to restricted format.

Question 4

What does the **CASCADE** option do in the following command?

```
ANALYZE TABLE mytable
  VALIDATE STRUCTURE CASCADE;
```

- ❍ a. Re-creates all indexes
- ❍ b. Verifies that no other schema in the database owns a table called **mytable**
- ❍ c. Validates the structure of indexes associated with the table
- ❍ d. Verifies existence of a primary key index associated with the table

Answer c is correct. When you use the **ANALYZE TABLE VALIDATE STRUCTURE CASCADE** command on a table with indexes, the structure of the index is verified. This command does not re-create indexes. The **ANALYZE** command does not re-create indexes, verify unique table names in the database, or ensure that tables have primary keys.

Question 5

Which data dictionary view shows the number of empty blocks in a table after issuing the **ANALYZE TABLE** command?

- ❍ a. **DBA_TABLES**
- ❍ b. **DBA_OBJECTS**
- ❍ c. **DBA_EXTENTS**
- ❍ d. **DBA_SEGMENTS**
- ❍ e. **DBA_FREE_SPACE**
- ❍ f. **DBA_TABLESPACES**

Answer a is correct. The **EMPTY_BLOCKS** column in **DBA_TABLES** records the number of empty blocks in a table after the **ANALYZE TABLE** command is executed. **DBA_OBJECTS** lists all objects in the database. **DBA_EXTENTS** lists the extents comprising all segments in the database. **DBA_SEGMENTS** contains information about storage allocated for all database segments. **DBA_FREE_SPACE** lists the free extents in all tablespaces. **DBA_TABLESPACES** contains descriptions of all tablespaces.

Question 6

You want to choose a datatype that allows you to store multiple contact names for each record in the **CONTRACTS** table. Which datatype would you choose for the **CONTACT** column?

- ❍ a. **REF**
- ❍ b. **TABLE**
- ❍ c. **VARRAY**
- ❍ d. **VARCHAR2**
- ❍ e. **NVARCHAR2**

Answer c is correct. Specifying a **VARRAY** datatype creates an array with a maximum number of elements, each of the same datatype. The **REF** type denotes a reference to an object, instead of the object itself. **REF** types can occur in relational columns and also in attributes of object types. It does not store multiple elements. **TABLE** is not a datatype. **VARCHAR2** stores character values as variable-length strings. **NVARCHAR2** is a variable-length character string having maximum length size characters or bytes, depending on the choice of the national character set.

Question 7

Which function of the **DBMS_ROWID** package would you use to find the relative file number of a **ROWID**?

- ❍ a. **ROWID_OBJECT**
- ❍ b. **ROWID_ROW_NUMBER**
- ❍ c. **ROWID_TO_EXTENDED**
- ❍ d. **ROWID_RELATIVE_FNO**
- ❍ e. **ROWID_BLOCK_NUMBER**
- ❍ f. **ROWID_TO_RESTRICTED**

Answer d is correct. **ROWID_RELATIVE_FNO** returns the file number of a **ROWID**. **ROWID_OBJECT** returns the object number of the extended **ROWID**. The **ROWID_ROW_NUMBER** function in the **DBMS_ROWID** package returns the sequence number of a given **ROWID** value. **ROWID_TO_EXTENDED** converts a **ROWID** from a restricted format to an extended format. **ROWID_BLOCK_NUMBER** returns the block number of a **ROWID**. **ROWID_TO_RESTRICTED** converts an extended **ROWID** to restricted format.

Question 8

Which parameter indicates the rate of growth for each subsequent extent allocated to a table?

- ❍ a. **NEXT**
- ❍ b. **PCTINCREASE**
- ❍ c. **MAXEXTENTS**
- ❍ d. **INITIAL**

Answer b is correct. **PCTINCREASE** is the percent by which the next extent will increase. **NEXT** is the size of the next extent to be allocated to the table. **MAXEXTENTS** is the maximum number of extents that can be allocated to the table. **INITIAL** is the size of the first extent allocated to the table.

Question 9

Which data dictionary view would you query to find out if an index is valid?

❍ a. **DBA_TABLES**

❍ b. **DBA_IND_COLUMNS**

❍ c. **DBA_SEGMENTS**

❍ d. **DBA_INDEXES**

Answer d is correct. **DBA_INDEXES** displays the status of each index. **DBA_TABLES** does not have any information on indexes. **DBA_IND_COLUMNS** shows the columns of an index, not the status of an index. **DBA_SEGMENTS** contains information about storage allocated for all database segments.

Question 10

Which statement is true about bitmap indexes?

❍ a. They should only be used for very small tables.

❍ b. They are slower than all the other indexing techniques.

❍ c. They use substantially less space compared to other indexing techniques.

❍ d. A unique bitmap index will outperform a B-tree unique index.

Answer c is correct. Bitmap indexes require less space than other kinds of indexes. Table size is not an issue for bitmap indexes. Bitmap indexes can out perform other indexing techniques when the data is of a low cardinality. A unique bitmap index does not exist.

Question 11

When a table is truncated, what happens to the index?

- ❍ a. The index is truncated and the index space is deallocated.
- ❍ b. Truncating a table does not affect the table indexes.
- ❍ c. The index is truncated, but the index space remains allocated.
- ❍ d. The index is not truncated, but the index space is deallocated.

Answer a is correct. The **TRUNCATE** command deletes all the rows in the corresponding indexes and deallocates the space. This is a trick question, because answer c could also be correct if the **REUSE** option is used. The question assumes the default action of **TRUNCATE**, which is to drop storage. Answers b and d are incorrect, because all indexes associated with the table will get truncated.

Question 12

What is the maximum number of columns allowed in a concatenated index?

- ❍ a. 1
- ❍ b. 5
- ❍ c. 16
- ❍ d. 32
- ❍ e. Unlimited

Answer c is correct. The maximum number of columns in a concatenated index is 32.

Question 13

How is a partitioned index different from a nonpartitioned index?

- ❍ a. Partitioned indexes do not perform as well when more than five partitions are present.
- ❍ b. Partitioned indexes work best on small tables.
- ❍ c. Partitioned indexes cause I/O contention during index lookup.
- ❍ d. Partitioned indexes allow an index to be spread across multiple tablespaces.
- ❍ e. Partitioned indexes allow an index partition to be created for only one table partition.

Answer d is correct. A partitioned index can have its partitions in multiple tablespaces. Partitioned indexes perform better with more partitions. Partitioned indexes work best on large tables. Disk contention is decreased in a partitioned index. Partitioned indexes are often used with partitioned tables. A partition is created for each table partition.

Need To Know More?

Ault, Mike: *Oracle8 Administration and Management.* Wiley and Sons, Inc., New York, NY, 1998. ISBN 0-471-19234-1. An easy-to-understand book that explains how to set up Oracle for optimal performance.

Loney, Kevin, and Marlene Theriault: *Oracle8 DBA Handbook.* Oracle Press, Berkeley, CA, 1997. ISBN 0-07882-406-0. See Chapter 4, "Physical Database Layouts," and Chapter 5, "Managing the Development Process."

See the Oracle documentation that is provided on CD with the Oracle RDBMS software. Pertaining to this chapter are:

Fee, Joyce: *Oracle8 Administrator's Guide.* Oracle Corporation, Redwood City, CA, 1997. See Chapter 8, "Managing Tablespaces," and Chapter 9, "Managing Datafiles."

Lane, Paul: *Oracle8 Reference.* Oracle Corporation, Redwood City, CA, 1997. See Chapter 2, "Static Data Dictionary Views," and Chapter 3, "Dynamic Performance (V$) Views."

Leverenz, Lefty: *Oracle8 Concepts.* Oracle Corporation, Redwood City, CA, 1997. See Chapter 2, "Data Blocks, Extents, and Segments."

Lorentz, Diana: *Oracle8 SQL Reference.* Oracle Corporation, Redwood City, CA, 1997. See Chapter 4, "Commands."

Raphaely, Denis: *Oracle8 Application Developer's Guide, Release 8.0.* Oracle Corporation, Redwood City, CA, 1997. See Chapter 10, " Using Procedures and Packages."

http://education.oracle.com/tbt/ocp8.html is the site from which you can order the Oracle Education CD-ROM bundle for Oracle8 Database Administration.

www.revealnet.com is the site where RevealNet Corporation provides Oracle Administration reference software.

13

Managing Users, Profiles, Grants, And Roles

Terms you'll need to understand:

- √ Users
- √ Profiles
- √ Resource limits
- √ Account locking
- √ Password history
- √ Password verify function
- √ Grants
- √ System privileges
- √ Object privileges
- √ Roles

Techniques you'll need to master:

- √ Creating users
- √ Altering users
- √ Dropping users
- √ Creating profiles
- √ Locking accounts
- √ Setting password history
- √ Using the password verification function
- √ Granting system privileges
- √ Granting object privileges
- √ Using roles

Database access begins with the creation of users, who are then assigned specific rights to perform actions either directly or through roles. These rights to perform actions are called *system* and *object privileges*. System privileges are rights to perform actions in a database, and object privileges are access rights to an object (table, index, synonym, procedure, and so on) within a database, including the columns within tables.

This chapter explains how Oracle uses object and system privileges, along with profiles and roles, to manage users and objects.

Users

To access an Oracle database, an account must be created. Although not always the case, normally all users have their own Oracle database account created by the database administrator (DBA). The exceptions to this are the **SYS** and **SYSTEM** users that are created by Oracle when the database is created. The following sections discuss the creation, alteration, and dropping of Oracle database users.

Creating Users

You must have the **CREATE USER** privilege to create a user. You can create users with the Oracle Enterprise Manager (OEM) or at the command line in SQL*Plus. The command syntax for creating a user is illustrated in Figure 13.1.

Here is an example of how you create a user for an Oracle database:

```
CREATE USER james IDENTIFIED BY abc1
DEFAULT TABLESPACE temp
QUOTA 1M ON users
PROFILE enduser;
```

You need to assign each new user a password or indicate that operating system (OS) authentication will be used. Passwords are stored in the database in encrypted format and cannot be read by any user. The use of OS authentication means that once your user has logged in at the OS level, no username or password will be required when logging into the Oracle database. Users who are not assigned an Oracle password must be designated as **IDENTIFIED EXTERNALLY**. Oracle depends on the OS for user authentication.

When you create a user, you can designate a specific tablespace to be the default tablespace for the user. The designation of a default tablespace means that all the objects created by the user will be placed in that tablespace, unless the user specifically indicates that the database object be placed in another tablespace. If no default tablespace is indicated for a user, the **SYSTEM**

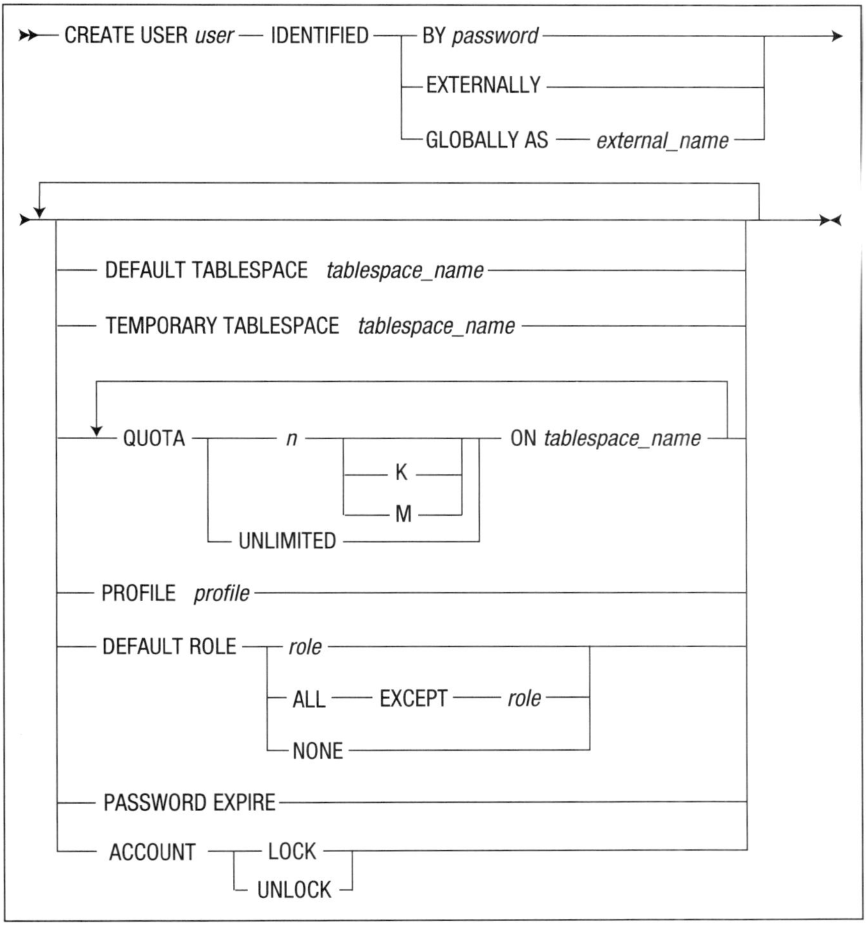

Figure 13.1 The syntax for creating a user.

tablespace is the default for the user. You should never let users create objects in the **SYSTEM** tablespace. Letting users default to the **SYSTEM** tablespace could cause it to run out of space, and thus cause database errors or input/output (I/O) contention for the data dictionary as well as other problems.

When you create a user, you can also designate a specific tablespace to be the temporary tablespace. This designation specifies the tablespace that will be used for any database actions that require use of a workspace for storage of intermediate results for actions, such as sorting.

If no temporary tablespace is indicated for a user, the **SYSTEM** tablespace is used. As stated previously, never let users default to using the **SYSTEM** tablespace. Designating a default tablespace, temporary tablespace, or quota on a tablespace does not implicitly grant any system or object privileges. You can give a user permission to create objects in tablespaces with the **QUOTA** clause.

As the DBA, you can access the **DBA_USERS** view for information on all users. All users can access the **USER_USERS** view for their own information. Tables 13.1 and 13.2 show the data stored in **DBA_USERS** and **USER_USERS**, respectively. To enable a user to create objects in a tablespace, you need to specify a quota for the user on the tablespace.

The tablespace quota can be limited to a specific amount of kilobytes or megabytes, or it can be designated as unlimited. An unlimited quota indicates that the user can have any portion of a tablespace that is not already in use by another user. If the user is not assigned the **UNLIMITED TABLESPACE** system privilege and the assigned limit is reached, the user will no longer be able to create additional objects or allocate new extents to any objects he/she owns in the tablespace.

> ***Note:*** *Remember that users granted the role* ***RESOURCE*** *are automatically granted the* ***UNLIMITED TABLESPACE*** *privilege as well, so only use this role when absolutely required.*

The **DBA_TS_QUOTAS** view provides tablespace quota information for all users in the database. The **USER_TS_QUOTAS** view provides tablespace

Table 13.1 The DBA_USERS view.

Column	Description
USERNAME	Name of the user
USER_ID	ID number of the user
PASSWORD	User encrypted password
DEFAULT_TABLESPACE	Default tablespace for data
TEMPORARY_TABLESPACE	Default tablespace for temporary table
CREATED	User creation date
PROFILE	User resource profile name
ACCOUNT_STATUS	Locked, expired, or unlocked
LOCK_DATE	Date the account was locked if **ACCOUNT_STATUS** = locked
EXPIRY_DATE	Account date of expiration
EXTERNAL_NAME	User external name used when a third-party service is used for authentication

Table 13.2 The USER_USERS view.

Column	Description
USERNAME	Name of the user
USER_ID	ID number of the user
ACCOUNT_STATUS	Locked, expired, or unlocked
LOCK_DATE	Date the account was locked if account status is locked
EXPIRY_DATE	Date of expiration of the account if **ACCOUNT_STATUS** = expired
DEFAULT_TABLESPACE	Default tablespace for data
TEMPORARY_TABLESPACE	Default tablespace for temporary tables
CREATED	User creation date
EXTERNAL_NAME	User external name

Table 13.3 The DBA_TS_QUOTAS view.

Column	Description
TABLESPACE_NAME	Tablespace name
USERNAME	User with resource rights on the tablespace
BYTES	Number of bytes charged to the user
MAX_BYTES	User's quota in bytes, or -1 if no limit
BLOCKS	Number of Oracle blocks charged to the user
MAX_BLOCKS	User's quota in Oracle blocks, or -1 if no limit

quota information for the current user. When you query **DBA_TS_QUOTAS** or **USER_TS_QUOTAS**, a designation of -1 in the **MAX_ BLOCKS** or **MAX_ BYTES** column indicates that the user has unlimited quota on that tablespace. Tables 13.3 and 13.4 show the data dictionary views associated with quotas.

Altering Users

To alter a user's characteristics, you must have the **ALTER USER** privilege. You can alter users with OEM or at the command line in SQL*Plus. The command-line syntax for altering a user is shown in Figure 13.2.

Table 13.4 The USER_TS_QUOTAS view.

Column	Description
TABLESPACE_NAME	Tablespace name
BYTES	Number of bytes charged to the user
MAX_BYTES	User's quota in bytes (-1 for **UNLIMITED**)
BLOCKS	Number of Oracle blocks charged to the user
MAX_BLOCKS	User's quota in Oracle blocks (or -1 or **UNLIMITED**)

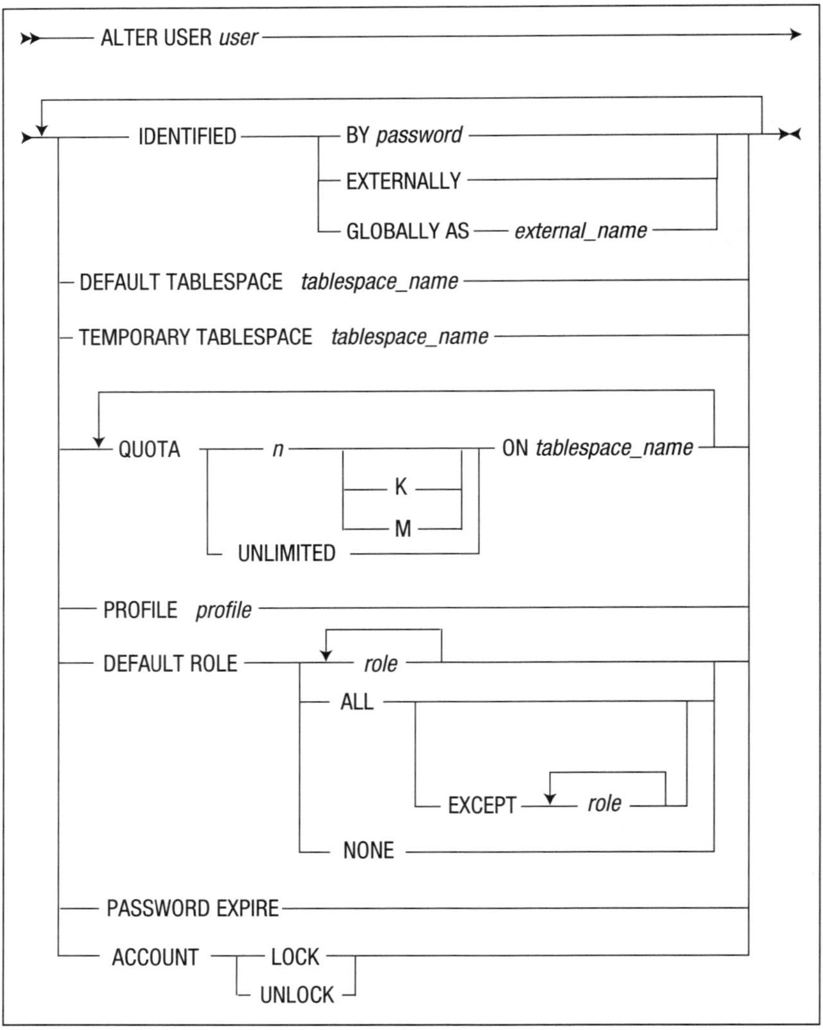

Figure 13.2 The syntax for altering a user.

Here is an example of how you alter a user for an Oracle database:

```
ALTER USER bill IDENTIFIED BY xyz2
DEFAULT TABLESPACE users
TEMPORARY TABLESPACE temp
QUOTA 1M ON users
PROFILE enduser
DEFAULT ROLE ALL;
```

After a user is created, the only thing that you cannot alter for that user is the username. You can alter the password, default tablespace, temporary tablespace, quota on the tablespace, profile, and default role with the **ALTER USER** system privilege. To force expiration of a user's password, for example, use this command:

```
ALTER USER bill IDENTIFIED BY billw PASSWORD EXPIRE;
```

To lock a user's account, use this command:

```
ALTER USER bill identified by billw ACCOUNT LOCK;
```

To unlock a user's account, use this command:

```
ALTER USER bill IDENTIFIED BY billw ACCOUNT LOCK;
```

These commands do not affect the current session; they are enforced the next time the user attempts to log in.

Each user can alter his or her originally assigned Oracle password, provided that the user is not identified externally (via the OS). In addition to the end user, users with the **ALTER USER** system privilege can issue the **ALTER USER** command to change their password. This privilege also allows the user to change the use of OS authentication. Any changes to a password take effect the next time the user logs into Oracle.

When you change the default tablespace for a user, all future objects the user creates will be created in the new default tablespace you designated (unless otherwise specified by the user at the time the object is created). Remember, a user must have a quota in a tablespace to create new objects in the tablespace. If a user reaches the maximum number of bytes assigned (specified in the quota), only a user with the **ALTER USER** system privilege can increase the quota limit.

Dropping Users

You must have the **DROP USER** system privilege to drop a user. You cannot drop a user currently connected to a database using only **DROP USER**; first, you have to terminate the user's sessions by means of either OEM or the SQL command **ALTER SYSTEM** with the **KILL SESSION** clause. You can drop users with OEM or at the command line in SQL*Plus. The command-line syntax for dropping a user is illustrated in Figure 13.3.

Here is an example of how you drop a user from an Oracle database:

```
DROP USER edward CASCADE;
```

If a user owns any database objects, you can drop the user only by including the **CASCADE** keyword in the **DROP USER** command, which drops the user and all objects owned by the user. If you are using OEM to drop a user, you need to indicate that the associated schema objects be included in the command. If a user owns objects and you fail to include **CASCADE**, you will receive an error message, and the user will not be dropped. You cannot drop a user who is currently connected to the database, until he or she exits or the session is killed. After a user is dropped, all information about the user and all objects owned by the user are removed from the database.

After you have issued the command to drop a user, you cannot perform a rollback to re-create the user and the user's objects. (**DROP USER** is a data definition language (**DDL**) command, which cannot be rolled back.)

If you need the objects created by a user, you can revoke the **CREATE SESSION** system privilege to prevent the user from logging on, instead of dropping the user. You can also copy the objects to another user by importing the objects from an export made before the user was dropped. To avoid the problem of dropping a user and losing your application tables, a separate application schema (instead of an actual database user schema) should own all application tables.

Profiles

Profiles are used to limit the database resources that can be used by a session or an individual call or SQL statement. When a database is created initially, all

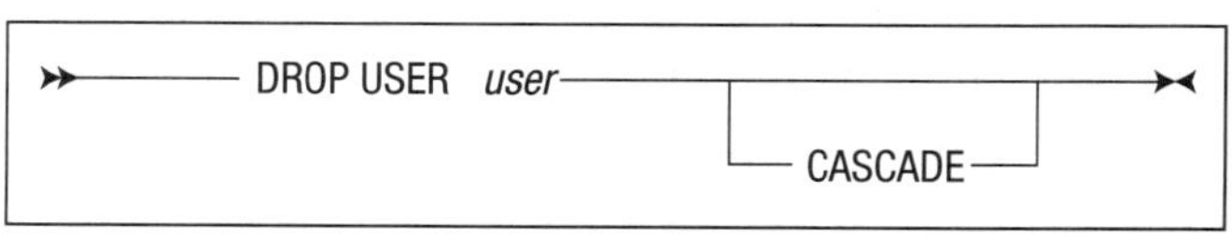

Figure 13.3 The syntax for the **DROP USER** command.

limits of the **DEFAULT** profile are set to **UNLIMITED**. Oracle handles enforcement of profile limits in the following ways:

- If a user exceeds the **CONNECT_TIME** or **IDLE_TIME** session resource limit, the current transaction is rolled back and the session is ended. On the next call to Oracle, an error message is returned.
- If an operation that exceeds the limit for other session resources is attempted, Oracle aborts the operation, rolls back the current statement, and immediately returns an error. A user can then commit or roll back the current transaction and must then end the session.
- If an operation that exceeds the limit for a single call is attempted, Oracle aborts the operation, rolls back the current statement, and returns an error message, leaving the current transaction intact.

Table 13.5 shows the resource limits that can be controlled through profiles.

The **RESOURCE_COST** view lists the cost for each resource. The view has two columns, **RESOURCE_NAME** and **UNIT_COST**.

Account Locking

Oracle can lock user accounts when they exceed a designated number of failed login attempts. The number of failed attempts is set by using the **CREATE PROFILE** statement. DBAs also specify the amount of time accounts remain locked.

In the following example, the maximum number of failed login attempts for the user jjay is four, and the amount of time the account will remain locked is one hour (the account will unlock automatically after one hour):

```
CREATE PROFILE prof LIMIT
FAILED_LOGIN_ATTEMPTS 4
PASSWORD_LOCK_TIME 1/24;
ALTER USER jjay PROFILE prof;
```

If the DBA does not specify a **PASSWORD_LOCK_TIME** for unlocking the account, Oracle uses a default value. If the DBA specifies **PASSWORD_LOCK_TIME** as **UNLIMITED**, then someone must explicitly unlock the account. After a user successfully logs into an account, the unsuccessful login attempt count is reset to 0.

The DBA can also explicitly lock user accounts. These locked accounts cannot be unlocked automatically.

Table 13.5 Resource limits that can be controlled through profiles.

Resource	Description
COMPOSITE_LIMIT	Specifies the total resources cost for a session, expressed in service units. Oracle calculates the total service units as a weighted sum of **CPU_ PER_SESSION**, **CONNECT_TIME**, **LOGICAL_ READS_PER_ SESSION**, and **PRIVATE_SGA**.
CONNECT_TIME	Limits the total elapsed time of a session, expressed in minutes.
CPU_PER_CALL	Limits the CPU time for a call (a parse, execute, or fetch), expressed in hundredths of seconds.
CPU_PER_SESSION	Limits the CPU time for a session, expressed in hundredth of seconds.
DEFAULT	Omits a limit for this resource in this profile. A user assigned this profile is subject to the limit for this resource specified in the **DEFAULT** profile.
FAILED_LOGIN_ATTEMPTS	Specifies the number of failed attempts to log in to the user account before the account is locked.
FUNCTION	Specifies the name of the password complexity verification routine.
IDLE_TIME	Limits periods of continuous inactive time during a session, expressed in minutes.
LOGICAL_READS_PER_CALL	Specifies the number of data blocks read for a call to process a SQL statement (a parse, execute, or fetch), including blocks read from memory and disk.
LOGICAL_READS_PER_SESSION	Specifies the number of data blocks read in a session, including blocks read from memory and disk.
NULL	Indicates that no password verification is performed.

(continued)

Table 13.5 Resource limits that can be controlled through profiles (continued).

Resource	Description
PASSWORD_GRACE_TIME	Specifies the number of days after the grace period begins during which a warning is issued and login is allowed. If the password is not changed during the grace period, the password expires.
PASSWORD_LIFE_TIME	Limits the number of days the same password can be used for authentication. The password expires if it is not changed within this period, and further connections are rejected.
PASSWORD_LOCK_TIME	Specifies the number of days an account will be locked after the specified number of consecutive failed login attempts.
PASSWORD_REUSE_MAX	Specifies the number of password changes required before the current password can be reused. If you set **PASSWORD_REUSE_MAX** to an integer value, then you must set **PASSWORD_REUSE_TIME** to **UNLIMITED**.
PASSWORD_REUSE_TIME	Specifies the number of days before which a password cannot be reused. If you set **PASSWORD_REUSE_TIME** to an integer value, then you must set **PASSWORD_REUSE_MAX** to **UNLIMITED**.
PASSWORD_VERIFY_FUNCTION	Allows a PL/SQL password complexity verification script to be passed as an argument to the **CREATE PROFILE** command. Oracle provides a default script, but you can create your own routine or use third-party software instead.
PRIVATE_SGA	Specifies the amount of private space a session can allocate in the shared pool of the only system global area (SGA), expressed in bytes. You can use K or M to specify this limit in kilobytes or megabytes. (This limit applies only if you are using multithreaded server architecture.) The private space for a session in the SGA includes private SQL and PL/SQL areas, but not shared SQL and PL/SQL areas.
SESSIONS_PER_USER	Limits a user to integer concurrent sessions.
UNLIMITED	Indicates that a user assigned this profile can use an unlimited amount of this resource.

Password Aging And Expiration

DBAs use the **CREATE PROFILE** statement to specify a maximum lifetime for passwords. When the specified amount of time passes and the password expires, the user or DBA must change the password. The following statement indicates that the user jjay can use the same password for 90 days before it expires:

```
CREATE PROFILE prof LIMIT
   FAILED_LOGIN_ATTEMPTS 4
   PASSWORD_LOCK_TIME 30
   PASSWORD_LIFE_TIME 90;
ALTER USER jjay PROFILE prof;
```

You can use the **CREATE PROFILE** statement to specify a grace period as well; this starts the first time the user attempts to log into a database account after his or her password has expired. During the grace period, a warning message appears each time a user attempts login; it continues to appear until the grace period expires. If the user does not change the password within the grace period, the account expires, and no further logins to the account are allowed until the password is changed.

For example, the lifetime of a password is 90 days, and the grace period is 5 days. The first time a user tries to log into the database after the 90th day, that user receives a warning message indicating that the password is about to expire in 5 days. If the user does not change the password within five days from the first day of the grace period, the user's account expires. The following statement specifies that the user must change the password within five days of its expiration:

```
CREATE PROFILE prof LIMIT
   FAILED_LOGIN_ATTEMPTS 4
   ACCOUNT_LOCK_TIME 30
   PASSWORD_GRACE_TIME 5;
ALTER USER jjay PROFILE prof;
```

Password History

The **CREATE PROFILE** statement can specify a time interval during which users cannot reuse a password as well as the number of password changes the user must make before reusing the current password. In the following statement, the DBA indicates that the user cannot reuse a password for 120 days:

```
CREATE PROFILE prof LIMIT
   PASSWORD_REUSE_TIME 120
   PASSWORD_REUSE_MAX UNLIMITED;
```

The next statement shows that the number of password changes the user must make before reusing the current password is five:

```
CREATE PROFILE prof LIMIT
PASSWORD_REUSE_MAX 5
PASSWORD_REUSE_TIME UNLIMITED;
```

Password Verify Function

You can specify Oracle's password complexity verification (password verify) function using the PL/SQL script (utlpwdmg.sql), which sets the default profile parameters. This function must be owned by **SYS**.

The password verify function makes sure passwords meet the following criteria:

- Has a minimum length of four characters
- Is not the same as the user ID
- Has at least one alpha and one numeric character as well as one punctuation mark
- Does not match simple words like *welcome*, *account*, *database*, or *user*
- Differs from the previous password by at least three letters

Here is an example of creating or altering a profile using the password verify function:

```
CREATE/ALTER PROFILE profile_name LIMIT
PASSWORD_VERIFY_FUNCTION routine_name
```

Privileges And Grants

You can grant two types of privileges:

- System privileges
- Object privileges

System privileges enable a user to perform a particular system-wide action or to perform a particular action on a particular type of object. For example, the privileges to create a table (**CREATE TABLE**) or to insert rows into any table (**INSERT ANY TABLE**) are system privileges.

Object privileges enable a user to perform a particular action on a specific object, including tables, views, sequences, procedures, functions, and packages. For example, the privilege to insert rows into a particular table is an object privilege. Object privilege grants always include the name of the object for which the privilege is granted and can extend down to the level of individual columns in a table. The following sections discuss these privileges.

System Privileges

All users require the **CREATE SESSION** privilege to access the database. This privilege is automatically granted to all users when you perform the grants using OEM. If you create users in SQL, you must remember to explicitly grant each user the **CREATE SESSION** system privilege either directly or through a role. Figure 13.4 shows the syntax for the **GRANT** command used to grant system privileges and roles.

System privileges can be granted to other users when the original grant made includes the **WITH ADMIN OPTION**.

Here is an example of granting system privileges with the **ADMIN OPTION**:

```
GRANT create session, create table
TO annie
WITH ADMIN OPTION;
```

Over 80 distinct privileges exist. Most of these are self-explanatory. Table 13.6 lists all the system privileges.

As the DBA, you can access the **DBA_SYS_PRIVS** view for information about the system privileges granted to users. The format of this view is shown in Table 13.7.

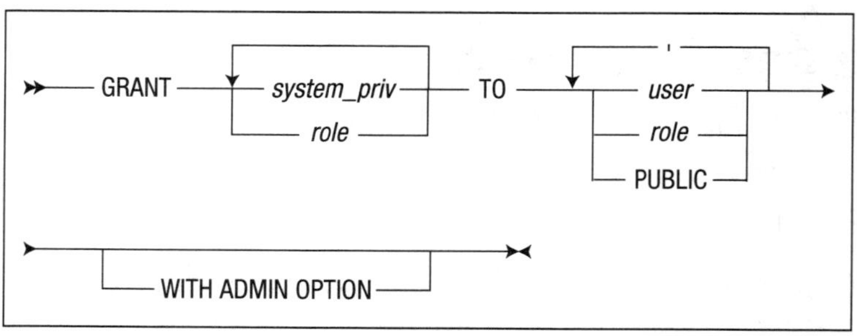

Figure 13.4 The syntax for the **GRANT** command to grant system privileges and roles.

Table 13.6 Oracle database system privileges.

Privilege	Permissible Operations
ALTER ANY CLUSTER	Change any cluster.
ALTER ANY INDEX	Change any index.
ALTER ANY PROCEDURE	Compile any stored procedure, function, or package in any schema.
ALTER ANY ROLE	Change any role.
ALTER ANY SEQUENCE	Change any sequence in any schema.
ALTER ANY TABLE	Change any table in any schema and compile any view in any schema.
ALTER ANY TRIGGER	Enable, disable, or compile any trigger in any schema.
ALTER DATABASE	Change the database and add files to the OS via Oracle.
ALTER PROFILE	Change any profile.
ALTER RESOURCE COST	Set costs for resources used in all user sessions.
ALTER ROLLBACK SEGMENT	Change rollback segments.
ALTER SESSION	Issue **ALTER SESSION** statements.
ALTER SNAPSHOT	Change any snapshot in any schema.
ALTER SYSTEM	Issue **ALTER SYSTEM** statements.
ALTER TABLESPACE	Change tablespaces and add datafiles to the OS via Oracle.
ALTER USER	Change other users. Change any user's password or authentication method, assign tablespace quotas, set default and temporary tablespaces, assign profiles and default roles in an **ALTER USER** statement.
ANALYZE ANY	Analyze any table, cluster, or index.
AUDIT ANY	Audit any schema object.
AUDIT SYSTEM	Enable and disable statement and privilege audit options.
BACKUP ANY TABLE	Perform an incremental export using the export utility. Perform in any schema.
BECOME ANY USER	Become another user. Any user performing a full database import requires this privilege.
COMMENT ANY TABLE	Comment on any table, view, or column in a schema.

(continued)

Table 13.6 Oracle database system privileges (continued).

Privilege	Permissible Operations
CREATE ANY CLUSTER	Create a cluster in any schema.
CREATE ANY INDEX	Create an index in any schema on any table.
CREATE ANY LIBRARY	Create callout libraries in any schema.
CREATE ANY PROCEDURE	Create stored procedures, functions, and packages in any schema. (User must also have these privileges: **ALTER ANY TABLE**, **BACKUP ANY TABLE**, **DROP ANY TABLE**, **SELECT ANY TABLE**, **INSERT ANY TABLE**, **UPDATE ANY TABLE**, **DELETE ANY TABLE**, and **GRANT ANY TABLE**.)
CREATE ANY SEQUENCE	Create any sequence in any schema.
CREATE ANY TABLE	Create tables in any schema. The schema in which a table is created must have space quota on the tablespace being used for the table.
CREATE ANY TRIGGER	Create any trigger in any schema associated with any table in any schema.
CREATE ANY USER	Create users. Assign quotas on any tablespace, set default and temporary tablespaces, and assign a profile as part of a **CREATE USER** statement.
CREATE ANY VIEW	Create a view in any schema. To create a view in another user's schema, you must have **CREATE ANY VIEW** privileges, and the owner must have the required privileges on the objects referenced in the view.
CREATE CLUSTER	Create a cluster in your own schema.
CREATE DATABASE LINK	Create private database links in your own schema.
CREATE LIBRARY	Create callout libraries in your own schema.
CREATE PROCEDURE	Create stored procedures, functions, and packages in your own schema.
CREATE PROFILE	Create profiles.
CREATE PUBLIC DATABASE LINK	Create public database links.
CREATE PUBLIC SYNONYM	Create public synonyms.
CREATE ROLE	Create roles.

(continued)

Table 13.6 Oracle database system privileges (continued).

Privilege	Permissible Operations
CREATE ROLLBACK SEGMENT	Create rollback segments.
CREATE SEQUENCE	Create a sequence in your own schema.
CREATE SESSION	Connect to the database.
CREATE SNAPSHOT	Create snapshots in any schema. You must also have the **CREATE ANY TABLE** privilege.
CREATE SYNONYM	Create any synonym in any schema.
CREATE TABLE	Create tables in your own schema and create indexes and integrity constraints on tables in your own schema. You must have a quota for the tablespace in which you are creating the table or the **UNLIMITED TABLESPACE** privilege.
CREATE TABLESPACE	Create tablespaces and add datafiles to the OS via Oracle.
CREATE TRIGGER	Create a trigger in your own schema.
CREATE VIEW	Create a view in your own schema.
DELETE ANY TABLE	Delete rows from any table or view in any schema.
DROP ANY CLUSTER	Drop any cluster.
DROP ANY INDEX	Drop any index.
DROP ANY LIBRARY	Drop callout libraries in any schema.
DROP ANY PROCEDURE	Drop any stored procedure, function, or package in any schema.
DROP ANY ROLE	Drop any role.
DROP ANY SEQUENCE	Drop any sequence in any schema.
DROP ANY SNAPSHOT	Drop any snapshot in any schema.
DROP ANY SYNONYM	Drop any synonym in any schema.
DROP ANY TABLE	Drop or truncate any table in any schema.
DROP ANY TRIGGER	Drop any trigger in any schema.
DROP ANY VIEW	Drop any view in any schema.
DROP LIBRARY	Drop callout libraries in your own schema.
DROP PROFILE	Drop any profile.
DROP PUBLIC DATABASE LINK	Drop public database links.

(continued)

Table 13.6 Oracle database system privileges (continued).

Privilege	Permissible Operations
DROP PUBLIC SYNONYM	Drop public synonyms.
DROP ROLLBACK SEGMENT	Drop rollback segments.
DROP TABLESPACE	Drop tablespaces.
DROP USER	Drop another user.
EXECUTE ANY PROCEDURE	Execute any procedure or function.
FORCE ANY TRANSACTION	Force the commit or rollback of any in-doubt distributed transaction in the local database.
FORCE TRANSACTION	Force the commit or rollback of own in-doubt distributed transaction in the local database.
GRANT ANY PRIVILEGE	Grant any system privilege.
GRANT ANY ROLE	Grant any role.
INSERT ANY TABLE	Insert rows into any table or view in any schema.
LOCK ANY TABLE	Lock any table or view in any schema.
MANAGE TABLESPACE	Take any tablespace offline, bring any tablespace online, and begin and end backups of any tablespace.
RESTRICTED SESSION	Connect when the database has been started using **STARTUP RESTRICT**.
SELECT ANY SEQUENCE	Reference any sequence in any schema.
SELECT ANY TABLE	Query any table, view, or snapshot in any schema.
UNLIMITED TABLESPACE	Use an unlimited amount of any tablespace. This privilege overrides any specific quotas assigned. If revoked, the grantee's schema objects remain but further tablespace allocation is denied unless allowed by specific tablespace quotas. This system privilege can be granted only to users and not to roles.
UPDATE ANY TABLE	Update rows in any table or view in any schema.

Table 13.7 The DBA_SYS_PRIVS view.

Column	Definition
GRANTEE	Oracle login name or role that received the privilege.
PRIVILEGE	System privilege granted to the user or role.
ADMIN_OPTION	Value = **YES**, grantee can pass along the privilege; value = **NO**, grantee cannot pass along the system privilege.

Users can see information related to them by accessing the corresponding user view named **USER_SYS_PRIVS**.

Object Privileges

Object privileges define a user's rights on existing database objects. All grants on objects take effect immediately.

To grant an object privilege, you must be the owner of the object, have been granted **WITH GRANT OPTION** on the object for the privilege, or have the system privilege **GRANT ANY PRIVILEGE**. You can also grant access to all users by granting the privilege to the **PUBLIC** account. Figure 13.5 shows the SQL syntax for the **GRANT** command and how to grant a table-level object privilege.

Here is an example of granting table-level grants:

```
GRANT select ON bob.emp TO derek;
```

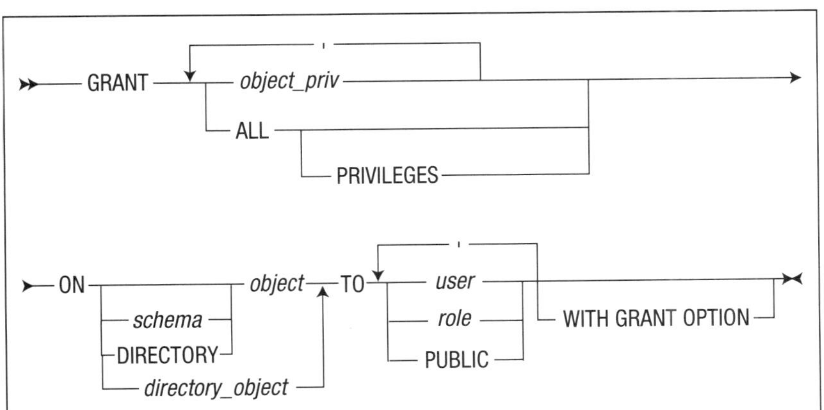

Figure 13.5 The syntax for the **GRANT** command used for a table-level grant.

As the DBA, you can access the **DBA_TAB_PRIVS** view for information on the object privileges granted to users. You should note that although it is named **DBA_TAB_PRIVS**, it also includes information on views and sequences as well as tables. Table 13.8 shows the contents of this view.

Users can see information on objects where they are the owner, grantor, or grantee by accessing the corresponding user view called **USER_TAB_PRIVS**. A user can see information for all objects where the user or the **PUBLIC** account is the grantee with the **ALL_TAB_PRIVS** view. The **ALL_TAB_PRIVS** view is slightly different from the **USER_TAB_PRIVS** and **DBA_TAB_ PRIVS** views. The contents of the **ALL_TAB_PRIVS** view are shown in Table 13.9.

A table owner can grant the following object privileges to other users:

- ALTER
- DELETE
- EXECUTE (for stored functions, procedures, and packages)
- INDEX
- INSERT
- REFERENCES
- SELECT
- UPDATE

All grants on objects and revoking of those grants are valid immediately, even if a user is currently logged into the database. The **SELECT** privilege can be granted only on tables, views, and snapshots. The **EXECUTE** privilege is used only for packages, procedures, and functions. Remember that packages, procedures, and functions are always executed with the permissions of the owner of the package, procedure, or function.

By granting other users **INSERT**, **UPDATE**, **DELETE**, and **SELECT** privileges on your table, you allow them to perform actions on the table. By granting the **ALTER** privilege, you can allow another user to modify the structure of your table or create a trigger on your table. By granting users the **INDEX** privilege, you can allow them to create indexes on your table. The **REFERENCES** privilege differs from the other privileges, because it does not actually grant the capability to change the table or data contained in the table. The **REFERENCES** privilege allows users to create foreign key constraints that reference your table.

Table 13.8 The DBA_TAB_PRIVS view.

Column	Description
GRANTEE	Name of the user who has been granted access
OWNER	Owner of the object
TABLE_NAME	Name of the object
GRANTOR	Name of the user who performed the grant
PRIVILEGE	Table privilege
GRANTABLE	Privilege can be granted

Table 13.9 The ALL_TAB_PRIVS view.

Column	Description
GRANTOR	Name of the user who performed the grant
GRANTEE	Name of the user who has been granted access
TABLE_SCHEMA	Schema of the object
TABLE_NAME	Name of the object
PRIVILEGE	Privilege on the object
GRANTABLE	If privilege is granted with **ADMIN OPTION**, value = **YES**, otherwise value = **NO**

A user can access the **USER_TAB_PRIVS_RECD** view for information about table privileges where the user is the grantee. The corresponding **ALL_TAB_PRIVS_RECD** view includes all grants on objects where the user or the **PUBLIC** account is the grantee. Table 13.10 shows the contents of the **USER_TAB_PRIVS_RECD** view.

Users can access the **USER_TAB_PRIVS_MADE** view for information about table privileges that they have granted to others. The corresponding **ALL_TAB_PRIVS_MADE** view includes information about all grants a user has made as well as grants made by others on the user's objects. Table 13.11 shows the contents of the **USER_TAB_PRIVS_MADE** view.

Column Privileges

Only **INSERT**, **UPDATE**, and **REFERENCES** privileges can be granted at the column level. When granting **INSERT** at the column level, ensure you grant access to all mandatory columns. Figure 13.6 shows the SQL syntax for the **GRANT** command.

Table 13.10 The USER_TAB_PRIVS_RECD view.

Column	Description
GRANTEE	Name of the user who has been granted access
OWNER	Owner of the object
TABLE_NAME	Name of the object
GRANTOR	Name of the user who performed the grant
PRIVILEGE	Privilege on the object
GRANTABLE	If privilege is granted with **ADMIN OPTION**, value = **YES**, otherwise value = **NO**

Table 13.11 The USER_TAB_PRIVS_MADE view.

Column	Description
GRANTEE	Name of the user who has been granted access
OWNER	Owner of the object
TABLE_NAME	Name of the object
GRANTOR	Name of the user who performed the grant
PRIVILEGE	Privilege on the object
GRANTABLE	If privilege is granted with **ADMIN OPTION**, value = **YES**, otherwise value = **NO**

Here is an example of granting updates on the columns of the EMP table belonging to the user named "edwin". **WITH GRANT OPTION** means that the user named "jone" can grant updates on this table to other users:

```
GRANT update ON edwin.emp TO jone WITH GRANT OPTION;
```

As the DBA, you can access the **DBA_COL_PRIVS** view for information about the column-level object privileges granted to a user. Table 13.12 shows the contents of the **DBA_COL_PRIVS** view.

Users can access the **USER_COL_PRIVS_RECD** view for information about column-level object privileges that have been granted to them. The **ALL_COL_PRIVS_RECD** view includes information about all column privileges that have been granted to them or to the **PUBLIC** account. The format of the **USER_TAB_PRIVS_RECD** view is shown in Table 13.13.

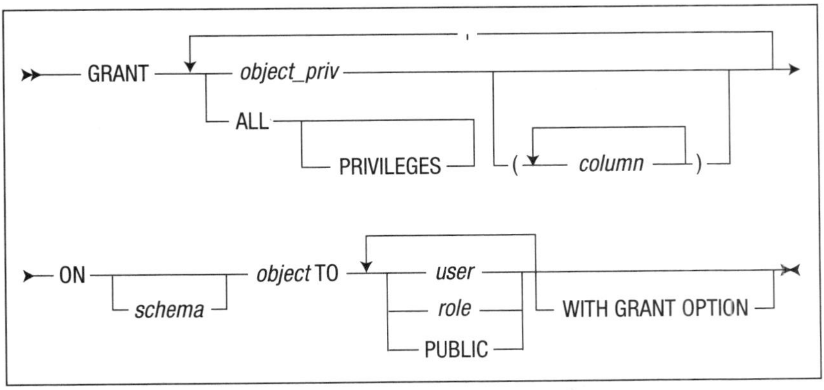

Figure 13.6 The syntax for the **GRANT** command used for column-level privilege grants.

Table 13.12 The DBA_COL_PRIVS view.

Column	Description
GRANTEE	Name of the user who has been granted access
OWNER	Username of the owner of the object
TABLE_NAME	Name of the object
COLUMN_NAME	Name of the column
GRANTOR	Name of the user who performed the grant
PRIVILEGE	Column privilege
GRANTABLE	If privilege is granted with **ADMIN OPTION**, value = **YES**, otherwise value = **NO**

Table 13.13 The USER_TAB_PRIVS_RECD view.

Column	Description
OWNER	Owner of the object
TABLE_NAME	Name of the object
GRANTOR	Name of the user who performed the grant
PRIVILEGE	Privilege on the object
GRANTABLE	Value set to **YES** if the privilege was granted with **ADMIN OPTION**, otherwise set to **NO**

Users can access the **USER_COL_PRIVS_MADE** view for information about column privileges that they have granted to others. The corresponding **ALL_COL_PRIVS_MADE** view includes information about all columns where the user is the owner or the grantor. The contents of the **USER_COL_PRIVS_MADE** view are shown in Table 13.14.

Users can access information about all columns where they are the grantor, grantee, or owner, or where access has been granted to the **PUBLIC** account with the corresponding **ALL_TAB_PRIVS_MADE** and **ALL_TAB_PRIVS_RECD** views.

Revoking Grants

The **REVOKE** command is used to take privileges away from users or roles. When system privileges are passed to others using **WITH ADMIN OPTION**, revoking the system privileges from the original user will not cascade. The system privileges granted to others must be revoked directly. In contrast, when object privileges are passed to others using **WITH GRANT OPTION**, the object privileges are revoked when the grantor's privileges are revoked.

> Only object privileges cascade when revoked; system privileges do not.

When **WITH ADMIN OPTION** or **WITH GRANT OPTION** has been included in a grant to another user, you cannot revoke the **WITH ADMIN OPTION** or **WITH GRANT OPTION** ability by itself. You must revoke the privilege and then issue another grant without **WITH ADMIN OPTION** or **WITH GRANT OPTION**. The SQL command-line syntax for revoking a system privilege is shown in Figure 13.7.

Table 13.14 The USER_COL_PRIVS_MADE view.

Column	Description
GRANTEE	Name of the user who has been granted access
TABLE_NAME	Name of the object
COLUMN_NAME	Name of the column
GRANTOR	Name of the user who performed the grant
PRIVILEGE	Privilege on the column
GRANTABLE	Value set to **YES** if the privilege was granted with **ADMIN OPTION**, otherwise set to **NO**

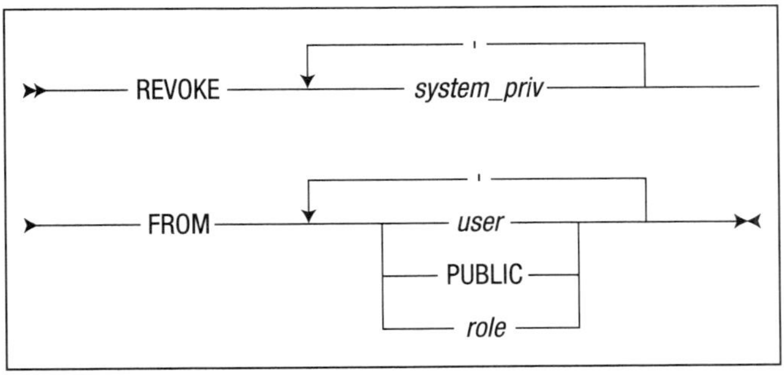

Figure 13.7 The syntax for revoking a system privilege.

Here is an example of revoking the **CREATE_TABLE** privilege:

```
REVOKE create table FROM judy;
```

To revoke an object privilege, you must either be the owner of the object, have granted the privilege to the user with **WITH GRANT OPTION**, or have the **GRANT ANY PRIVILEGE** system privilege.

You can revoke object and system privileges with OEM or at the command line in SQL*Plus. The command-line syntax for revoking an object privilege is shown in Figure 13.8.

Here is an example of revoking the **SELECT** privilege:

```
REVOKE select ON mike.emp FROM stan;
```

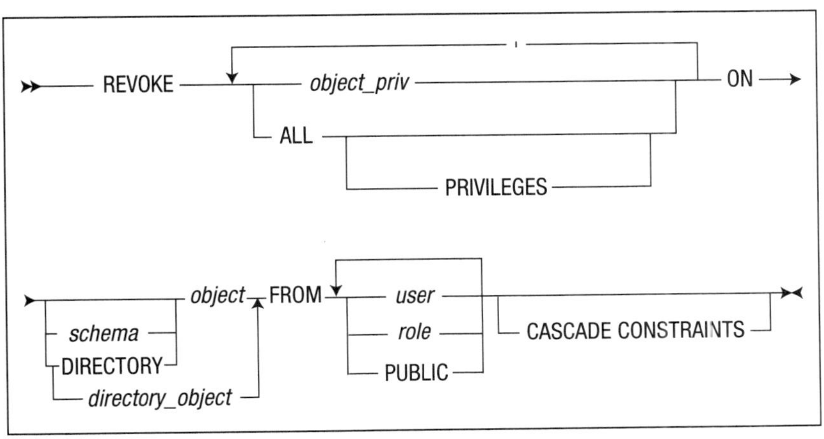

Figure 13.8 The syntax for revoking an object privilege.

When the object privilege **REFERENCES** has been granted, you must specify **CASCADE CONSTRAINTS** to drop the foreign key constraints that were created.

Use Of Roles

Using roles has several benefits, including:

- Reducing the number of grants, thereby making it easier to manage security
- Dynamically changing the privileges for many users with a single grant or revoke
- Selectively enabling or disabling depending on the application

Roles can be used for most system and object privileges. Privileges granted through a role cannot be used for creating views, packages, procedures, and functions. You instead need to grant privileges directly to the user.

Creating Roles

You need to create a role first and then grant system and object privileges to the role. When you create a role, there are three password options available:

- No authentication
- OS authentication
- Password authentication

You can set OS authentication either when the role is created or by using the database initialization parameters **OS_ROLES=TRUE** and **REMOTE_OS_ROLES=TRUE**. If you are using the multithreaded server option, you cannot use OS authenticating for roles.

To create a role, you must have the **CREATE ROLE** system privilege. You can create roles with OEM or at the command line in SQL*Plus. The command-line syntax for creating a role is shown in Figure 13.9.

The following is an example of creating a role in an Oracle database. **NOT IDENTIFIED** means that no password is associated with the role:

```
CREATE ROLE appusers NOT IDENTIFIED;
```

To alter a role, you must have the **ALTER ANY ROLE** system privilege or have been granted the role with **WITH ADMIN OPTION**. The creator of any role automatically has **WITH ADMIN OPTION** for the role.

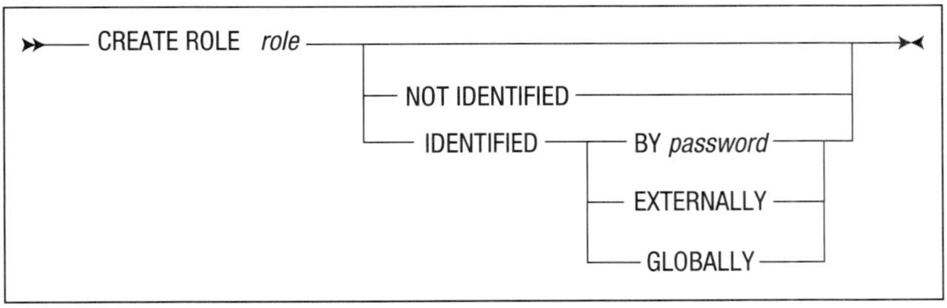

Figure 13.9 The syntax for creating a role.

Granting Roles

To grant a role to a user, you must either be the creator of the role or have the **GRANT ANY ROLE** privilege. You can grant roles to users with OEM or at the command line in SQL*Plus. Granted roles do not take effect for a user if the user is currently logged into the database with the role. When the user exits or sets another role, the changes take effect. Once roles have been granted to a user, they can be enabled and disabled.

The command-line syntax for granting privileges to a role is the same as the syntax for granting privileges to a user. Figure 13.10 shows the syntax for granting roles to users. Here is an example of granting a role to a user:

```
GRANT enduser TO patrick;
```

Figure 13.11 shows the syntax for granting system privileges to roles. Here is an example of granting a system privilege to a role:

```
GRANT create session TO enduser;
```

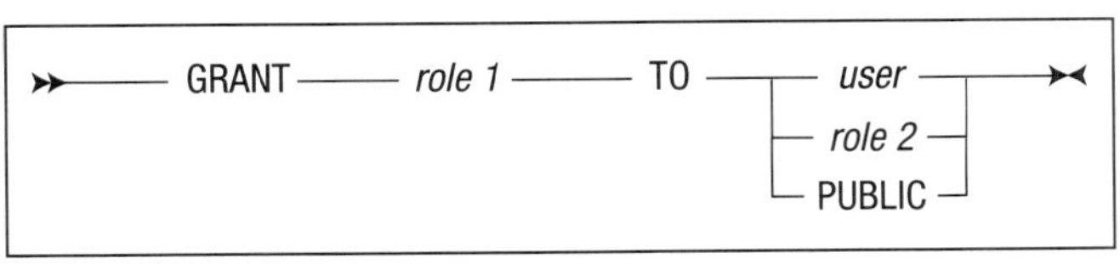

Figure 13.10 The syntax for granting roles to users.

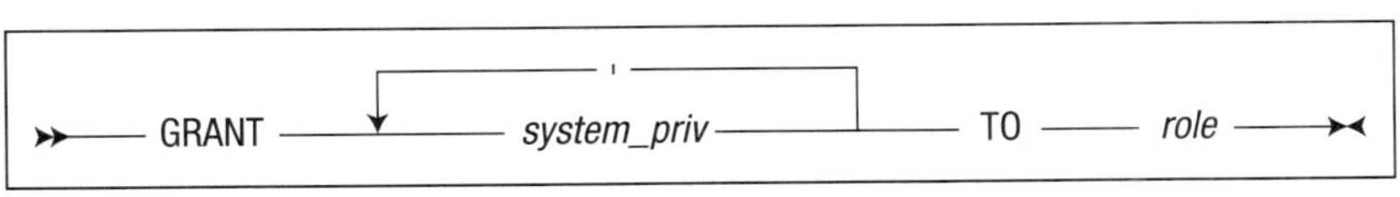

Figure 13.11 The syntax for granting system privileges to roles.

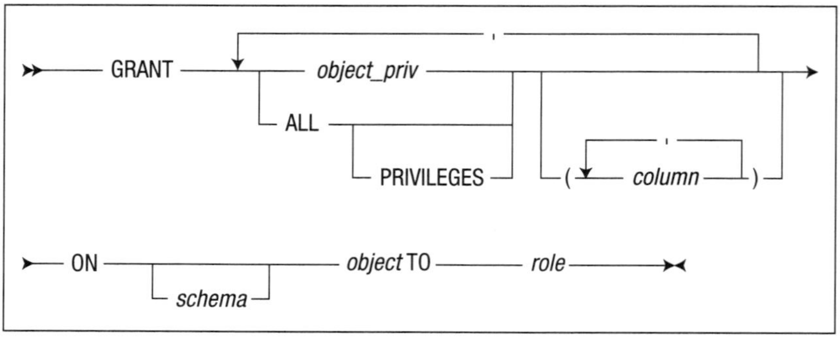

Figure 13.12 The syntax for granting object privileges to roles.

Figure 13.12 shows the syntax for granting object privileges to roles. Here is an example of granting an object privilege to a role:

```
GRANT select ON john.emp TO enduser;
```

System privileges can be granted to roles, with the exception of the **UNLIMITED TABLESPACE** system privilege. Grants on objects can be passed to other users or to roles if the grantee has been given **WITH GRANT OPTION**. However, you cannot assign a privilege that includes **WITH GRANT OPTION** to a role. The **INDEX** and **REFERENCES** privileges cannot be granted to a role; they must be granted only to a user. You can grant a role to a user or to another role. However, you cannot grant a role to itself.

See the data dictionary tables shown in Table 13.15 for information about views for roles.

Setting Roles

When a user is created, the default for active roles is set to **ALL**; this means that all the roles granted to a user are active. The DBA can change the default with an **ALTER USER** command. A user can enable multiple roles at one time and use the **SET ROLE** command to switch between roles or activate all roles with the command **SET ROLE ALL**. This command does not work if any of the roles assigned to the user requires either a password or OS authentication.

The SQL command-line syntax for setting roles is shown in Figure 13.13.

Table 13.15 Data dictionary views for roles.

Column	Description
DBA_ROLES	
PASSWORD_REQUIRED	Indication of whether the role requires a password to be enabled
ROLE	Role name
DBA_ROLE_PRIVS	
ADMIN_OPTION	Indication of whether the grant was with the **ADMIN** option (**YES**/**NO**)
DEFAULT_ROLE	Indication of whether the role is designated as a **DEFAULT ROLE** for the user (**YES**/**NO**)
GRANTED_ROLE	Granted role name
GRANTEE	Grantee name, user, or role receiving the grant
ROLE_ROLE_PRIVS	
ADMIN_OPTION	Indication of whether the grant was with the **ADMIN** option (**YES**/**NO**)
GRANTED_ROLE	Role that was granted
ROLE	Name of the role
ROLE_SYS_PRIVS	
ADMIN_OPTION	Indication of whether the grant was with the **ADMIN** option (**YES**/**NO**)
PRIVILEGE	System privilege granted to the role
ROLE	Name of the role
ROLE_TAB_PRIVS	
COLUMN_NAME	Name of the column, if applicable
GRANTABLE	Value set to **YES** if the privilege was granted with **ADMIN OPTION**, otherwise set to **NO**
OWNER	Owner of the object
PRIVILEGE	Object privilege granted to the role
ROLE	Name of the role
TABLE_NAME	Name of the object
SESSION_ROLES	
ROLE	Name of the roles that are currently enabled to the user

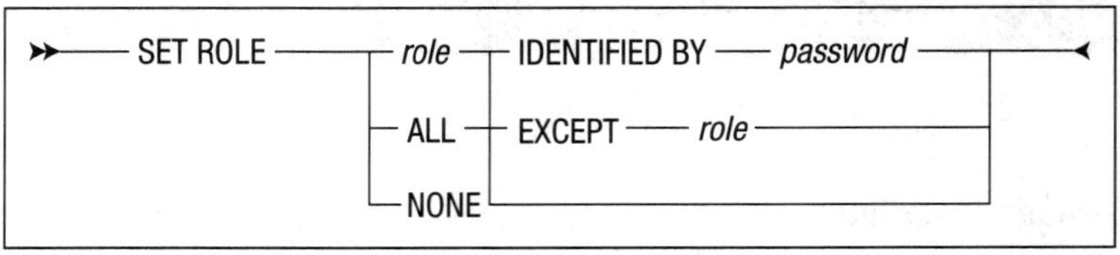

Figure 13.13 The syntax for setting roles.

Here is an example of setting a role with a password of "gucci":

```
SET ROLE bridge_update IDENTIFIED BY gucci;
```

Users can look at the **SESSION_ROLES** view to find the roles that are currently enabled for them, and at **SESSION_PRIVS** view to see the privileges available to their session.

If you determine that all control of roles will be at the OS level, you must set the database initialization parameter **OS_ROLES** equal to **TRUE**. All roles must still be created first in the database. Any grants you previously made using the database command line or OEM are still listed in the data dictionary, but they cannot be used and are not in effect. If the use of roles is determined at the OS level, the multithreaded server option cannot be used.

You can use the **MAX_ENABLED_ROLES** parameter in the database initialization file to set the number of roles that you will allow any user to have enabled at one time.

Special Roles

Oracle creates the following two roles when you install the Oracle executables:

- OSDBA
- OSOPER

Oracle creates the following three roles when you create the database:

- CONNECT
- DBA
- RESOURCE

When you execute the catalog.sql script, the following roles are created:

- DELETE_CATALOG_ROLE
- EXECUTE_CATALOG_ROLE
- EXP_FULL_DATABASE

- IMP_FULL_DATABASE
- SELECT_CATALOG_ROLE

For an explanation of the **OSDBA** and **OSOPER** roles, see Chapter 4. The following sections explain the other special roles.

CONNECT, **RESOURCE**, And **DBA** Roles

The **CONNECT**, **RESOURCE**, and **DBA** roles are predefined roles that are available for backward compatibility. Because the status of these roles might change, you may want to create your own roles rather than relying on these. These are created by Oracle when the database is created. When you create a user with OEM, the **CONNECT** role is automatically granted to the user.

The following system privileges are granted to the **CONNECT** role:

- ALTER SESSION
- CREATE CLUSTER
- CREATE DATABASE LINK
- CREATE SEQUENCE
- CREATE SESSION
- CREATE SYNONYM
- CREATE TABLE
- CREATE VIEW

The **DBA** role includes all system privileges, the capability to grant those system privileges to others, and **UNLIMITED TABLESPACE**. If the **EXP_FULL_DATABASE** and **IMP_FULL_DATABASE** roles have been created, they are granted implicitly with the **DBA** role.

When you grant a user the **RESOURCE** role, the user is granted the **UNLIMITED TABLESPACE** system privilege as well. The following system privileges are granted to the **RESOURCE** role:

- CREATE CLUSTER
- CREATE PROCEDURE
- CREATE SEQUENCE
- CREATE TABLE
- CREATE TRIGGER

You can grant additional privileges to or revoke privileges from the **CONNECT**, **RESOURCE**, and **DBA** roles just as you would any other role that you created.

Export/Import Roles

Oracle provides a script entitled catexp.sql to create the **EXP_FULL_DATABASE** and **IMP_FULL_DATABASE** roles. You can grant these to a user who will be executing the export and import utilities.

The **EXP_FULL_DATABASE** role has the **SELECT ANY TABLE** and **BACKUP ANY TABLE** system privileges. In addition, this role has **INSERT**, **DELETE**, and **UPDATE** privileges on the **SYS.INCVID**, **SYS.INCFIL**, and **SYS.INCEXP** tables.

The **IMP_FULL_DATABASE** role has the **BECOME USER** system privilege.

Catalog Roles

Users with explicit object privileges and the **SYSDBA** account can access dictionary objects. If you do not have explicit object privileges, you can be granted the following roles:

- DELETE_CATALOG_ROLE
- EXECUTE_CATALOG_ROLE
- RECOVERY_CATALOG_OWNER
- SELECT_CATALOG_ROLE

DELETE_CATALOG_ROLE enables users to delete records from the **AUD$** audit table. **EXECUTE_CATALOG_ROLE** provides execute privilege on packages in the dictionary. **RECOVERY_CATALOG_OWNER** is granted to the user, normally RMAN, that will own the recovery catalog. **SELECT_CATALOG_ROLE** enables users to select all catalog views and tables. Grant this role to users who must access all the views and tables in the data dictionary.

Practice Questions

Question 1

Which one of the following choices is a system privilege?

❍ a. **INSERT**

❍ b. **SELECT ANY TABLE**

❍ c. **REFERENCES**

❍ d. **EXECUTE**

Answer b is correct. **SELECT** is an object privilege, but **SELECT ANY TABLE** is a system privilege. **INSERT**, **EXECUTE**, and **REFERENCES** are all object privileges.

Question 2

Which command would cause this condition?

```
ERROR:
ORA-28000 the account is locked
Warning: You are no longer connected to Oracle
```

❍ a. **DROP USER**

❍ b. **ALTER USER QUOTA**

❍ c. **ALTER USER ACCOUNT LOCK**

❍ d. **DROP USER CASCADE**

❍ e. **ALTER USER QUOTA UNLIMITED**

Answer c is correct. A user account can be locked by changing a user's password or by locking the account. **DROP USER** eliminates the account from Oracle. **ALTER USER QUOTA** changes a users quota on a tablespace. **DROP USER CASCADE** eliminates a user account from the database and all the account's objects. **ALTER USER QUOTA UNLIMITED** gives the users unlimited usage of space on a tablespace.

Question 3

Which would be user Paul's default tablespace?

```
CREATE USER paul IDENTIFIED BY kilroy
TEMPORARY TABLESPACE temp01
QUOTA 20M ON data01;
```

❍ a. TEMP

❍ b. USERS

❍ c. DATA01

❍ d. **SYSTEM**

Answer d is correct. If the **DEFAULT TABLESPACE** clause is not used when a user is created, the user's default tablespace is the **SYSTEM** tablespace. TEMP and USERS are not referenced in the **CREATE USER** command and are not used. Paul is given 20MB of space on the tablespace named data01, but it is not defined as the **DEFAULT TABLESPACE**.

Question 4

Why would you query **SESSION_ROLES**?

❍ a. To display all roles in the database

❍ b. To determine the roles granted to a user

❍ c. To display the roles currently enabled for a user

❍ d. To display information about system privileges granted to roles

Answer c is correct. **SESSION_ROLES** displays the roles currently enabled for a user. All roles in the database are displayed by the **DBA_ROLES** view (answer a). Roles granted to a user are displayed by the **DBA_ROLE_PRIVS** view (answer b). System privileges granted to roles are displayed by the **ROLE_SYS_PRIVS** view (answer d).

Question 5

Which view would you query to display information about password expiration, locking dates, and account status for a user?

- a. **DBA_USERS**
- b. **DBA_TABLES**
- c. **DBA_OBJECTS**
- d. **DBA_PROFILES**
- e. **DBA_TABLESPACE**

Answer a is correct. **DBA_USERS** displays information about password expiration, locking dates, and account status for all the database users. **DBA_TABLES** displays information about tables. **DBA_OBJECTS** displays information about database objects. **DBA_PROFILES** displays information about database profiles. **DBA_TABLESPACES** displays information about tablespaces.

Question 6

How do you enable the password verification function?

- a. Use the **ORAPWD** utility.
- b. Execute the catproc.sql script in the **SYS** schema.
- c. Execute the utlpwdmg.sql script in the **SYS** schema.
- d. Set the **PASSWORD_VERIFY** initialization parameter to **TRUE**.

Answer c is correct. The utlpwdmg.sql script enables the **VERIFY_FUNCTION** function and alters the default profile. The **ORAPWD** utility creates a password file for users granted the **SYSDBA** or **SYSOPER** privileges. It does not check the password for every user. The catproc.sql script sets up the database to use PL/SQL. **PASSWORD_VERIFY** is not an initialization parameter.

Question 7

Which **CREATE USER** command clause would you use to give a user the ability to use 20MB on the USERS tablespace?

- ❍ a. **QUOTA**
- ❍ b. **PROFILE**
- ❍ c. **DEFAULT TABLESPACE**
- ❍ d. **TEMPORARY TABLESPACE**

Answer a is correct. The QUOTA clause defines the amount of space that a user can use to create and maintain objects in a specified tablespace. The PROFILE clause assigns a profile to a user. DEFAULT TABLESPACE assigns a default tablespace for a user but does not define space usage. TEMPORARY TABLSPACE assigns a temporary tablespace to a user for temporary segments.

Question 8

What is the setting **SESSIONS_PER_USER** in the **DEFAULT** profile if it has never been altered?

- ❍ a. 0
- ❍ b. 1
- ❍ c. 5
- ❍ d. 10
- ❍ e. Unlimited

Answer e is correct. User profiles can be created to limit the amount of system and database resources for a user. If a user is not assigned a profile, then the default database profile is used, giving unlimited access to resources.

Question 9

Which predefined role has all the system privileges?

- ❍ a. **DBA**
- ❍ b. **CONNECT**
- ❍ c. **RESOURCE**
- ❍ d. **IMP_FULL_DATABASE**
- ❍ e. **DELETE_CATALOG_ROLE**

Answer a is correct. The **DBA** role is granted all the system privileges with the **WITH ADMIN OPTION**. **CONNECT** allows users to establish sessions with the database and create objects in the accounts schema. The **RESOURCE** role assigns only the **UNLIMITED TABLESPACE** system privilege. **IMP_FULL_DATABASE** assigns only the privileges needed to do a full import. **DELETE_CATALOG_ROLE** does not grant any system privileges.

Question 10

Which object privilege do you need to grant privileges on an object not in your schema?

- ❍ a. **PUBLIC**
- ❍ b. **REFERENCES**
- ❍ c. **WITH GRANT OPTION**
- ❍ d. **WITH ADMIN OPTION**

Answer c is correct. To grant an object privilege to another user, you must have been granted the privilege **WITH GRANT OPTION**. **PUBLIC** is not a privilege—it is a special user account. **REFERENCES** is used for defining a foreign key integrity constraints on tables only. This question is tricky because **WITH ADMIN OPTION** is used for system privileges, not object privileges.

Question 11

Which statement is true about a role?

❍ a. It is owned by **DBA**.

❍ b. It can be granted to itself.

❍ c. It can consist only of object privileges.

❍ d. It can be granted to any role except itself (even circularly).

Answer d is correct. A role can be granted to a user, to another role, or to **PUBLIC**. **DBA** is a role and can't own roles. A role cannot be granted to itself. Roles can contain system and object privileges as well as other roles.

Need To Know More?

Ault, Mike: *Oracle8 Administration and Management*. John Wiley & Sons, Inc., New York, NY, 1998. ISBN 0-471-19234-1. An easy-to-understand book that explains how to set up Oracle for optimal performance.

Loney, Kevin, and Marlene Theriault: *Oracle8 DBA Handbook*. Oracle Press, Berkeley, CA, 1997. ISBN 0-07882-406-0. See Chapter 9, "Database Security and Auditing."

See the Oracle documentation that is provided on CD with the Oracle RDBMS software. Pertaining to this chapter are:

Fee, Joyce: *Oracle8 Administrator's Guide*. Oracle Corporation, Redwood City, CA, 1997. See Chapter 19, "Establishing Security Policies," Chapter 20, "Managing Users and Resources," and Chapter 21, "Managing User Privileges and Roles."

Lane, Paul: *Oracle8 Reference*. Oracle Corporation, Redwood City, CA, 1997. See Chapter 1, "Initialization Parameters" and Chapter 2, "Static Data Dictionary Views."

Lorentz, Diana: *Oracle8 SQL Reference*. Oracle Corporation, Redwood City, CA, 1997. See Chapter 4, "Commands."

http://education.oracle.com/tbt/ocp8.html is the site from which you can order the Oracle Education CD-ROM bundle for Oracle8 Database Administration.

www.revealnet.com is the site where RevealNet Corporation provides Oracle Administration reference software.

14

Maintaining Data Integrity

Terms you'll need to understand:

- √ CHECK
- √ FOREIGN KEY
- √ NOT NULL
- √ PRIMARY KEY
- √ UNIQUE KEY
- √ DISABLE
- √ ENABLE NOVALIDATE
- √ ENABLE VALIDATE
- √ SET CONSTRAINTS ALL
- √ SET CONSTRAINTS DEFERRED
- √ SET CONSTRAINTS IMMEDIATE
- √ ALTER TABLE

Techniques you'll need to master:

- √ Disabling constraints
- √ Enabling and validating constraints
- √ Enabling constraints with the **NOVALIDATE** option
- √ Deferring constraint checking
- √ Dropping integrity constraints
- √ Creating an **EXCEPTIONS** table
- √ Storing exception information in the **EXCEPTIONS** table
- √ Listing integrity constraint information from the data dictionary

You can maintain data integrity through application code, database triggers, or declared integrity constraints. Unless you can guarantee that all interactions with your data will happen through applications, it is a good idea to keep data integrity checking at the database level. Whereas database triggers allow you to define and enforce integrity rules, a database trigger is not the same as an integrity constraint. You can define a database trigger to enforce an integrity rule, but it cannot check data already loaded into a table. Therefore, you should use database triggers only when the integrity rule cannot be enforced by integrity constraints.

Managing Integrity Constraints

Oracle databases let you store rules about data, called *integrity constraints*, in the database and enforce those rules from the database. Table 14.1 describes the integrity constraint options that you can use to impose data restrictions on the input of column values.

A constraint checks data as it is entered or updated in the database and prevents data that does not conform to the constraint's rule from being entered. A constraint is not always enforced, however, for various reasons. For example, the constraint could have been added after the table was loaded, or it could have been disabled and enabled with the **NOVALIDATE** option. No matter what the reason is, in some circumstances data could exist in the database that violates the integrity constraints, causing the database administrator (DBA) to manage these integrity constraints.

An integrity constraint defined on a table can be in one of three states:

- DISABLE—A disabled constraint does not enforce the integrity constraint on the data values in the columns included in the constraint, but it does keep the definition of the constraint in the data dictionary. This mode is useful if you want to speed up loading data into the database.

- ENABLE NOVALIDATE—A table that has a constraint that is enabled with the **NOVALIDATE** option can contain invalid data, because the constraint does not validate existing rows. New rows, however, cannot violate the constraint. This mode is useful if you know that the data that was loaded does not violate the constraint and you do not want to incur the performance cost of validating the data.

- ENABLE VALIDATE—This is the default status of a constraint. It ensures that all new insert, delete, and update operations on the constrained data comply with the constraint. All existing data is checked to ensure that it obeys the constraint. An enabled and validated constraint guarantees that all data is and will continue to be valid.

Table 14.1 Integrity constraints.

Constraint	Description
CHECK	Requires that a specified condition be true or unknown for every row of the table. The condition of a **CHECK** constraint must be a Boolean expression evaluated by using the values in the row being inserted or updated. The condition also can't contain subqueries; sequences; **SYSDATE**, **UID**, **USER**, or **USERENV SQL** functions; or pseudocolumns **LEVEL** and **ROWNUM**.
FOREIGN KEY	Denotes the column or set of columns included in the definition of the referential integrity constraint. The foreign key column(s) can't be inserted or changed unless the primary key on the referenced trable has these same key values.
NOT NULL	Requires that every row have a value. The **NULL** value isn't allowed in this column.
PRIMARY KEY	Denotes the column or set of columns that uniquely identifies a table row. The column(s) must be unique and have values in each row. A table can have only one primary key.
UNIQUE KEY	Requires that no two rows of a table have duplicate values in a specified column or set of columns.

Disabling Constraints

Normally, integrity constraints are in the **ENABLE VALIDATE** state, but at times you might want to disable an integrity constraint. This could help the performance of large data loads or batch operations that do a great number of updates, or if an import is taking place on existing tables. While constraints are disabled, data that violates the integrity constraint can be inserted. Therefore, once any of these operations is completed, the constraint should be enabled and validated. Here is an example of disabling constraints:

```
ALTER TABLE city DISABLE UNIQUE (cityname, countyname, state);
```

Enabling NOVALIDATE

You can enable a constraint without validating the data in the table by using the **ENABLE NOVALIDATE** option. Using this option is much faster than enabling and validating a constraint. This option is very useful in cases where it is known that all existing data conforms to the constraint. Here is an example of enabling a constraint without validating it:

```
ALTER TABLE city ENABLE NOVALIDATE CONSTRAINT ck_cityname;
```

Enabling And Validating Constraints

When a constraint is enabled with the validation option (which is the default), all the rows in the table are checked to see that they conform to the constraint rules. No row that violates the constraint can be inserted into the table as long as a constraint is enabled. Here is an example of enabling a constraint and validating it:

```
ALTER TABLE ENABLE CONSTRAINT VALIDATE ck_cityname;
```

You can use the **EXCEPTIONS** table to examine any rows that violate constraints. You must create an appropriate exceptions report table to accept information from the **EXCEPTIONS** option of the **ENABLE CONSTRAINT** clause before enabling the constraint. You can create an **EXCEPTIONS** table by using the script utlexcpt.sql, which creates a table named **EXCEPTIONS**. This file can be found in the rdbms/admin directory under the Oracle home directory.

Deferring Constraint Checks

You can use the **SET CONSTRAINTS** statement to change the way Oracle checks constraints. The constraint can be checked when a transaction is committed (referred to as **DEFERRED**) or when each row is processed (referred to as **IMMEDIATE**). The set constraints mode stays in effect until the transaction commits or another **SET CONSTRAINTS** statement is issued. Using the **SET CONSTRAINTS** command does not change the default constraint checking specified when you created the constraint.

> Issuing a **SET CONSTRAINTS** statement inside a trigger is not allowed.

The **SET CONSTRAINTS** clause has the following three options:

- ALL—Sets all the constraints for this transaction to **IMMEDIATE** or **DEFERRED** checking.
- DEFERRED—Specifies that the rules of the deferrable constraint are checked when the transaction is committed.
- IMMEDIATE—Specifies that the rules of the constraint are checked immediately after each data manipulation statement (DML) statement.

The following is an example of setting all constraints for a transaction as **IMMEDIATE** in the current session:

```
SET CONSTRAINTS ALL IMMEDIATE;
```

If you have deferred constraint checking, you can check all constraints by using the **SET ALL CONSTRAINTS IMMEDIATE** before committing. The advantage of doing this is that if a problem arises with a constraint, the command will fail and the constraint causing the error will be identified without rolling back any transactions. If you validate during the commit and a constraint failure occurs, the transaction will roll back.

Dropping Integrity Constraints

You can use the **ALTER TABLE** command to drop integrity constraints if the rules they enforce are no longer needed. Use the **ALTER TABLE** command with the **DROP** clause as shown in the following example:

```
ALTER TABLE district
    DROP UNIQUE (dname, loc);
ALTER TABLE city
    DROP PRIMARY KEY;
ALTER TABLE city
    DROP CONSTRAINT district_fkey;
```

When you drop a unique key or primary key constraint, the indexes associated with the constraints are also dropped. When foreign keys reference a unique or primary key that is being dropped, the **CASCADE CONSTRAINTS** clause must be added in the **DROP** statement, or you cannot drop the constraint.

Managing Exceptions

When a constraint is enabled and fails the integrity check, an error is returned and the constraint remains disabled. If exceptions exist, you cannot enable the constraint until all exceptions to the constraint are either updated or removed. Use the **EXCEPTIONS** option in the **ENABLE** clause to store the **ROWID**, table owner, table name, and constraint name of all exception rows into a specified table. As stated in the "Enabling And Validating Constraints" section earlier in this chapter, you must first create the **EXCEPTIONS** tables by running the utlexcpt.sql script. You can modify this script to create multiple exception tables with different names. When managing exceptions, the goal is to eliminate all exceptions in the **EXCEPTIONS** table.

The following statement tries to enable the primary key of the **DISTRICT** table, and if exceptions exist, information is inserted into a table named **EXCEPTIONS**:

```
ALTER TABLE district
      ENABLE PRIMARY KEY EXCEPTIONS INTO exceptions;
```

If duplicate primary key values exist in the **DISTRICT** table, the rows inserted into the **EXCEPTIONS** table might look like this:

```
SELECT * FROM exceptions;

ROWID              OWNER      TABLE_NAME     CONSTRAINT
------------------ -----      ----------     ----------
AAAAZ9AABAAABvqAAB TWAY       DISTRICT       SYS_C00275
AAAAZ9AABAAABvqAAG TWAY       DISTRICT       SYS_C00275
```

You can join the **EXCEPTIONS** table with the **DISTRICT** table to produce a report of the rows that violate the constraint, as shown in the following example:

```
SELECT disno, dname, city FROM district, exceptions
    WHERE exceptions.constraint = 'SYS_C00275'
    AND district.rowid = exceptions.row_id;

DISNO      DNAME            CITY
-----      -------------    -----------
9          DISTRICT NINE    ST. LOUIS
9          DISTRICT NINE    KANSAS CITY
```

In order to enable a constraint, you should update or remove all rows that violate the rules of the constraint from the table. After doing so, you should delete the corresponding rows for the exception in the **EXCEPTIONS** table to avoid confusion with new exception rows. To correct the exceptions in the previous examples, you might issue the following commands:

```
update district SET disno = 4, dname='DISTRICT FOUR'
WHERE disno = 9 AND
dname = 'DISTRICT NINE' AND
city = 'KANSAS CITY';

DELETE FROM exceptions WHERE constraint = 'SYS_C00275';
COMMIT;
```

Table 14.2 DBA_CONSTRAINTS view.

Column	Description
OWNER	Owner of the table
CONSTRAINT_NAME	Constraint definition's associated name
CONSTRAINT_TYPE	Constraint definition type
TABLE_NAME	Name of table the constraint is affiliated with
SEARCH_CONDITION	Search condition text for table check
R_OWNER	Owner of table employed in referential constraint
R_CONSTRAINT_NAME	Owner of table employed in referential constraint
DELETE_RULE	Delete referential constraint rule
STATUS	Constraint's enforcement status (**ENABLED** or **DISABLED**)
DEFERRABLE	Indication of whether the constraint is deferrable
DEFERRED	Indication of whether the constraint was initially deferred
GENERATED	Indication of whether the name system is generated
LAST_CHANGE	Indication of when the constraint was last enabled or disabled
VALIDATED	Indication of whether all data conforms to the constraint (**VALIDATED** or **NOT VALIDATED**)

Listing Integrity Constraint Information

You can use the data dictionary views to look up information about integrity constraints. All the views have the same columns as the ones in Tables 14.2 and 14.3. The following list describes what each view shows:

- ALL_CONS_COLUMNS—Contains information about columns accessible to the user in constraint definitions.
- ALL_CONSTRAINTS—Lists constraint definitions on tables accessible to the user.
- DBA_CONS_COLUMNS—Contains information about accessible columns in constraint definitions.
- DBA_CONSTRAINTS—Contains constraint definitions on all tables.

- **USER_CONS_COLUMNS**—Contains information about columns in constraint definitions owned by the user.
- **USER_CONSTRAINTS**—Lists constraint definitions on user's tables.

Table 14.4 shows all the values for the **CONSTRAINT_TYPE** column in the data dictionary views.

Table 14.3 DBA_CONS_COLUMNS view.

Column	Description
COLUMN_NAME	Name associated with column or attribute of the object type column specified in the constraint definition
CONSTRAINT_NAME	Constraint definition's associated name
OWNER	Schema that owns the constraint
POSITION	Original column or attribute position in definition
TABLE_NAME	Name associated with table with constraint definition

Table 14.4 CONSTRAINT TYPE values.

Constraint Type	Character
CHECK, NOT NULL	C
FOREIGN KEY	R
PRIMARY KEY	P
UNIQUE KEY	U

Practice Questions

Question 1

Which data dictionary shows constraint definitions on all the tables of the database?

- ❍ a. **DBA_COL_PRIVS**
- ❍ b. **USER_CONSTRAINTS**
- ❍ c. **DBA_IND_COLUMNS**
- ❍ d. **DBA_CONSTRAINTS**

Answer d is correct. **DBA_CONSTRAINTS** displays the names and types of all the constraints in the database. The **DBA_COL_PRIVS** view lists all grants on columns in the database. The **USER_CONSTRAINTS** view lists constraint definitions on just the user's tables. The **DBA_IND_COLUMNS** view contains descriptions of the columns comprising the indexes on all tables and clusters.

Question 2

What three methods can be used to enforce business rules and maintain database integrity? [Choose three]

- ❑ a. Indexes
- ❑ b. Application code
- ❑ c. Database triggers
- ❑ d. Tuning
- ❑ e. Database backup and recovery
- ❑ f. Declarative integrity constraints

Answers b, c, and f are correct. You can define and enforce data integrity rules in application code, database triggers, and declarative constraints. Indexes are used to improve query performance. Tuning is also done to improve performance. Backup and recovery is used to restore the database after a failure.

Question 3

What actions can be taken on a constraint? [Choose three]

- ❑ a. Drop
- ❑ b. Alter
- ❑ c. Delete
- ❑ d. Enable
- ❑ e. Create
- ❑ f. Disable

Answers a, d, and f are correct. The three actions are drop, enable, and disable. The alter constraint command is nonexistent. Constraints are changed by the **ALTER TABLE** command. The create constraint command is also nonexistent. Constraints are created through the **CREATE TABLE** or **ALTER TABLE** command. This question is a little tricky. Although constraints can have their behavior changed and they are obviously created, the commands that do so are taking action on a table, not on the constraint directly.

Question 4

Which view would you query to determine if a constraint is enabled?

- ❍ a. **DBA_CONSTRAINTS**
- ❍ b. **DBA_OBJECTS**
- ❍ c. **DBA_SEGMENTS**
- ❍ d. **DBA_TABLES**
- ❍ e. **DBA_CONS_COLUMNS**

Answer a is correct. **DBA_CONSTRAINTS** displays the names and types of all the constraints in the database and their current status. The **DBA_OBJECTS** view lists all objects in the database. The **DBA_SEGMENTS** view contains information about storage allocated for all database segments. The **DBA_TABLES** view contains descriptions of all tables in the database. The **DBA_CONS_COLUMNS** view describes accessible columns in constraints.

Question 5

Which command would you use to disable a constraint?

- a. **ALTER TABLE**
- b. **DROP CONSTRAINT**
- c. **ALTER SESSION**
- d. **DELETE CONSTRAINT**

Answer a is correct. The ALTER TABLE command is used to disable a constraint. DROP CONSTRAINT is a clause of the ALTER TABLE command. ALTER SESSION cannot be used to disable a constraint; it only changes its validation behavior from immediate to deferred or deferred to immediate. DELETE CONSTRAINT is not a valid command.

Question 6

When possible, which method of enforcing business rules in a database is preferred?

- a. Application code
- b. Database triggers
- c. Integrity constraints

Answer c is correct. Integrity constraints are preferred because they can be easily enabled and disabled and are documented in the data dictionary. Application code is difficult to maintain and cannot be easily enabled or disabled. It is also not universally enforced for all database access methods. Database triggers should be used for business rules that cannot be enforced by declared integrity constraints.

Question 7

Which command is used to drop a constraint?

- a. **ALTER TABLE**
- b. **REMOVE CONSTRAINT**
- c. **DROP SEGMENT**
- d. **DELETE CONSTRAINT**

Answer a is correct. The **ALTER TABLE** command is used to drop a constraint. **REMOVE CONSTRAINT**, **DROP SEGMENT**, and **DELETE CONSTRAINT** are not valid commands.

Question 8

When will data be checked against a deferred constraint?

- a. At the end of every DML statement
- b. When a trigger fires
- c. At regular time intervals
- d. When a transaction commits

Answer d is correct. A deferred constraint is checked when the transaction commits. Constraints are checked at the end of every DML statement when checking is set to immediate. Triggers do not change when constraints are checked. Constraints are never checked in time intervals.

Need To Know More?

See the Oracle documentation that is provided on CD with the Oracle RDBMS software. Pertaining to this chapter are:

Fee, Joyce: *Oracle8 Administrator's Guide*, Oracle Corporation, Redwood City, CA, 1997. See Chapter 17, "General Management of Schema Objects."

Lane, Paul: *Oracle8 Reference Manual*, Oracle Corporation, Redwood City, CA, 1997. See Chapter 2, "Static Data Dictionary Views."

Leverenz, Lefty: *Oracle8 Concepts Guide*, Oracle Corporation, Redwood City, CA, 1997. See Chapter 24, "Data Integrity."

Lorentz, Diana: *Oracle8 SQL Reference*, Oracle Corporation, Redwood City, CA, 1997. See Chapter 4, "Commands."

http://education.oracle.com/tbt/ocp8.html is the site from which you can order the Oracle Education CD-ROM bundle for Oracle8 Database Administration.

www.revealnet.com is the site where RevealNet Corporation provides Oracle Administration reference software.

15

Sample Test

In this chapter, I provide pointers to help you develop a successful test-taking strategy, including how to choose proper answers, how to decode ambiguity, how to work within the Oracle testing framework, how to decide what you need to memorize beforehand, and how to prepare in general for the test. At the end of this chapter, I include a set of 63 questions on subject matter that is pertinent to Exam 1Z0-013, "Oracle8 DBA: Database Administration." In Chapter 16, you'll find the answer key for this test. Good luck!

Questions, Questions, Questions

There should be no doubt in your mind that you are facing a test full of specific and pointed questions. The Oracle8 DBA Database Administrator test consists of 63 questions that you must complete in 90 minutes.

Questions belong to one of two basic types: multiple-choice with a single answer and multiple-choice with one or more answers.

Always take the time to read a question at least twice before selecting an answer, and always look for an Exhibit button as you examine each question. Exhibits include graphics information that pertains to the question. (An exhibit is usually a screen capture of program output or GUI information that you must examine to analyze the question's scenario and formulate an answer.)

Not every question has only one answer; many questions require multiple answers. Therefore, it's important to read each question carefully—not only to determine how many answers are necessary or possible, but to look for additional hints or instructions when selecting answers. Such instructions often occur in brackets immediately following the question itself (as they do for all multiple-choice questions in which one or more answers are possible).

Picking Proper Answers

Obviously, the only way to pass any exam is to select enough of the right answers to obtain a passing score. However, Oracle's exams are not standardized like the SAT and GRE exams; Oracle exams are far more diabolical and convoluted. In some cases, questions are strangely worded and deciphering them can be a real challenge. In those cases, you might need to rely on answer-elimination skills. Almost always, at least one answer out of the possible choices for a question can be eliminated immediately because it matches one of these conditions:

- It does not apply to the situation.
- It describes a nonexistent issue, an invalid option, or an imaginary state.

After you eliminate all answers that are obviously wrong, you can apply your retained knowledge to eliminate further answers. Look for items that sound correct but refer to actions, commands, or features that are not present or available in the situation that the question describes.

If you're still faced with a blind guess among two or more potentially correct answers, reread the question. Try to picture how each of the possible remaining answers would alter the situation. Be especially sensitive to terminology, because sometimes the choice of words (*remove* instead of *disable*) can make the difference between a right answer and a wrong one.

Only when you've exhausted your ability to eliminate answers should you guess at an answer. An unanswered question offers you no points, but guessing gives you at least some chance of getting a question right. Just don't be too hasty when making a blind guess.

> You can wait until the last round of reviewing marked questions (just as you're about to run out of time, or out of unanswered questions) before you start making guesses.

Decoding Ambiguity

Exams are meant to test knowledge on a given topic, and the scores from a properly designed test will have the classic bell-shaped distribution for the target audience, meaning a certain number will fail. A problem with this exam is that it has been tailored to Oracle's training materials and not to the documentation. This causes problems where the training materials deviate from the documentation. The best strategy here is to try and answer every question correctly and not try to second guess the documentation over the training materials. This has been the strategy throughout this book.

The only sure way to overcome some of the exam's limitations is to be prepared. You will discover that many questions test your knowledge of topics that are not directly related to issues that the questions raise. This means that the answers offered to you, even the incorrect ones, are as much a part of the skill assessment as the questions themselves. If you do not have a thorough grasp of all the aspects of an exam topic (in this case, database administration), you will not be able to eliminate answers that are obviously wrong because they relate to a different aspect of the topic than the one the question addresses.

Questions can reveal answers, especially when dealing with commands. So, read a question and then evaluate the answers in light of common terms, names, and structure.

Another problem is that Oracle uses some terminology in its training material that isn't found anywhere else in its documentation. Whether this is a deliberate attempt to force you to take its classes to pass the exam or simply a case of sloppy documentation is unknown.

Working Within The Framework

The test questions appear in random order, and many elements or issues that receive mention in one question also crop up in other questions. It's not uncommon to find that an incorrect answer to one question is the correct answer to another question, or vice versa. Take the time to read every answer to each question, even if you recognize the correct answer to a question immediately. This extra reading might spark a memory or remind you about a feature or function that helps you on another question elsewhere in the exam.

You can revisit any question as many times as you like. If you're uncertain of the answer to a question, check the box that's provided to mark it for easy return later on. You should also mark questions that you think offer information that you can use to answer other questions. I usually mark somewhere between 25 and 50 percent of the questions. The testing software is designed to let you mark every question if you choose, so use this feature to your advantage. Everything you will want to see again should be marked; the testing software can then help you return to marked questions quickly and easily.

Deciding What To Memorize

The amount you must memorize for an exam depends on how well you remember what you've read, and how well you intuitively know the software. If you are a visual thinker and you can see the drop-down menus and dialog boxes in your head, you won't need to memorize as much as someone who's less visually oriented. Because the tests will stretch your recollection of commands, tools, utilities, and functions related to how Oracle works, you'll want to memorize—at a minimum—the following kinds of information:

- Various utilities and commands (for example, **svrmgrl**).
- Oracle instance and database creation and configuration procedures
- Data dictionary views
- The Oracle architecture, including the components of an Oracle instance and database emphasizing how they interact with each other

If you work your way through this book while sitting at a machine with Oracle8 installed, and you try to manipulate the features and functions of the various commands, tools, and utilities as they're discussed, you should have little or no difficulty mastering this material. Also, don't forget that The Cram Sheet at the front of the book captures the material that is most important to memorize, so don't forget to use it to guide your studies as well.

Preparing For The Test

The best way to prepare for the test—after you've studied—is to take at least one practice exam. I've included one in this chapter for that reason; the test questions are located in the pages that follow. (Unlike the preceding chapters in this book, the answers don't follow the questions immediately; flip to Chapter 16 to review the answers.)

Give yourself 90 minutes to take the exam. Keep yourself on the honor system, and don't look at earlier text in the book or jump ahead to the answer key. When your time is up or you've finished the questions, you can check your work in Chapter 16. Pay special attention to the explanations for the incorrect answers; these can also help to reinforce your knowledge of the material. Knowing how to recognize correct answers is good, but understanding why incorrect answers are wrong can be equally valuable.

Taking The Test

Relax. Once you're sitting in front of the testing computer, there's nothing more you can do to increase your knowledge or preparation. Take a deep breath, stretch, and start reading that first question.

There's no need to rush; you have plenty of time to complete each question and to return to those questions that you skip or mark for return. If you read a question twice and remain clueless, you can mark it. Both easy and difficult questions are intermixed throughout the test in random order. Don't cheat yourself by spending too much time on a hard question early in the test, which deprives you of the time you need to answer the questions at the end of the test.

You can read through the entire test and, before returning to marked questions for a second visit, figure out how much time you've got per question. As you answer each question, remove its mark. Continue to review the remaining marked questions until you run out of time or you complete the test.

That's it for pointers. Here are some questions for you to practice on.

Sample Test

Question 1

What does the **IDENTIFIED BY** clause do in the following command?

```
ALTER USER john IDENTIFIED BY doe;
```

- ❍ a. Specifies an alias for user john
- ❍ b. Specifies a new username for user john
- ❍ c. Specifies a new password for user john
- ❍ d. Specifies the current tablespace for user john

Question 2

Carol granted **SELECT** on the **DISTRICT** table **WITH GRANT OPTION** to Penny. Penny granted the privilege to Mark. If Carol's privilege is revoked, who else will lose his or her privileges?

- ❍ a. No one else will lose his or her privileges
- ❍ b. Only Penny
- ❍ c. Both Penny and Mark
- ❍ d. Only Mark

Question 3

Which statement about **CASCADE** in the following statement is true?

```
ANALYZE TABLE location
  VALIDATE STRUCTURE CASCADE;
```

- ❍ a. Re-creates all indexes
- ❍ b. Verifies any tables referenced by **REF** pointers in the table
- ❍ c. Re-creates any dropped indexes
- ❍ d. Validates the structure of indexes associated with the table

Question 4

If you set the **LOG_CHECKPOINT_INTERVAL** initialization parameter to 25, how frequently will a log switch occur?

❍ a. Every 25 seconds

❍ b. Every 25 minutes

❍ c. After LGWR writes 25 Oracle data blocks

❍ d. After LGWR writes 25 operating system blocks

Question 5

How can you show the current locations of the control files using Server Manager in line mode? [Choose three]

❑ a. Use the **SHOW SGA** command

❑ b. Query **V$CONTROLFILE**

❑ c. Use the **DESCRIBE** command

❑ d. Query **V$PARAMETER**

❑ e. Query **V$SYSTEM_PARAMETER**

❑ f. Use the **SHOW PARAMETER** command

Question 6

Which view would you query to find out the names of the tables and the names of the columns included in a cluster?

❍ a. **DBA_CLUSTERS**

❍ b. **DBA_CLU_COLUMNS**

❍ c. **DBA_OBJECTS**

❍ d. **DBA_CATALOG**

Question 7

Which requirement must be met for the following command to execute?

```
create database "HII4"
controlfile reuse
maxinstances 8
maxlogfiles  32
maxlogfiles  32
maxlogmembers 5
maxdatafiles 1022
maxloghistory 800
datafile
'/u02/oradata/HII4/system01.dbf'   size   200M
logfile
'/u05/oradata/HII4/redo01a.dbf' size 100M,
'/u05/oradata/HII4/redo02a.dbf' size 100M,
'/u05/oradata/HII4/redo03a.dbf' size 100M,
'/u05/oradata/HII4/redo04a.dbf' size 100M;
```

❍ a. All the log files must exist.

❍ b. The datafile must exist.

❍ c. The control files specified in the parameter file must exist.

❍ d. The user must have the **SYSOPER** privileges to create the log files and datafiles.

Question 8

When an instance fails, which type of segment is used to recover uncommitted transactions?

❍ a. Table

❍ b. Index

❍ c. Rollback

❍ d. Temporary

Question 9

Which OEM application would you use to give a user the **RESTRICTED SESSION** privilege?

- a. Data Manager
- b. Instance Manager
- c. Storage Manager
- d. Schema Manager
- e. Security Manager

Question 10

You created a SQL script that retrieves data from a table. Which Server Manager line mode command would you use to create the output file for the SQL script?

- a. **SET**
- b. **OUTPUT**
- c. **SPOOL**
- d. **EXECUTE**
- e. **WRITE**

Question 11

Which data dictionary view can you use to determine if an index is valid?

- a. **DBA_TABLES**
- b. **DBA_INDEXES**
- c. **DBA_SEGMENTS**
- d. **DBA_IND_COLUMNS**

Question 12

Which privilege do you need to audit objects in another user's schema?

- a. **AUDIT ANY**
- b. **ANALYZE**
- c. **AUDIT**
- d. **CREATE ANY AUDIT**

Question 13

Which **CREATE INDEX** clause ensures that redo generation will not affect performance when the index is created?

- a. **NOSORT**
- b. **UNIQUE**
- c. **NOSTORAGE**
- d. **LOGGING**
- e. **MINTRANS**
- f. **NOLOGGING**

Question 14

You have set the **REMOTE_LOGIN_PASSWORD_FILE** initialization parameter to **EXCLUSIVE**. Which view would you query to determine which users have been granted the **SYSOPER** privileges?

- a. **V$DATABASE**
- b. **V$INSTANCE**
- c. **V$PARAMETER**
- d. **V$PWFILE_USERS**

Question 15

Which characteristic describes a role?

- a. It can be disabled for each authorized user.
- b. It always requires a password.
- c. It is enforced by database triggers.
- d. It is stored in a schema.

Question 16

What would happen if you tried to start an Oracle instance and open a database with different database names in the parameter file and the control file?

- a. An instance would not start.
- b. An instance would start, but the database would not be mounted.
- c. The database would open without using the parameter file.
- d. An instance would start and the database would be mounted, but would not be opened.

Question 17

Which view shows the **SORT EXTENT POOL** status?

- a. **V$SORT_SEGMENT**
- b. **V$SORT_USAGE**
- c. **V$SESSION**
- d. **V$INSTANCE**

Question 18

If you want to find out if a role has a password, which view would you query?

- ❍ a. **SESSION_ROLES**
- ❍ b. **DBA_SYS_PRIVS**
- ❍ c. **DBA_ROLES**
- ❍ d. **DBA_ROLE_PRIVS**

Question 19

In the database buffer cache, which buffers are on the dirty list?

- ❍ a. Empty buffers
- ❍ b. Null buffers
- ❍ c. Buffers currently being accessed
- ❍ d. Buffers waiting to be written to disk

Question 20

Why would you use direct-load inserts when loading data into a table? [Choose two]

- ❑ a. Redo is generated in case of failure.
- ❑ b. Indexes are created to speed the data load.
- ❑ c. It loads data below the high watermark to reclaim disk space.
- ❑ d. Other rows in the same table can be concurrently modified by other users.
- ❑ e. Data can be quickly copied from one table into another within the same database, because it bypasses the buffer cache.

Question 21

Which operations can be taken on a constraint? [Choose three]

❑ a. **ALTER**

❑ b. **CREATE**

❑ c. **DELETE**

❑ d. **DISABLE**

❑ e. **DROP**

❑ f. **ENABLE**

Question 22

What part of a database block is a new table record inserted into?

❍ a. Header area

❍ b. Table directory

❍ c. Free space

❍ d. Row directory

Question 23

How would you drop a redo log member from an active group when archiving is enabled?

❍ a. After the group is archived, issue the **ALTER DATABASE DROP LOGFILE MEMBER** command.

❍ b. Before the group is archived, issue the **ALTER DATABASE DROP LOGFILE MEMBER** command.

❍ c. Issue the **ALTER SYSTEM SWITCH LOGFILE** command, then issue the **ALTER DATABASE DROP LOGFILE MEMBER** command.

❍ d. Before the group is archived, issue the **ALTER SYSTEM SWITCH LOGFILE** command, then issue the **ALTER DATABASE DROP LOGFILE MEMBER** command.

Question 24

What is the maximum number of control files that you can specify in the **CONTROL_FILES** parameter?

- ❍ a. 2
- ❍ b. 4
- ❍ c. 8
- ❍ d. 16
- ❍ e. 32
- ❍ f. Unlimited

Question 25

Which script is used to create the data dictionary views?

- ❍ a. catalog.sql
- ❍ b. catproc.sql
- ❍ c. dbmsutil.sql
- ❍ d. sql.bsq

Question 26

Which table contains the names of all the data dictionary views?

- ❍ a. **DB_VIEWS**
- ❍ b. **DBA_VIEWS**
- ❍ c. **DICTIONARY**
- ❍ d. **DBA_VIEW_DATA**

Question 27

Your database has a log group with three members. Two of the three members have become corrupted. What would happen when the database tries to write to this log group?

- ❍ a. The database will hang.
- ❍ b. LGWR will write to the available member.
- ❍ c. The instance will crash.
- ❍ d. Oracle will reformat the corrupt members.

Question 28

Where does Oracle store the database creation timestamp?

- ❍ a. Database file header
- ❍ b. Control file
- ❍ c. Parameter file
- ❍ d. Redo log files
- ❍ e. Rollback segment

Question 29

Which parameter would you use to control the space reserved in each data block for updates of existing rows?

- ❍ a. **INITRANS**
- ❍ b. **MAXTRANS**
- ❍ c. **PCTFREE**
- ❍ d. **PCTUSED**

Question 30

Which of the following methods can be used to enable automatic extension for an existing datafile?

- a. Use the **ALTER TABLESPACE** command.
- b. Drop the datafile and re-create it.
- c. Use OS commands to **AUTOEXTEND** existing files.
- d. Use the **ALTER TABLESPACE RENAME DATAFILE** command to rename the datafile to a larger file.

Question 31

Which is the correct sequence of steps to move a datafile to a new location?

- a. Take the tablespace offline, issue the **ALTER TABLESPACE** command, move the files using OS commands, and bring the tablespace back online.
- b. Issue the **ALTER TABLESPACE** command, take the tablespace offline, move the files using OS commands, and bring the tablespace back online.
- c. Take the tablespace offline, move the files using OS commands, bring the tablespace back online, and issue the **ALTER TABLESPACE** command.
- d. Take the tablespace offline, move the files using OS commands, issue the **ALTER TABLESPACE** command, and bring the tablespace back online.

Question 32

Which privilege do you need to execute the **ALTER SYSTEM ENABLE RESTRICTED SESSION** command?

- a. **RESTRICTED SESSION**
- b. **ALTER SYSTEM**
- c. **ALTER DATABASE**
- d. **ALTER RESOURCE COST**
- e. **ENABLE RESTRICTED SESSION**

Question 33

When you create a user, which clause would you use to control the amount of space the user can use in a tablespace?

❍ a. **DEFAULT TABLESPACE**

❍ b. **PROFILE**

❍ c. **QUOTA**

❍ d. **TEMPORARY TABLESPACE**

Question 34

If you want to deallocate some but not all of the unused space in a table, which option of the **ALTER TABLE** command would you use?

❍ a. **KEEP**

❍ b. **CACHE**

❍ c. **DEALLOCATE UNUSED**

❍ d. **MODIFY**

Question 35

You have a set of users who need to view the DBA data dictionary views. Which of the following roles would you use to give them this access?

❍ a. **DBA**

❍ b. **EXECUTE_CATALOG_ROLE**

❍ c. **RESOURCE**

❍ d. **EXP_FULL_DATABASE**

❍ e. **PLUSTRACE**

❍ f. **SELECT_CATALOG_ROLE**

Question 36

What clause of the **CREATE TABLE** command can you use to control how extents are allocated to a table?

- ❍ a. **PCTFREE**
- ❍ b. **EXTENT**
- ❍ c. **STORAGE**
- ❍ d. **LOGGING/NOLOGGING**
- ❍ e. **DEFAULT**

Question 37

Which view shows the constraint definitions for all tables in a database?

- ❍ a. **ALL_CONSTRAINTS**
- ❍ b. **DBA_CONSTRAINTS**
- ❍ c. **DBA_CATALOG**
- ❍ d. **USER_CONSTRAINTS**

Question 38

During which stage of starting an instance is the control file read?

- ❍ a. **MOUNT**
- ❍ b. **NOMOUNT**
- ❍ c. **OPEN**
- ❍ d. **RESTRICTED SESSION**

Question 39

Which of the following is not part of an Oracle instance?

- ❍ a. Shared pool
- ❍ b. Redo log buffer
- ❍ c. User process
- ❍ d. Data buffer cache

Question 40

You want to change the value of the **BACKGROUND_DUMP_DEST** initialization parameter. Which OEM utility would you use to accomplish this?

❍ a. Backup Manager

❍ b. Data Manager

❍ c. Instance Manager

❍ d. Schema Manager

❍ e. Security Manager

Question 41

Which of the following commands can be used to specify the default role for a user?

❍ a. **CREATE ROLE**

❍ b. **ALTER USER**

❍ c. **ASSIGN ROLE**

❍ d. **SET ROLE**

Question 42

You want to list all the users with the **ALTER ANY ROLE** command. Which view would you use to create the list?

❍ a. **DBA_ROLES**

❍ b. **ALL_COL_PRIVS_RECD**

❍ c. **USER_SYS_PRIVS**

❍ d. **DBA_SYS_PRIVS**

Question 43

Which category of data dictionary views does not have an **OWNER** column?

- ❍ a. **ALL_**
- ❍ b. **DBA_**
- ❍ c. **USER_**

Question 44

When are extents that are allocated to a sort segment released and the space returned to the tablespace?

- ❍ a. Never
- ❍ b. When the instance is shut down
- ❍ c. When the user process requesting the sort segment ends
- ❍ d. When the sorting operation ends

Question 45

Which view would you query to determine if any database user is close to exceeding their space limit on a tablespace?

- ❍ a. **USER_TS_QUOTAS**
- ❍ b. **USER_TABLESPACES**
- ❍ c. **DBA_TABLESPACES**
- ❍ d. **DBA_TS_QUOTAS**
- ❍ e. **DBA_USERS**

Question 46

What will happen to a user's tables if the quota for the tablespace containing the tables is altered to 0?

- ❍ a. The tables will be truncated.
- ❍ b. The tables will become inaccessible.
- ❍ c. No new extents can be allocated to the table.
- ❍ d. The tables will be dropped automatically when the quota is changed.

Question 47

Why does Oracle create temporary segments?

- a. For sorting that cannot be performed in memory
- b. So users can store temporary tables
- c. To store tables that are created without specifying a tablespace

Question 48

Which view would you used to determine if a constraint is enabled?

- a. **DBA_TABLES**
- b. **DBA_CATALOG**
- c. **PUBLIC_DEPENDENCY**
- d. **DBA_CONSTRAINTS**
- e. **DBA_CONS_COLUMNS**

Question 49

Which schema owns the data dictionary tables?

- a. **SYS**
- b. **SYSTEM**
- c. **SYSDBA**
- d. **SYSOPER**

Question 50

Which view would you use to find out the sequence number of the current redo log group?

- a. **V$DATABASE**
- b. **V$INSTANCE**
- c. **V$THREAD**
- d. **V$LOGFILE**

Question 51

What is the order in which objects are imported into a database from an export file?

- ❍ a. Table data, integrity constraints, triggers, bitmap indexes, indexes on the table, table definitions
- ● b. Table definitions, table data, indexes on the table, integrity constraints, triggers, bitmap indexes
- ❍ c. Indexes on the table, integrity constraints, triggers, bitmap indexes, table definitions, table data
- ❍ d. Table definitions, table data, integrity constraints, triggers, bitmap indexes, indexes on the table
- ❍ e. Table definitions, integrity constraints, triggers, bitmap indexes, indexes on the table, table data

Question 52

Which Oracle utility could you use to re-create Oracle tables and their associated objects under a new schema name and move the associated data from the previous schema to the new tables?

- ❍ a. SQL*Loader
- ❍ b. Direct-load insert
- ❍ c. Schema Manager
- ● d. Export/import utilities

Question 53

When you created the temporary tablespace, the **PCTINCREASE** was set to zero. How will this affect the size of new extents in the temporary tablespace?

- ● a. The second and all other extents will be the size of the **NEXT** parameter for the tablespace.
- ❍ b. All extents will be the size of the **INITIAL** parameter for the tablespace.
- ❍ c. The extents will be sized by the SQL*Plus **CREATE** command for temporary segments.
- ❍ d. No new extents can be allocated, because **PCTINCREASE** is zero.

Question 54

Which of the following could be determined by the **DBA_FREE_SPACE** view?

❍ a. The owner of a table

❍ b. The date an extent was created

❍ c. The size of an extent in Oracle blocks

Question 55

Which SQL*Loader file specifies the database tables to be loaded?

❍ a. Log file

❍ b. Discard file

❍ c. Control file

❍ d. Bad file

Question 56

Which two views could you query to list the names and locations of the control files? [Choose two]

❑ a. **V$DATABASE**

❑ b. **V$DATAFILE**

❑ c. **V$INSTANCE**

❑ d. **V$PARAMETER**

❑ e. **V$CONTROLFILE**

Question 57

Which command would you use to change the weights for each session's resource limit?

❍ a. **ALTER DATABASE**

❍ b. **ALTER RESOURCE COST**

❍ c. **ALTER SYSTEM**

❍ d. **UPDATE RESOURCE COST**

❍ e. **ALTER SESSION LIMITS**

Question 58

What is the order of precedence for storage clauses?

- ❍ a. Extent level, segment level, tablespace level
- ● b. Segment level, tablespace level, Oracle Server default
- ❍ c. Tablespace level, segment level, Oracle Server default
- ❍ d. Oracle Server default, tablespace level, segment level

Question 59

You have a table that has a data segment of 10,000 blocks. 7,000 blocks of the table were actually used for data. All the rows were recently deleted. Where is the high watermark for this table?

- ❍ a. 0 blocks
- ❍ b. 10,000 blocks
- ❍ c. 3,000 blocks
- ● d. 7,000 blocks

Question 60

Which background process writes changed buffers in the database buffer cache to the datafiles?

- ❍ a. SMON
- ❍ b. PMON
- ❍ c. ARCH
- ❍ d. LGWR
- ● e. DBWn

15/16 63 -15 48/63 = 76

Question 61

You need to add a rollback segment to your production database. Which OEM application would you use to perform this task?

- a. Storage Manager
- b. Schema Manager
- c. Backup Manager
- d. Data Manager
- e. Security Manager
- f. Instance Manager

Question 62

Which command would you use to drop a constraint?

- a. **DELETE CONSTRAINT**
- b. **REMOVE CONSTRAINT**
- c. **ALTER CONSTRAINT DROP**
- d. **ALTER TABLE**

Question 63

The database parameter **REMOTE_LOGIN_PASSWORDFILE** is set to **SHARED**. Which Oracle users will the password file recognize? [Choose two]

- a. **SYS**
- b. Any user with DBA privileges
- c. **SYSTEM**
- d. **INTERNAL**

16

Answer Key

1. c
2. c
3. d
4. d
5. b, d, f
6. b
7. c
8. c
9. e
10. c
11. b
12. a
13. f
14. d
15. a
16. b
17. a
18. c
19. d
20. d, e
21. d, e, f
22. c
23. c
24. c
25. a
26. c
27. b
28. b
29. c
30. a
31. d
32. b
33. c
34. a
35. f
36. c
37. b
38. a
39. c
40. c
41. b
42. d
43. c
44. b
45. d
46. c
47. a
48. d
49. a
50. c
51. b
52. d
53. a
54. c
55. c
56. d, e
57. b
58. b
59. d
60. e
61. a
62. d
63. a, d

Question 1

Answer c is correct. The **IDENTIFIED BY** clause of the **ALTER USER** command changes the user's password. Usernames do not have aliases. The **ALTER USER** command cannot change a username. No existing command sets the current tablespace.

Question 2

Answer c is correct. Object privileges that are granted **WITH GRANT OPTION** have their privileges revoked because the revoke cascades.

Question 3

Answer d is correct. When you use the **ANALYZE TABLE** command on a table with indexes, the structure of the index is verified. The **ANALYZE** command does not create indexes. The **ANALYZE** command only analyzes the table specified. Once an index is dropped, it can only be re-created by a **CREATE INDEX** statement.

Question 4

Answer d is correct. **LOG_CHECKPOINT_INTERVAL** specifies the number of OS blocks written by LGWR that will trigger a log switch. Answers a and b are incorrect, because **LOG_CHECKPOINT_TIMEOUT** specifies the number of seconds between checkpoints and the time period for checkpoints. **LOG_CHECKPOINT_INTERVAL** uses OS blocks, not Oracle blocks, for its value.

Question 5

Answers b, d, and f are correct. You can query the **V$CONTROLFILE** or **V$PARAMETER** view, or execute the **SHOW PARAMETER** command. The **SHOW SGA** command displays information about the current instance's system global area. You cannot use the **DESCRIBE** command on a control file. The **V$SYSTEM_PARAMETER** view contains information on system parameters, but does not include the control file location.

Question 6

Answer b is correct. **DBA_CLU_COLUMNS** displays the names of the columns included in the cluster and their corresponding table column. The **DBA_CLUSTERS** view contains a description of the storage information on all clusters in the database. The **DBA_OBJECTS** view lists all objects in the database. The **DBA_CATALOG** view lists all database tables, views, synonyms, and sequences.

Question 7

Answer c is correct. Because the **CREATE DATABASE** command uses the **CONTROLFILE REUSE** option, the control files listed in the parameter file will be reused. For this command to execute successfully, the control files listed in the parameter file must exist.

Question 8

Answer c is correct. Transaction recovery occurs after an instance failure. All uncommitted transactions are rolled back using the redo log files and the before images stored in rollback segments. A table is made up of a data segment and is not used for recovery. Indexes are made up of index segments, which also are not used for recovery. Temporary segments are used for sorting and are not used for recovery.

Question 9

Answer e is correct. Security Manager is used to grant privileges and roles to users. Data Manager is used to load and reorganize data. Instance Manager is used to start up and shut down the database and maintain initialization parameters. Storage Manager is used to maintain datafiles and rollback segments. Schema Manager is used to create and maintain tables, views, and other database objects.

Question 10

Answer c is correct. The **SPOOL** command spools the output to a named file. The **SET** command changes characteristics for the current Server Manager session. **OUTPUT** is an invalid Server Manager command. The **EXECUTE** command executes a PL/SQL statement. **WRITE** is an invalid Server Manager command.

Question 11

Answer b is correct. **DBA_INDEXES** displays the status of each index, as well as the name, owner name, type, table name, uniqueness, tablespace name, and more. The **DBA_TABLES** view contains descriptions of all tables in the database. The **DBA_SEGMENTS** view contains information about storage allocated for all database segments. The **DBA_IND_COLUMNS** view contains descriptions of the columns comprising the indexes on all tables and clusters.

Question 12

Answer a is correct. To enable auditing, you must own the objects to be audited or you must have the **AUDIT ANY** privilege. The **ANALYZE** command is used to collect statistics about schema objects used by the optimizer and store them in the data dictionary. **AUDIT ANY** is a privilege, but **AUDIT** is not. The **CREATE ANY AUDIT** is an invalid privilege.

Question 13

Answer f is correct. The **NOLOGGING** clause does not generate redo and increases the speed of the **CREATE INDEX** command. The **NOSORT** clause indicates to Oracle that the rows are stored in the database in ascending order; therefore, Oracle does not have to sort the rows when creating the index. Redo information is still created. **UNIQUE** specifies that the value of the column, or combination of columns, in the table being indexed must be unique. **NOSTORAGE** is an invalid SQL parameter. **LOGGING** specifies that redo information will be generated. **MINTRANS** is not a **CREATE INDEX** option.

Question 14

Answer d is correct. When password file authentication is enabled, **V$PWFILE_USERS** displays the names of users with the **SYSDBA** or **SYSOPER** privileges. The **V$DATABASE** view contains database information from the control file. The **V$INSTANCE** view displays the state of the current instance. The **V$PARAMETER** view lists information about initialization parameters.

Question 15

Answer a is correct. A role can be enabled or disabled for an individual user granted the role. Roles can have a password, but are not required to. Database triggers are used to enforce business rules and have nothing to do with roles. Roles are not owned by any schema.

Question 16

Answer b is correct. The instance would start, but when the control file is read to open the database, the mismatch in database names would stop the database from mounting. The database could not open or mount because of the name mismatch.

Question 17

Answer a is correct. **V$SORT_SEGMENT** displays the status of the sort extent pool for the current instance. **V$SORT_USAGE** view describes sort usage, but not the **SORT EXTENT POOL** status. The **V$SESSION** view lists session information for each current session. The **V$INSTANCE** view displays the state of the current instance.

Question 18

Answer c is correct. **DBA_ROLES** displays the names of all the roles in the database and indicates whether they require a password. The **SESSION_ROLES** view lists the roles that are currently enabled to the user. The **DBA_SYS_PRIVS** view lists system privileges granted to users and roles. The **DBA_ROLE_PRIVS** view lists roles granted to users and roles.

Question 19

Answer d is correct. Buffers waiting to be written to disk are on the dirty list and cannot be overwritten. Empty buffers are ready for use and do not need to be written to disk. The concept of a null buffer doesn't exist. Buffers currently being accessed are on the LRU list and are not dirty.

Question 20

Answers d and e are correct. During a direct-load insert, users can be concurrently modifying existing data in the table. Redo information is not generated during a direct-load insert. Also, the buffer cache is bypassed to speed up the insert. Direct-load insert does not create any indexes. Data is loaded above the high watermark.

Question 21

Answers d, e, and f are correct. The three actions are **DROP**, **ENABLE**, and **DISABLE**. An **ALTER CONSTRAINT** command does not exist. Constraints are changed by the **ALTER TABLE** command. A **CREATE CONSTRAINT** command does not exist. Constraints are created through the **CREATE TABLE** or **ALTER TABLE** command. This question is a little tricky, because, although constraints can have their behavior changed and they are obviously created, the commands that do so are taking action on a table and not on the constraint directly. Constraints cannot be deleted—they must be dropped.

Question 22

Answer c is correct. In a database block, row data is stored in the bytes allocated for free space, which then becomes part of the data space. The header contains general block information, such as the block address and the type of segment (for example, data, index, or rollback). The table directory holds information about the tables having rows in this block. The row directory contains information about the actual rows in the block.

Question 23

Answer c is correct. To drop a redo log member from an active group, cause a log switch first by using the **ALTER SYSTEM SWITCH LOGFILE** command and then use the **ALTER DATABASE DROP LOGFILE MEMBER** command after the archiving of the logfile is complete. You must cause a log switch so the log group is not active. The log group must be archived before you use the **ALTER DATABASE DROP LOGFILE MEMBER** command. If the database is in **ARCHIVELOG** mode, you cannot drop an online member until it has been archived. If the group is active, you must force a log switch before dropping one of its members.

Question 24

Answer c is correct. You can specify a maximum of eight control files.

Question 25

Answer a is correct. The catalog.sql script creates the data dictionary views to decode and summarize the data in the base tables. The catproc.sql script runs required scripts for PL/SQL use in the database. The dbmsutil.sql script creates the **DBMS_TRANSACTION**, **DBMS_SESSION**, **DBMS_DDL**, **DBMS_UTILITY**, **DBMS_APPLICATION_INFO**, **DBMS_SYSTEM**, **DBMS_SPACE**, and **DBMS_ROWID** packages. The sql.bsq script creates the base data dictionary tables.

Question 26

Answer c is correct. The **DICTIONARY** data dictionary view provides an overview for all the data dictionary views. **DB_VIEWS** is not a dictionary table. The **DBA_VIEWS** view contains the text of all views in the database. **DBA_VIEW_DATA** is not a dictionary table or view.

Question 27

Answer b is correct. If at least one member of the current group is accessible, the Oracle Server ignores the corrupt members. Because the database can write to the available log member, the database will not hang. The instance will not crash, because the log switch can take place with the one log member. Oracle will not reformat corrupted log members.

Question 28

Answer b is correct. The control file records the structure of the database, including the time that the database was created. Oracle has no database file headers. Tablespaces exist that have datafiles headers, which have information about the datafile and the last checkpoint. Oracle does not write back to parameter files. Redo log files contain information for recovery. Rollback segments keep before images of all changed data that is not committed.

Question 29

Answer c is correct. **PCTFREE** determines the percentage of space in each block that is reserved for updates. **INITRANS** specifies the initial number of transaction entries allocated within each data block allocated to the table. **MAXTRANS** is the limit of concurrent transactions allowed in a data block. **PCTUSED** is the the amount of space Oracle maintains in each data block for inserts.

Question 30

Answer a is correct. The **AUTOEXTEND** clause can be used with the **ALTER TABLESPACE** command to enable auto extension of an existing datafile. Datafiles can only be dropped if the tablespace is dropped. You cannot extend Oracle datafiles by using OS commands. When a datafile is being moved, the file in the new location must be an exact copy of the original file; it cannot be made larger.

Question 31

Answer d is correct. The correct sequence of steps to move a datafile is to take the tablespace offline, move the files using OS commands, issue the **ALTER TABLESPACE RENAME DATAFILE** command and then bring the tablespace back online. Answer a is incorrect, because you must move the datafile before using the **ALTER TABLESPACE** command. Answer b is incorrect, because the datafile must be offline before you use the **ALTER TABLESPACE** command. Answer c is incorrect, because the **ALTER TABLESPACE** command should be executed before the tablespace is brought back online.

Question 32

Answer b is correct. You need the **ALTER SYSTEM** privilege to use the **ALTER SYSTEM** command. The **RESTRICTED SESSION** privilege allows users to connect to a database that has been started or altered to be in restricted mode. The **ALTER DATABASE** privilege allows you to add datafiles to the database, but it does not give you the privelege to put a database into restricted mode. The **ALTER RESOURCE COST** privilege allows you to set costs for resources used in a session but does not give you the ability to put a database into restricted mode. **ENABLE RESTRICTED SESSION** is a clause of the **ALTER SYSTEM** command and not a privilege.

Question 33

Answer c is correct. The **QUOTA** clause defines the amount of space a user can use to create objects in a specified tablespace. The **DEFAULT TABLESPACE** clause specifies the tablespace to be used if a tablespace is not provided in a **CREATE/ALTER** statement. Profiles can be used to manage resources like CPU, session idle time, or logical reads per session, but not space allocation in tablespaces. The **TEMPORARY TABLESPACE** clause specifies the tablespace to be used for temporary segments.

Question 34

Answer a is correct. To deallocate unused space while keeping a specified number of bytes above the high watermark, use the **KEEP** option as follows:

```
ALTER TABLE table_name DEALLOCATE UNUSED KEEP integer K/M;
```

The **CACHE** option is used to control how rows from the table are placed on the LRU list in the buffer cache during a full-table scan. **DEALLOCATE UNUSED** deallocates all unused space above the high watermark unless the **KEEP** option is used. **MODIFY** is used to change the definition of existing columns.

Question 35

Answer f is correct. The **SELECT_CATALOG_ROLE** role grants select on the DBA data dictionary views. The **DBA** role is what makes this a tricky question. Although the DBA role gives users the ability to query the DBA data dictionary views, it also gives complete administrative capabilities to the database. The question states that you just want the users to be able to view the DBA dictionary views. The **EXECUTE_CATALOG_ROLE** grants execute privileges on package procedures supplied with the database. The **RESOURCE** role grants **CREATE CLUSTER, CREATE PROCEDURE, CREATE SEQUENCE, CREATE TABLE,** and **CREATE TRIGGER** to users. Grantees of **RESOURCE** also get a separate grant of **UNLIMITED TABLESPACE. EXP_FULL_DATABASE** allows users to do an export of the database with the **FULL** option. The **PLUSTRACE** role gives users the privilege to use the **AUTOTRACE** function in SQL*Plus.

Question 36

Answer c is correct. The **STORAGE** clause includes the **INITIAL**, **NEXT**, **PCTINCREASE**, and **MAXEXTENTS** values, which control how extents are allocated to a table. **PCTFREE** specifies the percentage of space in each data block of the table that is reserved for future updates to the table's rows. **EXTENT** is an invalid option of the **CREATE TABLE** command. **LOGGING/NOLOGGING** controls the logging of the **CREATE** statement to the redo log file. **DEFAULT** is used to provide a default value for a column when a row is inserted without a value for the column.

Question 37

Answer b is correct. **DBA_CONSTRAINTS** displays the names and types of constraints in the database. **ALL_CONSTRAINTS** lists constraint definitions on tables accessible to the user. **DBA_CATALOG** lists all database tables, views, synonyms, and sequences. **USER_CONSTRAINTS** lists constraint definitions on the current user's tables only.

Question 38

Answer a is correct. Because the control file records the database structure, the control file is read when a database is mounted by an instance. If the instance is started with the **NOMOUNT** option, the control file for the database will not be read. The database will mount before it is opened, so the control file will have already been read. **RESTRICTED SESSION** controls access to the database and has no effect on when the control file is read.

Question 39

Answer c is correct. User processes are not part of an Oracle instance. The shared pool, redo log buffer, and database buffer cache are part of the instance's SGA.

Question 40

Answer c is correct. OEM's Instance Manager can be used to maintain initialization parameters. Backup Manager is used in backup, restore, and recovery operations. Data Manager is used to load and reorganize data. Schema Manager is used to create and maintain tables, views, and other database objects. Security Manager is used to create users and manage user privileges.

Question 41

Answer b is correct. The **ALTER USER** command is used to specify the default roles for a user. The **CREATE ROLE** command is used to create new roles. **ASSIGN ROLE** is an invalid command. **SET ROLE** is used to enable a role that a user has been granted but is not being used.

Question 42

Answer d is correct. **DBA_SYS_PRIVS** displays system privileges granted to all users and roles. **DBA_ROLES** lists all roles that exist in the database. **ALL_COL_PRIVS_RECD** lists grants on columns for which the user or **PUBLIC** is the grantee. **USER_SYS_PRIVS** lists system privileges granted to the user.

Question 43

Answer c is correct. **USER** views provide information on objects owned by the user, so they do not contain the **OWNER** column, because this would be redundant. **ALL** views have an **OWNER** column, providing information on all objects accessible by the user. **DBA** views provide information on all the objects in the database and have an **OWNER** column.

Question 44

Answer b is correct. Temporary sort segment extents are released when the database is shut down. Otherwise, they are reused for the next sort request.

Question 45

Answer d is correct. **DBA_TS_QUOTAS** displays the names of tablespaces that any database user has a **QUOTA** on, the number of bytes and blocks used, and the users quota in bytes and blocks. The **USER_TS_QUOTAS** view lists information about tablespace quotas for the user doing the query. The **USER_TABLESPACES** view lists descriptions of accessible tablespaces. The **DBA_TABLESPACES** view lists descriptions of all tablespaces. The **DBA_USERS** view lists information about all users of the database, but does not contain quota information.

Question 46

Answer c is correct. The objects created by the user remain, but no new extents can be allocated to the objects. Altering a user's quota does not truncate tables. Altering a user's quota has no effect on table accessibility. Altering a user's quota does not drop tables.

Question 47

Answer a is correct. Oracle creates temporary segments when sorting cannot be done in memory. Tables are stored in data segments. Tables that are created without a specified tablespace are created in the user's default tablespace.

Question 48

Answer d is correct. **DBA_CONSTRAINTS** displays the names and types of all the constraints in the database and their current status. The **DBA_TABLES** view lists descriptions of all tables in the database. The **DBA_CATALOG** view lists all database tables, views, synonyms, and sequences. The **PUBLIC_DEPENDENCY** view lists dependencies to and from objects, by object number. The **DBA_CONS_COLUMNS** view lists information about accessible columns in constraint definitions.

Question 49

Answer a is correct. The data dictionary tables are created in the **SYS** schema. The **SYSTEM** user owns the data dictionary views that database users query. **SYSDBA** and **SYSOPER** are roles granted to a user and do not own any tables.

Question 50

Answer c is correct. **V$THREAD** displays the current redo log group, the number of online redo log groups, and the current sequence number. The **V$DATABASE** view lists database information, including the log mode, but not the current log group or the sequence number. The **V$INSTANCE** view lists the state of the current instance and does not contain any log group information. The **V$LOGFILE** view lists information about redo log files, but does not include the sequence number.

Question 51

Answer b is correct. The order of import is table definitions, table data, indexes on the table, integrity constraints, triggers, bitmap indexes.

Question 52

Answer d is correct. Export/import utilities are used to move tables, their associated objects, and their data from one user to another user. SQL*Loader is used to load data from external files into Oracle tables. Direct-load insert writes data directly into Oracle datafiles, without using the buffer cache. Schema Manager is an OEM utility used to create, edit, and examine schema objects. It cannot move data from one schema to another.

Question 53

Answer a is correct. Because **PCTINCREASE** is always zero, the second and all other extents will always be the size of **NEXT**. The **INITIAL** parameter will be used only for the initial extent. SQL*Plus has no **CREATE TEMPORARY SEGMENT** command. A **PCTINCREASE** of zero will not stop extents from being allocated.

Question 54

Answer c is correct. **DBA_FREE_SPACE** displays the tablespace name, relative file number, file ID, block ID, and size of the extent in Oracle blocks. The **DBA_FREE_SPACE** view does not contain any table information or extent creation dates.

Question 55

Answer c is correct. The control file used by SQL*Loader specifies the tables to be loaded. The log file holds information about the load, such as the number of records loaded/rejected, errors, and so forth. The discard file contains records that did not meet the specified selection criteria. The bad file holds records that are rejected because of incorrect data.

Question 56

Answers d and e are correct. **V$CONTROLFILE** lists the names and locations of the control files and their status. **V$PARAMETER** lists the information about the initialization parameters, including the control file name and location. The **V$DATABASE** view lists database information from the control file, but not the location of the control file. The **V$DATAFILE** view lists datafile information from the control file, but not information about the control file. The **V$INSTANCE** view lists the state of the current instance.

Question 57

Answer b is correct. To specify the weights assigned to each limit, use the **ALTER RESOURCE COST** command. The **ALTER DATABASE** command is used to for many DBA tasks, but cannot change weights for resource limits. The **ALTER SYSTEM** command can enable or disable resource limits, but cannot set or change the weighting. **UPDATE RESOURCE COST** and **ALTER SESSION LIMITS** are invalid SQL commands.

Question 58

Answer b is correct. The segment storage clause has the highest priority. If storage parameters were not specified at the segment level, then the tablespace parameters are used. If the storage parameters were not specified at the segment or tablespace level, then the Oracle Server default values are used.

Question 59

Answer d is correct. The high watermark in a table is the last block ever used by the table.

Question 60

Answer e is correct. DBWn writes changed buffers to the datafiles. The SMON process performs instance recovery at instance startup. The PMON performs process recovery when a user process fails. The ARCH copies the online redo log files to archival storage when they are full. The LGWR process writes redo log entries to disk.

Question 61

Answer a is correct. OEM's Storage Manager is used to administer tablespaces, datafiles, and rollback segments. Schema Manager is used to create and maintain tables, views, and other database objects. Backup Manager is used in backup, restore, and recover operations and to maintain the redo logs. Data Manager is used to load and reorganize data. Security Manager is used to create users and manage user privileges. Instance Manager is used to start up and shut down the database and maintain initialization parameters.

Question 62

Answer d is correct. The **ALTER TABLE** command is used to drop a constraint. Answers a, b, and c are invalid commands.

Question 63

Answers a and d are correct. If you use the **SHARED** option, the password file only recognizes users **SYS** and **INTERNAL**. Other **DBA** accounts, including **SYSTEM**, will not be able to connect as **SYSDBA** or **SYSOPER**.

Glossary

ALTER—A data definition language (**DDL**) command that changes database objects.

analysis—The step in the system development process where the users' needs are gathered and analyzed to produce documentation used to design a program system.

archive log—An archive copy of the redo log. The archive log is used to recover to an earlier point in time or to roll forward from a backup to the present time.

authentication—The process by which Oracle determines if a user should be allowed access to a database.

Backup Manager—An easy-to-use graphical user interface (GUI) for Recovery Manager, an Oracle utility that backs up, restores, and recovers database files. Backup Manager is part of the Oracle Enterprise Manager (OEM).

bad file—A file that contains records that were rejected either by SQL*Loader or by Oracle.

buffer—An Oracle memory area that holds data, redo, or rollback information. Usually the buffers are specified using the **DB_BLOCK_BUFFERS**, **DB_BLOCK_SIZE**, and **LOG_BUFFER** initialization parameters.

cache—A self-managing memory area that holds information about objects, locks, and latches. The caches are usually contained in the shared pool area of the system global area (SGA) and are preallocated as far as size, based on internal algorithms that control how the shared pool memory is allocated.

cardinality—A term used in relational analysis to show how two objects relate; it tells how many. For example, "A person may have zero or one nose" shows a cardinality of zero or one. "A person may have zero, one, or many children" shows a cardinality of zero through many. And, "A person has one or many cells" shows a cardinality of one or many. In reference to indexes, cardinality shows how many rows in an indexed table relate back to the index value. A low cardinality index, such as a person's sex (M or F), should be placed in a bitmapped index if it must be indexed, whereas a high cardinality value, such as a person's social security number or employee ID, should be placed in a standard B-tree index.

chaining—The process in which a row is split between two (or more) database blocks, occurring when a row is too large to be inserted into a single data block and Oracle stores the row in multiple blocks.

COMMIT—A data manipulation language (**DML**) command that marks a transaction as completed successfully and causes data to be written first to the redo logs and, once DBWR writes, to the disk. A **COMMIT** isn't complete until it receives word from the disk subsystem that the redo log write is complete. (Committed data cannot be rolled back using the **ROLLBACK** command, and must be removed using more **DML** commands.)

CONNECT—A Server Manager (**SVRMGRL**), SQL*Worksheet, or SQL*Plus command that enables a user to connect to the local database or to a remote database.

control file—An Oracle file that contains information on all database files and maintains system change number (SCN) records for each. The control file must be present and current for the database to start up properly.

conventional path load—The most commonly used form of the SQL*Loader database load utility. A conventional path load uses **DML** statements to load data from flat operating system (OS) files into Oracle tables.

CREATE—A **DDL** command that allows the creation of database objects.

data block—The unit in which Oracle manages datafile storage. A data block is the smallest unit of input/output (I/O) used by a database.

data definition language (DDL)—A SQL statement used to create or manipulate database structures. Examples are **CREATE**, **ALTER**, and **DROP** commands.

data dictionary—A collection of C structs, tables, and views that contain the database *metadata* (information about the database's data). The data dictionary is used to store information used by all database processes to find out about database data structures.

Data Manager—A GUI interface for the export, import, and load utilities.

data segment—A unit that holds all the data in every nonclustered table, index, or partition and every cluster in an Oracle database.

database—The logical and physical structures used to store and retrieve information.

datafile—An OS file created by an Oracle instance. A tablespace consists of one or more physical datafiles. A datafile can be associated with only one tablespace.

DDL—See *data definition language*.

DELETE—A **DML** command that removes data by rows (generally speaking) from database tables.

DESCRIBE—A SQL*Plus or Server Manager command that retrieves information about database structure. Any stored object (except triggers and indexes) can be described.

direct-load insert—A method of inserting data without logging redo or undo entries, which improves the insert performance significantly. Direct-load insert loads records above the current high watermark (HWM) and can waste space.

direct path load—A way of using the SQL*Loader data loading utility that inserts data directly into the table by prebuilding and then inserting data blocks. Triggers, some constraints, and indexes are disabled during the load, so a direct path load will generally be much faster than a conventional path load.

discard file—A file that contains records that were filtered out of a SQL*Loader load because they did not match any record-selection criteria specified in the control file.

DROP—A **DDL** command that removes database objects.

export utility—A utility that extracts the object definitions and table data from an Oracle database and stores them in an Oracle binary-format export dump file.

extent—A logical unit of database storage space allocation made up of a number of contiguous data blocks.

foreign key—A value or set of values mapped from a primary or parent table into a dependent or child table used to enforce referential integrity. A foreign key must be either **NULL** or exist as a primary or unique key in a parent table.

function—One of several structures. An *implicit* function is one that is provided as a part of the SQL language. An *explicit* function is one that is created by the user using PL/SQL. A function must return a value and must be named. As a part of the SQL standard, a function cannot change a database's or package's state, but can only act on external variables and values.

GRANT—A command used to grant object-level privileges to users and roles and system-level privileges to users and roles.

high watermark (HWM)—An indication of the highest level of a database table being utilized. A table can only reclaim empty space between currently filled blocks and the HWM through a rebuild or truncation process. To accurately get a reading on how much space is actually used in a table, you must count the blocks used, and not simply perform a count of used extents, because used extents are counted up to the HWM.

HWM—See *high watermark*.

import utility—This utility inserts the data objects extracted from an Oracle database by the export utility.

index—A structure that enhances data retrieval by providing rapid access to frequently queried column values. Indexes can be either B-tree structured or bitmapped. Two general types of indexes exist. A *unique* index forces all values entered into its source column to be unique. A *nonunique* index allows for repetitive and null values to be entered into its source column. Generally speaking, a column with high cardinality should be indexed using a B-tree type index (standard, default type of index), whereas low cardinality values should be indexed using a bitmapped index.

INITIAL—A storage parameter that sets the size in bytes (no suffix in Oracle), kilobytes ("K" suffix), or megabytes ("M" suffix) of the initial extent allocated to a table, index, rollback segment, temporary segment, or cluster.

INITRANS—A storage parameter that reserves space in the block header for the transaction records associated with a table's blocks.

INSERT—A DML command that enables users to place new records into a table.

instance—The SGA and the background processes make up an Oracle instance.

Instance Manager—An Oracle Enterprise Manager (OEM) application you can use to start up or shut down a database, place the database in archive log mode or no archive log mode, examine and edit database initialization parameters, manage in-doubt transactions, and manage users' sessions.

MAXEXTENTS—A parameter that sets the maximum number of extents an object can grow into. The default value for **MAXEXTENTS** is based on block size. Since version 7.3 of Oracle, this value can be set to unlimited.

MAXTRANS—A companion to the **INITRANS** storage parameter. **MAXTRANS** sets the maximum number of transactions that can access a block concurrently.

migration—An action that occurs when a row that originally fit into one data block is updated so that the row length increases and not enough free space exists for the update in the current block. When this happens, Oracle migrates the data for the entire row to a new data block. A pointer is maintained in the original row piece of the migrated row to point to the new block containing the migrated row. Thus, the **ROWID** of the migrated row does not change.

MTS—See *multithreaded server*.

multithreaded server (MTS)—Oracle allows multiplexing of database connections through MTS configuration. MTS consists of a listener process, one or more dispatcher processes, and multiple shared server processes. The server processes serve multiple user connections to the database. This multiplexing of database connections allows more users than would normally be serviced to use the database. It is especially useful on systems short on physical memory.

NEXT—A storage parameter that specifies the size in bytes (no suffix in Oracle), kilobytes ("K" suffix), or megabytes ("M" suffix) of the **NEXT** extent allocated to a table, index, rollback segment, temporary segment, or cluster. The **NEXT** parameter is used with the **PCTINCREASE** parameter to determine the size of all extents after the **INITIAL** and **NEXT** extents.

OEM Console—A graphical user interface (GUI) that allows you to manage multiple databases through a single interface.

ORAPWD—A generalized term for the Oracle Password Manager that creates and maintains the external password file. The external password file tells OEM and Server Manager who is authorized to perform database administrator (DBA) functions against a specific database.

OSDBA—A role assigned to users authorized to create and maintain Oracle databases. A user given the **OSDBA** role is authenticated by the OS.

OSOPER—A role assigned to users authorized to maintain Oracle databases. A user given the **OSOPER** role is authenticated by the OS.

package—A stored PL/SQL construct made of related procedures, functions, exceptions, and other PL/SQL constructs. Packages are called into memory when any package object is referenced. They are created or dropped as a unit.

PCTFREE—A parameter used in an Oracle block to determine the amount of space reserved for future updates. Too low a **PCTFREE** can result in row migration and/or possibly row chaining for frequently updated tables, and too high a value requires more storage space.

PCTINCREASE—A parameter determining the percentage each subsequent extent after **INITIAL** and **NEXT** grows over the previously allocated extent.

PCTUSED—A parameter determining when a block is placed back on the free block list. When used space in a block drops below **PCTUSED**, the block can be used for subsequent new row insertion.

PGA—See *program global area.*

primary key—In a relational database, the unique identifier for a table. A primary key must be unique and not null. A primary key can either be *natural* (derived from a column or columns in the database) or *artificial* (drawn from a sequence).

procedure—A stored PL/SQL object that can, but isn't required to, return a value. Procedures are allowed to change a database or package state. Procedures can be placed into packages.

profile—A set of resource allocations that can be assigned to a user. It limits idle time, connect time, memory, and CPU usage as well as enables password verification.

program global area (PGA)—The memory area allocated to each process that accesses an Oracle database.

RECOVER—A command used in Server Manager to explicitly perform database recovery operations.

redo log buffer cache—A memory structure inside the SGA that buffers writes to the redo logs. The redo log buffer cache is sized by the **LOG_BUFFERS** parameter.

referential integrity—The process by which a relational database maintains record relationships between parent and child tables via primary key and foreign key values.

rejected record—In SQL*Loader, a record that does not meet load criteria for the table being loaded, either due to value, datatype, or other restrictions.

role—A group of privileges that can be granted directly to users or to other roles.

ROLLBACK—A **DML** command that undoes uncommitted database changes.

rollback segment—A database object that contains records used to undo database transactions. Whenever a parameter in the database refers to **UNDO**, it is actually referring to rollback segments.

row chaining—An action that occurs when a row is too large to fit into one data block when it is first inserted. It is thus stored in more than one data block reserved for that segment.

Schema Manager—A GUI application supplied with OEM that creates, edits, and examines schema objects.

Security Manager—A GUI application supplied with OEM that creates, alters, and drops users, roles, and profiles.

segment—A set of extents that contains all the data for a specific logical storage structure within a tablespace.

SELECT—A **DML** command that retrieves values from a database.

Server Manager line mode—A mode that provides a command-line interface for database administration.

SET—A SQL*Plus or Server Manager command that changes the values of SQL*Plus or Server Manager environment parameters, such as line width and page length.

SGA—See *system global area*.

SHOW—A SQL*Plus or Server Manager command that shows the value of a variable set with the **SET** command.

SHUTDOWN—The command that shuts down the database. This command has three modes: **NORMAL** prohibits new connections, waits for all users to log off, and then shuts down; **IMMEDIATE** prohibits new connections, backs out uncommitted transactions, logs users off, and shuts down; **ABORT** shuts down immediately and not gracefully.

SPOOL—A SQL*Plus or Server Manager command that sends output to either a printer or a file.

SQL*Loader control file—A file that specifies how to interpret data to be loaded, the tables and columns to insert the data into, and, optionally, input datafile management information.

STARTUP—A command used to start up a database. A database can be started in one of several modes: **NOMOUNT, MOUNT, OPEN, EXCLUSIVE,** or **PARALLEL.**

STORAGE—The clause that Oracle uses to determine current and future settings for an object's extents. If a storage clause isn't specified, the object's storage characteristics are taken from the tablespace default storage clause.

Storage Manager—A GUI application supplied with OEM that performs administrative tasks associated with managing database storage. These tasks include managing tablespaces and rollback segments, and adding and renaming datafiles.

SYSDBA—A role that has the same privileges as the **OSDBA** role. Users assigned the **SYSDBA** role are authenticated through the Oracle password file.

SYSOPER—A role that has the same privileges as the **OSOPER** role. Users assigned the **SYSOPER** role are authenticated through the Oracle password file.

system global area (SGA)—The database buffers, shared pool, and queue areas that are globally accessible by all database processes. The SGA is used to speed Oracle processing by providing for caching of data and structure information in memory.

table—The structure used to store data in an Oracle database. Entities map to tables in relational databases.

table mode export—An export that makes only a logical copy of one or more tables and their related objects, such as triggers, constraints, indexes, and grants.

table mode import—An import that inserts tables and their related objects into an Oracle database from an export file.

tablespace—A logical storage unit in an Oracle database (the database can have multiple tablespaces).

temporary segment—A temporary workspace the database uses for intermediate stages of SQL statement parsing and execution. It is typically used for sorts that cannot be done in memory.

temporary tablespace—A tablespace that is used for temporary (sort) segments only. A permanent tablespace can contain either permanent or temporary segments, whereas a tablespace that has been designated by either the **CREATE TABLESPACE** or **ALTER TABLESPACE** command as a temporary tablespace can contain only temporary segments.

TRUNCATE—A DDL statement that removes all rows from a table. Because it is a DDL statement, it cannot be rolled back.

UGA—See *user global area.*

UPDATE—A DML command that allows data inside tables to be changed.

user global area (UGA)—The area used to store user-specified variables and stacks.

view—A preset select against one or more tables that is stored in a database and has no physical representation. Also known as a *virtual table.*

Index

Bold page numbers indicate sample exam questions.

B

C

E

F

J

K

L

M

N

Q

R

S

V